# How to Live
# on Other Planets

## A Handbook for Aspiring Aliens

**edited by Joanne Merriam**

# TABLE OF CONTENTS

# PREFACE
## Joanne Merriam, editor

Science fiction provides a natural backdrop for talking about movement across borders; immigrants are even called aliens. Many science fiction stories involve alien immigrants to Earth (*Superman*, *Men in Black*, *District 9*) and human immigrants to alien planets (Adams' *Hitchhiker's Guide To The Galaxy*, Cherryh's *Foreigner* series), and of course countless works have humans expanding across the universe and coming into conflict with each other and with aliens (Clarke's *The Songs of Distant Earth*, LeGuin's *The Left Hand of Darkness*, Bujold's *Vorkosigan Saga*, Leckie's *Ancillary Justice*) or otherwise transgressing borders that are supposed to be secure (*Logan's Run*, China Mieville's *The City & The City*).

Often, immigration in science fiction is represented as the threat of invasion (Wells's *The War of the Worlds*, Heinlein's *The Puppet Masters*, *Independence Day*, *Alien*). These threats tend to reflect the anxieties of their day (Communism, consumerism, etc.) as well as feeding into a more general cultural fear of the Other.

Borders are permeable political entities that require great effort to enforce, but are usually presented as inevitable and natural. Inside the borders are people and things that need protection when the border is perceived as under siege. Movement across borders must be monitored and controlled to protect against outsiders, so it's seen as justified when citizens must give up their usual rights if they wish to cross those borders, even if only temporarily.

As an immigrant to America who is white, middle class and English-speaking, I frequently find myself in situations where people assume I'm one of them and then retroactively define me as an Other when they find out I'm Canadian (a very harmless-seeming Other to Americans, and in the US South, preferable to a Yankee, as my East Coast accent would otherwise mark me).

My immigration experience has been relatively easy: the worst I've experienced is a border guard reading my diary and tossing my clothes in the road while searching my luggage, or the poverty that accompanied waiting for a work visa, or my home country disenfranchising me. Nobody wants to beat me up or legislate away my existence; nobody fears they'll catch a disease from me. That perception of my Otherness generally only manifests in teasing about my accent ("say 'about' again") or word choices ("what's a 'garburator'?"), but underlying that is an uneasiness with what people from my part of Canada call "come-from-aways."

People from foreign parts are always, even if just a little, suspect. Alien.

Despite the natural comparison of *alien* to *alien*, I'm not aware of any other speculative fiction anthology which has gathered together stories focusing exclusively on the immigrant experience.

In these pages, you'll find Sturgeon winner Sarah Pinsker's robot grandmother, James Tiptree, Jr., Award winner Nisi Shawl's prison planet and Nebula, Hugo, and World Fantasy Award winner Ken Liu's space- and time-spanning story of different kinds of ghosts. You'll find Bryan Thao Worra's Cthulhic poetry, and Pinckney Benedict's sad, whimsical tale of genocide. You'll travel to Frankfurt, to the moon, to Mars, to the underworld, to unnamed alien planets, under the ocean, through clusters of asteroids. You'll land on the fourth planet from the star Deneb, and an alternate universe version of Earth, and a world of Jesuses.

This is not a textbook. You will not find here polemics on immigration policy or colonialism. The most compelling fiction articulates the unsaid, the unbearable, and the incomprehensible; these stories say things about the immigration experience that a lecture never could. The purpose of this book is, first and foremost, to entertain the casual and the sophisticated reader, but its genesis is a response to the question: *Who do we become when we live with the unfamiliar?*

# KEN LIU
# Ghost Days

## 3.

### Nova Pacifica, 2313:

Ms. Coron pointed to the screen-board, on which she had typed out a bit of code.

```
(define (fib n)
    (if (< n 2)
        1
        (+ (fib (- n 1))  (fib (- n 2))))))
```

"Let's diagram the call-graph for this classic LISP function, which computes the n-th Fibonacci number recursively."

Ona watched her Teacher turn around. The helmetless Ms. Coron wore a dress that exposed the skin of her arms and legs in a way that she had taught the children was *beautiful* and *natural*. Intellectually, Ona understood that the frigid air in the classroom, cold enough to give her and the other children hypothermia even with brief exposure, was perfectly suited to the Teachers. But she couldn't help shivering at the sight. The airtight heat-suit scraped over Ona's scales, and the rustling noise reverberated loudly in her helmet.

Ms. Coron went on, "A recursive function works like nesting dolls. To solve a bigger problem, a recursive function calls on itself to solve a smaller version of the same problem."

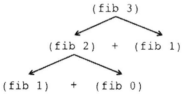

```
               (fib 3)


    (fib 2)  +  (fib 1)


(fib 1)  +  (fib 0)
```

Ona wished she could call on a smaller version of herself to solve her problems. She imagined that nested inside her was Obedient Ona, who enjoyed diagramming Classical Computer Languages and studying prosody in Archaic English. That would free her up to focus on the mysterious alien civilization of Nova Pacifica, the long-dead original inhabitants of this planet.

"What's the point of studying dead computer languages, anyway?" Ona said.

The heads of the other children in the classroom turned as one to look at her, the golden glint from the scales on their faces dazzling even through the two layers of glass in their and Ona's helmets.

Ona cursed herself silently. Apparently, instead of Obedient Ona, she had somehow called on Loudmouth Ona, who was always getting her in trouble.

Ona noticed that Ms. Coron's naked face was particularly made up today, but her lips, painted bright red, almost disappeared into a thin line as she tried to maintain her smile.

"We study classical languages to acquire the habits of mind of the ancients," Ms. Coron said. "You must know where *you* came from."

The way she said "you" let Ona know that she didn't mean just her in particular, but all the children of the colony, Nova Pacifica. With their scaled skin, their heat-tolerant organs and vessels, their six-lobed lungs—all engineered based on models from the local fauna—the children's bodies incorporated an alien biochemistry so that they could breathe the air outside the Dome and survive on this hot, poisonous planet.

Ona knew she should shut up, but—just like the recursive calls in Ms. Coron's diagram had to return up the call stack—she couldn't keep down Loudmouth Ona. "I know where I came from: I was designed on a computer, grown in a vat, and raised in the glass nursery with the air from outside pumped in."

Ms. Coron softened her voice. "Oh, Ona, that's not ... not what I meant. Nova Pacifica is too far from the home worlds, and they won't be sending a rescue ship because they don't know that we survived the wormhole and we're stranded here on the other side of the galaxy. You'll never see the beautiful floating islands of Tai-Winn or the glorious skyways of Pele, the elegant city-trees of Pollen, or the busy data warrens of Tiron—you've been cut off from your heritage, from the rest of humanity."

Hearing—for the millionth time—these vague legends of the wonders that she'd been deprived of made the scales on Ona's back stand up. She hated the condescension.

But Ms. Coron went on. "However, when you've learned enough to read the LISP source code that powered the first auto-constructors on Earth; when you've learned enough Archaic English to understand the Declaration of New Manifest Destiny; when you've learned enough Customs and Culture to appreciate all the recorded holos and sims in the Library—*then* you will understand the brilliance and elegance of the ancients, of our race."

"But we're *not* human! You made us in the image of the plants and animals living here. The dead aliens are more like us than you!"

Ms. Coron stared at Ona, and Ona saw that she had hit upon a truth Ms. Coron didn't want to admit, even to herself. In the Teacher's eyes, the children would never be good enough, never be fully *human,* though they were the future of humanity on this inhospitable planet.

Ms. Coron took a deep breath and went on as if nothing had happened. "Today is the Day of Remembrance, and I'm sure you'll impress all the Teachers with your presentations later. But let's finish our lesson first.

"To compute the n-th term, the recursive function calls itself to compute the (n-1)th term and the (n-2)th term, so that they could be added together, each time going back earlier in the sequence, solving earlier versions of the same problem...

"The past," Ms. Coron continued, "thus accumulating bit by bit through recursion, becomes the future."

The bell rang, and class was finally over.

§

Even though it meant they had less time to eat, Ona and her friends always made the long walk to have lunch outside the Dome. Eating inside meant squeezing tubes of paste through a flap in her helmet or going back to the claustrophobia-inducing tanks of the dormitory.

"What are you going to do?" Jason asked, biting into a honeycomb fruit—poisonous to the Teachers, but all the children loved it. He had glued white ceramic tiles all over his suit to make it look like an ancient spacesuit from the old pictures. Next to him was a flag—the old Stars-and-Stripes of the American Empire (or was it the American Republic?)—his artifact, so that he could tell the legend of Neil Armstrong, Moonwalker, at the Remembrance Assembly later that evening. "You don't have a costume."

"I don't know," Ona said, twisting off her helmet and stripping off her suit. She took deep gulps of warm, fresh air, free of the suffocating chemical odor of the recycling filters. "And I don't care."

Everyone presenting at the Remembrance Assembly was

supposed to be in costume. Two weeks ago, Ona had received her assigned artifact: a little, flat metal piece with a rough surface about the size of her palm and shaped like a toy spade. It was dark green in color, with a stubby, fat handle and a double-tined blade, heavier than its size would suggest. It was a family heirloom that belonged to Ms. Coron.

"But these artifacts and stories are so important to them," Talia said. "They'll be so angry that you didn't do any research." She had glued her artifact, a white veil, over her helmet and put on a lacy white dress over her suit so that she could enact a classical wedding with Dahl, who had painted his suit black to imitate the grooms he had seen in old holos.

"Who knows if the stories they tell us are true, anyway? We can never go there."

Ona placed the little spade in the middle of the table, where it absorbed the heat from the sun. She imagined Ms. Coron reaching out to touch it—a precious keepsake from a world she will never see again—and then screaming because the spade was hot.

*You must know where* you *came from.*

Ona would rather use the spade to dig up the past of Nova Pacifica, her planet, where she was at *home.* She wanted to learn about the history of the "aliens" far more than she wanted to know about the past of the Teachers.

"They cling to their past like rotten glue-lichen"—as she spoke she could feel fury boiling up inside her—"and make us feel bad, incomplete, like we'll never be as good as them. But they can't even survive out here for an hour!"

She grabbed the spade and threw it as hard as she could into the whitewood forest.

Jason and Talia stayed silent. After a few awkward minutes, they got up.

"We have to get ready for the Assembly," Jason murmured. And they went back inside.

Ona sat alone for a while, listlessly counting the darting shuttlewings overhead. She sighed and got up to walk into the whitewood forest to retrieve the spade.

Truth be told, on bright, warm autumn days like this, Ona wanted nothing more than to be outside, suitless and helmetless, wandering through the whitewood groves, their six-sided trunks rising into the sky, the vibrating silver-white hexagonal leaves a canopy of mirrors, their susurration whispers and giggles.

She watched the flutter-bys dance through the air, their six translucent, bright blue wings beating wildly as they traced out patterns in the air she was sure was a kind of language. The Dome had been built on the site of an ancient alien city, and here and there, the woods were broken by hillocks—piles of angular rubble left behind by the mysterious original inhabitants of this planet who had all died millennia before the arrival of the colony ship, alien ruins exuding nothing but a ghostly silence.

*Not that they've tried very hard,* Ona thought. The Teachers had never shown much interest in the aliens, too busy trying to cram everything about old Earth into the children's heads.

She felt the full warmth of the sun against her face and body, her white scales coruscating with the colors of the rainbow. The afternoon sun was hot enough to boil water where the whitewood trees didn't shade the soil, and white plumes of steam filled the forest. Though she hadn't thrown the spade far, it was hard to find it among the dense trees. Ona picked her way slowly, examining every exposed root and overturned rock, every pile of ancient rubble. She hoped that the spade hadn't been broken.

*There.*

Ona hurried over. The spade was on the side of a pile of rubble, nestled among some tinselgrass that cushioned its fall. A small spume of steam was trapped under it, so that it seemed to be floating over the escaping water vapor. Ona leaned closer.

The steam held a fragrance that she had never smelled before. The spume had blasted away some of the green patina encrusting the spade, revealing the gleaming golden metal underneath. She suddenly had a sense of just how ancient the object was, and she wondered if it was some kind of ritual implement, vaguely remembering the religion excerpts from Customs and Culture class—ghost stories.

She was curious, for the first time, whether the previous owners ever imagined that the spade would one day end up a billion billion miles from home, on top of an alien tomb, in the hands of a barely-human girl who looked like Ona.

Mesmerized by the smell, she reached for the spade, took a deep breath, and fainted.

## 2.

## East Norbury, Connecticut, 1989:

For the Halloween dance, Fred Ho decided to go as Ronald Reagan.

Mainly it was because the mask was on sale at the Dollar Store. Also, he could wear his father's suit, worn only once on the day the restaurant opened. He didn't want to argue with his father about money. Going to the dance was shock enough for his parents.

Also, the pants had deep pockets, good for holding his present. Heavy and angular, the little antique bronze spade-shaped token had been warmed by his thigh through the thin fabric. He thought Carrie might like to use it as a paperweight, hang it as a window decoration, or even take advantage of the hole at the handle end to turn it into an incense holder. She often smelled of sandalwood and patchouli.

Picking him up at his house, she waved at his parents, who stood in the door, confused and wary, and did not wave back.

"You look dapper," Carrie said, her mask on the dashboard.

He was relieved that Carrie had approved of his costume. Indeed, she did more than approve. She had dressed up as Nancy Reagan.

He laughed and tried to think of something appropriate to say. By the time he settled on "You look beautiful," they were already a block away, and it seemed too late. So he said, "Thank you for asking me to the dance," instead.

The field house was festooned with orange streamers, plastic bats, and paper pumpkins. They put on their masks and went in. They danced to Paula Abdul's "Straight Up" and then Madonna's "Like a Prayer." Well, Carrie danced; Fred mostly tried to keep up.

Though he still moved as awkwardly as ever, the masks somehow made it easier for him not to worry about his lack of the most essential skill for surviving an American high school—blending in.

The rubber masks soon made them sweaty. Carrie drank cup after cup of the sickly-sweet punch, but Fred, who opted to keep his mask on, shook his head. By the time Jordan Knight began to sing "I'll Be Loving You (Forever)," they were ready to get out of the dark gym.

Outside, the parking lot was filled with ghosts, Supermans, aliens, witches, and princesses. They waved at the presidential couple, and the couple waved back. Fred kept his mask on and deliberately set a slow pace, enjoying the evening breeze.

"Wish it could be Halloween every day," he said.

How to Live on Other Planets

"Why?" she asked.

*No one knows who I am,* he wanted to say. *No one stares at me.* But instead all he said was, "It's nice to wear a suit." He spoke carefully and slowly, and he almost could not hear his accent.

She nodded, as if she understood. They got into the car.

Until Fred's arrival, East Norbury High School had never had a student whose first language wasn't English and who might be illegal. People were mostly friendly, of course, but a thousand smiles, whispers, little gestures that each individually seemed so innocuous added up to *you don't belong.*

"You nervous about meeting my parents?" she asked.

"No," he lied.

"My mom is really excited about meeting you."

They arrived at a white raised ranch behind an immaculate lawn. The mailbox at the mouth of the driveway said "Wynne."

"This is your house," he said.

"You can read!" she teased, and parked.

Walking up the driveway, Fred could smell the sea in the air and hear the waves crashing against the shore nearby. There was an elegant, simple jack-o-lantern on the steps before the front door.

*A fairy tale house,* Fred thought. *An American castle.*

§

"Is there anything I can do to help?" Fred asked from the kitchen door.

Mrs. Wynne ("Call me Cammy") was shuttling between the kitchen table, which was being used as a cutting/mixing/staging station, and the stove. She smiled at him quickly before turning back to her work. "Don't worry about it. Go chat with my husband and Carrie."

"I really can help," he said. "I know my way around a kitchen. My family runs a restaurant."

"Oh, I know. Carrie tells me your Moo Shu Pork is excellent." She stopped and looked at him, her smile even wider. "You speak such good English!"

He never understood why people felt it important to point that out. They always sounded so surprised, and he never knew what to say. "Thank you."

"It *really* is very good. Go on now. I have this all under control."

He retreated back to the living room, wishing he could stay in the warm, almost-familiar heat of the kitchen.

§

"A terrible thing," Mr. Wynne said. "Those brave students in Tiananmen Square. Heroes."

Fred nodded.

"Your parents," Mr. Wynne continued, "they were dissidents?"

Fred hesitated. He remembered his father reading the Chinese newspaper they got for free from Chinatown up in Boston, showing the photographs of the protesting crowds in Beijing.

*"Stupid kids," he had said, contempt making his face red. "Wasting their parents' money to riot outside like the Red Guards just so they can pose for the foreigners and their cameras instead of studying. What do they hope to accomplish? They're all spoiled, read too many American books."*

*Then he turned to Fred and shook his fist threateningly. "If you ever dare to do something like that, I'll beat you until you can tell your ass apart from your head again."*

"Yes," Fred said. "That's why we came here."

Mr. Wynne nodded, satisfied. "This is a great country, isn't it?"

Truth be told, he had never really understood why, one day, his parents had woken him up in the middle of the night; why they had gotten on a boat, then a truck, then a bus, then a big ship; why, for so many days, they had ridden in the dark, the tossing and tumbling of the sea making him sick; why, after they landed, they had hidden in the back of a van until they emerged in the dirty streets of Chinatown in New York, where some men spoke with his father in menacing tones while he nodded and nodded; why his father had told him that now they all had different names and were different people and they must never talk to foreigners or the police; why they had all lived in the basement of a restaurant and worked there for years and talked endlessly of how to save money to pay off the debt to those menacing men and then make more of it; why they had then moved again, to East Norbury, this small town on the coast of New England, where his father said there were no Chinese restaurants and the Americans were too stupid to know that he wasn't much of a cook.

"A great country, sir," he said.

How to Live on Other Planets

"And that's the face of a great man you're holding," Mr. Wynne said, indicating his mask. "A real fighter for freedom."

After that week in June, his father had gotten on the phone every evening, whispering deep into the night. And suddenly his father told him and his mother that they had to memorize a new story about themselves, about how they were connected to the students who had died in Tiananmen Square, believed the same things, and were hopelessly in love with "democracy." "Asylum" was mentioned often, and they had to be prepared for an interview with some American official in New York next month, so that they could make themselves *legal.*

*"Then we can stay here and make lots of money," his father had said, satisfied.*

The doorbell rang. Carrie got up with the bowl of candies.

"Carrie is always adventurous," Mr. Wynne said. He lowered his voice. "She likes to try new things. It's natural, being rebellious at her age."

Fred nodded, not sure what he was really being told.

Mr. Wynne's face lost its friendly expression, like a mask falling off. "She's just going through a phase, you understand. You're a part"—he waved his hands vaguely—"of ... of how she wants to get a rise out of me.

"It's not serious," he added. But his expression was very serious.

Fred said nothing.

"I just want there to be no misunderstandings," Mr. Wynne continued. "People tend to belong with their own kind, as I'm sure you'll agree."

Over by the door, Carrie gasped and pretended to be scared by the trick-or-treaters and expressed admiration at the costumes.

"Don't get the wrong idea about what she's doing with you."

Carrie returned from the door.

"Why so quiet?" she asked. "What were you two talking about?"

"Just learning about Fred's family," Mr. Wynne said, his face again friendly and smiling. "They were dissidents, did you know? Very brave people."

Fred stood up, his hand in his pocket, fingers wrapped around the little bronze spade. He fantasized throwing it at the face of Mr. Wynne, which strangely bore some resemblance to his father's.

But instead, he said, "I'm sorry. I didn't realize it's so late. I should go."

# 1.

## Hong Kong, 1905:

"Jyu-zung—" William's father called again. He was as loud as their neighbor futilely attempting to quiet her colicky child.

*Why does everyone in Hong Kong have to shout? It's the first decade of the twentieth century, and everyone still acts like they live in villages.*

"It's *William*," William muttered. Even though his father had paid for his expensive education in England, the old man still refused to use his English name, the name he had gone by for more than a decade.

William tried to focus on the book in front of him, the words of the 14th-century Christian mystic:

*For thou hast brought me with thi question into that same derknes, and into that same cloude of unknowyng that I wolde thou were in thiself.*

"Jyu-zung!"

He plugged up his ears with his fingers.

*For of alle other creatures and theire werkes—ye, and of the werkes of God self—may a man thorou grace have fulheed of knowing, and wel to kon thinke on hem; bot of God Himself can no man thinke.*

The book, *The Cloude of Unknowyng,* had been a parting gift from Virginia, who was surely the most radiant of His works and one William longed to have "fulheed of knowing."

"Now that you're going back to the mysterious Orient," she had said as she handed him the book, "may you be guided by the mystics of the Occident."

"Hong Kong is not like that," he had said, unhappy that she seemed to think of him as a mere *Chinaman,* though ... he kind of was. "It's part of the Empire. It's civilized." He took the book from her, almost, but not quite, touching her fingers. "I'll be back in a year."

She had rewarded him with a bold and radiant smile, which, more than all his high marks and the praise from his tutors, made him feel like a proper Englishman.

*And therfore I wole leve al that thing that I can think, and chese to my love that thing that I cannot think. For whi He may wel be loved, bot not thought. By love may He be getyn and holden; bot bi thought neither.*

"Jyu-zung! What is the matter with you?"

His father stood in the door, his face red with the exertion of having climbed up the ladder to William's attic room.

William pulled his fingers from his ears.

"You're supposed to help me with the preparations for *Yu Lan.*"

After the mellifluous music of Middle English in his head, his father's Cantonese grated on his ears like the clanging of cymbals and gongs in *Jyut kek,* the native "folk opera" that was undeserving of the name, a barbarous shadow of the real operas he had attended in London.

"I'm busy," William said.

His father looked from his face to his book and then back again.

"It's an important book," he said, avoiding his father's gaze.

"The ghosts will be parading tonight." His father shuffled his feet. "Let's make sure the spirits of our ancestors aren't ashamed, and we can try to comfort the homeless ghosts."

To go from reading Darwin, Newton, and Smith to *this,* to *appeasing ghosts.* In England, men were contemplating the possibility of knowing all the laws of nature, the end of science, but here, under his father's roof, it was still the Middle Ages. He could easily imagine the look on Virginia's face.

He had nothing in common with his father, who might as well be an alien.

"I'm not asking," his father said. His voice grew hard, like the way the Cantonese opera actors ended a scene.

*Rationality suffocates in the air of superstition in the colonies.* His determination to go back to England had never been stronger.

§

"Why would grandfather need this?" William asked, staring critically at the paper model of an Arrol-Johnston three-cylinder horseless carriage.

"Everyone appreciates things that make life more comfortable," his father said.

William shook his head but continued the task of gluing headlights made of yellow paper—intended to simulate brass—to the model.

Next to him, the surface of the table was covered with other offerings to be burnt later that night: a paper model of a Western-style cottage, paper suits, paper dress shoes, stacks of "underworld money" and piles of "gold bullion."

He could not resist commenting, "Grandfather and great-grandfather must have poor eyesight to confuse these with the real thing."

His father refused to take the bait, and they continued to work in silence.

To make the tedious ritual tolerable, William fantasized that he was polishing the car in preparation for a ride through the countryside with Virginia ...

"Jyu-zung, could you take out the sandalwood table from the basement? Let's lay out the feast for the ghosts with some style. We shouldn't argue any more on this day."

The pleading note in his father's voice surprised William. He noticed, suddenly, how bent his father's back had become.

An image came unbidden to him of himself as a young boy sitting on top of his father's shoulders, which had seemed as broad and steady as a mountain.

*"Higher, higher!" he shouted.*

*And his father lifted him over his head so that he could be above the milling crowd, so that he could see the exciting costumes and beautiful makeup of the folk opera troupe performing for Yu Lan.*

*His father's arms were so strong, and kept him lifted high in the air for a long time.*

"Of course, *Aa-baa*," William said, and stood up to go to the warehouse in the back.

The warehouse was dark, dry, and cool. This was where his father temporarily stored the antiques he was restoring for customers as well as the pieces he collected. The heavy wooden shelves and cubbyholes were filled with Zhou bronze ritual vessels, Han jade carvings, Tang tomb figurines, Ming porcelain, and all manner of other wares that William did not recognize.

He made his way carefully through the narrow hallways, looking impatiently for his prize.

*Maybe in that corner?*

In this corner of the warehouse, a ray of slanting light from a papered-over window illuminated a small workbench. Behind it, leaning against the wall, was the sandalwood dining table.

How to Live on Other Planets

As he bent down to pick up the table, what he saw on the workbench stopped him.

There were two identical-looking *bubi,* ancient bronze coins, on the table. They looked like palm-sized spades. Though he didn't know much about antiques, he had seen enough *bubi* as a child to know that this style was from the Zhou Dynasty or earlier. The ancient Chinese kings had cast coins in this shape to show a reverence for the earth, from which came life-sustaining crops and to which all life must return. Digging in the earth was a promise to the future as well as an acknowledgement of the past.

Given how large these *bubi* were, William knew they must be very valuable. To have an identical pair was very rare.

Curious, he looked closer at the coins, which were covered in dark green patina. Something didn't seem right. He flipped over the one on the left: it gleamed bright yellow, almost like gold.

Next to the coins was a small dish with some dark blue powder inside, and a paintbrush. William sniffed the powder: coppery.

He knew that bronze only looked bright yellow if it was freshly cast.

He tried to push away the thought. His father had always been an honorable man who made an honest living. It was unfilial for a son to think such thoughts.

But he picked up the pair of *bubi* and put them in his pocket. His English teachers had taught him to ask questions, to dig for the truth, no matter what the consequences.

He half-dragged and half-carried the table up to the front hall.

§

"Now this looks like a proper festival," his father said as he placed the last plate of vegetarian duck on the table. The table was filled with plates of fruit and mock-versions of every kind of meat. Eight place settings had been arranged around the table, ready to receive the ghosts of the ancestors of the Ho family.

*Mock chicken, vegetarian duck, papier-mâché houses, false money...*

"Maybe we can go to see some opera performances in the streets later," his father said, oblivious to William's mood. "Just like when you were little."

*Forged bronzes...*

He took out the two *bubi* from his pocket and placed them on the table, the gleaming side of the unfinished one facing up.

His father looked at them, paused for a moment, and then acted as if nothing was wrong. "You want to light the joss sticks?"

William said nothing, trying to find a way to phrase his question.

His father arranged the two *bubi* side by side and flipped them over. Carved into the patina on the reverse side of each was a character.

"The character forms from the Zhou Dynasty were a bit different from later forms," his father said, as though William was still only a child being taught how to read and write. "So collectors from later ages would sometimes carve their interpretations of the script on the vessels. Like the patina, these interpretations also accumulate on the vessels in layers, build up over time."

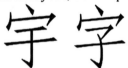

"Have you ever noticed how similar the character 'jyu'—for the universe, which is also the first character in your name—is to the character 'zi'—for writing?"

William shook his head, not really listening.

*This entire culture is based on hypocrisy, on fakery, on mocking up the appearance for that which cannot be obtained.*

"See how the universe is straight forward, but to understand it with the intellect, to turn it into language, requires a twist, a sharp turn? Between the World and the Word, there lies an extra curve. When you look at these characters, you're convening with the history of these artifacts, with the minds of our ancestors from thousands of years ago. That is the deep wisdom of our people, and no Latin letters will ever get at our truth as deeply as our characters."

William could no longer stand it. "You hypocrite! You are a forger!"

He waited, silently urging his father to deny the charge, to explain.

After a while, his father began to speak, not looking at him. "The first ghosts came to me a few years ago."

He used the term *gwailou* for "foreigners," but which also

meant "ghosts."

"They handed me antiques I had never seen before to restore. I asked them, 'How did you get these?' 'Oh, we bought them from some French soldiers who conquered Peking and burned down the Palace and took these as loot.'

"For the ghosts, a robbery could give good title. This was their law. These bronzes and ceramics, handed down from our ancestors for a hundred generations, would now be taken from us and used to decorate the homes of robbers who did not even understand what they were. I could not allow it.

"So I made copies of the works I was supposed to restore, and I gave the copies back to the ghosts. The real artifacts I saved for this land, for you, and for your children. I mark the real ones and the copies with different characters, so that I can tell them apart. I know what I do is wrong in your eyes, and I am ashamed. But love makes us do strange things."

*Which is authentic?* he thought. *The* World *or the* Word? *The truth or understanding?*

The sound of a cane rapping against the front door interrupted them.

"Probably customers," said his father.

"Open up!" whoever was at the door shouted.

William went to the front door and opened it, revealing a well-dressed Englishman in his forties, followed by two burly, scruffy men who looked like they were more at home in the docks of the colony.

"How do you do?" the Englishman said. Without waiting to be invited, he confidently stepped inside. The other two shoved William aside as they followed.

"Mr. Dixon," his father said. "What a pleasant surprise." His father's heavily accented English made William cringe.

"Not as pleasant a surprise as the one you gave me, I assure you," Dixon said. He reached inside his coat and pulled out a small porcelain figurine and set it on the table. "I gave you this to repair."

"And I did."

A smirk appeared on Dixon's face. "My daughter is very fond of this piece. Indeed, it amuses me to see her treating the antique tomb figurine like a doll, and that was how it came to be broken. But after you returned the mended figurine, she refused to play with it, saying that it was not her dolly. Now, children are very good at detecting lies. And Professor Osmer was good enough to confirm my guess."

His father straightened his back but said nothing.

Dixon gestured, and his two lackeys immediately shoved everything off the table: plates, dishes, bowls, the *bubi*, the food, the chopsticks—all crashed into a cacophonous heap.

"Do you want us to keep looking around? Or are you ready to confess to the police?"

His father kept his face expressionless. *Inscrutable,* the English would have called it. At the school, William had looked into a mirror until he had learned to not make that face, until he had stopped looking like his father.

"Wait a minute." William stepped forward. "You can't just go into someone's house and act like a bunch of lawless thugs."

"Your English is very good," Dixon said as he looked William up and down. "Almost no accent."

"Thank you," William said. He tried to maintain a calm, reasonable tone and demeanor. Surely the man would realize now that he was not dealing with a common native family, but a young *Englishman* of breeding and good character. "I studied for ten years at Mr. George Dodsworth's School in Ramsgate. Do you know it?"

Dixon smiled and said nothing, as though he was staring at a dancing monkey. But William pressed on.

"I'm certain my father would be happy to compensate you for what you feel you deserve. There's no need to resort to violence. We can behave like gentlemen."

Dixon began to laugh, at first a little, then uproariously. His men, confused at first, joined in after a while.

"You think that because you've learned to speak English, you are other than what you are. There seems to be something in the Oriental mind that cannot grasp the essential difference between the West and the East. I am not here to negotiate with you, but to assert my rights, a notion that seems foreign to your habits of mind. If you do not restore to me what is mine, we will smash everything in this place to smithereens."

William felt the blood rush to his face, and he willed himself to let the muscles of his face go slack, to not betray his feelings. He looked across the room at his father, and suddenly he realized that his father's expression must also be his expression, the placid mask over a helpless rage.

While they talked, his father had been slowly moving behind Dixon. Now he looked over at William, and the two nodded at each other almost imperceptibly.

*And therfore I wole leve al that thing that I can think, and chese to my love that thing that I cannot think.*

William jumped at Dixon as his father lunged at Dixon's legs. The three men fell to the ground in a heap. In the struggle that followed, William seemed to observe himself from a distance. There was no thought, but a mixture of love and rage that clouded his mind until William found himself sitting astride Dixon's prone body, clutching one of the *bubi,* poised to smash its blade into Dixon's head.

The two men Dixon had brought with him looked on helplessly, frozen in place.

"We don't have what you're looking for here," William said, breathing deeply. "Now get out of our house."

§

William and his father surveyed the mess Dixon and his men left behind.

"Thank you," his father said.

"I suppose the ghosts got a good show tonight," William said.

"I'm sure grandfather is proud of you," his father said. And then, for the first time that he could remember, his father added, "Jyu-zung, I'm proud of you."

William did not know if what he felt was love or rage, and as he looked at the two characters on the upturned *bubi* on the ground, they seemed to waver and merge into one as his eyes grew blurry.

## 2.

### East Norbury, Connecticut, 1989:

"Thank you for having me to your house," Fred said. "I had a great time tonight." He spoke stiffly and carefully kept his distance from her.

The waves of Long Island Sound lapped gently at the beach at their feet.

"You're very sweet," she said, and held his hand. She leaned against him, and the wind lifted her hair against his face, the floral scent of her shampoo mixing with the smell of the sea, like promise mixed with longing. His heart thumped. He felt a tenderness in the middle of his chest that he was frightened of.

Across the bay, they could see the bright red lights of the Edley Mansion, which was being run as a haunted house for the week. He imagined the delighted screams of the children, willingly thrilled by the lies told by their parents.

"Don't worry too much about what my dad says," she said.

He froze.

"You're angry," she said.

"What do you know about it?" he said. *She is a princess. She belongs.*

"You can't control what others think," she said. "But you can always decide for yourself if you belong."

He said nothing, trying to comprehend the rage in himself.

"I am not my father," she said. "And you're not your parents. Family is a story that is told to you, but the story that matters the most you must tell yourself."

He realized that this was the thing about America that he loved the most: the utter faith that family did not matter, that the past was but a *story.* Even a story that started as a lie—a fib—could become authentic, could become a life that was real.

He reached into the pocket of his pants and took out his gift.

"What is it?" She held the little bronze spade uncertainly in her hand.

"It's an antique," he said, "a spade-shaped coin used a long time ago in China. It used to belong to my grandfather, and he gave it to me before we left China, for luck. I thought you might like it."

"It's beautiful."

He felt compelled to be honest. "My grandfather said that his father had saved it from foreigners trying to steal it from the country, and the Red Guards almost destroyed it during the Cultural Revolution. But my dad says it's a fake, like many things from China, and not worth anything. See this mark on the bottom? He says it's too modern, not really old. But it's the only thing I have from my grandfather. He died last year and we couldn't go back for the funeral, because of ... immigration problems."

"Shouldn't you keep it?"

"I want you to have it. I'll always remember giving it to you, and that's a better memory, a better story."

He bent down and picked up a small, sharp rock from the beach. As he held her hand with the spade coin in it, slowly, he etched the letters of their initials into the patina, next to the older character. "Now it has our mark, our story."

She nodded and solemnly put the coin into her jacket pocket. "Thank you. It's lovely."

He thought about going home, about the questions from his father and the worried silence from his mother, about the long hours ahead of him in the restaurant tomorrow and the day after and the day after that, about college, now a possibility if he could show his citizenship papers, about one day making his own way across this vast continent, now still hidden under a cloud of unknowing darkness.

But not yet. He looked around and wanted to do something big, to commemorate this night. He took off his jacket, his shirt, kicked off his shoes. He was naked, maskless, costumeless. "Let's go for a swim."

She laughed, not believing him.

The water was cold, so cold that diving in made him gasp and think his skin was on fire. He dove under and then popped back up, and shook the water from his face.

She called for him, and he waved back, once, and then swam towards the bright lights on the other side of the bay.

The reflection of the red-lit Edley Mansion in the water was streaked, mixed with the bright white from the moon. As his arms moved through the dark blue sea, jellies glowed against his skin, like hundreds of little stars.

Her voice faded behind him as he swam through the stars and stripes, fractal, ambiguous, tasting of salty hope and the deliberate sting of leaving behind the past.

## 3.

**Nova Pacifica, 2313:**

Ona woke up in the middle of a busy street. The light was dim, and it was cold, as though it were dusk or dawn.

Six-wheeled vehicles shaped like sleek finned sea-darts rushed by both sides of her, seeming to miss her by inches. A glance inside one of the vehicles almost made her scream.

The head of the creature inside had twelve tentacles radiating from it.

She looked around: thick, six-sided towers around her rose

into the sky, as dense as the trunks of the whitewood grove. She dodged around the speeding vehicles and made her way to the side of the street, where more of the twelve-tentacled creatures ambled by, paying no attention to her. They had six feet and a low-slung torso, with a shimmering skin that she wasn't sure was made of fur or scales.

Overhead, cloth signs etched with alien markings fluttered in the wind like leaves, the individual symbols made up of line segments intersecting at sharp and obtuse angles. The noise of the crowd, consisting of incomprehensible clicks, moans, and chirps, coalesced into a susurration that she was sure was a kind of language.

The creatures paid no attention to her, sometimes barreling right into her, through her as though she were made of air. She felt like a ghost in the stories that some of the Teachers used to tell when she was younger, an invisible being. She squinted to find the sun in the middle of the sky: it was dimmer and smaller than she was used to.

Then, suddenly, everything began to change. The pedestrians on the sidewalks stopped, swung their heads skyward, and lifted their tentacles towards the sun—at the tip of each appendage was the black orb of an eye. The traffic in the street slowed and then ceased, the occupants of the vehicles stepping out to join the sun-gazing crowd. Silence fell across the scene like a veil.

Ona looked around the crowd, picking out individual groupings frozen in tableaus like photographs. A large creature wrapped its forearms protectively around two smaller ones, its tentacles trembling noiselessly. Two aliens leaned against each other, their tentacles and arms entwined. Another one, its legs unsteady, supported itself against the side of a building, its tentacles lightly tapping against the wall like a man sending a message.

The sun seemed to glow brighter, and then brighter still. The creatures turned their faces away from the sun, their tentacles wilting in the new heat and light.

They turned to gaze at *her.* Thousands, millions of dozens of eyes focused on Ona, as though suddenly she had become visible. Their tentacles reached towards her, pleading, signaling.

The crowd separated, and a small creature, about her size, walked towards her. Ona held out her hands, palms uplifted, uncertain what to do.

The small alien reached her, deposited something in her hand, and stepped back. Ona looked down and felt the ancient, rough metal against her scaled skin, absorbed its heft. She flipped the spade around and saw a mark that she did not recognize: sharp angles, hooks, reminding her of the markings on the fluttering signs.

A thought came into her mind like a whisper: *Remember us, you who treasure the old.*

The sun glowed even brighter, and as Ona felt warm again, the creatures around her melted into the blinding, bright light.

§

Ona sat under the whitewood tree, fingers wrapped around the small bronze spade. White plumes of steam continued to erupt from the hillocks around her, each perhaps another window into a lost world.

The images she had seen went through her mind again and again. *Sometimes understanding comes to you not through thought, but through this throbbing of the heart, this tenderness in the chest that hurts.*

As their world was about to die, the ancient people of Nova Pacifica, in their last days, focused all their energy on leaving behind tributes, memorials of their civilization. Knowing that they themselves would not survive the sun that burnt hotter and hotter, they embedded their six-fold symmetry into every species around them, hoping that some would survive and become living echoes of their cities, their civilization, their selves. In their ruins, they hid a record that would be played when triggered by the detection of something made, aged, layered, still preserved because it was valued, so that they had some reasonable expectation that the owner would have a sense of history, of respect for the past.

Ona thought of the children, frightened and uncomprehending as their world burnt up. She thought of the lovers, poised between regret and acceptance, as the world outside collapsed against the world between them. She thought of a people trying their hardest to leave behind a trace of their existence in this universe, a few signs to mark their passage.

The past, ever recurring, made up the future like layers of patina.

She thought of Ms. Coron and the naked faces of the Teachers, and for the first time, she came to see their expressions in a new light.

It was not arrogance that made them look at the children the way they did, but fear. They had been stranded on this new world, where they could not survive, and they clung to their past as fiercely as they did because they knew that they would be yielding their places to a new race, the People of Nova Pacifica, and live on only in their memories.

Parents fear to be forgotten, to not be understood by their children.

Ona lifted the small bronze spade and licked the surface with the tip of her tongue. It tasted bitter and sweet, the fragrance of long-dead incense, of sacrificial offerings, of traces left behind by countless lifetimes. The spot where the steam had blasted away the patina, next to some ancient etched marks, was shaped like a little person, gleamed fresh and new, the future as well as the past.

She got up and pulled off a few pliant branches from nearby whitewood trees. Weaving carefully, she made them into a crown with twelve radiating branches, like tentacles, like hair, like olive branches. She had her costume.

It was but a brief scene glimpsed through the cloud of unknowing, a few images that she could barely comprehend. Perhaps they were idealized, sentimental, constructed; yet was there not a trace of authenticity, an indelible seed of the love of a people whose past meant something? She would show them how she now understood that digging into the past was an act of comprehension, an act of making sense of the universe.

Her body was an amalgam of the biological and technological heritages of two species, and her very existence the culmination of the striving of two peoples. Nested inside her was Earth Ona and Nova Pacifica Ona and Rebellious Ona and Obedient Ona and all the generations that came before her, stretching back into infinity.

Steeped in memories and the beginning of understanding, a child of two worlds picked her way through the woods and among the hillocks towards the Dome, the surprisingly heavy little spade cradled in her palm.

How to Live on Other Planets

# SARAH PINSKER
# The Low Hum of Her

Father built me a new grandmother when the real one died. "She's not a replacement," he said, as if anything could be. This one was made of clay and metal all run through with wires to conduct electricity, which Father said made her a lot like us. At her center, where we have hearts and guts, she had a brass birdcage. I don't know how he made her face look right. He put my real Bubbe's clothing on her, and wrapped one of my real Bubbe's headscarves around her iron-gray hair, and put Bubbe's identification papers into her skirt pocket and told me to call her Bubbe.

"Does it cook?" I asked him. "Does it bake, or sing?"

"She can," said Father. "Those are exactly the things she can do. You just have to teach her. She can look after you and keep you company when I'm working."

"I won't call it Bubbe."

"Call her what you like. Maybe you can say 'the new Bubbe' and 'she' when you're around me, though. I worked hard to make her for you."

He had spent months at his workbench. Long evenings after days spent teaching, and then long days after he was no longer allowed to work at the university. I had heard him cry sometimes, when he thought I was asleep. "She," I repeated, eyeing the machine.

That night, it offered help as I prepared beets for soup.

"Just stand in the corner and watch," I said. "You don't know how."

It followed my instructions. I stained the kitchen red with my messy chopping while it stood in the corner. How strange to see something that looked so much like Bubbe lurking in the dark corner where Bubbe never would have been found. "Too much to do," she would have said. "I'll rest when I'm dead." Now she was dead, and her absence was an ache in my chest.

The fake Bubbe was quiet for a while, then spoke again. "Teach me the songs you're singing, Tatiana. We can sing together while you cook."

I hushed it and sang the old songs softly to myself, imitating my grandmother's quavering soprano. There was no "we," I told myself. There was Father and there was me and there was the hole that Bubbe had left. No machine could replace her, even one that

31

looked and sounded like her. It didn't even know to call me my nickname, Tania. Or perhaps Father told it that would be too familiar.

I had started a notebook of recipes and songs back before my real Bubbe took ill. She hated that notebook. She said I should remember with my hands and heart and not leave a book to do the remembering for me. Each night after she was gone, I flipped through the pages and chose something to make, trying to recreate her recipes precisely. I made new notes to myself when the recipes went wrong, trying to recapture the little details that hadn't made it to the page. On the page for challah, my original transcription said "knead." "Use your back to knead," I remembered Bubbe saying when she first showed me how. "Your hands will get tired without the help of your back." She threw her whole body into the effort. Her whole front was coated in flour by the end. "Bosoms," she sighed in false despair, dusting herself off.

I wrote "use back" next to "knead." Still, the dough never worked out as well for me as it had for her. The other recipes were the same way. My father ate each meal without complaint, but I longed to make us something that tasted as good as my grandmother's cooking. I tried and tried, with the new Bubbe looking on from her corner.

And then Father came rushing home early one afternoon. "Tania, we must leave the house now as if we are going for an afternoon stroll. We can take only what we can fit into Bubbe." I started to correct him, to say "new Bubbe," but something in his tone silenced me.

The new Bubbe unbuttoned its blouse and opened the birdcage for us. For the first time, I understood what it was for. Father filled it with what little gold we had: my real Bubbe's rings and necklaces and the shabbos candlesticks, all wrapped in headscarves so they wouldn't rattle. Father's prayer book. I put in the picture of my parents at their wedding, and a portrait of Bubbe with the grandfather I never knew, and my book of songs and recipes.

I saw my father glance back, just once, and I looked back too. The house looked sad. The eaves drooped and the window boxes sagged empty. Father had been too busy to fix the eaves, and I had not known when to plant seeds for spring flowers. Bubbe had always done that. What if my memories of my mother and grandmother were so tied to that house that they stayed behind? I whispered one of Bubbe's songs under my breath, to show the memories they could come with us.

We walked away. The trees still had more flowers than leaves, but rain the night before had driven some of the petals to the ground. The petals were soft underfoot and muted our footsteps on the cobblestones. The streets smelled like lilacs and rain and I listened for screams and jackboots that I never heard and the three of us strolled down to the river and along its bank as if there were no hurry in the world. We walked away from home, just like that, just kept walking with nothing but the valuables that traveled inside the cage of the new Bubbe's chest.

One of Father's friends met us outside the city as evening fell. He gave us black bread and cheese and drove us through the night. We stopped once to show papers. A soldier shined a light into the car and looked at our documents while another held a rifle at the ready. They opened all of the doors and the boot of the automobile.

"Where are you going, Grandmother?" the one soldier asked the new Bubbe. I held my breath.

"My son, he has all the answers," she said. It was something Bubbe had always said. I didn't even know this one knew how to say it. I didn't hear father's explanation for our travel over the pounding of my heart. The light lingered in our faces another moment, then went out.

"No bags," said the one soldier to the other. They raised the gate to let us through.

We drove on. I wished father had sat in the back seat with me, to stroke my hair and reassure me. Instead, the new Bubbe reached for my hand in the darkness of the car; for the first time, I let it. I fell asleep on its lap listening to the low hum of it and pretending it was a lullaby.

Father's friend left us in a strange city in the morning. There, Father purchased a small trunk and a suitcase and clothing for us, then tickets aboard a steamship for the following day. He only bought two tickets. I watched from our hotel room's single sagging bed as he dismantled the new Bubbe.

"I'm sorry I have to do this," he said to it. It shrugged and sighed a very Bubbe-like sigh, weighted with suffering and understanding. I shivered when the light went out of its eyes.

"Why didn't you just buy it -her- a ticket?" I asked.

"There will be closer quarters on the next part of our journey, Tania, and inspections. She can fool anyone who is not expecting a person to be something other than a person, but she would not pass a medical examination."

He separated it into several parts, tying and braiding wires back in on themselves in neat bundles. I averted my gaze when he took its face. He left the torso intact, like a dressmaker's form, with its birdcage core and all of our valuables hidden within. Disassembled, she fit into the small trunk he had purchased that afternoon.

At the docks, we were assigned numbers and a group. We descended a steep staircase to the steerage compartment, pushed and prodded the whole way like cattle. Father needed both hands for the trunk that contained the new Bubbe, so I gripped his coat with one hand and the suitcase with the other, trying not to get separated from him in the crush of people. Two more levels down we found the family quarters, where we were permitted to claim two iron bunks and the narrow gap between them.

That night, Father placed the trunk at the foot of his straw mattress. He slept curled up like a baby in the space that remained. I tried not to think about the collection of parts in the trunk, which had once seemed so close to alive. Life was a fragile thing. I had seen my grandmother's body after her passing, but I was not there to witness the light leaving her eyes.

Our quarters smelled like sweat and wet wool and sick. And so many noises! Other families murmured. Babies cried, and somewhere an old woman moaned. The steam engine churned and clanked. I struggled to sleep at first, but I soon learned to tune out the families and let the sounds of the ship lull me. The engine sounds from the deepest parts of the ship's belly reminded me of the new Bubbe, and that in turn reminded me of my own Bubbe's voice. I let the sounds blur together: real and imaginary, alive and almost alive.

I did not count the days, but gave over to the indignities of the situation. We had no dining area, but ate on the floor or on our bunks. We gnawed hard biscuits and picked insects out of our soup. My cooking was fit for royalty compared to the ship's fare, and at least I had never lost a hairpin into my stew. After each meal I waited in line to dunk our tin plates in a basin of sea water, and in another line to wash my face and hands. I considered the new Bubbe, in pieces in the trunk, whenever I felt too cramped.

We arrived in the place Father said would be our new home. As he had warned, there were physical inspections. They checked our hair, face, neck, and hands, which the new Bubbe might have passed, then our eyes, which she might not have. The doctors had chalk in their hands, and marked the clothing of some. I tried to regulate my breathing, tried to turn myself into a machine incapable of weakness, and hoped Father was doing the same. We passed the doctors, and the interrogators, and then we were in the new place with nothing but our trunk and our suitcase.

Father had the address of a colleague from his old university, and we walked for an hour to reach his house. Mr. Levitan embraced my father despite what must have been the overwhelming stink of us. He helped us secure an apartment that very day. Perhaps the odor sped his actions. Still, he took the time to ask me questions about our journey, and he gave me a candy that tasted both sweet and citrus-sour at once.

The new apartment was much smaller than our old house. That didn't matter, since we had fewer things. The building smelled like lemons and pickles and cigarettes, and the sunlight that filtered through the windows was more intense than the light where we had come from. Bells rang often throughout the day.

Father reassembled the new Bubbe. I did not admit it to him, but when he reconnected her circuits I was relieved to see that she had survived her travel without any damage. I listened as he explained our new situation. She shrugged and nodded.

Father said not to leave the apartment, which was easy since we had no place to go. The new Bubbe was my only company now that Father was away working even longer hours than he had at home. She had not asked her questions since we moved to the new place. Father brought home only bread and herring, so she had no reason to help with the cooking. He bought me a radio. I listened to that in place of singing, though I recognized few of the songs and didn't know the language the announcers spoke.

The electricity in our building was inconsistent, surging and dropping at various points throughout most days. For the most part the power would resume mere moments after the interruption, but one morning it went out and didn't come back on. My radio cut out in mid-song. I paced the floor, at first in boredom and then in fear. Hours passed, and the room grew dark.

"What if something happened and Father can't come home?" I asked the new Bubbe. "What if we're alone?"

"Ssha," she said. For the first time since the car ride, I let her take me in her arms. The whir of her inner workings reassured me; she was something the outage couldn't touch.

It took a minute to realize she was singing. Quietly at first, then louder when I didn't make her stop. She sang one of Bubbe's songs, the ones I had sung under my breath when I didn't want her to hear. Her voice cracked like porcelain on high notes.

I wanted her to sing another, and she seemed pleased when I asked her to do so. I joined her on the chorus. We sang another, and another, the old songs and the ones from the radio, and passed the day in that way. I didn't even notice when the electricity came back on.

Late that night, Father arrived with a chicken and an onion and a sack of kasha.

"Get your recipe book, Tania," he said. "We'll have a feast."

I shook my head.

The real Bubbe said to remember with my hands, so I showed the new Bubbe how the secret to kasha was to mix in the chicken fat. She got grease on her blouse, like the real Bubbe. I taught her to say "bosoms," and sigh, as the real Bubbe always had.

My thought that day was if I taught her hands the recipes, if her lips knew Bubbe's songs, then there would always be two of us to remember, even when Father was away. My real grandmother had been my teacher, but this one needed me to teach her.

"You can call me Tania," I said to her. It might have been my imagination, but I thought she looked pleased.

"What will you call me?" she asked. I considered. Bubbe did not fit any longer, nor "the new Bubbe," as I had addressed her with such derision.

"What would you like to be called?"

She shrugged. "You choose. Call me something with meaning to you."

I gave her the name Chaya, alive. She was no longer just a reminder of the grandmother I had lost, but her own thing.

She will be with me always, I hope. Someday she and I will show my children and grandchildren how to make kreplach and kasha varnishkes. Someday they will wonder at the birdcage in her chest, which still holds my old book of recipes and the photo of my grandparents. Someday I will have hair as gray as hers, and then grayer. I will lean over the table and cover my own blouse with flour, and sigh and say "bosoms" with the right note of false despair, so the children around me will giggle. When the others go to sleep, she and I will remember together, and I will listen to the low hum of her, and we will sing each other lullabies.

## BOGI TAKÁCS
## The Tiny English-Hungarian Phrasebook For Visiting Extraterrestrials

*Now with transliterations—a true lifesaver!*

**Yes** — Igen — *EE-gehn*

**No** — Nem — *NEHM*

**My automatic translator does not support Hungarian.** — A fordítógépem nem tud magyarul. — *AH FOUR-dee-toh-gay-pehm NEHM tood MAH-dyah-roohl.*

**I speak Chinese/English/Russian/German.** — Beszélek kínaiul/angolul/oroszul/németül. — *BEH-say-lehk KEEH-nah-ee-ool/AHN-go-lool/OH-raw-sool/NEH-meh-tuehl.*

**Do you speak Chinese/English/Russian/German?** — Beszél ön kínaiul/angolul/oroszul/németül? — *BEH-sail oehn KEEH-nah-ee-ool/AHN-go-lool/OH-raw-sool/NEH-meh-tuehl?*

**My apologies.** — Elnézést kérek. — *EHL-nay-zaysht kay-rehk.*

**I am not from Earth.** — Nem a Földről jöttem. — *NEHM ah FOEHLD-roehl yoeht-tehm.*

**That's (not) an integral part of my body.** — Ez (nem) a testem szerves része. — *EHZ (nehm) ah TESH-tehm SEHR-vesh ray-seh.*

**I am not interested in politics.** — Nem érdekel a politika. — *NEHM ehr-deh-kehl ah POH-lee-tee-kah.*

**I am not affiliated with the Left/Right.** — Nem vagyok baloldali/jobboldali. — *NEHM vah-dyohk BAHL-ohl-dah-lee/YOHB-ohl-dah-lee.*

**Do you support the radical Right?** — Támogatja a radikális jobboldalt? — *TAAH-moh-gaht-yah ah RAH-dee-kah-leesh YOHB-ohl-dahlt?*

How to Live on Other Planets

**I cannot answer that question. I need to talk to a telepath first.** — Erre a kérdésre nem tudok válaszolni. Előbb beszélnem kell egy telepatával. — *EHreh ah kayr-daysh-reh NEHM too-dohk VAH-lah-soul-nee. EH-loeb BEH-sail-nehm kehl edy TEH-leh-pah-tah-vahl.*

**I am not Jewish.** — Nem vagyok zsidó. — *NEHM vah-dyohk ZHEE-daw.*

**Please do not touch me. My tentacles produce a neurotoxin.** — Kérem, ne érjen hozzám. A csápjaim idegmérget termelnek. — *KEH-rehm, NEH ayr-yen hohz-zahm. Ah TSHAH-pyah-eem EE-dehg-mayr-geht tehr-mehl-nehk.*

**I mean no harm.** — Nem áll szándékomban kárt okozni. — *NEHM ahl sun-dei-kohm-bahn KAHRT oh-kohz-nee.*

**Please step back.** — Kérem, lépjen hátrébb. — *KEH-rehm, LAYP-yen HAHT-rayb.*

**I have no intent to have sex with my family members.** — Nem szándékozom családtagjaimmal közösülni. — *NEHM sun-dei-koh-zohm TSHAH-lahd-tahg-yah-eem-mahl koeh-zoeh-shuel-nee.*

**If you continue to threaten me, I will have to resort to self-defense measures.** — Ha tovább fenyeget, kénytelen leszek önvédelmi módszerekhez folyamodni. — *HAH TOH-vahb feh-nieh-geht, KEHNY-teh-lehn leh-sehk OEHN-vay-dehl-mee MODE-seh-rehk-hehz FOH-yah-mohd-nee.*

**Officer, I was acting in self-defense.** — Rendőr úr, önvédelemből cselekedtem. — *REHN-deur OOHR, OEHN-vay-deh-lehm-boehl TSHEH-leh-kehd-tehm.*

**Despite the occasional small incident, I appreciate the hospitality of the Hungarian people and of Earth.** — A néhány apróbb incidens ellenére értékelem a magyar nép és a Föld vendégszeretetét. — *AH nayh-hahny ahp-rawb EEN-tsee-densh eh-leh-nay-reh EHR-tay-keh-lehm ah MAH-dyahr nayp aysh ah FOEHLD vehn-dayg-seh-reh-teh-tayt.*

How to Live on Other Planets

# TOM GREENE
## Zero Bar

"Even the best birth control fails sometimes," the doctor says. "It's a good thing you found out early, while you still have options."

"I guess I won't be showing for a while yet?"

"It varies. Maybe a month or two. Let me give you some literature."

She starts pulling brochures off the rack on the wall.

I lean over and point. "Can I have *that* one?"

She gives me a knowing look and hands me the brochure.

On the front is a picture of a smiling baby—fair skin, blue eyes, and a tuft of corn silk hair—nestled in a pile of white linens. The title says, "What Will Your Baby Look Like?" It doesn't mention plasmids until you look inside.

"If you want to go with this," the doctor says, "you'll have to decide right away."

"Like, how soon?"

"It's already kind of late, but the next few days should be okay. The longer you wait, the riskier it gets."

I nod and shove the brochure into the hip pocket of my jeans. The doctor thinks she knows what's going on—with the father's race, I mean. She must see a lot of women with something to hide. If I do nothing, there's a chance my child will look more like its father's ancestors, and a chance it'll look more like mine.

§

"Okay, boys. Ante up."

The building manager comes up to us with a datafly. One at a time, the three men on my crew press their thumbs onto the print pad.

"You all understand it don't matter to me," the manager says. "But immigration's been cracking down."

The *jefe's* father came from Bogota, but Jorge and Rudy are my cousins—hometown boys for generations back. They're all going to check out.

"Be right back," the manager says, then leaves us standing in the office building's lobby.

41

I meet Rudy's eyes for a second. He looks troubled.

"You okay, *meja*?" he says.

Actually, there's nothing I'd rather do at the moment than go curl up in bed at home and cry. But that wouldn't do anybody any good. Least of all me. I try my best to give Rudy a smile. I think it comes out okay.

"Sure," I say.

"Elsa said you went to the doctor this morning," he says.

The brochure is still in my hip pocket.

"It's nothing," I say. "Just a check up."

He exchanges a glance with his brother Jorge, but lets it drop. They've always been protective of me. When they were teenagers and I was a little girl riding my bike around the streets in the old neighborhood, they watched out for me. They used to rescue me from fire ants and garter snakes in the vacant lot where the neighborhood kids played. They know part of the story of why I came back and asked for this job at the HVAC company their father owns. I can tell they're troubled. I want to tell them that the familiarity of just being around them is helping me feel better. But I don't think it would reassure them.

The manager comes back and says. "All right, then. Bring your truck around." Then to me he says, "You can come through the building with me, missy."

Technically, he's supposed to offer the thumbprinter to me too. But he doesn't.

§

"Dad, what are we?"

I'm riding in the car with my father. He picks me up every day after school on his way home from the community college where he's a professor. At about twelve years old, I'm already at my full adult height of five-eight. I bump into everything. I'm too smart, and I'm persuaded none of the boys at school will ever find me interesting.

"What do you mean?"

"What race are we?"

He flinches, but doesn't take his eyes off the road. He shifts his hands on the steering wheel.

"Well, your mother's grandparents came from Mexico. That's the easy one. My family, it's hard to explain without a history lesson."

I throw up my hands and flop back in the seat. "Why does every question always have to be so complicated?"

"We were already here," he says, squinting down the road like he's looking at something in the distance. "In North America, I mean."

"So like Native American?"

He shakes his head. "We were on the wrong side of a map line when they handed out that label. When the Spaniards came, they called us *Indios.* When the Mexicans kicked out the Spanish, they called us Mexicans. When the whites came, they renamed the place 'America,' but they still call us 'Mexicans.' Why is this coming up now?"

"We took a state test today. We were supposed to bubble in our race on the form, and I didn't know what to put."

"You didn't just put 'white'?"

"I was going to, but Paul Gomez said I couldn't."

"And what was Paul Gomez's reasoning?"

"He said I was a Zero Bar. What is that?"

My father mutters something about Paul's father. When he speaks, his voice is clipped.

"It's a kind of candy bar. I think you can still get them."

"What does it mean?"

"A Zero Bar is white on the outside, and brown on the inside."

§

I'm fifteen, and it's my first day at the new school. Even though my mom has hinted about 'fresh starts,' I'm wearing my usual threadbare jeans and hoodie because—as I tell Mom to her dismay—I Don't Care About Superficial Appearances.

At my old school on the west side, everything looked like it had been beaten up, patched, and then the patches beaten up again. Where the paint chipped, you could see layers of institutional pastel colors underneath. I was afraid to go into the girls room or touch a banister for fear of catching something.

But here, the halls have bright lights. The door handles work. The windows don't have steel mesh. I go to class, and there are enough dataflys for everyone, and they're not even leashed to the desks. And there's something else bugging me—something I can't place. Then finally I get it. Everybody is white. From the back of the class, I'm looking out over rows of blond heads. Instead of giving us a worksheet and then sitting at her desk, the English teacher stands at the front and asks us what we think. The kids raise their hands and answer, like they're used to this.

Years later, I look back at my class pictures. Through eighth grade, it's always easy to find myself, one of a handful of white faces in the sea of brown. Then after the move, my face is lost in the crowd. I had always looked whiter than anybody in my class. Now, among real white people, I'm the ethnic one.

§

"They're hard workers," the manager says, opening the utility room door so I can go through. "You know what I mean?"

"What?"

"I mean, I can't get the teenagers in my neighborhood to mow my lawn."

"Oh," I say. "Yeah, kids don't want to work."

"But these guys, they come up here, they know how to put in a day's labor."

I don't say anything.

"I admire it," he says. "I really do."

I still don't say anything. We're at the back door now, and the manager pauses with his thumb over the door button.

"I apologize in advance if I'm saying something bad here, but a lot of people been coming to this country for a long time. All kinds, you know? But at least the blacks learned to speak English."

§

My cousin Jesse screams. He's about three years old—I'm a year older. I'm watching him scream, his mouth an inverted bean shape, his face purple. My mother rushes over, picks him up in her arms. She's babysitting while my Aunt is out of town.

"Why did you hit him?" she says.

"He won't speak English."

"He can't speak English."

I don't know what to say. I never thought of this before. My cousin pauses long enough to take a breath, then howls again.

I say, "Well then I don't want to play with him."

§

The door opens, and the heat from outside washes the utility room. The guys use a hand truck to wheel in the crate, over to the spot the manager indicates. I want to say something to him. Do I say something to him? I'm missing my chance. I've never been good at this kind of thing.

The guys start to unbox the unit. The manager's job is done at this point and he could just leave us to work. But he lingers.

When I took over this job from my cousin Elsa so she could go back to reception, she told me that my main responsibility was keeping the clients out of the way so that the guys could work. She said she hated the job because she felt like nobody respected her as a foreman.

"But you won't have that problem," she said.

§

It's because of the new school that I find out what's been done to me. Because of sophomore biology class where we actually do things, instead of reading silently at our desks and answering the questions at the end of the chapter.

We're studying genetic inheritance, drawing Punnett Squares of our hair and eye color for two generations back. My father's grandparents both had brown eyes and hair. My mother's grandparents both had brown eyes and hair. So that means that I should have...

I raise my hand. "Mr. Kreiger? Am I doing this right?"

He comes over and looks at my datafly. "Hmm, that's all correct. Human eye and hair color is actually more complicated than Mendel's peas—" He stops suddenly. I get the feeling he's realizing something. Connecting the dots.

His eyes shift away from me. "Recessive genes can sometimes lie dormant for generations."

My father picks me up after school and I tell him what happened. He doesn't look at me until I get to the end and say, "So I should have brown hair and brown eyes, right?"

"Yes," he says, "And brown skin. You have the genes for those. And from your mother's Spanish ancestors you also have genes for green eyes, fair hair and white skin, which are actually expressed."

"Huh?"

"We were wondering when to tell you. It had just been approved by the FDA when you were—you know, before you were born."

"What had been approved?"

"A way to swap—or not actually to swap out genes—they can't do that yet. But a way to control which genes are expressed by inserting an extra piece of DNA. A 'plasmid.'" He glances at me. "So you would have brown hair and eyes, and darker skin. But those genes were switched off." He looks back at the road. I take a moment to figure out what to say.

"You messed with my genes? To make me look white?"

"You gotta understand, Zoe. As a parent, you want your child to have every possible advantage." *Narrator*

"What advantage?"

"Demographics don't lie. Race and poverty are still correlated for Latinos almost as strongly as for African Americans. So we do everything we can. Good nutrition. A safe neighborhood. Strong schools. So when we had the chance to do this—you understand, right?"

§

"So tell me about this," the manager says.

"The fuel cells are in there," I say, pointing to the chromed box about the size of a mini-fridge that the guys are levering into position.

"That little thing gonna power the whole building? All the offices?"

"Yep, it'll cut in when the grid goes out, like any emergency generator, but this—" I point to a little box on the side, "—monitors the price of electricity, and cuts the generator in automatically when natural gas is cheaper."

The manager looks worried. "They're gonna tap the gas line?"

Jorge is a state-certified gas fitter. Rudy is a master electrician. They're probably the two most skilled tradesmen in this business within a hundred miles. But when the manager looks at them, all he sees is some Mexicans.

I really want to smack him right then.

But I remind myself—this is for the family. Assault charges are bad for business. I'm going to knuckle under, do whatever it takes to

How to Live on Other Planets

get through today.

I say, "So how about we go take care of the invoicing?"

"Yeah, okay," he says. He gives the guys a final eyeballing, then leads me back through the fire door to the lobby.

§

"I didn't want Dad to find out about this," I say. "He would have a meltdown."

I'm eighteen, in my bedroom with my mom, and the stack of papers in her lap is my acceptance forms from a school in Massachusetts.

"It's a lot of money," she says, looking at the forms. "But how did you apply for this?"

"I'm not sure."

I go to the window to make sure the driveway is empty. Dad's still at work.

I say, "I'm never sure what bubbles to fill in. I guess whatever combination I put down got me in for this minority student thing."

I sit on the bed next to my mom.

"I can't take the money, right? I mean, I'm basically white in some ways—"

She shakes her head so hard that her dark curls flop into her face. "Listen, you don't have anything to be ashamed of."

"But isn't this what Dad always says? The whole problem is people accepting privileges that they didn't earn themselves?"

She sighs. "This, from the man who gets pulled over all the time for driving in his own neighborhood in a car that's too fancy. He knows even when he says it—all this 'post-racial' stuff is nonsense. People see brown skin, they act the same way as always."

"So I can take the money?"

She tucks the papers back into the envelope. "Listen, my mother always used to tell me that we don't know how much longer this stuff is going to be around. Any day somebody could decide that the problem is over and take it all away. So I say, take advantage of it while it's here."

"And Dad?"

She shrugs. "We just won't tell him."

§

"Whereabouts you from?" the manager asks.

"I grew up here, but I went to school in Massachusetts."

He hitches up his belt as we walk through the lobby. "My nephew had an offer from a school up north once. He could of gone on a football scholarship."

"Oh really?"

"Yup. Come to find out they give the football scholarship to a black boy. I mean, I reckon they can do what they want with their money," he says. "But that don't seem quite fair to me."

"Must have been a while ago," I say.

"Maybe ten years?"

"They took away the last of those programs a couple of years ago," I say. "That's all gone now."

We arrive at his office door. He fumbles with his keys.

"So you came all the way back here for the summer?"

"I graduated," I say. "I'm here to stay."

"Just a home town gal, eh?"

My gut twinges. Sometimes it's possible to nearly forget for a little while.

"Something like that," I say.

§

It's the usual story. We meet in history class, senior year, a group project together. He makes a corny joke. I laugh. He impresses me by actually doing his share of the work. Afterward, he calls me for a date. He's into music, has actually heard of Timba and Conjunto. We share a bottle of Martini & Rossi Bianco one night. He reads me Bukowski; I read him Zinn. We go to a bad art film and laugh, annoying everyone else in the theater. → boyfriend

I warn Jeff early-on about my quirks, my old-fashioned affection for actual paper books, the way I never really learned how to use the features of my cell phone, don't really use the social media nets. He isn't scared away. He's comfortable with it. With my boyfriends before, everything was drama. But Jeff is easy to be with.

*A white guy* I think at first, and then I hate that I've thought it. I decide to be post-racial, to go with it. When spring comes and he wears shorts, I tell him it reminds me of middle school gym class, where we all had to dress out and the other kids would make fun and call me *"leche legs."*

To see such an expanse of white skin, with its fine, fair hair, on someone else is a new experience. Even his junk is white. That takes some getting used to.

I'm nervous telling him about my heritage. I give him the complete version, with the history lesson. He says I'm exotic. I like him even more.

§

"So you don't consider yourself to be basically just white?"

I look across the bed at Jeff in surprise. His roommate is off studying somewhere, so we have the room to ourselves. The sun slants through the blinds with that honey-colored New England afternoon light that I never got used to.

"I guess I spent a lot of time avoiding the issue," I say. "I never learned Spanish. My mom wouldn't teach me because of the trouble she had, going to school not knowing English. My dad wanted me to learn, but he was working his way through school with three jobs."

"So you're kind of white by default?"

I frown. "Well it's mostly about the attitudes now. I mean, the 'No Mexicans' water fountains and bathrooms are gone—"

"I thought that was blacks."

"Uhhhh, no. There's a whole history of the same segregation against Latinos in the southwest." I poke him in the chest. "Y'all Yankees just don't read about it."

He laughs and leans back on the pillows. I lean back beside him.

I say, "That's why we get touchy when people say Latinos are white. Until the supreme court told them no, Texas laws said it was okay to segregate us because anti-segregation laws didn't apply to 'Mexicans.' Because we're white."

He thinks for a minute. Then he says, "History."

I stare at the sunlight on the ceiling. I want to tell him about how, even now, my father is careful to meet his white female students in the college cafeteria instead of his office because of what any accusation, however false, could do to his career. Or about how, still today, when people knock on the door of our big house in the nice neighborhood and my mother answers it, they ask to talk to her employer.

But I don't want him to think I'm creating drama. I don't say anything.

§

Jeff tells me he's interested in marriage, in kids. I've already been thinking the same things. The American Dream—someone you love, a house of your own, kids growing up safe and happy. Doing better than your parents.

I tell my friends that I think he might be The One. They're envious. When I go home for winter break, we text every day and exchange silly phone pictures. In the spring, with graduation coming, we talk about the future. He gives me a ring tucked between the dog-eared pages of my copy of *A People's History.* I say yes. We make plans.

§

The manager's office is a tiny closet off the lobby mostly filled by a huge cluttered desk. Photos of his family in mismatched frames. Last year's calender on the wall still open to December. He uses a lot of paper—writes me out a physical check, tears it out of the binder and hands it over.

"So what's it like up north?"

I shrug. "Like on TV. Leaves in the fall, snow in winter. Liberals."

He does one of those belly laughs. "Surprised you didn't stay up there. My kids can't wait to get out of the Texas heat. The 30-year drought, the economy..." He shakes his head.

"Nothing open in my field right now. This is the family business, so I'm mostly doing it just to help out."

"Pretty close with your family, eh?"

I shrug. "I guess."

§

"You don't understand," I say. "Moving would be a big deal for me. My whole family lives within a few dozen miles of each other."

"You don't think maybe it's time to branch out?" Jeff says.

We're walking on a beach—a New England beach, so rocks

under our boots and we're bundled up against the wind. A late cold snap has turned the sky gray, and the ocean is like rippled slate.

I say, "Moving away to set up your own nuclear family is a middle-class white American thing. I had kind of planned to move back after graduation."

"Really?" he says. "You'd want to be that close to your family?"

"What's wrong with staying near your family?"

He picks up a pebble without breaking stride, tosses it out into the water. "Connecticut has really good schools. We want all the possible advantages for our kids, right?"

We walk. I find the courage to say what I'm thinking.

"Speaking of advantages, you know there's a chance any kids we have will resemble my family? Physically, I mean."

"Yeah."

"Connecticut isn't exactly the most diverse place on earth."

"Maybe it won't matter."

"What do you mean?"

"I don't know. Maybe race won't matter as much anymore, now that anybody can be any color."

I hesitate. Then I say, "You mean now that everybody can be white."

"Not necessarily—"

"What parents would choose to make their children black? Or Latino? Would you?"

He doesn't answer.

"And anyway," I say, "if I'm proof of anything, it's that having white skin doesn't make you white."

A seagull glides down and fixes us with one red-ringed eye to see if we have anything to eat. When neither of us takes our hands out of our coat pockets, it loses interest and banks away.

I say, "So everything is arranged with your parents?"

"They're really looking forward to meeting you," he says.

"I've never been to a country club."

He nods.

"Wow, the meeting of the parents." I punch him in the arm. "So how does your mom feel about you bringing home a Latin girl?"

He doesn't say anything for a minute. Then he says, "I'm sure it'll be fine."

§

I'm crying, and the fact that I can't stop just makes me angrier until I can feel myself shaking. Jeff crosses the lawn to where I am in the gazebo and puts a hand on my elbow.

"I told them you're not feeling well. Are you okay?"

"No," I say. I twitch his hand off my elbow.

He says, "I'm really sorry."

"I don't know how to answer that."

"It's just talk. They don't know what they're saying."

I look up the hill at the white pavilion where they sit, their expressions faint in the distance: Jeff's parents and uncle and aunt, pale khakis, pastel polo shirts, summer dresses.

"Really? A casual lunch conversation about how the Rodney King rioters got what they deserved, about shooting Mexicans before they get across the river. And that crap about 'the Values that Made this Country Great—'"

"They usually never talk like this," he says. "They're just repeating back stuff they've heard."

"But you didn't even stand up for me!" I turn toward him. "How can they say all that stuff right to my face?"

He looks down. It dawns on me, and I have to hold my fist across my mouth until I get enough control to speak.

"You didn't tell them. They think I'm white."

He starts toward me, but stops when he sees my look.

"You need to take me home," I say.

"What am I going to say to them?"

"Take me home, or I'm calling a taxi."

He goes back up the hill and talks to them. The uncle gets up, as if to come over, but Jeff gestures him back down. I can't hear what he's telling them. He comes back and we get in the car and drive. It's a long time before he speaks.

"I told them you weren't feeling well," he says.

I don't answer.

He says, "Sometimes it's hard to remember. You know."

I look out the window.

"I don't understand why you're getting worked up about this," he says. "What difference does it make?"

"Were you trying to hide it?" I say.

"What? No. I just though it would be easier."

"Easier for who?"

He doesn't answer.

"Did you think they wouldn't figure it out?" I say. "What about the wedding? Were you going to tell them I was adopted or something?"

"Forget my family. We'll only see them a couple of times a year anyway."

"Is this why you wanted to move?"

"Look, it's good to have ideals and everything, but we're graduating pretty soon. You're going to need to get over this."

"*Over this?*" I say. "Stop treating my race like a disease."

"That's not what I meant."

"Who did you think you were marrying?"

"Lets just stick to the plan."

We ride past the entrance to campus without saying anything. I'm understanding something new. I see myself and Jeff in our two-storey, four-and-a-half-bath colonial outside Hartford or wherever. I teach history or work for a museum part time. He commutes to the city. I do Yoga three times a week. He golfs on weekends. Our kids make good grades. I take them to dance class, hockey, tutoring, lacrosse. They grow up and get good jobs. We retire to Florida, and none of our friends ever suspects.

I feel like the ground is opening up under my feet. Not because it would be wrong, but because it terrifies me that it would be so *easy.*

When Jeff pulls up outside my dorm, I get out of the car. I leave the ring on the seat.

That night I dream we're were married and I'm washing his shirts for him, but I can't get them clean.

"They're not white!" I keep saying.

And in the dream, he pats my arm and says, "Yes they are. Yes they are."

§

The manager walks me back out through the utility room, past the new generator, now all hooked up and running, and to the back door. He shakes my hand.

"Pleasure doing business with your family, young lady."

I nod and step out into the heat. The guys are packing the last of the stuff back into the truck, closing the door on the cap. I'm pretty sure the manager sees the name of the HVAC company on the side panel—family business, family name. He gives me a funny look. I feel a tiny sense of triumph.

§

At home, dinner is ready, and Mom and Dad are waiting. I tell them I'll be down in a minute and run upstairs. In my room, there's all my childhood stuff: the battered furniture, the old paper books, the academic trophies that my mom dusts religiously. When I first got back, feeling numb and bewildered, it was comforting. But now it all looks different to me, like stuff that belongs to another childhood. The stuff of a girl who never had to think about "What Will Your Baby Look Like?"

I take the brochure out of my pocket and look at it. I didn't think I would ever even consider this. But now that it's me—my child—it's different. My father was right. You do want all the advantages.

I think about the building manager, and about Jeff's parents. I think about Paul Gomez and his 'Zero Bar,' and the world my child is going to have to live in.

I crumple the brochure and drop it in the trash, then go downstairs for dinner.

# NISI SHAWL
# In Colors Everywhere

*Clients must not be killed. WestHem has opted to destroy their original bodies while preserving psychoemotional components. Transport to Amends completes the allotted punishment, taking into consideration the impossibility of return to Earth, along with the harsh experiences certain to arise from atechnical living conditions. On this account, however, minimal attempts should be made to ameliorate these conditions.*
                    —*Mission Guidelines,* Psyche Moth, *2055*

Trill walked home through the Rainshadow Mountains with Adia, her former mentor. Not alone.

The sky had been high all day. Now, with evening, it came low, wetting them and their surroundings with mist. Silver beaded the fuzz beneath their feet.

Adia was tough, though an elder. She walked steadily, without complaint. She ought to have been tired even before they started; she and Trill had spent the week teaching a cohort of tens-to-thirteens how to weave buildings.

Jubilee, the largest settlement of prisoners on Amends for two generations now, had decided to bud a new village. As expected, the tens-to-thirteens were eager for adventure, the fourteens-to-seventeens hardly less so. The site they chose, where the peninsula joined the mainland's western coast, fronted a beach on Unrest Bay, quieter waters than Jubilee's open ocean. "Unrest" might well be picked as the new place's name; the selection would be finalized by those who ended up living there.

The first wave had big plans. They would build boats and fish there, these two age-groups claimed. They'd start double the Fisher *Dopkwes* and beat the older settlement's harvest. The eighteens-to-twenty-fours were of course more skeptical, having just discovered cynicism. The few twenty-fives-to-forty-fives—Trill's age cohort—who had chosen to emigrate with them smiled and nodded encouragingly whenever the idea came up. And then returned to the work of their current dopkwes: rope spinning, planting, preserving, and so on.

Trill and Adia had left to go home late that morning with no urgency. No Rogues or Solitaries had been sighted in the area for months. And it was summer; even when the sky came down to kiss them they were sure that leaflight would last long enough for their trip. They'd eaten a big lunch at the halfway point, so they wouldn't be hungry till they arrived—

Trill stopped before she knew why. Adia, ahead of her, kept walking moments after the sound became audible to Trill: a scream, a shriek sinking lower, louder—closer, Trill realized. She shrank to crouch under a dripping Chrismas tree while looking up, frightened but curious. Like a tooth or a knife the sound bit through the air. A flock of prettybirds burst out of a fall of redvines hanging from a bluff and flew south. The sound grew, grew, the rising roar of someone who never needed a new breath.

Adia still stood in the open, face tilted up as if she could see the screaming. Trill staggered to her feet to coax the Lady who had trained her to shelter, to safety.

**BOOM!**

On her hands and knees, Trill looked around. Nothing had changed—except that she had to piss from fear. But Adia stood stubbornly upright in the same place, on the same rough path just beginning to be worn between Jubilee and the new settlement. She stood calmly, relaxed, as if facing nothing more serious than a test— though she'd become a Lady decades ago. As though nothing threatened her.

The elder shook her head and glanced at Trill over her shoulder, then came to help her rise. "Long time since I heard anything like that." Adia's words were soft as whispers. Why? "Poor shang. You got no clue, do you? That come from Dr. Ops."

Trill stepped back off the path to release her water. She whispered too. "From *Psyche Moth*?" Her clothes didn't rustle. Her water made no sound striking the fuzz.

"What? Speak up!"

"Dr. Ops on the *Psyche Moth*?" Trill shouted. She understood now. Adia wasn't whispering, so she didn't have to. It was just that the huge noise had made it hard to hear anything else afterwards.

"He the one. It ain't a bomb or nothin—mission guidelines say he ain't spozed to kill us. Naw, he just sent us another drone, sounded like. First since I had my final period. I wish I coulda seen it. Fuckin Chrismas trees in the way. Wonder what kinda trouble he put inside it?"

§

*Low intrusion surveillance recommended. High-orbit
monitoring to be supplemented by trustee insertion at
periodic intervals keyed to instructions relayed from
verified WestHem government facilities via translight. If
no such instructions are received for over 20 years, refer
to procedures for establishing surface stock.*
—*Mission Guidelines*, Psyche Moth, *2055*

Trill was working out a design when they sent for her, an idea about
something to help the Hunters Dopkwe that had come from talking
with her ex-lover Hett, LeeRai's father. It was a sort of a box that
became a basket when its walls dried out. A strap over the forehead
and the high-climbing sixes-to-nines could pack one of them as full of
phibian eggs as they liked. Hang the box-baskets from a line and
even with the lids left on, there'd be enough air getting inside to cure
the leathery eggs slowly, the way she liked them.

"Lady?"

Trill looked up from her workbasin. Dola, an eighteens-to-
twenty-fours identifying as female, leaned tentatively in at the shed's
entrance. "Will you come with me to the baths?"

A summons. Trill nodded. "Just let me—" She did what she
needed to without further explanation: tied off her project's last side
panel, laid it on a rack, emptied her workbasin's water into the
shop's barrel, and wiped dry her hands.

Outside, the sky had mellowed to a gold like beer. Evening. She
should have stopped work long ago to visit the kitchen for food.
There would always be something, though. More tempting was the
urge to find the fives-and-unders before they went to sleep. She
hadn't spent the night with LeeRai since coming home four days—
almost a full week—ago.

That morning they had raced each other on the hard-packed
sand of the beach. Trill had laughed, the breath hot and easy in her
lungs, her daughter big and plump and bronzed by the sky. And
getting so strong! So fast! Always moving—it would be strange and
lovely to see her lying still, asleep—

But the other Ladies wanted her now.

She followed Dola up the hill. This neighborhood of Jubilee, up against the Rainshadows, had drawn people to it from the settlement's main site because of the hot springs. As they walked the sun disappeared, ducking behind the mountains, though the sky's grace and the leaves' first radiance provided plenty of light.

Dola had applied to become a Lady that spring, shortly after conscripting Trill to help the Gardeners Dopkwe. Having recently completed her entry trials she was now an apprentice, in training for her final test. Many Ladies were part of the Gardeners Dopkwe, since plant lore was intimately tied to their power.

Trill didn't mind helping Inker, Dola's main mentor. She liked the girl. They had sung together while working, and since then, too. The eighteens-to-twenty-fours had a good voice and knew all the verses to "Billie Jean." She wore her hair in bunches of thin braids braided together into three thicker ones these days, the same as Trill did. Around her neck hung a necklace woven of Redvine tendrils, one of those things Trill made when she had nothing else to keep her busy.

They climbed a fuzz-covered slope and descended into a shallow, wooded valley. Steam rose from the dark water pooled at its center. Around the water's edge several of the Jubilee Ladies lounged. In the leaves' glow Trill saw Adia's sharp-chinned face; the elder next to her, braiding her long, white hair was Robeson, Adia's friend. She recognized others, too, such as Kala and True, also from Trill's cohort. On Earth, the groups the Ladies modeled themselves after wouldn't have considered admitting Trill, Kala, or True, let alone an applicant Dola's age. But the empty clone bodies given to the first prisoners had all been twenty-fives-to-forty-fives. "You don't have to be old to be wise," they said. That was why the younger cohorts were welcome to at least ask to belong.

One person in the pool wasn't a Lady. Standing in the middle of the spring was an unfamiliar eighteens-to-twenty-fours—from another settlement? She didn't know everyone here; Jubilee was home to almost 32,000 people. If not for the Ladies there would have been twice that number—too many to prosper.

She folded her dress and underwear and left them on a bench. The dark water washed warmly over her feet, calves, knees—

"Stop." Trill obeyed. The voice was Robeson's; she held the bright, dying branch of a Hannakka bush, meaning she was the Ladies' speaker for now. "Don't need to stand no deeper. You ain't makin no report; we got Adia's. And Odell's. We called you for a different reason. Work."

"Work?"

"We want you to go where that thing Dr. Ops sent landed."

The Ladies had used her before for duties not obviously connected with her dopkwe, of course. After her test, when she became one of them, they told Trill that honesty was her particular power; lies made her weak. Because since then she'd told the truth scrupulously, paying almost obsessive attention to conveying details, she was their best reporter. But— "But—but—where? Where is it? How do you know?"

"Odell a trader comin here from Hamza. Six of em together on the road an they think it dropped down between where they camped at and us. They was gonna radio—" Eefay, to the far south, had supplied Hamza, Jubilee, and the nine other settlements on Amends with crystal sets. "—but that didn't seem real safe. *Psyche Moth* mighta changed orbit. Dr. Ops mighta heard. They split up instead."

"You want me to go with—" Odell wore no clothing, which meant Trill had no way of telling if the stranger was a him or a her. "You want us to go together and find out...what?"

Adia put her hand over Robeson's tiny one, sharing the speaker's branch with her. "What kinda trouble he put inside," she said, echoing the words she'd spoken on the path from the new place.

Dola would go too, with Trill as her mentor. Training. It made sense. The girl was due for her final test soon. She needed fieldwork, a task to take her outside the settlement.

Trill acknowledged to herself that she'd rather stay home and weave. The men and women in her dopkwe had interesting ideas that kept them talking some nights long after the last leaves faded. But she waded out of the water and dressed again without protest. The three of them would depart at flowerlight. She had just a short time to eat and sleep.

§

*Offspring produced by clients during their sentences have committed no crimes but must serve with them, as they are likely to be contaminated with clients' views. Under no circumstances are they to be allowed to develop extraplanetary capabilities. Similar caution must be*

*exercised regarding any later generations coming into direct contact with clients.*
—*Mission Guidelines,* Psyche Moth, *2055*

Trill woke as the flowers' buds were barely beginning to unfurl. Beside her, Odell stirred gently, driven from sleep's depths by the growing light. Their sex had been excellent. According to his estimate—Odell was currently male, and apparently had been since the age of six—the stretch of shoreline they now neared was close to the waters where whatever Dr. Ops sent must have come down.

She sat up, twisting, lifting one buttock and then the other to free her dress, and pulled it on over her head. "Dola!"

"Yes, Lady!" The eighteens-to-twenty-fours girl had climbed a bottle tree like a much younger person. "Is it time for breakfast?"

"Come and find out."

Odell rose and left silently to relieve himself. Dola descended and did likewise, then returned to eat the tofruit they had brought as provisions for their trip. Tasteless but somehow more satisfying than ordinary garden crops, tofruit grew from seeds that had arrived on Amends years ago in a drone sent to Nunavut Island. So Dola said.

Trill went a little ways off to make her own water and earth. She buried them quickly, yet Dola had again climbed a tall tree when she got back. For a member of the Gardeners Dopkwe she spent very little time on the ground. "What are you searching for up there?"

The bottle tree's leaves shivered as Dola scrambled down to the forest floor. "A flock of prettybirds. They were looking at us while you slept. Then they flew away."

Odell frowned and pushed the blond fronds of his hair back from his temples. "Anything else? Smoke or—or glints of metal? Or is some part of the ocean an unusual color?"

"No."

Not till noon did they come upon a sign of Dr. Ops's intrusion: trustees talking loud enough they could be heard ten arms away. Two of them. At first Trill thought they were Rogues, though none had been reported north of Hamza. But they were arguing about what Dr. Ops wanted like they knew. According to the elders he told trustees his secrets.

"How come you ain't let us start with that other place, the closer one? Coulda got clients carryin our equipment. Be quicker than us havin to lug evvathing, an we spozed—"

A high, decisive voice cut the other off. "Dr. Ops sent us here to take care a business, not be goin all over, back an forth. We start up in Jubilee, get clients there to help us an head on south, we be fine. Like I said yesterday, an the day before. Like we already *doin.* Now stop askin me am I sure."

Both spoke the way many elders did, so they, too, must have originally occupied black bodies.

Trill, Dola, and Odell stepped softly to within three arms of the pair. She saw the strangers through the day-dull leaves: both men, judging by their overalls, with the pale skin of babies. They faced each other over four stacks of four smooth grey-and-black boxes. She edged closer and one box lit up like a tiny, square Chrismas tree. The men fell suddenly silent. After a long while the high-voiced one called out that he could see them, then contradicted himself by asking them to show themselves.

Odell emerged into the open from behind Trill.

"Come on. Where's the other two?"

Trill was impressed. Adia's claims of accuracy for Dr. Ops's tracking equipment held up. Could his weapons kill as horribly as she and Robeson said? The hand of one man now held something—without waiting to learn what, Trill followed Odell. So did Dola.

"Well. That's much better. Have a seat." The high-voiced man gestured at the fuzz to one side of the stacks with what Trill assumed was a weapon. "We trustees come from the *Psyche Moth.* Been waitin here for you—you stay in Jubilee?"

Trill nodded. "Me and Dola do; Odell here belongs in Hamza."

"Well, I'm Isabelle and this is Freddie. Dr. Ops figured you could use a more permanent installation at this point, so he picked us to set one up. After we take care a Jubilee we can help the other settlements."

Did the man think they were stupid? "Take care of us how?"

Isabelle patted the top of one of the stacks. "With the latest advances in knowledge just come from Earth, transmissions got sent to us only a few years back. These here banks contain blueprints—um, that mean models, plans—"

Trill tried to look as ignorant as Isabelle obviously believed she was.

"—for improvements, medicines, time-saving devices—"

"Of course, only Isabelle and I be able to access things for you," Freddie added. Maybe he was afraid he'd be murdered if he didn't make that plain.

What the trustees *said* they wanted in exchange for their "improvements" was safe conduct to Jubilee. They *said* they were worried about Rogues and Solitaries. Which made no sense; they'd been fine for the week-and-a-half since Trill heard them arrive, and they'd just demonstrated they could tell when someone approached their camp. And Isabelle carried a weapon.... Again Trill pretended like she had no mind.

Going along with the lie about Rogues and Solitaries though none were known to be nearby, the three took turns "scouting." This consisted of getting far enough away that they no longer registered on the trustees' tracking instruments and then spying on what they said and did.

Sixteen boxes. Either Freddie or Isabelle stayed with their "equipment" at all times. Trill's attempts to wander off aimlessly with the four boxes she carried mostly failed. Twice she managed to open a box's latched drawer to reveal mysterious black slabs of identical lightweight material: plastic, like a lot of things the Scavengers Dopkwe in Dinetah used and traded. The second time, Isabelle caught her and she pretended it had been an accident. The last time.

At night, the sky showed them *Psyche Moth's* orbit. It hadn't changed. They calculated when it would most likely fly overhead; that was when Freddie and Isabelle could learn their "guides'" locations easily from Dr. Ops. That was when the prisoners took care to be where expected.

Climbing trees in pursuit of prettybirds, Dola discovered that above the height of seven arms she was undetectable. Trill in her underwear was almost as agile as the eighteens-to-twenty-fours girl. One afternoon the trustees thought they were completely alone. Stretched out on a branch—almost within eyesight, if they'd bothered to look for her—Trill listened closely.

Freddie was grumbling about having to walk. Elders reminisced about easier ways of traveling, too. And faster ones. "We takin so *long.*" he complained. It had only been five days—just a week. "We know where Jubilee is—cain't we do the job right here?"

"You wanna set up equipment an tear it down again inna middle a nowhere on the chance one a these the best bet? An explain that to em how? Look, Dr. Ops say do one in every settlement. So we go to Jubilee. With the clients we with. Then we probably have a lot more success gettin a big bunch of em to buy what we sayin."

"Awright." But Freddie wasn't through complaining. "Still wish they'd hurry up. Or we had a auto, hover, *somethin.* Ain't it spozed to be more sunshine when we get there? So tired a these goddam fuck-ass clouds an this mothafuckin fog I could strangle the shit—"

Despite the danger—or maybe because of it—Trill laughed so hard she fell ten arms to the ground. Cursing the *sky?* What good was that going to do? The sky was *there,* always would be.

She lay giggling on the fuzz, unhurt. Good thing Chrismas tree branches were so thick and soft.

But here came the two trustees thrashing through the Hannakka bushes—of course they'd heard her crashing down. Trill crawled away and "returned" to their camp by another route. She called them back there and told a tale of chasing off a dangerous Rogue from the spot where she'd fallen.

§

*Given a timelag for Earth-Amends communications of nearly a decade, and a minimum duration of almost a century for any physical return trip, rehabilitation efforts made after clients are settled should consist of observation and counseling only. None will have even the slightest effect on WestHem paradigms. Natural tendencies as embedded in the provided genetic material will eventually assert themselves.*
—*Mission Guidelines,* Psyche Moth, *2055*

They arrived at the new settlement as the sun was about to rise over the Rainshadows. New gardens lined the rough path, rosetoo blooms shining their last yellows, reds, blues, and shocking pinks. They passed the two eighteens-to-twenty-fours on perimeter watch without either of the trustees noticing them. Trill had sent word ahead about their arrival via Dola. They were expected.

The two houses Trill and Adia had helped the emigrants start were fully woven. Beside them, five more half-finished ones curved in a line like a barely-bent bow around the central workshed. Or where the workshed would be—the posts were set, cured redvines pulled tight in their notches, but the actual weaving had yet to begin. At either side three more ranks of seven house foundations each curved around relatively flat areas.

On sixteen of the house sites, members of various of the new settlement's dopkwes were dressing, rolling up blankets, laying out tools for their day's work. In the middle of a space surrounded by unoccupied sites, people holding bulbs from bottle trees circled around baskets full of sweetly steaming food—rosetoohip porridge, from the smell.

Isabelle stopped and put his hands on his hips, turning, looking around. "This ain't Jubilee! What you tryna pull?"

"We just stopped here on our way," Trill told him. "Jubilee's close, though. People came here because it got too crowded—"

"How close? How many people come here?"

"Through the mountains," Dola said. "One more day, right?" Trill nodded. "And—how many?" The girl looked helplessly at Trill. "All the dopkwes, most cohorts. And more people every time they want to...." Her words trailed off.

"You alla sudden cain't count?" Freddie asked.

Of course they could. The Ladies knew exactly how many there were of every kind of woman, man, boy, girl, gardener, hunter, elder, under-six—but Dola was just an apprentice, and Trill hadn't checked for changes recently. "347," she said, the last figure she'd been given.

This did nothing to ease Isabelle's suspicious expression, but all he did was demand who to see about where to set up. The trustees expected to take over one of the two finished houses. The Weavers Dopkwe offered theirs as a courtesy to Trill.

Black, silver, grey, and clear were apparently the trustees' favorite colors. All the boxes she handed Isabelle, and all the things coming out of them, looked like that.

When Freddie and Isabelle came outside to set up a giant, silver fake flower in back of their house she followed them to help, but they shooed her off. Skirting their house's half-woven neighbor she circled around for a short, uninformative peek through the door. It would be rude and unexplainable to enter uninvited. Besides, the biggest box, which the trustees had always carried themselves, was as yet unopened. The noise they'd been making as they worked behind the house ceased and she walked away before they could see she was still there.

Dola seemed to have connected well and quickly with the new settlement's Gardeners Dopkwe. Trill joined them a while to make sure. The eighteens-to-twenty-fours girl sat with several others around a pile of dried bottle bulbs, cutting them open with sharp plastic tools. Trill helped pull out the spoor masses and spread them flat so the wind would blow them clean enough to spin. Already some in the group were leaning close to Dola, telling her their troubles. Not long, Trill thought, till Dola was able to function as a full Lady, a junction of secrets. Satisfied at her charge's progress, Trill considered the loose ends of the main panel she was weaving, her true work.

She decided to try to find out more about the trustees' equipment that night, after leaflight, when at least one of them slept. In preparation she napped on the site of the workshed. Odell offered to lie down with her awhile, though it wasn't the same as snuggling with LeeRai, or her dopkwe. What she needed was a friend, someone like Adia had in Robeson. Not a sex partner. Someone more. Someone….

She woke alone. The sky was still bright, but close again, the bay swallowed in mist. She got up and rolled her sleeves down against the chilly dampness. She was tired of being away from home.

Trill walked downhill till she saw the walls of a house to her left, the one being used by the Gardeners Dopkwe. Just beyond that the fake flower had opened wider, flattening—and turning to the west? The trustees' house *hummed,* a low, hard-to-notice noise. If this was an elder's memory instead of something happening right now, that sound would be coming out of a machine.

The house's doorway was filled with a grey curtain. Trill had never seen anything like it. She tried to pull it aside. It wouldn't move. Caught? Tied? She ran her hand along the seam where wood met cloth.

"Can I help you?"

Freddie! Fear panged through her like salt. She turned and smiled. "I only wanted to make sure you got everything you need."

"Come on in. You here for the health test?" He reached past her and drew the curtain aside easily. The house's interior was much brighter than it ought to be.

"Sure," Trill said. She entered the house. Clear baskets hanging from the roof beams burned white, canceling out each others' shadows. Two short stacks—including the big box—still stood in one of the house's quarters, but the rest must have been unpacked and then somehow rewoven or folded into these odd furnishings.

Freddie pointed to a long, low surface. "Sit on that table and pull your sleeves up." He took a pair of white gloves from a box and put them on and started touching her, proceeding from her hair to her ears, face, throat, and downwards. He lifted her dress.

"Oh. Uh. Oh."

"Somethin wrong?" But she knew there wasn't. Unique checked everyone every five weeks—once a month, regular as leaflight. Doctors out of Uluru backed him up when they came through the settlement. Trill was fine.

"It's just—I can't, uh—I thought you were a woman."

"I am. Since I was a tens-to-thirteens."

"Of—you—of course—"

A whisper of cooler air as Isabelle pushed the curtain aside and walked in. "What Freddie mean is a course we knew gender assignments among you all be pretty fluid—that's why come summa us original clients wound up here, after all. Among other crimes. But he never suspected *you*, that you wasn't born what you say you are."

The elders were right again. "But it won't be a problem? People put here were allowed to live on Amends anyway we wanted, so—"

Freddie had recovered his ability to talk in sentences. "The only difficulty is that summa my treatments are for *biological* females." He stripped the gloves off and rolled them up without touching their outsides. Isabelle held open a grey bag and he dropped them in. "Guess we're done, then."

Trill didn't frown till she was well away from the house. She sat on the shore side of a tangle of roots sticking out of the sand, the remains of a broken and upended tree. The sky caressed her, bathed her in dew, in coolness, yet she felt no easing of her...anger? No. Fear? Much closer to that feeling, but stiller, deeper.

Dread.

Different kinds of women and men had different kinds of genitals. Like colors. Elders said that most places on Earth, that had mattered. Mattered enough to get some women—some men, too—murdered.

What treatments would the trustees—or rather, Dr. Ops working through them—want to impose based on those differences?

The Ladies would need to know. She'd have to find out. Somehow.

Tonight she'd investigate further. But she'd already expected to do that, so why this sudden, awful feeling? She looked at the sky for comfort.

A flock of prettybirds wheeled close overhead. Unusual to see them here in the open, Trill thought. They stayed in the woods and mountains, generally, though the elders said that when they'd first been brought down to the surface prettybirds were in the thick of everything, always. Much easier then to find their eggs, she imagined. Adia had told her Wayna practically lived on them when she was alive and pregnant with Trill. But now the Ladies had asked everyone to leave the eggs alone.

A rush of wings in front of her and Trill involuntarily shut her eyes. A small weight rocked on her head, balanced, then two more fell on her shoulders, a fourth on her left knee. Breathing as softly as she could, she opened her eyes.

Prettybirds had landed on her, were using Trill as a perch. At the edges of her sight, gold and orange and scarlet flashed, fluttered, made her want to turn her head—but would that scare them off? And without moving at all she could clearly see the last one who had arrived, aquamarine and a dazzling green, impossibly bold. It cocked its head and stared her in the face.

A visitor from Hamza who studied the animals of Amends said that elders in her dopkwe hadn't wanted to call them pretty*birds* because their eyes weren't on the sides of their heads. And they had hollow hairs instead of feathers, which no one else cared anything about.

And the visitor thought they shouldn't have been so good at flying since they had to turn their heads to look anywhere but forward.

The prettybird on Trill's knee blinked once. A pause and it blinked twice more. Another pause. Four times. Another pause. Eight. Another pause, longer. Evidently that ended the sequence.

She wanted to shake herself. Was she dreaming? Awake?

The Ladies had suspected. Dola had come up with her own theories and they'd encouraged her to investigate them. Here was proof! Skin tingling as if she lay over hot spring bubbles, Trill lowered her lashes once, waited—twice, waited—four times—

—and they were gone, flying off. Someone had frightened the flock. She listened closely, and soon she heard another person approaching. He came into view: Lou, a tens-to-thirteens member of the Food Dopkwe, holding a limp bag. Well, she hadn't walked that far from the settlement. She'd have to get someone else, another Lady, to follow up on what had probably—maybe—happened. Sighing, she got up and stretched, ready for her night's work.

§

*A record of cooperative rehabilitation is the first requirement for trustee selection, with acceptance of the tracking and communication equipment necessarily incorporated into the body another nonnegotiable issue. Utilization of the selected subject's psychoemotional predilections can help when other factors indicate a less desirable fit, and indeed can form the basis for stronger than usual loyalty ratings.*
               —*Mission Guidelines,* Psyche Moth, *2055*

The roofing made her knees and shins itch unbearably. Quietly, Trill shifted her position, lowering herself to lie on her side. Now her dress shielded her. That helped. She re-aimed her mirror so she could see through the sky vent.

Sky vents penetrated roofs' layers of casing-bundles at angles meant to keep the rain from entering. Trill peered upwards to where her long-handled mirror reflected the house's interior. Outside, full night reigned: leaflight had died down, and flowerlight wouldn't come for many hours. Inside, though, the clear baskets burned whitely.

Trill thought she might have been able to open a more direct spy-hole into the clinic, sheltered by their glare. But this would do. She saw plenty. More than she really wanted to.

Dola lay silently on the table where earlier Trill had sat. Perhaps she was asleep? Drugged? Trill's view of her was only from the girl's midsection down, and the other sky vents showed even less. But Dola's bent legs and scantily haired mons barely moved, and the pale belly rose almost imperceptibly with her long, slow breaths.

Breaths Trill couldn't hear above the sound of Freddie's, quick and harsh, as he pumped his penis between Dola's feet. In and out, in and out of the hollow he formed by clasping them together.

From Dola, nothing indicating refusal or rejection. No moans of joy or instructions or encouragement, either. From Freddie, faster breathing, harder fucking. He slammed to a stop, grunting. Semen spilled from his penis over Dola's tanned ankles and he bent forward.

Slurping sounds. Was he licking up his come? He kept slurping long after it must be gone, though.

"You about rehabilitated?"

Isabelle's voice. Trill had made sure he was in the house, too, before she climbed to the roof. But this was the first time he'd spoken.

"Come on. Do the implants. And then see if you can bring yourself to fuck her pussy; she never gonna believe she got pregnant cause a you pervin over her way down there."

"Why don't you do it, you in such a hurry?" Snorts of laughter were Isabelle's only answer. Freddie pulled up and fastened his overalls and left the reflection of Trill's mirror.

Implants. Pregnant. What had she gotten Dola into?

Freddie came back into view carrying a—Trill couldn't figure out the thing he cradled in his arms. She'd never seen it before, so obviously it had been hidden inside the big box. It seemed to be covered in skin. Kind of a cube but vaguely oblong, about the size of her LeeRai, it showed a puckered opening on the side she saw best. With the—skin?—darkening slightly around it, the opening looked like an anus. Freddie plopped the thing unceremoniously on the table between Dola's still open knees, and left again.

Was that hair? Yes, two small, sunken circles of hair—black, scantier than Dola's, and rimming what seemed to be recesses in the thing's top—

Freddie returned more quickly than before; this time he carried a white speculum and a clear rope with shining metal ends. One end—it was hard to tell from where she lay, but it looked like he somehow stuck it into the face of the cube nearest to Dola's mons. He draped the rest around his neck. Then, with an odd expression of disgust on his face, Freddie pulled apart the lips sheltering Dola's vagina and inserted the speculum.

Trill imagined a muted squeaking as she watched Freddie crank it open.

He did something she couldn't quite make out with the rope's remaining end and fed it through the speculum, into the girl's vagina. Bending over, he seemed to make a few sharp adjustments to the arrangement of things. Then he caressed—no other word would do—caressed the skin-covered oblong. With both hands he rubbed the side Trill couldn't see—gently, repeatedly. Soon the clear rope turned red. The color ran from its cube end to vanish into the speculum's white maw. And into Dola.

After some moments Isabelle spoke again. "Ain't gonna try an implant this first client with all of em, is you?"

"We got plenty. Over a hundred embryos stored in here. I'm spozed to set ten into every breeder so we make sure at least one of em lives."

"If you call that livin. No mind."

"You know what I mean."

Trill didn't. But she had faith one of the other Ladies would.

She was finding out something important tonight. Though that didn't exactly make up for the horror being inflicted on Dola. Which was Trill's fault.

Cool rain threaded down from the lightless clouds. She wanted to accept the sky's blessing, but kept wishing she had done things differently that day. Not told her apprentice about the prettybirds' intelligent behavior. Kept from mentioning in the same conversation how she'd been thwarted in her assignment. Made herself lie or omit part of the truth. One or the other. Really, there was no connection between those two things, though the girl had acted like receiving confirmation of her belief in the prettybirds' sentience obligated her to take on Trill's assignment. As if the two of them were involved in a trade.

She reminded herself that Dola had volunteered to go through the trustees' treatment in Trill's place. That as her mentor Trill had followed tradition in accepting Dola's help. Nothing got rid of her guilt.

Freddie and Isabelle lifted Dola from the table and moved her to a place Trill couldn't see. They made the table lower and wider and moved her back. In a new position; Dola's face was visible now. Her eyes were shut, as Trill had feared.

Her apprentice had been raped.

Now Freddie took off his overalls completely and lay down naked beside the naked girl. "What if the baby that come out be one a mine?" he asked.

"We be able to tell right away if it do more than breathe. Brain gonna be empty as what they put you in. An your body sterile, too. Doan worry. Dr. Ops took care a everthang. Now kiss her. Harder— wake her up!"

§

*When a permanent installation is deemed optimal, operational success will almost certainly derive from creating appropriate transfer stock in situ.*
    —*Mission Guidelines,* Psyche Moth, *2055*

"The baby will be his—"

"No!" Trill raised a hand as if she could snatch Dola's complacency out of the air, then dropped it to her lap. "Even if he claims the birth, it will also belong to Dr. Ops. The baby will be a blank space for him to write another person onto. That's what they're planning."

The girl twisted the necklace Trill had given her, looking puzzled. "All babies are blank, aren't they?" She seemed not to believe that she had been raped, not to mind—probably because she didn't remember it. Only the consensual sex afterwards. Which Trill had felt obligated to watch till a more natural sleep claimed her apprentice and flowerlight dawned.

Not till then did she descend from the roof and go to Odell, who had spent the night with the new settlement's Traders Dopkwe. She sent him to the Jubilee Ladies with the best words she could come up with to describe what had happened. When she went back to the trustees' house the door's curtain was pulled back, and no one was inside except Isabelle. It took time to find Dola helping to construct a terrace on steep slopes, laboring away as if nothing were amiss, smelling pleasantly of sex and sweat. Trill had drawn her aside and insisted on talking with her out of the dopkwe's hearing, alone.

"No one is born blank, not exactly. We say the soul is building itself, a process going on before birth—and after—but these are things you can learn later." Rote knowledge was rarely important when it came to an apprentice's final test. "All I want now is to let you know what has happened soon enough that you can have an easy abortion."

Dola's palms curled protectively over her young, pouting belly. "You're sure?"

Should she lie? "Almost. I need to ask the elders. And the Ladies. They'll decide what to do. We have to go back to Jubilee; Unique could test you, treat you—"

Here came Isabelle, Freddie right behind him.

"You don't know!" The girl stood up from the fuzz in one enviably smooth motion. "You're just jealous!"

"What?" Trill stood up, too, but stayed where she was as Dola hurried to her rapist's embrace. Jealous? Of whom? Of what? Dola's pregnancy? But Trill already had a child, though LeeRai'd been born out of Hett's womb....Jealous of Freddie? "I go with men," she murmured to herself. Dola didn't hear her. She was too far away.

The rest of that day the girl kept her distance. And the next. At Trill's approach she would scowl and leave her soup untasted, her seeds unsown, her conversations with her cohort unfinished.

In the following morning's flowerlight, though, Trill woke to find Dola snuggled against her side, her warm breath heaving hard with pain but her whispers quiet in Trill's ear. "—like you—said—it was—like you—said it was—I know—it was—"

"Shhh." She soothed the girl's scalp, brushing back a few tiny brown braids that had escaped their arrangement. "Now. Now." She was glad to hear the girl acknowledge she was right. That was what she'd been waiting for, why she hadn't returned to Jubilee. But she wished she'd been wrong.

The trustees had tested the eighteens-to-twenty-fours girl's urine to make sure their procedure worked. They hadn't thought Dola would overhear or understand when they gloated about the results.

Trill told Isabelle she and Dola were going home the next day, and he and Freddie started repacking. Lou took Odell's place, bearing his former load. Knowing what was inside the big box, Trill was glad not to be asked to carry it.

At noon they stopped only briefly to eat and continued on. Again the trustees seemed not to notice the sentries in the Chrismas trees, though Trill smelled and even heard at least four. They were much further out than she'd expected. Then they came upon Adia waiting for them. Trill was glad; otherwise, she would have brought the trustees to Jubilee's main site. Instead, they descended from the mountains slightly to the west of the hot springs, where Unique lived.

This was better. Treatment could start right away. She put a hand on Dola's tense shoulder, felt its warmth through the fabric of the girl's thin dress.

On Jubilee's outskirts, with so many gardens around, the danger of quill-throwing grazers was higher than at the settlement's center. People built houses here anyway, but not the nicest ones. Haphazard weaving, uneven roofs... Unique's was small enough he wouldn't be able to share it with more than two or three members of his dopkwe. Dola and Trill sat on the bare dirt floor, without mats. Freddie and Isabelle had invited themselves in only to be politely ignored until Adia offered to show them where they could stay.

Always smiling, slender as the branch of a bottle tree, Unique lowered himself apologetically to the house's one piece of furniture, a stool Trill and Dola had insistently refused.

"I appreciate your consideration," he said, "though it's going to make refusing you more difficult."

"You think you know what we're going to ask for?" Had he heard a rumor? From whom? Trill looked sideways at Dola's expressionless face.

"Women of your age cohorts generally come to me for one of two things: an abortion or fertility aids. It could be the latter, but being aware of Trill's preferences...."

Dola flushed, probably with anger. "You're right. I've been raped and I want lookoutforthelily. I'll take a pregnancy test."

Unique's pleasant expression remained in place yet faded. "What about talking this idea over with the Ladies first?"

"I *am* a Lady," Trill said. "As you're aware."

"*A* Lady. Only one. The others, though, have yet to be consulted. They—"

"What? What? You give her that plant! You have no right to do anything else!"

"I have no choice. Unless you are able to tell me the girl's condition has nothing to do with what the Ladies sent you off for." As silence dragged in the wake of his words, Unique's smile become smaller and more ironic.

He addressed Dola. "If the Ladies allow it, later, come back to me for an abortion, child. With your mentor or without her. Now, though, I think you should attend the meeting."

"What meeting?" But through the house's door she saw Adia returning, silhouetted by leaflight.

"Come," she said. They went.

§

*Resource extraction may be greatly improved by the wide*

*establishment of surface stock suitable for hosting*
*multiple-generation downloads of reliable trustees.*
*However, anticipated benefits must be weighed against*
*highly probably costs such as lander production; fuel*
*expenditure; embryo manufacture, storage, and*
*implantation tools; remote downloading equipment; and*
*of course against the risk of hostile client reaction to this*
*initiative's primary agents.*

—*Mission Guidelines*, Psyche Moth, *2055*

Adia, Robeson, Kala, True—even in the shimmering half-dark she knew their faces easily, their names. But it was Dola she looked at while she told the gathering of Ladies how her apprentice had lain helplessly unconscious under the trustee's assault as she, Trill, responsible for her, could only watch.

Black creases angled down between the girl's eyebrows and her thin lips pinched together. Her chin lifted, her head tilted back, but tears spilled down her cheeks anyway, reflecting the pastel shine of the Hannakka bush branch in Trill's hand. She tried to pass it to Dola. The eighteens-to-twenty-fours refused it; evidently she didn't want to talk yet.

Kala took the bright branch. "We should kill them. But we can't. Dr. Ops's guidelines won't protect us from him if we do."

Adia's turn. "We have to stop em. Back before the final trustee died, our work was too hard! Let em get a new toehold now and we ain't never gonna have no peace.

"What we gotta do is this: have the babies but keep the downloads from happenin right. Corrupt em. Hide the mothers an kids afterwards till it's no more danger—maybe find a island for that down near Nunavut or Panonica."

Hands waved in the darkness like lightless leaves. Questions: Affect the downloads how? With what? Suggestions: Allow the downloads and then raise the newborn trustees as double agents. Or abandon them, isolate them where they could do no harm. Objections: Dr. Ops would only try again.

And at last Dola accepted and held the Hannakka branch. Her head lowered. Tears spattered into the water, sent ripples of darkness through the bright refelection. Head up again, she spoke. "I want an abortion."

Robeson reached out. "But you can't—"

Dola snatched the branch away from the Lady's grasp. "I can! I will! I know the plant—I'll figure out the dosage—"

Trill shivered, cold in the warm water. So many had died proving the pharmacopeia of Amends that first generation, despite all the Ladies' precautions. Her own mother, for one.

"Listen!" Robeson grabbed again and this time tore the top of the Hannakka branch free. "If you don't stay pregnant they'll do some other girl the same way they done you! That what you want?"

"No! No!" Shouting, waving the stub of branch she held, Dola backed out of the pool. "I don't! I don't want anybody hurt but I—I won't—I can't—No!" And she was gone.

Silence ruled the meeting for long moments.

"She pass. Yall agree?" Adia asked. The other Ladies nodded.

"Trill, you go tell her. She a Lady now." But Trill couldn't move yet. She waited for the news to sink in. This had been Dola's test. The girl had passed.

Trill hadn't known. She hadn't known. They hadn't told her—mind crawling into movement again she understood why: because she couldn't lie.

Even so, she should have known. Because there was no reason Dola couldn't have an abortion. Not logically, and not according to any precedent, and no, no reason at all. Absolutely none.

§

*When setbacks occur to planned or in-place operations, best practice is to inquire as to their causes, even when they are assumed to be known. Worst practice is immediate retaliation. Biological entities are limited in their abilities, scope, and lifespans. Orders are orders, and must be carried out—eventually.*
    —*Mission Guidelines,* Psyche Moth, *2055*

Leaflight died. Unique's little house looked dark and sounded quiet. Trill knocked on the doorpost and called Dola's name, but only he answered. He had not seen her. The girl had not come there.

Under the sky's last scattering of grace she walked slowly, quietly, toward where the trustees were supposed to sleep. Soon Trill saw their white glow breaking through poorly woven walls. Dola would never have gone to them willingly. If they had managed to compel her—

A shadow shifted, became the tens-to-thirteens named Lou. Touching his ear she led him off a safe distance to talk. Dola was not in there, either. And Isabelle was awake.

The sensible thing to do would be to wait till flowerlight. Lookoutforthelilies grew somewhere nearby. Didn't they? She could find them in plenty of time. Dola would need to prepare them somehow. Wouldn't she? Plenty of time.

She tried to wait sensibly. That didn't last.

Instead of asking for help as she should have, Trill left on her own. Anyone else would only slow her down. While the path met her feet firmly she walked east. Downward. After a while the scent of the sea informed her of where she was. Sinking in suddenly looser soil, she trod forward a few more steps. The terrain rose very slightly, confirming that this was the edge of the dunescape. Where, if she remembered correctly, the plants Dola was looking for could be found. And, hopefully, Dola.

Who might not want Trill to find her.

Now that she needed the cover of full night, now the buds unfurled, shining, showing themselves to their pollinators. Showing the gentle slopes and hollows lying between her and the distant water. And—oh, wonderful!—another woman's back bending low over the ground, dress fluttering, a long stick in her hands.

Closer, she was sure. Dola.

The wind's direction helped. It was too early for the girl to expect anybody to have followed her here, and facing the ocean as she did, neither sight nor sound provided her with clues of Trill's presence.

It was the prettybirds who betrayed her. A rainbow flash caught the corner of her eyes; it grew and filled the air, a huge flock of them streaming out of the trees, over her head, over Dola and then circling around, reversing their flight path. Trill followed them with her eyes. When she turned her gaze on the girl again she saw that Dola, too, had tracked the flock and of course noticed Trill, just ten arms away by now.

The girl frowned as she lifted a handsome basket, green stalks peeping over its lip. "You can't stop me—I won't let you. Keep away." She backed up several steps and seemed about to turn and run.

"Wait! No!" Trill did the least threatening thing she could think of: sat down. "The Ladies are fine with an abortion."

"They're not! They said—"

"It was lies! They lied—we had to find out if you'd give in. If you'd do something you knew was wrong because the Ladies told you to, we couldn't let you join."

"You—you lied? You *lied*—to *me?*" The basket slumped in the girl's grasp.

Trill rose to her knees. "No. I didn't realize what the others were doing. I didn't know till after you left."

"How could they do that to you? To *me?*"

Trill shrugged. "I'm no good at not telling the truth. All the Ladies understand. So if they told me, they told you. It wouldn't have worked. Wouldn't have been a test."

"But—aren't you angry?"

"Yes. I should have known. A little. Yes."

"Not at yourself—" Dola stopped midsentence. Trill opened her own mouth to ask why and prettybirds surrounded them, their colors everywhere: swirling rainclouds and ripe gold seeds brushed against their arms, night and ivory and crimson filled the sky above and on their either side. And now a red luminousness hovered before them, its bright yellow wings beating the air as it blinked once, twice, four times, eight—not the same bird, but the same sequence!

Trembling, Trill repeated it. Received it in answer. Again. Again.

And then the prettybirds were gone. Her fingers hurt. Dola held them, crushed them in her hands. How had that happened?

§

"I saw! I saw! Trill—I'm a Lady now. We're equals. I can be your friend? And we can make a dopkwe, a new one, talk to them—oh, Trill! I saw!"

Counting. That was all the prettybirds had done so far. It was a long way from that to conversation.

A long way, but a good one. A good trail to walk. And not alone. She laughed softly to herself without opening her mouth, gently loosening the tight hold on her hands. Not remotely alone.

## CELIA LISSET ALVAREZ
## Malibu Barbie Moves to Mars

Why? Overpopulation. Too many
Barbies to one Ken, Joe on some macho
trip involving videogames. As one
of the eldest and most rugged, I felt
it was my duty to lead the way. Here,
I have some weight. There's so much space. A girl
can have twenty walk-in closets if she
wants them, although what's the point? There's no one
watching. Doesn't matter if you have two
hundred outfits, one for every million
miles connecting us, as if you could mount a
catwalk between planets. Walk that plank. No,
all you need is the one suit to protect
you from the toxic atmosphere. Here, I
don't have to be all things to all people,
just one thing to myself. The red dust's charged
with minerals unknown, and the strange plants
I've grown feed me—they feed me. Here, I can
look straight at the sun and let it burn. When
I see all the damage in the mirror,
all the wrinkles and the spots, my eyes fixed
on this vast, empty loneliness, at least
here, there is an explanation for it.

# BENJAMIN ROSENBAUM
# The Guy Who Worked for Money

Nera waited for Malka in the big outer living room of 534a.tower5.loverslump.frankfurt.de—Jörg's place. It had been six months since Nera was last here. Four months ago, she'd forced herself to stop watching and commenting.

She used to sleep in this room. Then it was spare, full of light from the big window, vintage Ikea daybeds and electric lamps and side tables. Jörg used to scavenge them, fill cracks in the pasteboard and pine with archaic wood-goo. Now a forest of columns of fungus blocked the light. They were as wide as trees, crimson and magenta and burnt-sienna. They smelled like sausage. Tomas must be growing them, beta-testing gene splices. It was the kind of thing he'd do.

Jörg was in the library—she'd checked, scanning the party before she arrived. He was talking to some guy named Sergei Balduri. Nera's services weren't offering many predictions about whether she'd like this Sergei. No weightings available for intellectual stimulation, stabilized admiration, social usefulness, practical alliance—nothing, except that they'd be good in bed together (with 89% compatibility—hUBBUB summarized, "Run That Bunny Down!"). He was 45, three years older than Nera, rated in the 500s at Moody's and Snopes and in the 700s at hUBBUB. Nera only had a 453 at hUBBUB.

Anyway, she'd gestured that window closed. She didn't want to stand around in the middle of the party with a glazed expression, watching an ex-boyfriend in another room over in-eye. Instead she was standing around with a glazed expression trying to catch up on work. Colette had messaged her: *Sabine needs a breakdown on what the historical construction style is really going to mean for energy impact. It needs to be better than canned agent estimates, because Slow Growth and Big Frankfurt are trying to pull us into their bullshit ideological fight. Sabine has friends at the Autie Girls collective who can get us some custom-evolved estimates, but you know what they're like—they're going to have a million super-literal questions. Can you figure it out?*

It was insane, in Nera's opinion, to be doing 1990s-style artisanal re-creationist construction—steel frame and drywall—three kilometers above ground. If they just printed bamboo and carbon thread out of compost like everyone else, the rest of the project might still get slagged for showboating, but at least their energy use wouldn't be over the top. But it wasn't Nera's decision. Nera was lucky to be involved at all.

She heard Malka's theme song before she saw her. Nera had Moody's Clamor service on audio, and its theme song for Malka was a peppy, sizzling cryohaka beat—up-to-the-minute, fun, powerful, a little out of Nera's league. Moody's had their relationship pretty well down, in other words. Nera closed her in-eye windows.

"Hey," Malka said. She was in a short-sleeved ocean t-shirt (rolling waves, blues and greens) and matte black slacks. It suited her.

"Hey babe," Nera said, maybe a little too cheerful. She wondered, for the nth time, what Malka's services played in Malka's ears for Nera's theme song.

A woman in a sparkly blue chador pushed between them, followed by an old white guy in a top hat. They were arguing in Bäyerish. When Nera focused on them, Clamor played something dark, ominous, and classical: they were trouble. They threaded through the fungus columns.

"So, that guy Jörg's talking to?" Malka said.

"Yeah?" Nera said. She wondered if she was blushing—it was apparently obvious to Malka that she'd be watching Jörg. Did all her commenters know, too?

"He works for money," Malka said.

"He what?" Nera felt a hint of queasy vertigo.

"I know, weird." Malka smiled. "Come on, let's go meet him." She winked, and her fingers flickered in the air. The green of an incoming flashed in the lower right corner of Nera's vision, and with a flick of her tongue she pulled Malka's message open: *come on, princess, let's get this over with.* Malka meant seeing Jörg again.

Malka set off towards the library, and Nera followed. At the base of a deep purple column, a little blond boy stuffed strips of fungus into his mouth. He examined his hands while he chewed. For him, Clamor played turn-of-the-century pop: sweet and bouncy U.S.-Anglo music from Nera's parents' childhood. As her eyes lingered on him, her infospace started whispering: Torsten Hughes, 6 years old, born in Edinburgh, Scotland—

Nera looked away to shut it up, resisting the urge to google his parents. She took some fungus herself—soft and spongy, red as blood. It tasted like bratwurst, the texture of angel's-food cake.

They paused as a flock of nine- and ten-year-old kids pushed past them, chattering in Chinese, none of them Chinese: tongue-slaved to some server. There never used to be kids at these parties. But who knew where kids went or why, nowadays? When Nera was a kid, you knew where kids were during the day. They were in school. Or with their parents. Torsten Hughes's parents were probably across town at some other party. They probably had him on a kidcam. They probably just deputized whoever was dumb enough to stop and talk to him.

When Nera and Malka were teenagers, back in the tumult of '33, they'd helped remake the world, cheering each other on long before they ever met in person. They were commenters on each other's video streams, that year when everyone was phoning in earring footage of eviction standoffs, food riots, praise-ins, convoys, patentbreaking spontos. Later, when they'd finally met in person at Uni, they'd charged across the mensa to fall into each other's arms.

"Are you following Sven?" Malka asked, as Nera caught up.

"Sven from the old days? Sven who was in the Pie Squad?" The Pie Squad happyslapped statist politicians with cream pies, assassination-style, in '33–'36. Sven was a beauty, and Malka had been sleeping with him in Berlin, when her tribe unfirewalled the national surveillance network.

"Yeah, that Sven," Malka said. "He's fallen apart since then. He gets in fights, drinks, won't work, takes things uninvited—he's in the red, nobody will feed him but the kitchens, and the Security Committee is talking about calling a vote for deportation, gang work, or dosing him on moodies..."

"Oh shit," Nera said.

"Yeah," Malka said. "It's a mess. I was commenting for a while, rooting for him, asking him to shape up, but he's so bitter—now I'm really just watching for the trainwreck value. It's sad."

Through the kitchen: Schwarzwälders at the bar, Bavarians around the fridge, and Finns and Peruvians cooking something loudly at the grill. There was a purple flash at the corner of Nera's vision. Did she want to contribute some of her energy ration to the barbecue? No. She did not.

Why had Malka brought up Sven? Was it some kind of warning, about the limits of old loyalties? An uncomfortably high proportion of Nera's ratings hinged on Malka's yes-votes. That had gotten her accepted into Cambergerstrasse project. And if *that* would only go well, it ought to break her into the mid-500s, maybe beyond.

How was it Malka's life had kept growing after Uni, while Nera's stayed like a potted plant? At sixteen, they had both driven party shuttles, done megaphone duty, matchmaker, and groupie work with union shop stewards and farmhands, in the Work For Love campaign to keep German agribusiness from collapsing. Now, at 42, Malka was an industrial facilitator with an 803 on hUBBUB. When she posted about shortages, Frankfurt's entire ratings landscape shifted.

Nera had spent the last two decades mostly just partying, media-surfing, commenting on other people, and doing pick-up jobs pulled from the services—enough to keep her ratings out of the gutter. Couriering a package across town, stopping to help fix lunch at a buffet, visiting with some officially at-risk lonelies (work most people hated but Nera often didn't mind, so a big ratings win), getting babysitting-delegated, bit-part acting in flash dramas, gardening, or just hauling crap from place to place. That life was soothing: waking up at one party, spending the day drifting and doing whatever Frankfurt told her to do, whatever her services predicted would help her ratings (and assured others she could handle)... ending up at some other party and going to sleep in some comfortable nook—with or without some new friend vouched for by hUBBUB.

"Maximize joy," that was the old slogan of '33, the byword of the Free Society. Nera had thought that that was what she was doing.

When they entered the library, Clamor played Jörg's theme song—brassy, sexy, big-band Montevideo jazz. At two-meters-oh-five, Jörg towered over Sergei. He had shaved his skull except for a long blond queue, down to his hips. He was dressed in brown, a crisp new leather sleeveless vest—it must have come from a printer, too new to be vintage salvage, but it sure looked real—and leggings. On his hard, broad triceps there was a new lifebrand tattoo—the pyramid-eye of Illuminatus, above the steaming spoon of De Gustibus and the bicycle of Ergo. He was keeping up *three* lifebrands! With that and neighborhood stuff and leading the rez committee for this floor of tower5, he must be clocking thirty contrib hours a week. He had to be in the 1100s by now.

Her hands were stained red from the stupid sausage mushroom.

Jörg's eyes widened. "Nera!" His broad face spread into a grin, a cascade of wrinkles. He saw her hands. "So what do you think of Tomas's garden?"

"It stinks," she said. "I'm going to smell like wurst for a week." She turned her attention decidedly to Sergei. Bristling eyebrows, dark eyes, a strong nose plummeting straight from a raised bridge— a Dravidian-Slavic mix. His hair was a black ear-length mop, his shirt flowing blue silk opening to show the softness of his throat. Maybe she *should* run that bunny down. No predictions from Clamor, though, so no audio. When she focused on Sergei, all she heard was the party around her.

Malka and Sergei kissed cheeks. "Nera wanted to meet the guy who works for money," she said.

"Oh, thanks, nice wingman work there, Malka," Nera said, mock-outraged. "Make me look like a total banker." Jörg and Malka simultaneously strangled a laugh. "What? Oh —"

Sergei inclined his head in a gracious nod and smiled. "You have gotten it in one."

"I didn't mean it like—you're a *banker?*" Nera sent an urgent message to her mouth to stop talking, but apparently it had to go by carrier pigeon. "Literally? Is that even legal?"

"Oh Nera, come on," Malka said, laughing. "Do you read *anyone's* page before you meet them?"

"It's definitely legal," Jörg said, "Outlawing money exchange would lead to even more extreme distortions in our metrics than we've got." His fingers flicked, his eyes briefly on a point above her head, and more incoming green pinged at the corner of her vision, but she wasn't going to read his goddamn footnotes in the middle of the party. "The Free Society doesn't compete on force or fiat, it outperforms on joy. Wherever there's a reversion to the money economy, that's a signal of a deficit of either trust, satisfaction ability, or information flow. It's better to let that signal manifest rather than —"

"All right, all right," Malka said, patting Jörg on the shoulder. Jörg smiled his goofy grin.

Startlingly—though his theme song blared out pulse-warming and strong, and though he still had the fine glint of gold stubble on his chin, and smelled as good as ever—Jörg was a bore. Maybe it was because of the Cambergerstrasse project. Now that she finally had a hold on something solid, Nera didn't feel intimidated by Jörg's footnotes anymore, or jelly-kneed with longing. It was like a tight band around her chest had been loosened, and she could breathe.

She grinned, and turned to Sergei. "What do you even buy with money anymore?"

"Are you kidding?" Sergei smiled. He cupped his hands, enclosing a swarm of mites. They glinted, swift and metallic; in the darkness, you could see tiny flares of laser communications. "These need gallium, tantalum, rubidium... delicate nano components you can only make in orbit..." He opened his hands, and the mites wisped away. "Nobody mines rubidium in the Sudan just to impress their friends or make a lifebrand quota. Right? China doesn't send up taikonauts to low orbit to get a good rating at hUBBUB..."

"I thought the metals could be salvaged out of old gear," Nera said, shocked.

"Oh no," Jörg said. "Not enough of them, not for years. Probably every pre-2030 laptop and cell phone in Europe outside of deep landfill has been recycled by now, but we're way past that point, and back to extraction. There's a robust debate in the import-export committee wiki..." More little green footnotes, flashing like the mites' lasers.

"Always need more mites," Malka said drily. "How else are we going to be sure not to miss any neighbor picking her nose..."

Nera felt the queasiness return. How had she not known this? What the hell had they had a revolution for anyway, if they were all living on the backs of wage-slaves in Africa again? Should she say that? As she hesitated, she saw the brass flash of a neutral comment in the corner of her vision. People were following this conversation; she should be careful. Nera didn't have many regular followers, and most of them were friendly mutuals, plus some contextuals (who usually were more interested in Jörg or Malka or others of her buzzier friends), and a few tourists from overseas who'd picked her at random. But there were always the inevitable drive-bys when she did something truly bloat. Her savvy rating wasn't the best anyway; all she needed was a spike in buzz on a collapse in savvy.

"Did you two see that Nera's a signer on a construction request-for-comment?" Malka asked. Nera couldn't tell if she was being supportive—trying to help Nera land Sergei in the sack—or catty, or just maneuvering off the topic of Sergei's job before Nera put her foot in it.

"Oh yeah?" Jörg said, his eyes twinkling. He honestly had no idea. These last four thrilling months, she'd been planning, facilitating, consensus-building, detail-checking—things she'd done in '33, things she'd forgotten she missed. Clearly, Jörg hadn't paid any attention. She'd had to force herself to stop following him—it had never occurred to him to follow her.

Sergei's eyes had the telltale drift-to-the-right of someone googling something. "You're building a music space on the 300th, on Cambergerstrasse..."

"Well, I'm a minor player," Nera said. "The big wheel is Sabine Heuspross, the music historian? She's a major scholar in late-twentieth-century U.S. alternative music. Originally we wanted to do it specialized on Washington, DC punk, late 1980s? But we got major flak from the Niederrad punks —"

"Oh right." Jörg nodded. "You don't want to tangle with them." It was unbelievable—all this time, she'd imagined him forced to see her in a new light, not just as this bubblehead drifter who'd wandered in at a party one night and stayed to warm his bed. She'd imagined the loverslump crowd talking about her. She'd imagined Jörg's fanboy commenters teasing him, giving him credit for her transformation: "Jörg can't even *sleep with* bubbleheads without turning them into prosocial contributors! Our brother over here *ejaculates* impulsiveness suppressants!"

"Yeah?" asked Sergei. "A lot of clout? I don't really follow re-creationists..."

"They're not *exactly* re-creationists," Jörg said.

"Yeah, that's the problem!" Malka said. "Punk is like a religion in Niederrad. They're the authentic inheritors of the true flame, they don't need any academic poseurs butting in..."

"So... we switched to Seattle grunge," Nera said. "Same general period, less contentious. There's an academy for original grunge ensembles and karaokists in Stuttgart, but all we've got are re-enactors up here. I mean, so far. If we get approved—it ought to change."

"The 300th, though? Isn't it a little high up for a performance space?" Sergei said. "That's quite a climb..."

"Especially for hauling steel girders," Malka said, pursing her lips.

"It's big, too," Jörg said. He stroked a hand in the air, scrolling through the plans.

"It's not all performance space, it's also party and squat," Nera said. She saw a flutter of brown flashes, three negative comments in a row, in the corner of her vision.

"Wow," Sergei said. "Are you guys going to reserve it to live in yourselves at all, or is it going straight to general squatright?"

"We don't know yet," Nera said. She felt her chest tighten again. It would be so good to live there with the project group! But they'd been accumulating disses—not that many people cared about 20th century music, and everyone cared about energy and airspace.

Malka looked sour. Maybe she regretted bringing the topic up. "What do *you* think?" she asked Jörg.

Jörg nodded. "It's good, it's good. People should take risks. Good to see you stretching, Nera."

Nera felt a stab of anger. She slid open a message tray with her tongue and fingered a message to Malka: *Porky jesus, he's patronizing!*

Malka shrugged, looked away. "Back to the banker thing, Sergei," she said, "since Nera did bring it up. I get why you work *with* money—it still makes a lot of the world go round. You take Frankfurt's various exports and patents and Swiss bank accounts and whatever, and buy us whatever we can't make here. I get that, and I get why it would be a high-rep job; we need it, and most people would find it boring. But you told me you worked *for* money—not just *with* money." She crossed her arms beneath her breasts, where her top shimmered electric blue. "Why?"

Sergei smiled the long-lipped, eyebrow-cocked smile of someone who is amused in advance at the reaction they're about to get. "I like money," he said.

"What, you mean, like, physical money?" Malka said. "Like you collect coins and bills? That's cool, I guess."

"No," Sergei said. "I mean I like *money*. I like exchange. Abstracted exchange. Simplicity. You give me something, I give you something. We're quits. You don't have to decide what kind of person I am, if you like me, how distant I am from you in social space. We could be masked strangers in a privacy zone. You want something from me, you give me money. I don't care who you are. I don't care what you want it for."

Comments were flashing in, but Nera didn't stop to read them. Queasy, she thought of the hunch of her father's shoulders in his starched white uniform and red tie, behind the florist counter at the supermarket. She recalled the burn of tear gas at the back of her throat, the sound of shattering windows.

Jörg looked like he was the proud owner of a performing dog; Malka, like she was equally disgusted and turned on. Or maybe a little more turned on.

"Huh," Malka said. "'Masked strangers in a privacy zone'...? You know the 'raw swingers'? They hook up with strangers for sex with their services totally turned off. No peeking at comments or reviews or social map—so they have *no idea* if it's going to be a total nightmare, right? That's the point, I guess, part of the thrill. They've got this whole thing about how it's so much better when it does work, because of the risk and the authenticity and whatever. So are you saying this is like that, Sergei? You do stuff just for a marker of hoarded value... you don't even know why. You don't know what the effect of your actions are, what you're contributing towards, or what people will say..."

"All you know is you want the money," Nera said.

Malka nodded. "Pure greed, no connections, heedless of consequences. That's it? It's a kink? Like a... sick thrill?"

Sergei laughed. To his credit, he looked a little discomfited. "I guess you could look at it like that."

"Oh, don't underplay it," Jörg said. "Sergei—you've written about this. It's a philosophy." Nera glanced at him, and she recognized his expression. A year ago she would have called it an eager openness—his fascination with the unending variety of people and ideas Frankfurt's flow brought bobbing to his door. But she'd been in his collection of flotsam. Drifter Nera, banker Sergei, autie-genius Tomas, the Finns and Peruvians grilling in the kitchen; they all ended up part of Jörg's menagerie, and by means of them all, he somehow ended up rating as a life-artist instead of a pompous, lecturing do-gooder.

"Well," said Sergei. "Okay. I think it's more than just kinky." He glanced sidelong at Malka. "Money is... clean. It severs connections. That's not always a bad thing. You *say* you know what the effect of your actions are. But you don't really know—you don't trace them all in detail. You don't have time. You just go with the consensus. With fashion."

"Sure, sure, ratings and fashion are all we have," Malka said. "That's not a new argument or anything, and we are all concerned, I'm sure, with the plight of the low-rated. Nera has done quite a bit of visiting with at-risk lonelies, did you know that? But *money* seems like a weird solution to that problem, doesn't it?"

"No," he said, and there was a little bit of a quiver in his voice that made Nera wonder what history it pointed to, "no, it doesn't. With money, poverty is empty of meaning. It's not a judgment on your life and works. It doesn't mean no one likes you, that you're obnoxious or boring. If you're poor in a money economy, you know what you need to do: make money. It's not as... wounding."

"That's stupid," Nera said. Jörg and Malka turned to look at her, eyebrows raised—her voice was too loud, too harsh. Her heart was beating fast. "It's dead easy to get your ratings up when they fall. Your services tell you how."

"Your services tell *you* how," Sergei retorted. "You have skills, you're charming. You're rated as trustworthy. People want you to babysit their kids. Carry their packages. Cook their food. It's not that easy for everyone."

"Well I don't understand what you're saying," Nera said, flushing. "If people, or the networks, don't trust someone to watch kids or cook *food*— well, there's probably a good fucking reason for that then! There are other things they can do instead that are contributive. This is ridiculous. You want to return to a world where you can—I don't know, push people off bridges and as long as you can steal some jewelry and convert it into cash, you get to have everything you want?"

"I don't think that's quite what Sergei means," Jörg said. The zookeeper interposing himself between two fighting animals.

"I'm not saying we should go back to just having money," Sergei said, smiling uncertainty. "Not only. But it's—freeing. It's like—maybe sometimes you don't need to know what something's for. You don't always need to be beholden to people, to have all these tribes and affiliations. All these people arguing about what to do, imposing on you. Don't you get tired of the politics? Of being second-guessed, of... positioning everything? Maybe it's just that I've travelled quite a bit, and the world beyond Frankfurt and the Free Society Zone is different. Not maybe better, but... yeah, *freer,* in some ways. In China and the 'Stans, you know..."

"Yeah, I know," Nera said, "you can get baby hookers there with your precious *money,* and plenty of privacy."

There was a beat. Sergei's smile vanished. Jörg lost his patronizing zookeeper look.

Malka looked as if she'd bitten into something rotten. "Nera, cool it. That's an awful thing to say."

"Well how do you know?" Nera said, her blood pounding in her ears. "How do you know what he does with his freedom, with his rubidium, out there where people have to work or die..." A flurry of brown flashes in the corner of her vision. The vultures descending on her comment space. Then a few gold, positive comments.

"He's doing all that for Frankfurt —" Malka said.

"Fuck that," Nera said.

Sergei raised his eyebrows, tried a smile. Malka and Jörg exchanged a glance. Their fingers twitched. Discussing what to do with problem Nera.

Her ears burned. Fine. She'd lost her cool.

She was quivering with anger, and she couldn't open her jaw to say hey, I'm sorry, I know you don't mean it like that, I've had a bad day. The comments were splotching into her vision like shit bombs. But she couldn't open her mouth.

The cryohaka beat hissed and rumbled, repetitive, slick, and meaningless. Malka put her hand on Sergei's shoulder.

Nera turned and walked away.

§

Nera's dad was a florist. Her mom was a pharmacist, who moved up to managing process architecture generation for a chain of drugstores. They'd immigrated as kids, from the Balkans, to a rich, safe, First World, EU country: Germany. For *their* parents—Nera's grandparents—Germany was a hard and lonely heaven. Long hours, disapproving looks from the neighbors, the officious and unmusical language, refugee paperwork. But safe. No snipers on the rooftops, no land mines in the soil. Computers in every house, fresh fruit from South America and New Zealand in the shop on the corner. Fitness clubs and GPS cell phones, and softly humming BMWs in the streets.

Nera's father used to tell her about their summer trips back to the Balkans: fields of sunflowers, dappled forests, bomb craters from the last century, villages of half-built houses. Parties long into the night, rich homemade food and aunts fussing over you. But he never took Nera back there.

He worked long hours. Her mother, once Nera was in school, worked even longer hours. Nera's prototypical memory of her: hunched over a tablet, late at night, in a curvy, designer orange leather chair by the front parlor window.

Her father, at least, had the flowers, which you could touch and smell, and the customers, who were sometimes—rarely—enthralled by the flowers' beauty. But those were brief moments in a day filled with sneers; with bitching coworkers and an angry, disapproving boss. His German was perfect, he was punctual and polite, he cheered the Frankfurter Fussballclub and drank Hefeweizen. But they acted as if he didn't understand, couldn't think, and didn't belong. He kept arriving every day to cut and bundle and ring up flowers, through an ulcer and graying hair and a permanent, heartbreaking, conciliatory flinch-smile. Because it was his job.

Nera's mother was more assertive, slicker, better at claiming her place in Germany. She rose through the ranks. She was rewarded with weekends shuffling numbers, running simulations, and playing office politics over instant messaging. She was proud of her work. She was glad when she could prove that her candidate process had evolved better than her rivals.' It was all ephemeral. At best, it meant a few more shoppers loaded a few more plastic tubes and bottles of chemicals into their shopping carts in a few more narrow, fluorescent-lighted aisles. She gave her life over to that.

That, and money, and a place in the system promised by the state. The state would educate their child. It would care for them when they were sick, when they were old. If they could not find work, it would feed and clothe them for a while, while they looked for work. The state would defend them from violence. It would protect from theft all the things they acquired: the tablet computers and phones and leather chairs, the shapely anodized aluminum pans hanging above the induction stove in their beautiful open-plan kitchen/living room. In exchange for these protections, they would feed the state with taxes. And for food, for electricity, for clothes, for videos, for the internet, for rented cars and ice skates and piano lessons, they would feed the market a constant stream of money.

It was a bargain. We will give you our lives; we will spend our lives obediently doing things we wouldn't choose, things that probably do not really matter to anyone. And in return we will get money. And money will take care of us.

The United States of America defaulted on its debt in 2026, destroying the dollar. The Euro Zone bet on propping up its banks the following year, and lost its bet. Martial law kept the shaken house in order another year, until the pandemics hit, and the soldiers fled the cities. Nera was ten the hungry year that super-resistant TB and goose flu kept everyone home. She was already on Tribes then. She already had people around the world and around the block who she could count on for help even if they'd never met, even though it was all guesswork and the crudest of relational metrics on Tribes, not predictive at all. Her parents, who had never made the transition from Facebook and LinkedIn, did not understand why strangers were dropping off food.

Nera's parents knew that the state had betrayed them. They knew that their savings had vanished, that the promises of health care and support in old age had turned out to be lies. They never understood that the market had betrayed them as well. Even though their money had stopped being worth anything, they kept looking for a money that would be worth something: yuan, or Swiss francs, or real solid gold, or the virtual-gold currencies of fantasy games which briefly, perversely, served as the world's lingua-franca medium of exchange.

They never understood what their grandparents had known: that the only thing you could trust was people.

They didn't understand why Nera was in the streets in '33.

They died looking for jobs and money, trying to find a way back, trying to find someone to sell their lives to.

§

Flashes of brown, brown, brass, brown. One last consoling flash of gold.

Back in the kitchen, dry-mouthed, Nera forced herself to send an answer: *I'm sorry, I just needed to get away from that bullshit banker.*

Malka's response was a long time coming. Nera pulled open a window and watched the three of them. Jörg leaned towards Sergei, laughed his abrupt booming laugh. Sergei smiled. Malka stood a little stiff, but intent, listening, her hands twitching. Clamor had a theme song now for Sergei—harsh, almost atonal, like grunge guitars playing Schönberg. Apparently she'd given it enough data, now, to figure her and Sergei out.

Finally, among the brown flashes, Malka's green: *Nera, I'm really sorry. I'm pulling my support on reliability and trust. I care about you, but you keep doing things like this—attacking poor Sergei, who's doing important work... wallowing in glory from the good old days... risking my rep on Sabine Heuspross's ego-splurge. It's ridiculous. I liked it better when you were just drifting. Let's not talk for a while.*

On hUBBUB, Nera's aggregate rating was now 358.

In her queue: messages from drive-by ratings advisors, attracted by her sharp plunge. They'd have suggestions for her; probably they'd want her to shift her friendships around, invest in relationships with other narrow-minded ideological assholes like herself. That would improve her numbers. Also in her queue: a lot of private messages from friends worried about her behavior, and a couple of random gig offers. She scrolled to the gold comments in her comment stream. They were from drunk losers who liked the idea of baby hookers, or conspiracy-theory ravings from incoherent, bitter old Thirty-three'ers.

Incoming, from Colette:

*Um, Nera, I don't know how to say this so I'll just say it. We all know it's really important to keep ratings up when the project's in such a risky place. It doesn't really cohere for us, to have RFC signers who are under 400 at hUBBUB. I'm sorry, I know it's a pile-on, but it's really best if you take a break. You've done good work and we'll still vouch for that. Maybe later when things are more stable, you can get involved again. I'll find someone else to talk to the Autie Girls. Really sorry.*

She checked hUBBUB again: still 358, and for a few crazy seconds she thought that getting booted from the Cambergerstrasse team would have no effect—maybe people hated the project that much? But it was just lag. Soon she was down to 302 on hUBBUB, 288 on Moody's, 268 on Snopes.

Tears stung in her eyes, so that the crisp in-eye windows were overlaid on a blurry world. She rubbed her eyes, angry. Now the Schadenfreude voyeurs who got off on watching the tragic, weeping de-rated would swarm.

She scrolled to the last gold comment in her comment stream.

*I read what you said on a kidfilter so maybe I don't understand it all. But I agree with you. Money was dumb. People shouldn't be able to make other people play with them just because they have points in that kind of game. I'm asking my parents to delegate you. I'm in the fungus room if you want to play.*

Sure enough, one of the gig offers was a babysitting offer from Torsten's parents.

§

"Hi Torsten," she said brightly, squatting down. "What do you want to play?"

He was slouched against a fungus pillar, his eyes blank, whole body twitching—shoulders, chin, elbows jerking—playing some in-eye game. He blinked, his vision cleared, and he looked at her cautiously. His cheeks were stained red from sausage mushroom.

She wiped her palms on her knees. There was a kid's version of Clamor, he could probably hear that she was less trustworthy than before. "We could play tag, or I could tell you a story..."

"Are you really sad?" he said. "I'd be sad if that happened to me."

She blinked. He was looking at her as if he was wondering if she was about to lose it. Should she shrug it off, reassure him? Who wanted a sad babysitter?

But they used to say, in the revolution: we take our allies where we find them.

"Yeah," she said. "I'm sad."

Torsten stood up. "Why did they do that? Weren't they your friends?"

She shrugged. "I said some dumb things."

He frowned, and nodded. A grim expression. She remembered her mother, looking up from the orange leather chair when Nera wanted to play, smiling falsely, returning to her tablet. "Nera, I have to work." She remembered knowing that that was what adult life was like.

Any ratings consultant would tell her she needed to sound apologetic now, not defiant, or she was going to get de-rated further.

But she could see Torsten bracing himself to live in this world they'd made.

"What happened to me, Torsten... it wasn't okay," she said. "My friends made a mistake. Your friends should stick by you always."

Torsten looked up and grinned. He looked enormously relieved. He reached out and took her hand. "I'm hungry," he said.

"You've been eating the mushrooms though," she said.

"They're kind of yucky."

"I know a yummy soup place straight up from here, if you can climb."

Torsten puffed his chest out. "I can climb *great.*"

She smiled. His small hand folded in hers, warm and confident. "Let's go play," she said.

# ANIL MENON
# Into The Night

The island of Meridian was still thirty minutes away, but Kallikulam Ramaswamy Iyer had already done enough neck stretches, shoulder shrugs, hand wiggles and toe scrunches to limber his joints for this lifetime and the next.

He was tired. He was eighty-two years old and had relaxed his ancient Brahmin joints through many a stressful hour, but the last few days had been some of the worst: first, a thirteen-hour flight from Mumbai to Sydney with a three-day layover at Singapore, then a four-hour flight in a boomerang-shaped aeroplane from Sydney to Fiji's Nadi airport followed by a two-hour ride in a catamaran ferry to Meridian. Far away.

Ramaswamy shook his head. Why had Ganga decided to settle so far away? She'd always been peculiar, his daughter, this bright-eyed girl they had raised from mustard seed through plaits and school bag to first-class first and first menses, this wild daughter of theirs that squeezed their hearts so, squeezed it till he'd sworn not to love her anymore, but of course it was all talk, as the missus would verify, for wasn't he here in the belly of a fish, going to a land of cannibals for the sake of their bright-eyed girl who only thirty-seven years ago had begun a mustard seed as modest as an ant's fart.

"Think in English," advised his wife. "Tamil will only make it harder for you to adjust."

Oh, listen to the Queen of England. Who was the matriculate, madam? And who was the Sixth Standard twice fail?

A wave of laughter surged through the boat. It was beginning to irritate him, these periodic laughs. What were they laughing at? And why was it funny? A passenger in the adjacent seat, a sleek cheetah of an Indian girl who'd been gesturing with her silver thimbles throughout the last half-hour, lifted her head, blinked rapidly and smiled. She looked tired too. What was she doing here, alone, so far away from home and husband?

He continued to brood. She could've stayed. There were plenty of jobs for Hindus in India. Even a job in Europe would've been acceptable. But the South Pacific! Meridian was so new it wasn't even listed in his Rand McNally 1995 World Almanac. Who could've foreseen when he left Kallikulam in 1962, barely nineteen years old and with ninety rupees in his pocket, when he'd left his parents, dressed in their starched best, left them behind and forever at the Thrichedur railway station, who could've foreseen this final migration, three score and three years later, to a land without elephants, to a land without ancestors, who could have foreseen?

"Stop beating that drum, sir," said Paru. "Fall on your knees and thank your Krishna-bhagavan that you have such a sterling daughter. You're in her care now. So chin up and get ready for the next innings."

You? What had happened to the 'we'? His wife Paru had been younger by ten years. By all logic she should have been on this boat, not him. But of course, the 'we' of sixty years plus had ended at the Sion Electric Crematorium in Mumbai.

He flexed his neck. No. That had just been the disposal of the end. The end had come with a shopping list. Paru had sent him to buy groceries and when he returned, it was to a world without— No, it was no use dwelling on that day. Today was the first day of the rest of his life.

He sat, resigned, as another rash of laughter broke out. The girl was also laughing. She must've sensed his inspection, because she turned her head in his direction. Her eyes were milked over, like the white, dead corals he'd seen near Fiji. Pity struggled with revulsion in his mind. O God, what was the matter with the girl's eyelids? Why was she rolling them up? Almost like a lizard. Poor girl. Ramaswamy quickly turned his head. So there were handicapped people in the West as well. But then, Earth itself was handicapped now, broke and broken.

People may say what they want, thought Ramaswamy, but fate was blind. Why else would this beautiful girl be blind, why else would he have had to leave India, and why else would the last conversation with his wife have been about potatoes, brinjals and coconuts, and would he, for God's sake, please, please check the tomatoes before buying them, because the last batch had been overripe and practically rotten. It could've been about anything, and it had been.

He didn't mind that his wife had died. She'd become tired, worn out. Nothing had interested her anymore, not even their fights, and her insults had stopped being insults and begun to feel like the instructions of someone departing for an immensely long journey. She'd become weary, Paru had, his wife of sixty years and seven lives, weary of waiting for Ganga to amass the papers and travel-credits 'to

How to Live on Other Planets

bring you home, Amma. I love you, please, please hang in there, okay?' Why, had his house been any less of a home? Had he not taken care of his wife? Paru wanted to let go, and he'd gotten tired of holding on for the both of them. He didn't mind. But she hadn't left empty handed. She'd taken his memories with her. That he did mind.

It meant that he now had to recollect things, and could no longer rely on a shout ("Paru!") and an answer. For instance, what was the name of the school he'd attended in the 1940s? Had they first talked in the Esso canteen, or had it been that monsoon day when he'd offered her his umbrella? What was the name of his last American boss at Esso, the year before it became Hindustan Petroleum? He clearly remembered the fellow. Especially his laugh. The fellow would laugh, a great big honk of pure evil, revealing a panoply of white, red, yellow, lead glint and a couple of canines sharpened by decades of insatiable meat-eating. But what was his name?

There was an announcement being made, but the accent was impossible to understand. It was clear though they'd almost reached. Through the giant windows, he could see bits and pieces of the skyline. Passengers were busy getting their things together; a few were busy blinking at each other. Maybe that's how they said goodbye in this part of the world. The blinking reminded him of ants on a sugar trail. The catamaran docked with a bump and jerk.

"We've reached," said his co-passenger. "You can unbuckle now."

"I know," said Ramaswamy, smiling and blinking. "That's what I want, that's what you want, but that's not what the buckle wants."

"Here, let me help. It's been a long journey, huh?"

And before he could say anything, she leaned over and began to struggle with the belt. Her hair glistened as if they were coated with glass. He couldn't help touching a strand, and she glanced at him. "Careful. The alloy coat is not quite stable yet."

"Are you married?" he asked.

She frowned and didn't answer. "There!" She detached the belt. "Come, Appa. I'll call Aaliyah and let her know we've reached."

Appa? Yes, of course. This was Ganga, his daughter. How could he not have recognized her? The hair was a factor, yes. But still. What was happening to him? He was so astonished by the lapse in memory, he forgot to be terrified.

"I'm okay," he said, furious with Paru. It was all her fault. Fresh resentment began to ooze from the wound of his recent loss.

§

He'd been here before, a stranger in a strange land. In 1962, he'd stepped out on Platform No. 3 at the Victoria Terminus in Bombay, with the smell of soot in his nostrils, a roll of bedding and an aluminum trunk full of good advice. He'd survived the first strange day, and the second, and the third, till a season had passed, and he'd become part of the very strangeness he'd seen on the first day. On his way to work, he'd sometimes see himself stepping out of a train, on this platform, on that platform, from this village, from that village, going everywhere and going nowhere at all.

So why did this transition feel so different, as if he were doing it for the very first time? Perhaps strangeness simply could not be gotten used to. Especially if the strangeness lay, not in the miracles of the place, but in its small-small things.

The miracles were manageable, because they all had a familiar feel. Buildings that supposedly chatted to each other about energy, politics and life. Or, for example, the 'bubbles.' They were cars with skins that quivered and become teardrop-shaped as they picked up speed. His daughter had tried to explain how it all worked: drive-by-wire, gyroscopic gaddabaddoo, Gandhi's loincloth, and pure unadulterated ghee. Who knew how it worked? He could tell she had no idea either. But they were just inventions.

Ditto for the hearsee. It was just a binoculars and headset rolled into one. With the hearsee, you could see what other people were seeing, hear what other people were hearing, assuming they had hearsees too. It used a "nictating membrane" and of course wireless. Wireless was a must. He'd had the idea himself one afternoon, so he wasn't too surprised.

No, the strangeness lay in other things, once familiar things. It lay in Ganga. She had so many friends. He'd always hated that word: friend. It excused everything and expected nothing.

One friend— Aaliyah— seemed to be a permanent guest. Another "friend" was practically an animal; she lay curled on the sofa, her skinny, thimbled hands working ceaselessly— thinking about the mathematics of relatives in general, Ganga claimed— getting up only to feed, and that too eating things directly from the fridge, all the while standing on one leg like a flamingo and eyeing him cautiously, as if she half-expected an ambush. They were many others, all women, with made-up names, Tomi, Rex, Lace, Sharon, and once, just once, a slender man with a sharp Aryan nose, high forehead, and a girl's name. Ramaswamy had asked him why.

"Because I am a girl," he'd replied.

Dinner was a nightmare: meat and wine all around him, overcooked rice, undercooked vegetables (they crunched! ), rubbery yogurt, and cold metal spoons. The first time he ate with his hand— thoroughly mixing the rice and buttermilk by hand, relishing every wet squelch, and licking the fingers at the end— it'd been impossible to ignore the long watchful silences, rapid blinks, the Flamingo's high laugh, and most hurtful of all, Ganga's startled expression. As if she didn't know. As if she too hadn't eaten the Tamil Brahmin way, his way, the correct way, once. As if she'd forgotten.

He had a room at the end of the hall on the first floor, tucked away from the rest of the house. The girls mostly lived upstairs, rarely coming down, and if they did talk to him, it was only to ask him idiotic questions about festivals, the caste system and Hinduism. He had to watch his answers. Otherwise:

"That's rubbish," Ganga would begin, knitting her brows. "If you look at the facts..."

The facts were these: Brahmanism was bad. The West was good. Everything he said was superstition. Everything she said was science. Those were the facts. S'all right. He had his beliefs, she had hers. She called her beliefs 'facts,' and that was all right too. If science was all-powerful, then why she did grovel before the Evolution God? Evolution this, Evolution that. The girl knew a lot, but she understood nothing. As people said, just being able to talk about a trunk didn't make you an elephant.

But most of all, it was the silence that was intolerable. So many circuits of the house, so many cautious in-the-doorway peeks into bedrooms, so many against-the-light inspections of their mail, so many cups of microwave chai, so many naps and then to painfully go up, down, around and about the house circumnavigating the hours, the day, the month. Occasionally the house would pass on messages in Ganga's voice or Aaliyah's voice, and he'd feel like a house pet, expected to mewl and bark at the sound of his master's voice. He never responded when they called, shuffling around silently, refusing to be happy for their sake, and fully aware that irrespective of whether he responded or not, every room in the house was visible to their lizard eyes.

The silence of his Mumbai apartment had always been bordered with far-away horns, shouts of neighborhood children, Paru's telephone gossip and the imminent possibility of tea. This silence had weight. Sometimes he cried.

§

Ramaswamy lay in bed, facing the wall, the coverlet pulled all the way to his neck, and quietly burbling in a mix of English and Tamil:

"Appa?"

He froze.

"Who are you talking to? Are you alright? Are your legs hurting?"

When he turned, he saw Ganga in her nightdress, her face lit from below by the room's night light.

"I'm okay. Just thinking, that's all. About the good old days."

She sat down besides him and put a hand on his chest. "Not able to sleep?"

"How much sleep can I do?" He hesitated, and then spoke in a rush. "Ganga, I want to go back to Mumbai. I can't live here in this freezing cold and twenty-four hours of rain. Everything is backwards and upside down. From the nose via the back of head to the ear, as people say. A simple man like myself only needs his two servings of rice-curds and a glass of water. That I can get for myself. Why I should be a burden to you? I am going back."

"We can't have this conversation over and over again. Haven't you been watching the news from India? And there's no one there to take care of you. In a few years, your health problems are only going to get worse. If anything happens—"

"Krishna-bhagavan will take care of me as he has all these years."

"Don't be childish! Amma took care of you all these years, not your bloody bhagavan. So at least give credit where it's due."

He was pleased to see her voice rise and her accent veer into its natural roly-poly South-Indian roundness. Ha! Not such a suit-and-boot madam after all. He remembered roly-poly; he'd walked this little girl back from kindergarten every day, pig-tails and upturned face, hopeful smile and Appa, Appa, please can I have some kulfi, Appa.

Where had it all gone wrong with Ganga? Was it the day he'd found her smoking with the sweeper's boy, a Shudran, whose polluting dirty hand also happened to be inside her unzipped pants? Or was it when she'd burnt her Maths degree merely because her college had changed its name from the Indian Institute of Science to the Hindu Institute of Science? Or was it that black day when she'd left India, a month after renouncing her citizenship— he hadn't know it was possible— and in her fierce embrace, he'd sensed an irreversible letting go.

"I should've disciplined her more," thought Ramaswamy, "but as people say, a donkey never has a tiger for a father."

"Can we go to a doctor?" he asked.

"Now?"

She nictated and geometric patterns flashed across her eyelids; the room seemed filled with a new awareness. He sensed there were others in the room, watching, listening, perhaps even commenting on him.

"Appa? Are you in pain? I can call an ambulance—"

"No, no. I just wanted to get an estimate of how much time I have left."

"No one can tell you that!"

"Not even science?"

She smiled and touched his face. "Not even science."

What was the use of it then? He lay back on the bed and turned to face the wall.

"Appa? Look at me." She shook him. "Look at me." And when he did, she continued in the same calm voice. "I know it's all very strange and new to you. And Amma is not here to make it easier. But life is change, and we have to adapt. Otherwise, we might as well be fossils. Evolution—"

"What is this evolution-evolution you keep brandishing like a stick?"

"It's a theory that says we don't need a story to explain how we all got here. It was first clearly explained by Darwin—"

"Speak in Tamil, Ganga. Speak in Tamil."

He listened to her fantastic tale about fish that had grown lungs and learned to walk on earth, a Xerox machine called DNA in every atom and what not. As she talked, her alloy-treated hair furled outwards, a controlled motion that had nothing to do with the wind or any natural shake of the head. Somebody was playing with her hair. He closed his eyes.

When she said 'cells,' he imagined tiny telephones, but when she said 'chromosome,' 'molecule,' 'recombination,' and 'species,' nothing came to mind at all. He marveled that she could swallow so incredible a story but refuse to accept the simplest, most obvious explanation understandable by the stupidest child: God did it. But he didn't want her to stop talking.

"Ganga, this Evolution God, is it Christian or some other religion only? And if it is Christian, then who is Jesus?"

She was silent for a few long seconds, and when she spoke, it was quiet enough to be almost a sigh. "Aaliyah is right, Appa. If you're to see, you must have the right eyes first. The first step is to set you up with a visor. It won't be as good as having a hearsee, but it's better than nothing. It'll be easier to see how it all fits together. Maybe a tour of Galapagos, my research lab, fossil museums. Let's see."

§

He was here, on the battered bench of a battered park, banished for the day, because the house was being energy-audited, and they didn't want him blurting something to the inspector.

It was good to be out, even though the sky was a sickly bluish-gray and the wind was one tooth too sharp. The park was bordered by book shops, clothing stores, cafes and open-air restaurants. He'd picked a spot on a deserted side of the park, because the smell of burning meat reminded him of the ghats of Benares.

Ramaswamy carefully removed the visor and the thimbles from their case. As he stared at the "vision field," it began to shear, as if it was being stretched from opposite corners. The eye had to keep moving, otherwise the visor would lose focus. His arthritic fingers found it hard to gesture the thimbles to manipulate the visor's controls, and after a while he began to get confused with the colored flags, training wheels and little rotating astrology-type signs. The view filled with tiny windows and he blinked helplessly as he tried to regain the original view.

"Don't worry," said Paru. "A spectacles is no match for a Senior Clark from Esso."

Abruptly, a gut-wrenching image of water, wood, blue and sky filled his vision field. And tentacles. He caught a glimpse of lettering:

"Marine Research Institute." He jerked back in his seat, reaching out to clutch something tangible.

"Hey! No linking," said a voice. "This is a research channel."

And then his view shifted back to the park and its threadbare green. He regained his breath, and with it, triumph. He'd just used somebody else's visor, or more likely, hearsee. So this is what "surfing" the I-net was all about.

It took a while to retrace his steps, but he managed to get the screen full of windows again, and as it scrolled past, he blinked. And blinked. And blinked. In most cases, he got wobbly images of edges, shadows and corners of rooms. But even when he got a nice view, such as the one from the tourist staring up at the statues on Easter Island, or merely a bizarre one, like that young girl who stared fixedly at different parts of her naked body, what did it matter? Most people seemed to be sitting on equally battered benches staring out over equally battered parks. What did he and they have in common after all, other than a mutual acknowledgment of being lost? He was everywhere and nowhere.

"It is not our time," said Paru, sounding subdued. "Give it a chance."

His visor filled with fifty scattered circles. Ganga had explained that in "idle mode" the visor would show the GPS coordinates of people in a half-a-mile radius. A window popped up, reminding him to "fill in his profile."

"Do what it says," said Paru. "Put up a sign saying you want to chit-chat."

"Keep quiet! You should be sitting here suffering, and I should be in your Madras-coffee loving head. Irresponsible, selfish cow."

He tried to describe himself but didn't get very far. The "wizard" asked for his Myers-Briggs type, whether he was an introvert or extrovert, whether he was an active or a passive voyeur, and on and on. What kinky things turned Ramaswamy on?

Elephants, thimbled Ramaswamy. Temples. Obedient children. Early morning showers. India. Brahmin culture. Decent women. But then he got diverted with the memories of all the delicious foods he would never eat again.

The bench was still slightly wet, perhaps from the early morning rains. The colony's park in Mumbai had always been chock full of people: retirees, teenage lovers, food vendors, toy vendors, mating dogs, laughing clubs, children running about everywhere.

The sky looked dark, swollen, a child about to cry. Perhaps global raining was around the corner.

The visor queried his current mood. He selected the most depressed face he could from the samples in front of him.

"I took it all for granted," he thought. His head had begun to ache.

A teenager sat down at the far end of the bench. He had an open, cheerful face framed by a halo of curly black hair. He nodded in Ramaswamy's direction.

"Waz," said the kid. Then he stretched out his legs and made himself comfortable.

The visor claimed the kid's name was Krish and then went on to bug Ramaswamy with a variety of options. Irritated, he took off the visor.

"Excuse me, is your name Krish?"

"Like da tag sez, heya?" The boy seemed a little puzzled, and his eyelids nictated. His expression brightened. "Ya-i-c. Welcome to Oz, uncle."

"I'm Ramaswamy. I'm from India. Tamil Nadu. Are you also from same?"

Krish shrugged. "Maybe. Me's from Wooshnu's navel, maybe."

The boy's accent was not Indian. In fact, Ramaswamy could barely understand what he was saying. "Are you having school holiday today?"

Krish grinned and shook his head. "Waz school? You's the headmaster? What you be teaching, Master Bates?"

Ramaswamy laughed. Kids were scoundrels no matter where they were. "Bad boy. You need to be more disciplined."

"Nuff sport." Krish scooted over. "You's wanting da elephant, heya?"

The boy's eyes were so merry and his smile so infectious, Ramaswamy also found himself smiling. "Heya. Heya. What's this 'heya'?"

"Gimme the izor, dear." The kid reached for the visor, but something about his expression made Ramaswamy snatch it away and put it in his shirt pocket.

Krish shrugged and unbuttoned his pants. "Assayway you's want." He grabbed Ramaswamy's hand and shoved it into his pants. "Go on. Sample all you's want. 100% desi juice on da tap, uncle-dear."

Later, Ramaswamy would puzzle over the fact that the boy's

penis had been hard and erect. But it was only one of the many puzzles.

A police car swooped out of nowhere, a blaze of whirling blue lights and piercing siren. The next ten minutes were a terrifying blur. Two officers jumped out of the car; one ran after Krish, and the other fumbled for his handcuff.

His boss from Esso! How was it possible? The same beefy expression, the same grayish-white whiskers, the same sozzled eyes. Mr. Gregory! Just remembering the name after all these years was mildly orgasmic.

"Mr. Gregory, Sir!" Ramaswamy shot to his feet and was ready for dictation.

"Move again asshole, and you'll make my day." The cop pointed an object that resembled a TV remote at Ramaswamy.

But Ramaswamy had already realized his mistake. Of course this policeman wasn't Mr. Gregory. His boss had already been middle-aged when he, Ramaswamy, had joined as a young assistant clerk.

"I'm sorry, I thought you were my boss from Esso. I came here to take some fresh breeze only."

Ramaswamy tried to explain how his hand had ended up in the boy's pants. The boy clearly needed a doctor, he had a rash of some kind. Perhaps he'd thought an Indian would help. But he was only a retired clerk from Esso, his daughter's dependent, practically a beggar himself. Esso's health insurance had barely covered Paru's treatment; there was nothing he could do for random lost-eyed Indian boys. If the officer would be kind enough to call his daughter, Ganga could confirm every detail. When Ramaswamy reached for the visor in his pocket, the officer tasered him.

§

In time, the pain faded, as did all direct memory of the incident. In time, a woman in blue came to apologize, and she began to talk about punking clubs, sadistic voyeurs and clockwork porn. He understood little, and was grateful when Aaliyah stepped in to keep it that way.

"Do you remember, Appa," Ganga asked him, a few days after the nightmare, "do you remember a terrace, a girl, and a sweeper's boy?"

Of course he remembered. It was the day his daughter's eyes

had begun to terrify him. The boy had been beaten to an inch of his life. Deservedly so. There was no comparison.

"Why do you drag up that incident over and over. Nothing happened."

"Do you know that his hands were just as accidentally placed as yours? That I was the guilty one?"

"I don't know anything. Tell me what to say."

"Maybe it was karma." She nictated and turned away. "Things haven't changed as much as we think."

It did comfort him a little, the idea that karma mattered and that she believed it did. Or pretended to.

When the cold rains came, as they often did in this age of carbon, he liked to sit by a corner window of the house and watch the banana tree in the yard make short work of the water. The rain, as thin as cow's milk, rolled off the tree's bright green plates, as ineffective as a mother's Tamil on a child's unrepentant back. Sometimes the Flamingo would creep up and crouch by him, her eyes blind in thought, her bony fingers ceaselessly working on the general problem of relatives.

"What is the solution?" he once asked the Flamingo, in Tamil, "if the ones I love hate what I love?"

The Flamingo said nothing. Perhaps she hadn't heard. It was moot in any case, for the problem was intractable. Change was inevitable; it hadn't been, but now it was. Call it evolution, fate, choice or chance. If that was the only way the world would turn, so be it.

But acceptance wouldn't come. The darkness crowded him from all corners, the light of his understanding curving upwards along its walls and returning in an ever-tighter loop. Soon, he would be beyond the reach of all stories.

"Amma," Ramaswamy would shout, forgetting himself in his despair. His mother: a chequered six-yard sari, a raspy voice, wrinkled hands, jasmine-scented hair and the comfort of her sari's corners. "Amma!"

Sometimes his daughter would turn up with a glass of Horlicks. In her nightdress and short-hair, she resembled one of those Goan ladies in India, brown as a coconut but all white inside. She would pretend to listen to his burbling, her eyes blinking absent-mindedly, her hair furling like snakes as they flexed and re-flexed into one of her many styles. She had many styles, but she looked a widow in all of them. She would tell him fantastic tales from science and biology, offering truth when he longed for comfort. He would pick a fight, say outrageous things, insult her friends and all that she held dear, and sometimes Ganga would lose her temper.

"Speak in Tamil," he'd urge. "Speak in Tamil."

Then Ramaswamy would relax. Ah, familiar words. So familiar, so sweetly familiar. He let the ferocious alphabet fall, splish-splosh, all around and galosh, the rain of words, in one ear, out the other, the gentle splash of words, how he missed her, Paru, his comfort, his eyes, how he missed her, his compass, his all, as he walked, ever faster, into the night.

# MARGE SIMON
## South

You promised me no problems
when the temperatures dropped,
assured me that we were prepared.
Holding hands we watched
the great migration south.

With synthetic skins, cryo foods,
and prefab domes, you said we couldn't lose.
There was little need to leave the domes.
Safe from the fierce glacial winds,
we made love on autumn colored furs.

Yet you were the first to grow restless,
to stand all night at the southern window
following the great move of stars.
We shared the bitter smoke of silence
until one morning, you were gone.

I waited for you, my fingers
tracing love symbols on the icy glass.
I slept with the red wing of your guitar.
Then moon-shadow tall, you came home.
Inside the door, I didn't know your eyes.

This year, I read while you play solitaire.
Our conversations are textured with frost.
I ache for your laughter,
the taste of grass on your skin,
a bouquet of crocuses in a blue vase.

# DEBORAH WALKER
# Speed of Love

In the National Trust play-area, in the sight of the immense Neolithic stones that have stood for five thousand years and whose purpose was lost and now is understood, the sisters watched the children playing. November air bit the children, turning un-gloved fingers cold and red and numb. The children were indifferent. They hurtled around the play-area, engrossed in the convoluted pecking-order games they'd devised. No strangers here. Children find their play-mates quickly. They understand the rules.

At unmeasured distance, the triangles converged in apex aligning space. The Neolithic stone gate nearest the playground opened in a hiss of >c-light, splitting and reforming, and delivering the passenger.

"Look at that," said Penny, the elder sister, mother of the two girls galloping around the playground. "That's another one." She watched the slow man unfurl from a foetal position. "They're so damn slow. I can't stand them being so slow."

"It's the time dilation," said Maggie. "They can't help living near a white hole."

"I can't think why you wanted to meet us here," said Penny.

The slow man was tall. Probably Elska class thought Alice, like the engineers who'd mapped the intersecting triangles of space and re-discovered the void-spanning short-cut to this whirling, speeded planet.

"Slow as a snail," said Penny. "It's a wonder they get anything done."

The slow man turned his head. He walked towards the sisters.

"They're only slow from our perspective," said Maggie. "Anyway, I asked you here for a reason. I've got something to tell you, Penny."

"Hmm?" Penny was momentarily distracted by a scream from the playground. "Darling, don't do that," she shouted to her younger daughter, who was punching a small un-chaperoned boy.

"I've met someone. Moved in with him, in fact."

"Hey, that's great. What does he do?"

"His name's Arille." There—she'd said it.

The children screamed as Patricia, the eldest of Penny's daughters, championed an attack on the occupied wooden fortress/slide.

The shell of the slow man's naked body glinted in the harsh air.

"Arille?" Penny said. "Oh, Maggie, why do you do it?"

"Do what?"

Penny shook her head. "You've always been like this. You've always made bad choices."

"This is good for me. Me and Arille have a good relationship."

"It's not really a relationship is it, Maggie?"

"Arille's good for me." Maggie thought of the relationships she'd had in the past. All her bad choices, as Penny called them. Arguments, words used like knives. Arille was good for her. Restful. He completed the hole in her life. "I love him," she said. That should tell Penny all she needed to know.

"You're fooling yourself. God forbid you have any children."

Maggie glanced across to her nieces riding wild with the excitement of their games. "I'm sorry you don't approve."

"Have you registered?"

"Not yet."

"I should report you."

"You won't will you?" Slow/human relationships had to be registered. But it had always been difficult for Maggie to do the things she had to do. Why should she have to register? Why should she try and make people understand? But she was here, trying to explain to her sister. Maggie stared at her nieces, spinning on the roundabout. Spinning so fast. "I knew you wouldn't understand."

"I don't understand. Time to go, kids," Penny shouted to the children. "Maggie, I think we better not see each other for a while. I don't want the children exposed."

The slow man had finally reached them. Their comprehension was astounding, truly the most alien thing about them. In the glint of his spiral eye, the wink he gave to Maggie was like the melt of frozen water, a glacier of understanding.

§

When she got home, Maggie saw that Arille hadn't done the washing-up. She thought about complaining, but instead she did it herself. It was hard to be angry when a conversation extended over hours, or even days.

Arille watched the TV slowed down to the speed of his

comprehension, on a special device that he'd designed himself.

Maggie sat down beside him. She just breathed. She thought of her sister and her nieces and everyone outside. They were spinning as fast as they could, just to stand still. And she didn't have to anymore. "I love you, Arille."

Five minutes later, he squeezed her hand. Maggie smiled. It was good, and it was quiet, and it was slow, and it felt like home.

# MARY ANNE MOHANRAJ
## Jump Space

**_Grains of Sand_ Freighter. Deneb, planetary approach. Three weeks ago.**

"Do you really want to stop here?" Kate sat in the pilot's chair, twisted around to face them, with Amara nursing quietly in her lap. "We don't have much to trade that they want—and even if we did, this planet is barbaric. I don't want the girls exposed to this culture."

Iniya was playing in her room. Hopefully. A precocious four-year-old could get into a frightening amount of trouble, even on a small ship where she'd lived her entire life. Joshua kept an ear open, just in case—he was on Ini-watch right now. Honestly, he'd rather be sitting on the floor, playing knights and dragons with her—but the adults needed to have this conversation.

"You say culture like there's just one," Sarita said sharply. "What about the engineered species and their cultures?"

"Sarita, c'mon," Joshua said. "The engineered species and their treatment here are her _point._"

"Exactly," Kate snapped. "The dominant culture on this world is disgusting."

Sarita said primly, "We're supposed to avoid value judgments."

"Kate's right. It's appalling, really," Joshua said. He tried to keep his tone mild, though Sarita in uppity mode would make a saint want to slap her.

Sarita deflated suddenly, flopping down into the co-pilot's chair. She reached out an apologetic hand to Kate, who, after a moment, took it. Joshua breathed a covert sigh of relief. Sarita said, "I know. They're awful—but it's not as if I want to take the girls down there. You can all stay up here; I just need one more vocal grouping...and no one's ever studied any of the genetically engineered serf-species here."

"Because no one civilized can stand to be around them. Poor things," Kate said.

Joshua knew Kate was right, but he also knew that Sarita was going to get her way. She almost always did. She just wanted things so passionately, so intensely, that it became impossible to say no to her. She wasn't even saying anything now—just looking at Kate with those big dark eyes steady, silently pleading.

How to Live on Other Planets

Kate sighed. *"One week.* That's it. Maybe we can find an isolated beach somewhere in the world to take the girls to while you're working. Ini's never seen an ocean, and this world is practically all water."

Sarita wisely didn't say anything more—just jumped up and wrapped Kate in a hug, careful not to disturb the baby. Joshua turned and headed back to Ini's room, grateful that the women had worked it out with only minimal intervention from him. That seemed to work best; when a man was partnered with two alpha females, it was generally wise to keep his head down and count his blessings. Besides, there were several knights and dragons waiting for him, along with one strong-willed princess.

## University of All Worlds. Pyroxina major. Seven years ago.

"Professor?" The girl stood before him, her eyes downcast. Dark skin, like so many of his students here; all the locals on Pyroxina were of South Asian descent, from the third wave of Old Earth colonists. The University drew from all the colonies, of course, but it was still tremendously cheaper for the locals to attend. No space fare, for one thing, and a discounted tuition rate.

Joshua smiled gently. "I've told you all before, you don't need to be so formal with me. I'm not even a real professor—just a visiting instructor. Please, call me Joshua."

The girl ducked her head even lower, her long black braid swinging. "Sorry, professor. I forgot."

He wished she would look up. All the local girls seemed trained not to make eye contact with strange men; after ten weeks, it had gotten pretty frustrating trying to have conversations with so many tops of heads. It also made it a lot harder to learn their names. "It's okay. Sarita, right? What can I do for you?"

"I love this class. It's the best one I've taken at University. They should make you a real professor."

"That's very kind of you to say." In fact, his chair had dropped a hint that maybe he should stick around, teach some summer classes, apply for the job that was opening up for next year. But that would mean dealing with all the department politics, working his way slowly up the totem pole. Joshua had seen how hellish that could be in other departments, how much time it took away from your real work. He wasn't sure he wanted to make that kind of compromise.

Besides, he wasn't ready to settle down in one place, not yet. There was so much of the universe still to see...

"I particularly enjoyed the Grommer-Twince tributary modulations. The way they evoke the musicians' desperate sense of planetary limits, given their distance from any other system —"

Joshua cut her off, confused. "You wrote a fine paper on the subject, yes." It was based on that paper that he'd recommended her for the grad student fellowship. "But did you have a question for me?"

"I was wondering..." Sarita looked up then, her eyes meeting his for the first time in the conversation—the first time that semester. "...would you like to have dinner with me?"

Joshua drew in a quick breath, his face flushing. Her eyes was astonishingly dark brown, almost black. Dark like the empty spaces between the stars; the vertigo was dizzying. Before he could answer with the obligatory *no,* a response Joshua was surprised to find he did not want to give, Sarita had gone on, speaking quickly, her eyes locked on his.

"You've graded everything except the final exam, and I've gotten straight A's. I'm going to get an A on that too, and I know you have to have a second-grader on the final anyway, so even if you wanted to give me a better grade than I deserve, you can't, so it wouldn't be a breach of ethics to go out with me. I would have waited to ask you until the semester was over, but I checked the flight records and you're scheduled to leave Pyroxina the day after finals, so if I waited it would be too late. So I had to ask now."

The only thing he could think to say was, "Those flight records are sealed."

She smiled then, a wicked grin that he would never, not in a million light-years, have imagined on her. It transformed her serious face. "Not if you know how to hack your way in."

Joshua found himself fighting back the very unprofessional urge to laugh. "You don't have a lot of respect for the rules, do you?"

She said solemnly, "I'm actually very law-abiding. My parents would tell you that I've been an obedient daughter. I only break the rules when there's an excellent reason to do so."

"And I'm an excellent reason?" His pulse quickened.

She hesitated—the first pause he'd seen in her since the day she walked into his class, so serious and confident. "I'm not sure." And then she smiled again, an uncertain smile that caught at him, made him swallow. "But I think so."

Joshua knew, knew that he shouldn't say it. But the words came out anyway, spilling from his mouth as if spoken by someone else entirely. "You know, I've recently decided to stay at the university a little longer, teach a summer class or two. So if you have any questions for me once the semester is actually over..." And he was smiling too, helplessly. He had a feeling he was in big trouble.

## Deneb IV, Katchari Quarters. Three weeks ago.

Sarita was in trouble. The house-master who had agreed to let her interview some of them (provided that she pay the full sexual use-fee, of course), had warned her she might find it difficult to concentrate on her work. Sarita had thought he was exaggerating, but no. She'd interviewed seven Katchari so far—five females, two males. Even when she kept her head down focused on her notes, kept a broad wooden table between them, the pheromones still had an effect in the small, enclosed bedroom. Quite an effect.

Sarita crossed and uncrossed her legs, trying to get comfortable. It was just so *hot* here. Sweat dripped down her spine, sliding under her sari's silk border. She took another long drink from the glass of iced fruit juice on the table, and glanced up, briefly, at the new Katchari entering the room. Gods. This one might be the most beautiful yet. Deep, dark brown fur, and a long, muscular body, at least a foot taller than she was. She had a weakness for tall men.

Professional. The key was to stay professional. She tapped the recorder, setting it going. "Name, please?"

He answered in a low voice, "Chocolate."

Sarita glanced up, startled. "You must be joking! Seriously? Did your parents actually name you that?" They had discussed the girls' names for months before naming them, and had been very careful to choose names that couldn't easily be mocked.

"I never knew my parents." He stared straight ahead, his tone carefully neutral. "My crèche-leader felt *Chocolate* accurately described my fur, both in color and silky texture."

"Well, yes," Sarita had to admit, trying not to think about touching that fur. "Accurate, maybe. But it's no name for a person!"

"I'm not a person, mistress. Not legally." And there it was. He glanced down at her from under long lashes, and on those last words, a spark of anger flashed in his eyes. The others had sung for her, just as she'd asked, and she'd recorded the songs, but they'd all been so sad, so despairing, so *broken*. Sarita didn't know whether this one could even sing, but one thing was clear—despite his circumstances, he wasn't broken yet. She felt her interest stirring.

"I can't call you Chocolate. Or Choco. Umm...would it be okay if I called you Cho?"

He blinked, slowly, and then a smile curved its way along his face, taking him from beautiful all the way to drop-dead gorgeous. "I would like that." He stepped closer, and closer yet, until he was suddenly all the way across the room, inches away, on absolutely the wrong side of the table. "I would like that very much."

## Sarita's parents' house. Pyroxina major. Six years ago.

"You don't have to do this," Kate said.

Sarita frowned. "What, you want me to just run off, leave the planet without even saying goodbye?"

"But they're not speaking to you," Joshua protested.

"That's *their* choice. I've been a good daughter. I've done everything I can to make them happy. I found a nice professor —"

"— agnostic, white-skinned, and can't even speak Tamil —" Joshua interjected.

"— introduced them to him, or tried to. Didn't even have sex with him until we were contracted..."

"That depends on how you define sex, don't you think?" Kate asked, lifting an eyebrow.

"...stayed in school, kept majoring in Engineering, the way they wanted —"

"Sneaking in a second major in Music & Ethnology," Kate continued.

"Engineering. Where I happened to meet a very nice freighter captain while interning at the spaceport." Sarita smiled, too brightly. "You could argue that it was actually *all their fault* that I met Kate, fell in love, got you to redefine our contract as a threesome—"

"— and in the process, broke your poor parents' hearts. Not that I'm complaining," Joshua added hastily. He definitely thought he'd come out ahead in that deal.

"It's not like I'm the first in the family to have multiple spouses," Sarita said, with just a little too much defiance in her voice.

"I'm not sure your parents will think that our situation is exactly comparable to your many-times-great-great-grandfather and his three wives, back on Old Earth. I don't think I'd recommend that as your first line of attack," Joshua said. "How do you know that after not speaking to you for over a year, that they're going to be willing to talk now?"

"I *don't* know," Sarita said, her voice finally breaking. "But they're my parents, and I love them. I have to try. Okay?"

"Okay," Kate said, her own voice shaking a little. She reached out and took Sarita's hand in hers.

"Okay," Joshua said, taking a deep breath. "Let's do this." He reached out to push the doorbell, bracing himself for the coming storm.

## Deneb IV, Katchari Quarters. One week ago.

Sarita sank down into the bed. "They've agreed to stay another week. It took some convincing, but Josh told Kate that it really wasn't unreasonable for the work to take another week, especially if it was going well."

"When was the last time you actually recorded a song?" Cho asked, his face unwontedly serious.

She smiled. "Two weeks, six days, and seven hours ago. Just before I met you. Unless you count the noises you've been making..."

"Have you told them about me?" He curled around her, his hands reaching to massage her back, claws retracted.

"Not yet. But I will." Sarita's eyes closed, involuntarily, at his touch. They'd trained him in massage, but it was more than that— Cho seemed to have an instinct for exactly the right places to touch. *Animal instincts,* she thought. But she would never say that out loud.

"You don't have to tell your family," he said.

"I want to." She opened her eyes, reached out to stroke a finger across the short creamy fur of his cheek, marveling again at its softness.

"It's pointless." His voice was dark, empty.

Sarita reached out, trying to hold as much of his long body in her arms as she could. "Shh..." She didn't want to talk about that, didn't want to think about the end that was inevitably coming. Racing towards them, like the nose of a great ship, diving through space towards a Jump gate.

Cho said softly, "As you command, mistress."

She stiffened. "Don't ever call me that. Never, never, never. Do you understand me?" Her voice rose; her fingers clenched, digging into his pelt.

"Shh..." Now it was his turn to pull her into an embrace. They sank deeper into the bed.

### *Grains of Sand* Freighter. Deneb, fourth planet, stable orbit. Two nights ago.

"Amma. Amma. Amma."

"Amma's not here, baby. Shh... Do you want me to read you your story?" The girl's father sat by her bedside, stroking her forehead.

"Amma! Amma amma amma amma amma!"

Joshua glanced over to where Kate stood in the doorway, her hands twisting together in front of her. She was the calm one, but she'd never make a good poker player. Her hands always gave her away. "Maybe Mommy will sing you a song?" They were usually careful not to break the routine—bath, book, song, bed, in strict order. The adults had long ago agreed that the children needed as much routine as possible in their itinerant lives. But Sarita hadn't come home for three nights now. The story was *her* job.

Kate came forward, her voice lifting in a low croon, soft and wordless. The baby quieted. This would be enough for her, for now. It wasn't the first time Sarita had disappeared for a night, after all. Sarita had warned him when he met her—she wasn't the type to settle down. Joshua understood that. And it wasn't as if she was in any danger—the planet might be cruel to the engineered species, but Sarita should be well protected as a Pyroxina citizen. But still—three nights. Three days and three nights. What the hell was she doing?

### *Grains of Sand* Freighter. Saltair Expanse. Four years ago.

"Try this," Sarita said, bringing over a bowl to Kate's bunk. "My mother sent the recipe; she swears by it for nursing mothers. Of course, she's not happy that I'm not the one nursing Ini, but still—can't let her only granddaughter starve, can she? It's a white curry, full of coconut milk. Milk to bring in the milk, they say. Although it's actually the fenugreek that does the trick; stimulates milk production."

"Can't I just take some pills?" Kate asked. "I'm not hungry." She lay sideways on the bunk, eyes closed, Iniya curled naked against her chest.

Sarita poked her arm gently. "That's just the exhaustion talking. Who would have thought the tough freighter captain would be laid low by a little baby! C'mon, try a bite. For me? It took me hours to find all the ingredients on that last planet we stopped at, and they cost a fortune."

Kate opened her eyes, sighed, and then opened her mouth and let Sarita spoon the curry in. She chewed wearily and swallowed. "You'd think after all these years they'd have found some better way to feed babies."

Sarita kept feeding her, one bite after another. "*You* were the one who insisted on breast-feeding. Joshua and I would have been fine using formula. They've duplicated the ingredients found in breast milk, you know. Perfected the recipe two decades ago."

"It's not the same," Kate insisted. "I can't prove it, but I'm sure it isn't."

"And so we bow to your motherly instincts," Sarita said, smiling. "After all, you're the one who has to wake up every three hours and stay awake until she's done eating. We're just the support team."

Kate bit her lip. "Neither one of you has gotten any work done in months; I'm so sorry..."

"Shh..." Sarita brushed damp hair away from Kate's forehead. "That was the deal. It's *fine.* We knew what we were getting into—as much as any parent does, anyway. Besides, the little monkey's actually kind of cute." Sarita put down the bowl and gently scooped Ini up into her arms, bending down to smell the baby's hair. Vanilla. She'd swear Ini's hair smelled like vanilla.

Kate yawned and rolled over onto her stomach, her eyes closing again. "If they could just figure out a way to make babies' stomachs bigger, so they could eat more at a go. It ought to be a simple engineering problem."

Sarita laughed. "How about you work on that when you wake up, okay? After another hour or two of sleep, I'm sure you'll be able to solve it." Sarita bent down and pulled the blanket up to cover her partner, dropping a kiss on her forehead.

"Okay," Kate said, and went to sleep. Sarita walked away, carrying Ini up to visit Joshua in the pilot's chair. Three more weeks until they made planetfall again. Three more months until they could start the baby on solids. She thought they would make it. Probably.

She had *no* idea how two-parent households survived.

## Deneb IV, Sea of Frustrated Desire. Yesterday.

Kate checked her comm unit again. "She's not even answering her comm now."

"Stop worrying. Probably ran out of power; she always forgets to charge it."

Kate called out, "Ini, stay where we can see you!" The sleepy baby on her chest muttered, "Amma....amma."

"Hush, baby. Hungry?" Kate offered her breast, and Amara took it peacefully enough, though she didn't look happy.

Joshua blinked at the peaceful picture—Kate with light-brown Amara bare against her pale skin. Thinking again how lucky he was. "She's always hungry. She's going to be tall, I think, like her mother."

"Her mother who ought to be back by now." Kate's voice was even more acerbic than usual.

"Aren't you enjoying our little seaside vacation? Pink sand, turquoise water."

"Three weeks of vacation is plenty. Why hasn't she called?"

"Deep in her research, probably. You know how I get when I'm working on a project."

"And what about your work! Selfish, that's what she is."

"I'm mostly on paternity leave now anyway, you know that."

"You love your work."

"I do, but it was miserable enough trying to work when Ini was an infant—I didn't need to do that again. Tenure is a wonderful thing. Be patient with Sari; it's different when you're still in grad school—much more anxiety-provoking. And she's been a grad student a long time now."

"Where's Ini?" Kate sat up. "Ini? INI!"

Joshua jumped to his feet, scanning the sand and ocean around them. No sign of the child. He started walking, then running in the direction they'd seen her last, clambering over a rocky outcropping. His heart was racing; he couldn't breathe. But somehow he was still shouting out her name, "INI! INIYA!"

"Papa?" And there she was, toddling back around the rocks, not so far away after all.

Joshua swept her up in his arms, hugging her sticky, sandy

body close. "We told you to stay in sight! Foolish child! You could have been drowned! Or eaten by dragons!"

Ini just giggled. "There aren't any dragons here, papa."

He carried her back to Kate in long strides, sinking down on their blanket with Ini still cradled in his arms. Kate scanned her for any possible injuries, and then, finding her daughter intact, lay down again. Joshua relaxed his own grasp a little. "What were you doing, going so far without us, monkey?"

"Looking for Amma. I want her to come home."

Joshua swallowed. "Us too, monkey. She'll be home soon, I promise. But you can't go wandering off like that again, okay?"

"Okay," she said, nodding her head several times.

"Good. Now go play in the water." He thumped her bottom and sent her off towards the gentle wavelets. The water here was incredibly calm—the most peaceful shore he'd ever seen. He said, "Sea of Frustrated Desire. Why do you think they called it that?"

Kate sighed, her eyes closed. "They probably had children. Or a wife."

## *Grains of Sand* Freighter. Deneb, fourth planet, stable orbit. Five minutes ago.

"I signed a term contract," Sarita said. She stood silhouetted in the open hatchway, gasping for breath as if she'd just run a mile, the stranger behind her. She hadn't even called up first—just banged on the hatch door until they all came running, Joshua and Kate trying to keep Ini behind them until they looked out the porthole and saw Sarita there. Then they couldn't get the door open fast enough, but this was not what Joshua had expected to hear.

"You what?" Joshua asked.

Iniya clung to her leg, murmuring 'amma amma amma,' and Sarita stroked her hair as she talked, her voice low. "Shh…baby…shh. It's okay. I missed you too, monkey." She looked at Joshua. "It was the only way to get him out. I signed over five years of my service, in exchange for thirty years of his. Engineering work only, which they value highly. That's specified in the contract. I'll be fine."

"Like hell you will!" Joshua said.

Kate frowned. "Josh, hush. Iniya's upset…we can finish this conversation later."

"Kate—this concerns the kids too. Whatever she's got to say, she needs to say it in front of them."

"Josh, no. You're angry, and you're wrong. Ini, sweetie, c'mon." Kate bent down and peeled Iniya off Sarita's leg. The poor kid immediately started howling, and Kate shushed her as she walked away, down the corridor. Sarita stared after them, looking lost, her hands clenching and unclenching at her sides, as if she wanted to grab Ini back. The alien brought his hands together in front of him and laced his fingers together, as if he wanted to reach out and touch her, but was deliberately refraining.

Joshua was grateful for that—if the man said or did anything, Joshua wasn't sure *what* he would do in response. He bit his tongue, waiting until Ini's wails quieted down before asking in a fierce whisper, "Sarita, what possible excuse can you have for all this?"

She squeezed her eyes shut for a moment, then opened them. "I couldn't leave him there, like that. I love him."

"You *lust* after him. That's what he was built for." Joshua had never been attracted to men, but even he could feel the pull of the cat-man, with his lithe, perfect body. His soft fur was chocolate brown streaked lightly with copper. He looked utterly edible. But that was programming, biology, pheromones. It didn't mean anything.

Sarita insisted, "It's *not* just lust. That's why you haven't heard from me, the last three days—I needed to enter the bondservant quarters where no comms are allowed. I needed to live with him, to be sure. It's love. The real thing."

How could she betray them? Joshua couldn't even think, he was so angry. He wanted to just shove the man out the hatch, drag Sarita in, by her damned hair, and take off before she could say one more idiotic thing. "How long have you been seeing him?" He was proud that his tone was steady.

Her voice was soft. "Three weeks. Since the day we landed."

"You've lied to us for three weeks!" All this time, when they thought she'd been working, she'd been going down to the planet every day to see *him*. Those last three days, she hadn't even bothered to come back up…

"I know, I know. And I'm sorry, I really am. But I had a good reason. I *love* him."

Joshua found himself shouting, "You can't love him—you barely know him!"

Sarita smiled then, a smile with tears in it. "I barely knew you, or Kate. But I knew who you were, deep down. Was I wrong?"

Joshua's hands were shaking. "None of this makes any sense. Why did they even let you leave the compound with him? Do they have a tracer on you?" His mind was spinning with questions. How could she do this to them? How could she betray them like this, without even a warning? Had she ever really loved them?

Sarita bit her lip. "They didn't let me leave. I hacked the security codes on the gates. Spliced in a tape of us in bed. It should hold them about an hour, and then they'll realize. It took us twenty minutes to get here—we ran. So Cho and I need to go back, now." She took a deep breath, and Joshua could see the tears in her eyes. "I—I wish we had more time."

Cho was silent through it all, a quiet presence at her back, his eyes and stance saying that he would follow her anywhere. Sarita whispered, "I just had to say goodbye. Let me say a proper goodbye to the girls, and then we'll go. I'll comm you from the surface, so you can reach me to fill out all the paperwork. I'd like to stay in touch with Ini. And Amara. If it's all right with you both. You can send me holos of them, and I'll send holos back to them, I promise."

"*Holos?* As if that's a replacement for a mother? Never mind about us—how can you do this to them! You have responsibilities!" Joshua slammed a fist into the bulkhead, barely feeling it split the skin on his knuckles. He was glad to have an excuse to hit something.

Now the tears broke, flowing down her face. "I know—but I can't *leave* him. Not to that life. The girls—they'll be okay without me. They'll have both of you, a mother and a father, a perfect little family. You'll all be okay without me, and he won't. Can't you see I don't have a choice here!" Sarita hesitated, as if she wasn't certain whether to continue. But she'd never lacked courage. She said, her voice dropping again to a whisper, "You—you don't *have* to dissolve our contract. It's only five years. Depending on how you felt, at the end of the term, you could come back here..." Her eyes were wide and her hands were balled into fists at her sides, as if she were afraid to open them, afraid that asking was going too far.

It was. Joshua was ready to let her go. Just take the goddamned cat-man who had screwed up their lives and get off the ship for good. Joshua opened his mouth to say so, to squeeze the words past the choking lump in his throat, but before he could say anything Kate stepped out of the hatchway to stand beside him and say, "Don't be an idiot. You're not going anywhere with him."

## University of All Worlds. Pyroxina major. Five years ago.

Joshua rolled over in bed, sliding his right arm under Sarita, pulling her close. "I want a baby."

She tucked her head in his shoulder, in that spot where she fit so well. "What, right now?"

"No, not right now. But soon. What do you think?"

Sarita raised an eyebrow. "Do you think we're stable enough?"

"We've lasted almost two years. It's the longest relationship *I've* ever been in. Feels stable to me."

"Me too." Sarita grinned. "If Kate's up for it…"

Kate raised her head from the far side of the bed, where she lay curled against Sarita's side. Her face was drawn, ten years older than it had looked moments ago. "I can't have children."

"What?" Joshua asked, startled. He'd assumed that Kate would be the one…

"I tried. Miscarried four times. The last time, uterus ruptured, almost died. So that's it." She lay her head down again, turned away, so they couldn't see her face. "Maybe you two should go ahead, do this without me. Always knew this was too good to last. Probably time for me to be lifting off again anyway, head for the empty stars. The short hauls were starting to get to me."

Sarita thumped a gentle hand against Kate's head. "Don't be crazy. I don't want to be a mom."

Kate turned back, confused. "But you just said…"

"Not the *main* mom. I'd like to help, but I'm not ready to be tied down, feeding some brat twenty-four/seven. I've got years of fieldwork to do, and itchy feet."

"But you're willing to bear a child…"

"I guess. If I have to. But as soon as that thing is born, it's all you. You take the hormones, get the milk pumping, feed the kid, sing it songs, change the diapers, the whole bit."

Joshua interjected, "I can sing songs and change diapers too."

Sarita sighed, fluttering her eyelashes. "Oh, I *suppose* I can change a diaper or two. Once in a while."

Kate was silent, her fingers twisting. Sarita took her hand in hers, interlacing their fingers, stilling them. After a long silence, Kate said, in a voice almost too soft to hear, "So you're both in this. For the long haul."

"Looks like it," Sarita said, squeezing her hand.

How to Live on Other Planets

Kate glanced at her—then looked up at Joshua, finally smiling, "Well, they say that the gods bless lovers and fools."

"Does that mean yes?" Joshua asked.

"I suppose so." She bent down, dropped a kiss on Sarita's cheek. "Yes."

## *Grains of Sand* Freighter. Deneb, fourth planet, stable orbit. Now.

*Grains of Sand, come in. Come in, star-freighter Grains of Sand. You are not cleared for departure.*

"Josh, shut that damn thing off." Kate' voice was tense as she worked the pre-Jump checklist, flipping switches, turning knobs. Joshua reached up to the far right of the co-pilot's chair, shut down the ship-to-planet comms.

Sarita stood behind their chairs, saying tensely to Kate's back, "You don't have to do this. Please, please don't. We can go back."

Kate turned her head, raised one eyebrow. "It's true—Amara would forget you soon enough," Kate said, deliberately cold. "But Ini is too old. She'll always remember that her mother didn't love her enough to stay with her. She'll always know that her mother *abandoned* her."

"I don't *want* to leave her!" Sarita had tears in her eyes again, which made them look even larger and darker than ever. Space between the stars.

"So don't," Kate said softly.

"But your ship—nine years of work to buy this ship, another nine of sweat and tears building up the business...to risk losing it all?" Sarita gulped. "I can't ask that of you."

"So you'd ask us to let you go instead." Kate took a deep breath, trying to steady her voice, but despite her best efforts, it cracked on the next words, "Are you *trying* to break my heart?"

"I'm sorry, Kate, I'm so sorry!" Sarita was sobbing now, great gasping sobs that had to make it hard to breathe.

"Just go!" Kate snapped. "Get in back, check on the kids, prepare *him* for his first Jump. Jump in ninety."

Sarita turned and fled out of the cabin, leaving them alone with the screens.

Joshua waited until she was well down the corridor, out of earshot, before asking, "You were a little hard on her, weren't you?"

His hands moved automatically through the final checks. The first wave of fury had passed, once he realized that they weren't actually going to lose Sarita. He didn't know how he felt now. Relieved. Numb. Worried.

Kate shrugged, frowning. "She's made us all into criminals. We'll never be allowed back into this system, that's for sure. If it weren't for the fact that nobody else likes these folks, I'd be seriously worried for the business."

Joshua raised an eyebrow. "You didn't tell her that. She probably thinks we're going to turn pirate."

"Good," Kate said sharply. "Let *her* worry for a change. Once we get through this Jump, I'm going to tear some strips out of her hide for scaring us like that. She is *never* going to go out of contact like that again. Idiot. And god knows what we're going to do with *him*— I don't even know where we're going to put him. He's going to have to sleep on the engine."

"But you were never going to leave her here." Joshua said the words as if he had no doubt—but if Kate hadn't stepped in, he would have let Sarita go, would have thrown her out, off the ship, out of their lives. Maybe.

Kate paused a long moment. Then she sighed and said, "Of course not."

Joshua nodded, feeling the tension sliding away. "It's in a good cause, anyway."

"What? True love?" Kate looked as if she wanted to spit, if there had been anywhere safe on the control board *to* spit. "Bet it doesn't last a month. She barely knows him."

Joshua frowned thoughtfully. "I'm not so sure. Remember when you two were like that? All she could talk about was you." He could tease about it now, but he remembered how he'd felt at first. Angry. Scared. If he'd known then what he knew now—well, maybe he'd be just as scared. But he wasn't sorry. "I was ready to scratch your eyes out; I was sure you were going to take her away with you, up to the stars on your big, fancy ship."

"Don't mock my ship," Kate said, frowning a warning. "It's saving your butt."

"I would never mock the ship—or its beautiful, gallant captain." Joshua blew her a kiss from across the cabin.

"Oh, hush. Idiots, the both of you. Sometimes, I don't know why I bother." She flicked the last switch, poised her finger over the final button. "Prepare for Jump." She paused, took a deep breath, and said, "I love you."

And that was why. They always said it before a Jump. Jumps had been mostly reliable for close to a century now, but still. Just in case. They always said the words. Joshua flicked on the intercom, so they could hear the rest of it throughout the ship. Sarita, the children, and now this new one, this stranger. Beloved of Sarita, gods knew why, and so. "We love you."

Kate's steady voice read out the final count. "Jump in five. Four. Three. Two. Jump."

# ERICA L. SATIFKA
## Sea Changes

The room my father dies in is green: green like his eyes, green like the carpet of the house we used to live in, when we lived under the sea. He dies with those green eyes open, gone milky under a film of cataracts. The nurse who comes to take away the body looks at him with disgust, but then, they all do.

"Are you the daughter?"

"Yes."

She inspects me with her bureaucracy eyes, and I sense her grudging approval. I only spent two years there, two years in the pressurized dome that was our family's refuge. I am not like him. I'm not like her either, but at least I'm not like *him.*

My father was not a strong man. His limbs were rubbery and slack from the years spent underwater. Some people, like my old foster parents, said his brain got rubbery too, clogged with the seawater seeping through his eardrums. That's nonsense, of course. My father was always well protected whenever he left the airlock, in the bulky scuba suit that made him look like Superman instead of the hundred-pound weakling he really was. But people will believe what they want to believe.

While the nurse rolls my father onto a gurney and heads for the incinerator, I gaze out the window at the skyscrapers that line the avenue, polished black surface as far as the eye can see. I don't turn around until I cease to hear the nurse's squeaky shoes, and then I slip away.

§

On Tuesday afternoons I take the bus out to the suburbs, to attend my support group. They have all kinds there: sea people, glacier people, people who grew up in floating villages the size of three square city blocks. It is hard for people to adjust after living in these conditions, they say. It is a state requirement to attend.

It takes all kinds of people to build America.

A woman named Dolores leads our motley group. She is young and eager and hopeful and mindless. Every session begins with a variation on the same question:

"When did you figure out you were different from other people?"

*When you told us,* I want to say. But if you do that, you don't get your subsistence check. "I... I was nine years old. Some kids pushed me down into the mud on the playground. They called me mermaid. They were so cruel." I hang my head, putting my hand over my mouth so she doesn't see the smirk.

That's the kind of answer she loves to hear. Her pleasure is evident. "And how did it make you feel?"

*"Awful,"* I say. "Awful."

Dolores grew up in a split-entry house in a subdivision called Mulberry Creek, with fifty other families exactly like hers. Despite its name, there is no water in Mulberry Creek. Just a lot of split-entry houses.

In the ocean, there are no subdivisions. That's only one of the things that make it so dysfunctional.

"Today we're going to do a little bit of art therapy. I want you to draw a picture of your ideal home. What would it look like? What would it contain?" Dolores passes around pads and crayons, enough for the entire group.

Also, there is no art therapy in the ocean, as there are no counselors there.

The secret I don't tell them is this: I loved it there. I loved every second of it.

§

When you grow up in one of Earth's most uninhabitable locations, you don't expect much in the way of amenities. That's why they house us in dormitories, one person to a postage-stamp-sized room. Communal bathrooms and kitchen, a small backyard for us to pace around in and tend. It's not much, but between the monthly checks and the free medical care, it's a pretty sweet life for someone like me.

But it makes some things hard. Dating, for one. Can you imagine bringing a guy back to a place that's designed to mimic your abusive childhood home under the sea, and trying to convince him you're a nice, normal girl? That's why we usually date each other, though that has problems of its own. Namely, the self-pity patrol.

"I grew up on an ice floe near Greenland," a guy named Mark or Matt, says.

"Okay."

"It was a very traumatic experience. I mean, I was really affected by it."

"Takes one to know one."

"I don't think I'll ever get over it," Mark-or-Matt says, shaking his head. "There's just no way."

"I don't blame you."

"It was a terrible way to grow up."

It's a good thing I like being alone.

§

When night comes, they turn on the wave machines in the ocean peoples' wing, to remind us of home. We'll go crazy if we aren't immersed in our natural environment, no matter how dysfunctional our natural environment is. That's what the top experts say, so it must be true. At first it kept me up, but now I'm indifferent. You don't really hear it after a while.

But when it does keep me up, I like to pretend that I'm back there, back underneath the ocean, in the thick wool blankets my mother used to wrap us in. Together in our aloneness, my brothers and me, the only children for miles.

A hologram of a fish swims past me, on the wall above my cot. You can't even see fish in an underwater sea-floor dome, but they don't care.

I don't know where my brothers are now. They probably live a life a lot like me, in the cities they were taken to after we were all rescued and separated. I wouldn't know how to contact them if I wanted to.

Sometimes memories are enough.

§

When I met my father for the first time in thirteen years, he was starving and homeless, having hitchhiked from Albany, New York, which is where he was placed after we were rescued. He bribed my address out of a state worker sympathetic to our case. They exist, though they still don't like to touch us. He was dying of cancer. I took him out for coffee, and we got to talking.

"I never should have made your mother move." His walrus

mustache trailed into his coffee cup.

"You don't have anything to apologize for."

"I've ruined your life. You can't ever be normal because of me. I'm the one that made us move."

"I liked it there. I wouldn't change a thing."

"You can't get a good job because you didn't go to school. Because of me."

"Drink your coffee," I said.

"We shouldn't have run. Things aren't so bad here." I followed his gaze out onto the street. His breath quickened as he watched the riot of flesh and metal streaming down the street, the crowded angry world. "We thought they were bad. There were too many people, too much noise. Life wasn't exciting anymore. But excitement doesn't matter. We should have stayed put."

With a quick gesture I turned his attention back to the table, back to me. "I love you, Dad."

He sighed, added cream to his coffee, and swirled it around, a miniature Charybdis.

I touched his gnarled hand with its delicate network of veins and looked out the window, up to the sky. The stars weren't out right then, but they would be soon. And I thought then that someday I would like to be among them. In my mind, I buried my feet in the soil of a virgin planet, strange waters lapping at my shinbones. Here and now, I traced the blue highways of my father's hand.

# SONYA TAAFFE
## Di Vayse Pave

*Lyu-lyu,* it sings, its feathers a shiver of light
when it rises on your path like a daymoon,
white as annealing glass,
as the salt of a look over your shoulder,
searching for the world that slept beneath its wing.
*You closed my eyes to dream of your longing,*
*blind as limelights on a bare stage.*
*My eyes were the white heat of pages*
*in a summer of honey and almonds,*
*the white nights in a winter of sorrel and empty shirts.*
*My eyes were the lines between your letters,*
*the ones you left inside the ink.*
*You can write with your fingers stained from eating cherries*
*of mending windows, old snapshots and new bread*
*until my eyes open,*
*black as the dip of a quill;*
*there is no way back over so much sea.*
*My eyes will be white as sails or a wall at morning*
*when you write from a city of lighthouses,*
*each verse a wing, watching the harbor*
*where ships still come in.*

# LISA BOLEKAJA
# The Saltwater African

*Bola Ogun.*

Tchula Walker rolled the name on her tongue. It was a thick name. Had weight. Texture. She hadn't heard a pureblood African name in years. Purebloods fresh off the boat were a risk for slave owners, because they remembered what it was like to be free. The sweetness of it was still fresh as black strap molasses for them, and that sweetness could infect others. There were legendary stories about Africans along the Georgia coast who had escaped their bondage. Stretched out their arms and flew away. But this was Mississippi, and homegrown niggers had clipped wings.

The washerwomen were whispering about the arrival of the Saltwater African, Bola Ogun, that morning when Tchula was rubbing a poultice made of burdock root and comfrey onto her twin sister Celestine's right hand. Celestine had a boil above her left knuckle that pussed over and stunk to high heaven, seeping yellow, orange, and pinkish-red fluid. Tchula chewed up more pieces of burdock root, fished the moist pieces off her tongue and pressed them onto the infected area before wrapping it with a clean strip of cotton.

Sitting on Tchula's uneven oak table, Celestine blocked off her nose with a lavender handkerchief that was embroidered with her initials. She made a great show of it to Tchula, fluttering her hand so that the silken cloth was always within eyesight. It was a gift from their owner, Master Lyle Stewart.

The two solidly built washerwomen with sun-scorched indigo skin were heaving large baskets of laundry on top of their heads when they passed by Tchula's cabin door, clucking their tongues, giddy with excitement.

"He a big man," one woman said.

"For true. Long time since a big man walked these parts," the other said, and then they tittered, shushing themselves. Tchula's tiny splintering cabin was near the main house, and the women didn't want their laughter stirring up the Stewart household.

Celestine eyed the women outside and wiped her brow with the handkerchief.

"You seen him yet?" she asked.

"No," Tchula answered.

"You think he knows English?" Celestine asked.

"Dunno," Tchula said. She stood up from the stool she squatted on and rubbed her hands on her dress.

"That oughta hold you. Try and keep it clean if you can. I have wash to finish."  ⌐→ Tchula sister

"You're not curious?" Celestine asked.

"A slave is a slave," Tchula said.

"Not this one. He saltwater. I'm gonna see him. So are you."

Celestine grabbed her sister's hand and pulled her out of the cabin gingerly, mindful of Tchula's bad hip and limp.

The sisters went together towards the front of the spacious colonial-style house. Stewart was talking to the owner of Bola Ogun, a flinty-eyed man known as Mr. Harper. Stewart's slightly receding hairline had turned a splotchy crimson from the heat, and he had a look on his face that let the sisters know he was annoyed with Harper.

"I'm telling you Mr. Stewart, this slave is worth every penny. He was seasoned in Barbados for the last three years. They broke him in real good down there. And he's a damn fine blacksmith. A skilled slave with a trade, and—" Harper moved over to Bola and slapped his hand on the slave's arm and chest, "—he'd make a good breeder if you want to stud him."

"Healthy?" Stewart asked.

"Got his papers right here, sir. He's a dream investment. I'd keep him myself if I could afford to. If you don't want him, Mr. Trammel over in Noxubee County wants a gander at him."

"Trammel? That hump wouldn't know what to do with a quality slave. Hand over his papers."

Harper reached into his dingy coat and pulled out a folded paper. Stewart frowned at the soiled condition of the health record, but read it anyway.

Bola stood shackled next to two tired horses and a field hand named Luther. The new arrival was dusty, and streaks of sweat striped his face. His flared nose was pointed on the end, and his eyes were slanted and deep set. His lips were puffy, almost like a woman's, and his head shaved bald.

"He's a looker, eh, Tchula? Tall and solid," Celestine said, sucking in her teeth.

"For true. Seem like he could fly off right now if he didn't have those chains—"

How to Live on Other Planets

"What are you two doing here?" Stewart demanded.

"Tchula was helping me with my hand Master Stewart, sir. We're just passing through, sir. Sorry," Celestine said, linking her arm with Tchula's and moving them past the carriage.

Walking past Bola, Tchula smelled the sour stench of long travel on him. She kept her head down, but her eyes upon him. His gaze was like a gentle fondling on her cheek, and she shivered as if he had actually touched her. There was a mindfulness about him, something familiar in the way he regarded her. What impressed her most was that he didn't have the bearing of a slave. His hands and legs were shackled, but his back was straight and his head held high. Unlike her, he was primordial, undiluted and unadulterated.

And then he smiled at her.

Not with teeth, but the curling up of those abundant lips. She found herself licking her own lips, and felt as if he'd made her do that. She tasted invisible blood in her mouth. It was a vulgar display of power on his part, and she felt compelled to smile back at him. *Yes, there it is,* she thought. She knew his kind well. He was a two-headed man, and she could sense his Vodun strength spilling off in waves. He had recognized her as a two-headed woman, although she veiled this knowledge publicly.

When she and Celestine headed back around towards the kitchen, Tchula knew she would have to talk to the saltwater conjure man and ferret out his mojo. She felt like she had met her match at last.

§

Bola stood hitting iron on a fairly new anvil in the smithy barn. It was his first official day, and Stewart had asked for new horse shoes for his entire stable. Luther, the slave who had briefed Bola on the lay of the plantation, worked by his side along with a stocky young teen named Teak who chopped wood and kept the forge fires blazing. Luther wiped his mouth and glanced out of the smithy.

"Here come trouble," he said.

Bola finished pounding the iron shoe and slid it into a barrel of water. He saw one of the twins making her way to the smithy. This one didn't limp. She wasn't the one he wanted to see.

"Ain't nothing worse than them red niggers, hear me, Bola?" Luther said.

"Why?"

"That one there is Celestine. She's a cook for the house, and she sleep with the master. Watch what you say 'round her, 'cause it might get back to him if she can make it benefit herself some kinda way. The crippled one, Tchula, now she's nice and all, but she's not to be toyed with. She obeah, a black magic woman—"

"You flapping your gums, Luther?" Celestine said, fanning her face with her hand. Bola noticed she dressed nicer than the other slave women, and she wore real shoes. Her hair was wrapped like the women he remembered back home. But the tufts of hair sticking out were thinner and straighter. She didn't look like most of the women on the plantation who had made excuses to walk past the smithy, trying to catch Bola's eye.

"Thought you'd be making Master Stewart his biscuits by now, gal," Luther said.

"He gone for the day. Now stop pestering me man, I came to talk to Bola."

"Watch yourself," Luther whispered to Bola. He left them alone.

"Teak, you can rest," Bola said. Teak nodded and headed out.

"You do know some English. I was worried we couldn't talk." His *Ibo* accent was heavy but understandable. Celestine closed the gap between them.

"I know enough," he said. Celestine inched closer.

"Good. You know something? My daddy was African too. My mama was Choctaw. You know what that is? You know what Indians are?"

"Red peoples."

Celestine laughed, a full-throated belly laugh.

"Yeah, Bola. Red people. My name is Celestine." She held out her hand.

"I hear your name is Neshoba." he said.

"It's Celestine," she said with a snap, her smile faltering.

"Careful," he said. "Iron still hot." He pushed her back from the anvil.

"I go by Celestine now. It's prettier."

"What you want, Celestine?"

"Get to know you. It's boring around here. We don't get much news about the outside world, so I thought you could talk to me about it. Not now, since you're working, but later."

"I need my rest."

"I know."

He liked looking at her. She was attractive and her voice was soothing, but there was a sharpness beneath her that he didn't care for. He'd have to be on his toes with her.

"Something wrong?" she asked, stepping close again.

It had been a long time since he had been with a woman. He was allowed to sleep in the smithy, so he would have plenty of privacy. He glanced down at her flushed cheeks and the swelling of her breasts. She was eager. It would be easy. But this was a kept woman. He wouldn't risk his life for sex. He stepped away from her, and his right arm struck the anvil, burning his flesh.

"Oh, God," Celestine said. Bola ran to the clean water bucket, and thrust his arm inside.

"I'll go get Tchula!" Celestine yelled, running out of the smithy.

## §

After wrapping his wound with cloth, Tchula made Bola drink willow bark tea in her cabin. Celestine wanted to assist, but she had a late supper to help the head cook with, so she left them alone.

Bola was surprised at how clean Tchula could keep her cabin when so many slave quarters were infested with vermin. She had a lopsided wooden table and three chairs, a lumpy pallet with faded quilts in a corner, a fireplace with a stool in front of it, and a chamber pot near the front door. There was shelving on one wall that housed various jars of dried herbs and a few plates and bowls. A black kettle sat in the fire boiling water. She stuck a ladle in the kettle to draw out some hot water to make him more tea.

"You have a man?" he asked.

"Had one. He's dead," she said. Her voice was firm, but still had a melancholy lilt to it. He could tell that it had happened awhile ago.

"How he die?"

"We tried to run from here and find my mother's people. Got caught. They hung him on that Tupelo tree out there by the well."

"And you?" he asked. Her eyes never wavered from his.

"Master tied me to that tree while my man still swinging, and had another slave beat me in front of everyone. I was pregnant. The baby didn't live. Now I have a limp and a half tooth."

Tchula poured the hot water into his tin cup and sat down in a chair beside him.

"I'm sad for your baby." he said.

"I'm not. Glad it's dead. I didn't want to raise Master Stewart's seed."

They sat for a moment in silence. He drank the tea. She watched him. He regarded the room again.

"What's that?" he said, pointing to another corner. A small checkered cloth covered something on the dirt floor near the fireplace.

"That's how I do my real healing," she said.

She stood and walked over to the cloth, squatted down and lifted it up. From where he sat, Bola saw bundles of dried tobacco sitting next to a pipe, a turtle shell, and several polished stones. There was also a small plate filled with dried corn near a wooden bowl filled with clear liquid. Familiar tools to him. He reached deep into his pants pocket and pulled out a small leather pouch. Tchula covered her altar and sat down next to him. He opened the leather and revealed a lock of dark curly hair tied with thread, bits of iron and other metals, along with a small tobacco leaf stained with dried blood.

"Strong medicine?" she asked.

"The strongest I know," he said, fingering the lock of hair. He tied the pouch back up and placed it on her table. She picked it up.

"I think our gods should meet," she said. She took his pouch and placed it on her altar next to the tobacco. She returned to her seat.

"You hungry?" she asked.

"Yeah," he said.

"I can go to the kitchen, and get you a plate of leftovers. You can wait here for me...."

"Not that kinda hungry, Tchula."

He traced the shape of her oval face with his right index finger until it rested on her lips.

"I'll be your man now, if you want," he said.

"I want," she said, taking his hand and leading him to her pallet.

§

The next morning when she awoke, Tchula found a tiny metal bird sitting on the pillow where Bola had slept. A tiny metal bird made of copper and pewter with mechanical wings that moved when the bird's head was touched. It was half the size of her thumb.

She could smell the burning of iron and hear Teak chopping wood to keep up with Bola's work. She stretched out on the pallet that now smelled of his musk and her own sweat. She allowed herself a small sliver of happiness, just a little bit, no bigger than a thimble. To increase its size would risk more Tupelo trees and bitter tears. She touched the bird's head again, and watched the metal wings flutter.

§

Tchula worked with the washerwomen, boiling clothes and sheets in big iron pots at four-thirty in the morning, then beat them against brick blocks with cleaning sticks that looked like boat paddles. Their rhythmic pounding filled the air with a cacophony of sound. Some of the women clucked their tongues at her because she didn't tie her hair up. Instead she allowed her black silken strands to blow freely, making her look younger than her twenty-four years.

At noon she took a break to eat with some friends out near the cotton fields before heading back to boil more sheets and fold up dried clothing. She saw Bola pounding iron with a hammer, creating sparks that twinkled like fireflies. Teak hovered near him, watching and learning. Moving closer to the smithy barn, Tchula noticed her sister sashaying over to Bola and Teak. Celestine carried a basket, probably with the pretense of doing an errand, Tchula thought.

Bola's body looked relaxed. He was listening to Celestine, and then he was back to pounding metal. Tchula saw Celestine's neck roll and she walked away so fast that Tchula understood she was upset with Bola. Tchula knew her twin wouldn't give up until she had a taste of him. She wasn't mad at her sister. She felt sorry for her twin now that Celestine had replaced her in Stewart's bed. Because of Tchula's bad hip and broken tooth, she was damaged goods in Stewart's eyes. The last time he raped her, she was told that her raggedy teeth hurt him "down there" when he used her mouth. No man wanted either sister because of Stewart. It was the reason why Celestine was housed as a permanent cook inside the main house, away from the slave quarters and the fields.

Tchula wanted to talk to Bola. And when she arrived at the smithy he was grinning at her, rubbing his chest. Teak chopped more wood, ignoring them.

"You like my gift?" he asked.

"How you make it so life like?"

He showed her his pouch hung around his neck.

"You have to be careful with that. If Master Stewart sees that he'll get real nervous. Sell you off or worse."

He nodded and squeezed the pouch again.

"The first day you was here, you was showing off to me. You put blood in my mouth. I tasted it."

He shrugged, but her face was strained. He tucked the pouch back into his shirt.

"I don't want to see you on no tree, Bola. He won't let me live next time."

Now she made him taste blood in his mouth where there was none. She pulled out the bird from her apron.

"Can you make me something else? A turtle?" she asked.

"Whatever you want."

"Good," she said.

She wanted to kiss him, but Teak was nearby. Bola put down his tools, pulled her to the side and away from prying eyes.

Tchula knew that Celestine was none too pleased to see them like this when she returned to have another go at Bola. It was the gentleness of Bola's hand stroking Tchula's arm that knotted Celestine's stomach into a twisted mass. Paulo, Tchula's former lover, had done that often, and it frightened Celestine. It meant that Tchula cared about something other than herself. It meant that her sister would try to run again. Escape the plantation without her. Unlike Paulo, Bola was strong and healthy, not likely to slow Tchula down and get them caught. And where would that leave Celestine? Alone and further alienated from the other slaves. Tchula was her one true, faithful companion, her only blood relative. Unlike Tchula, Celestine was not a runner. She was too afraid of Master Stewart and the pain of a whip.

Tchula watched Celestine slip away. She would have to force Celestine to run with her this time. Force the wolf back into her sister's blood.

§

There was the turtle, and then the pair of frolicking rabbits. Next was the group of pewter washerwomen beating sheets with miniature wooden paddles. Each week, when he had time, Bola shaped figurines for Tchula. Each gift strengthening their bond. They were discreet around their owner's family and the boisterous overseer during the day, but entwined their arms and legs in her cabin at night. Other slaves knew of their couplings, but said nothing. They respected Tchula but feared her, too. They needed her to tend to their cuts and heal all wounds since the nearest doctor was miles away.

The older slaves remembered her mother, Itta, the Choctaw woman who emancipated herself away from the forced Indian migration back in 1831. The Choctaw were the first ones removed, and Itta, a woman who carried strong medicine in her bones, walked away from her tribe and their own parcel of West African slaves, hauling two twin girls in her belly. There were no tears when she made her way further south, passing herself off as a tawny-skinned white woman when needed. If it came down to it, she preferred to be a slave on the land of her ancestors than be free somewhere foreign, without them.

When Itta reached the Stewart property in 1832, she had babies strapped to her front and back, and when they asked for her name, she told them "Itta, the walker". Her girls were Tchula and Neshoba Walker. The fox and the wolf. And that was that.

Despite their fears of obeah and darker forces, the slaves let Tchula be. Other women who may have gnashed their teeth for Bola gave her a wide berth.

The true fear was of their owner, who was slowly selling off small groups of slaves to cover gambling debts, poor financial planning, and the lack of a good cotton season two years in a row. Lyle Stewart liked to pass himself off as a big man, owner of the most slaves in Yazoo County, but he was hemorrhaging money at an alarming rate. He had to bring home his eldest son from a prestigious boarding school to learn the trade of overseeing the slaves in his absence, and the current overseer, Rankin, was more interested in sleeping with slave women and drinking corn liquor than teaching Junior slaving skills. The opportunity to acquire Bola had been a lucky break.

§

Word came down in late August that Stewart had made a deal to exchange Bola's labor to an owner in a New Orleans parish that was known to work slaves to death. The owner needed a skilled iron man for his shipbuilding enterprise, and in exchange for Bola's labor, Stewart would get twenty male slaves for the duration of Bola's stay. Twenty slaves that would be clothed, fed, and housed with compensation from the shipper, and not out of Stewart's pocket. Any children born on the Stewart plantation during Bola's service in New Orleans would be split between the two men and vice versa. Stewart ceded first choice to the shipper. Plans were in the works for Stewart to travel to New Orleans with Bola so both owners could sign binding legal contracts in person. They both wanted to look over their merchandise, finger the goods to make sure they were suitable for the new jobs they would undertake.

Tchula became anxious with the news of Bola's imminent departure from her life. Other slaves began to talk, and wondered how she would handle another man taken from her. She spent her days washing, healing those who needed healing, and admiring Bola's metalwork. Celestine admired them too, and one day she slipped the washerwomen figurines into her apron pocket to show the head cook, and Mrs. Stewart saw them. She demanded to know where Celestine got them from. Celestine told. Mrs. Stewart made such a fuss over them, that she took every last one she could find in Tchula's cabin and placed them in her own parlor.

Tchula was furious. She accosted Celestine in front of their mother's gravesite. Celestine was placing flowers on the headstone when Tchula pounced on her.

"You bitch!" she screamed, clawing at Celestine's arm.

"Let me go!"

"Why did you take my things? He made them for me. For my eyes only."

"I was only going to show them to Ouida."

"You should've asked me. Now she'll never give them back."

"He can make you some more—"

"There's no time for him to make that many again!"

Celestine pulled out the metal bird from her apron.

"Here, she didn't take all of them. I hid this one. I'm sorry."

Tchula took the bird from Celestine's hand.

"Maybe if you sweet talk Master Stewart, he'll let you have them back, or maybe you can come look at them—"

"I'm not like you. I can't have that man on me—" Tchula said.

"You think I like it? He only took me because you left! You did this to me. And I hear everyone whispering about you running off again. If you leave again, he'll hurt me worse."

Tchula let her eyes look towards the ground.

"I know it's bad." she said. She felt deep shame. Glancing over at their mother's grave, she also felt a deep loss. Itta had been gone for twelve years. Tchula reached down and touched the headstone.

"Yeah? Well I take it. I lay there and pretend he's doing it to someone else. It ain't fair. You get Bola, and I get that maggot's filth all in me. How many more babies you gotta shake outta my womb? If you leave, I'll have his children, and he will sell them. I'll be stuck."

"Mama didn't want this for us," Tchula said.

"She died and left us, Tchula! This how it's gonna be."

"Neshoba," Tchula said.

"Celestine. My name is Celestine."

"I can't stay here anymore."

"What about me? You would leave me here all alone?"

"You can run with me. Mama would want you to come with me—"

"No—"

"I'll die if I stay here. I know it," Tchula said.

"I'm already dead," Celestine said.

§

A week before Bola was to leave, Tchula asked him for one more metal figurine.

"My mother used to take spider webs and put them inside of cuts to bind the flesh. She liked spiders. They were good luck. Make this for me. It will remind me of you."

Within three days Bola handed Tchula the inch long metal spider. In her quarters she ran her fingers over it, marveled at the elaborate detail he put into the piece. She kissed it, and then hugged him.

"Tonight, you have to ask your gods to help me with Celestine. I'm not strong enough to do it alone," she said.

"She has no faith; it won't work," he said.

"It has to," she said.

He looked unsure. Worry lines creased his brow. She stood on bare tiptoes and kissed his forehead.

"We need two backs to carry this weight. Together we are powerful, Bola," she said.

She unfastened his pants and let them drop to the floor. Holding his penis, she pulled back the dense foreskin, feeling the wide purplish head stiffen.

"*Chi hollo li,*" she said, the Choctaw words rolled off her tongue, "You know that right? I love you."

He felt small droplets of semen pooling at the tip.

"Yes." he answered, his breath quickened.

"This will hurt," she said, and jammed a finger in. He bled like a virgin.

§

It was easy to coax her out of the kitchen.

Bola had purposely missed the communal noon meal by working through it. Stewart had no problem with that when he went to check on him, and praised Bola's work ethic, chastising the other slaves whose bodies ached because of their continuous movement from can-see to can't-see each day. Some of the slaves cut their eyes at Bola as they passed by the smithy to get to the feeding tables. When meal time was over, and weary bodies headed back to the fields, Bola snuck around to the kitchen door that led to Celestine's quarters.

"What you want, Bola?" she asked, her face dusted with cornmeal, her hands wringing a cooking rag. Ouida the head cook eavesdropped on them, making loud cleaning noises to cover their conversation from the owners but not herself.

"I ain't eat yet. Can you fix me somethin'?"

"What makes you think there's some leftovers waitin' on you, man?"

He put a bold foot on the bottom step that led to the inside. She looked down at his foot, then up at him. She smiled.

"Master Stewart see that foot, you'd be in trouble."

"Then help my foot not get in trouble."

Ouida saw this and rolled her eyes at them both. Celestine pushed past the older woman, grabbed a clean table napkin, and wrapped a chunk of cornbread dipped in pot liquor and a thick piece of fatback inside. She had been saving it for her own dinner. She handed it to Bola.

"You gotta live on that for now; the beans are all gone."

"Thank you," he said.

"Mhmmm...."

"Did you eat yet?"

"No."

"I'll be over by the chicken coop. Come eat with me."

Her eyes narrowed. She looked over her shoulder.

*"Telemi kalo,"* he said.

"What did you say?" she asked.

"Come with me."

Ouida shook her head. Glared at Bola.

"Master Stewart come through, don't tell him where I am." Celestine said.

"You playin' with fire, gal," Ouida said, handing Celestine a smaller chunk of cornbread.

Bola walked ahead of Celestine just in case anyone else was watching them. He casually passed Tchula's cabin. He could hear Celestine's heavy footsteps behind him, and he picked up his pace to distance himself until they were in the clear, hidden by the chicken coop behind the smithy.

Bola leaned against a tree and ate the bread and swallowed the fatty meat that greased his lips. Celestine slid her cornbread in her apron.

"I thought you wanted me to eat with you," she said.

"I'll watch you eat."

"Why you sniffin' around me?"

"C'mere," he said. He grabbed for her arm. She pulled back. But not too far.

"Quit playin' with me, man."

"I got no time to play. Only two days left before I'm gone."

"My sister—"

"She don't want me no more."

"Why not?"

*"O rewa gan lobinrin,"* he said.

"What are you saying to me?"

*"Moferan e...* I like you."

"Master Stewart—"

"Ain't here."

His accent was more pronounced. Celestine wavered. To want

to do it freely and not because she was forced—that was a gift. Bola held out his hand. She took it.

"*Oda,*" he said.

She wondered if he felt like he was kissing Tchula. Her body would feel new, and yet it would not be new, not really. She fumbled with the buttons on her blouse as he lifted her skirt and apron and fingered her slowly. She spun herself around so that she was facing the tree and holding it with her hands.

"We have to watch out in case someone finds us. Master Stewart is talking with the overseer in the parlor," she said, but he was busy nibbling her earlobes, his hands running up and down her heavy breasts.

"Hurry," she said. He pulled down his pants and she reached around and guided him in.

"*Be' ni—yara, yara—*" he said with gritted teeth.

"English, Bola, please say it in English," she moaned.

"Yes, faster, faster," he yammered

She came before he did. He made sure of that.

Later that day, he slept with Tchula. They held one another, their heartbeats pounding in their ears. Earlier Tchula had smoked tobacco leaves in a tightly wrapped cigar and blew the smoke into a mound of dirt on her altar. Bola gave the mound holes for eyes, a mouth, and a nose. Tchula blew smoke into the dirt mouth and opened the way for their deities to come through.

Tchula had stolen a chicken from the coop, slit its throat and fed their gods with the gushing of blood and prayers on her altar. The presence of heavy Red and Black Gods mingling together and meeting for the first time bent Tchula's and Bola's backs. The spirits rode them, exhausting their limbs. Requests were made to the Red and the Black, and she felt their escape was imminent. There was no turning back.

"What if I never see you again?" he asked Tchula in the twilight of their rest. She didn't answer him. A tingling in her stomach let her know she was afraid to. Any doubt released from her lips would taint their bond. Instead, she placed her lips on his. Maybe she could make him plant a new seed in her. One that she could grow in free soil.

She slid on top of him. Tired limbs or not, she would remember every part of his body. He was asleep when she whispered in his ear, "I will find you."

The overseer and Junior came for Bola at nine that evening. They shackled his arms and legs and transported him onto a supply carriage. Tchula watched Junior strike his horses and carry Bola away into the dark. Master Stewart would follow them in a few days.

Celestine consoled Tchula when she threw herself down on her pallet.

"He'll use you tonight," Tchula said when her tears finally dried up.

"I know," Celestine said, resolved to her endless fate.

"Promise me something," Tchula said.

"What?"

"Think of mama's grave."

"Why would I want to do that?" Celestine asked.

Tchula reached out and hugged Celestine. Huddled on the disheveled pallet, Tchula squeezed Celestine's shoulders.

"Just think of Itta for me, please."

Celestine pulled herself free from Tchula's smothering arms. She gazed into Tchula's piercing eyes.

"I will," Celestine answered, still puzzled with the request.

§

Stewart summoned Celestine to his private bedroom in a downstairs wing of the main house. Mrs. Stewart had retired only a half hour earlier after having a nightcap in their parlor, so Celestine was a little thrown off by the scheduling. He would usually wait until his wife had been asleep for some time before crawling out of their marital bed to enjoy his debauchery with Celestine.

She arrived in a pale blue housedress that doubled as a nightgown. Stewart smoked a cigar and watched her undress. She flung the dress across a divan near the full-sized bed. Pulling back the satin bed linens, she positioned herself on her back. She watched Stewart methodically remove each article of clothing and place it on a wing-backed chair across from the bed. He was a man of average height, with a slender physique, but his stomach was bloated and looked like it belonged to a much heavier man. Lying there, Celestine wondered if he had worms.

Stewart kneeled before Celestine and parted her knees, lifting her limbs over his shoulders. Celestine felt her back and buttocks sliding on the cool sheets, and the lips of her lightly haired vulva opened to the warmth from Stewart's hands. Candles flickered, illuminating her body, her skin taking on a deep orange glow that contrasted with the stark white sheets. Stewart took his right pinky finger and parted her dusky inner labia to reveal her pink insides. He gripped his penis with his left hand and inserted himself, enjoying the fact that Celestine was moist so early.

Her eyes were closed, her lips pursed into a thin line. Stewart partially pulled out, then thrust again, engrossed in the grip of her sex and the light/dark interplay of his penis and her slick orifice. He shifted his weight, driving his knees into the mattress. He moved her legs to wrap around his waist.

"Open your eyes," he said.

Celestine obeyed. Stewart's face bore down on her, his passionate tempo faster. Celestine studied his tense expression, his eyes mere slits. She tried to imagine what Bola's face looked like in the midst of his pleasure, their coupling against the tree still vivid in her mind. She tried to recall the words he whispered in her ear in his native tongue, the calloused grip of his hands on her nipples, the muscles of his chest pressing on her back. She felt her vaginal walls quiver then squeeze, a surge of tension racing down her spine as Stewart grabbed her hair from the back, pulling her head forward. He reached his peak. He would finish soon. She pumped her hips furiously to hurry him.

He opened his eyes.

"Oh!" he gasped, his eyes widening. Celestine stopped moving. This wasn't his usual response to climax. He gazed down below her navel, down to his penis. He drew out his glistening member, grabbed it with both hands. There were two visible bite marks on the tip of the glans. Two tear-sized drops of blood pooled on the skin and dripped down onto the sheets.

"What have you done?" he barked, color draining from his face. Stewart's penis swelled, turning deep purple. His breath became ragged chirps. He stared between her legs. Celestine felt a fullness pulsating inside her. She shifted her weight, and raised herself up with her hands.

Her labia pushed open. Two long segmented limbs, thin like twigs, poked out hauling out six more brown legs. Eight feral-looking black eyes shined up at Stewart. Its venomous fangs throbbed as it drew out its entire body from Celestine's vagina. Its abdomen was as big as a man's fist. Each spider leg was a foot long. Stewart's naked body fell backwards to the floor, and Celestine jumped off the bed, screaming. The spider regarded her coolly. Knowingly.

She heard the stampede of feet from upstairs. Muffled shouts were moving down towards her. The overseer and a sallow-faced male house servant burst into the room. Celestine draped her house dress around her nakedness and stood on the divan. The overseer knelt down by Stewart.

"What did you do to him?"

"He was bitten by a spider."

"Where is it? Did you kill it?"

"On the bed!" She pointed.

The house servant cautiously smoothed down the bed linen with one hand while holding a kerosene lamp with the other. A small glint caught his eye. He squinted, moved his hand to the bed and held up a miniature metal spider. He stared at Celestine, then hid the metalwork in his bed clothes and sank to his knees on the floor. He gaped at the bite marks on Stewart's blackened penis.

"Lyle!" Mrs. Stewart staggered into the room. Celestine took advantage of the distraction. She pulled on the housedress and slipped out.

§

Celestine ran to Tchula's cabin and found it empty. A small fire blazed in the fireplace, burning off mounds of herbs. All of Tchula's jars were smashed on the floor. Her altar was gone. On the oak table, Celestine saw a stuffed burlap bag and the little metal bird, Bola's first gift to Tchula.

Outside, the commotion of the main house rose to a loud din, waking slaves in their quarters. Beyond the door she could see dark bodies striding towards the chaos. Ouida shuffled into the cabin, out of breath and holding her side.

"We need your sister," Ouida said.

"She's gone."

"God help us," Ouida said, and rushed back to the house.

Celestine picked up the bird and tapped its beak. The wings flapped with a tinkling sound. Her eyes caught sight of the empty pallet. She remembered Tchula's tears, her strong arms squeezing her shoulders, and—

"Itta," Celestine said. A fearful smile spread across her face.

Itta's grave. Tchula would be there, waiting for her. She closed her hand around the bird and held it to her breast.

"Let's get free," she said.

Draping the burlap bag around her shoulder, she ran out of the cabin, past the smithy and the chicken coop. She ran past the Tupelo trees and cotton fields, past all the pain. In the distance, she saw Tchula standing behind a group of maple trees, waving for her to run faster. Celestine ran so fast that she felt like she could extend her arms and soar.

And she did.

# JOANNE MERRIAM
# Little Ambushes

Practically the first thing she did when she took in the alien was to give him a new name. He looked at her outstretched hand long enough to annoy her, and then grasped it with his four opposable fingers and hung on limply until she wrenched her hand out of his moist and over-jointed grip. *→ Narrator took in alien*

She said, "I'm Sarah," and he said his name, or what she assumed was his name, in return, rolling the syllables around in his mouth like so many rough pebbles. His name was too long, something like Shperidth with extra grunting noises in the middle, like a car backfiring very far away. She tried to repeat it and couldn't, while he stood on her doorstep sweating and folding his fingers around each other. She frowned at him.

"I can't say that," she said.

He twisted his fingers together as though emphasizing his alienness, every one of them looking like a slender thumb, and she thought his hands looked like a big, black spider wriggling at the end of its thread. *→ narrator can't pronounce alien name so calls him that*

"How about I call you Spider instead?" she said. "It kind of sounds the same."

He inclined his head, and she took that as agreement and stepped back to let him in the house. She wondered how they'd chosen him: their first artist. How did you test for an ability you didn't understand?

Their culture was a coin made of soft metal, rubbed featureless by long use, with no further worth, but they didn't come for ours, no matter how politely they listened while we tried to explain ourselves to them. They came for no particular reason, or maybe because they were bored, or maybe for some other reason. They had suggested the exchange program, but hadn't shown anything other than polite interest in the things we'd suggested exchanging. Sarah didn't even know if her guest wanted to be here. She supposed it didn't matter.

A smaller alien followed him and placed several smooth black boxes on the floor, bowed, and left the house. His luggage and art supplies, presumably.

The people who had brought the aliens stood by their car and talked into headsets, eyes scanning the road. She closed the door on them.

The refrigerator kicked on in the kitchen, and the alien's ears swiveled toward it. "Are you thirsty?" Sarah asked. "Would you like something to drink?"

Spider inclined his head again and just stood there, looking at the floor. Sarah stamped on her irritation with him—he was several month's mortgage payments, if nothing else—and led the way, coming back to take his arm when he didn't follow her. In the kitchen, he sat down, either expecting to be waited on or not understanding where they were.

"The glasses are here," she said firmly, indicating them as she pulled down two. "Help yourself to anything in the fridge." She handed him a glass, and he looked at it, and then at her, his chin raising a little as his nostrils flared. She poured juice in her own glass. "Juice?" she said. He just looked at her. She put the pitcher down next to him and walked away. When she heard him drinking, she turned to see him holding the pitcher to his lips. She showed him the right way to drink. "It is the custom," she kept saying, hoping he wouldn't take offense. Who knew what would happen if she offended him. The aliens hadn't been hostile yet—not when the Prime Minister had mistaken their leader for a child, not when we'd pointed our nuclear weapons at them, not when one of their ships had been covered in rude graffiti—but the program director had impressed upon her the need for civility. "With the technology they have," he'd said, "they could probably destroy our planet without blinking."

The alien pointed out a squirrel on her lawn, which was eating something with the nervous intensity of small mammals. Its tiny hands turned the little bit of food around and around. Spider imitated it, and she smiled back, relieved the alien had a sense of humor, however baroque. "That's a squirrel," she told him.

"Squirrel," he agreed. "Very like our—" and here he made a noise like a truck skidding on loose gravel. "I like to watch them hunt each other," he said, and she explained that squirrels weren't carnivores. "Nevertheless, they hunt, as all things do," he said, and she shrugged. She wasn't being paid to teach him biology.

They started on drawing first. "Before I can teach you how to paint like a human," she told him, "you need to learn how to see."

"I can see."

"No. I've seen your work. You don't see the way we see. You see the way a camera sees. If you want to be able to reproduce our style, you need to understand us."

Spider nodded, a little awkwardly, as though he'd never done it before but had been told it was something humans did. They sat at separate easels, and she showed him how to draw an orange, and then she showed him how to draw an orange like Rembrandt might, and then Picasso, and so on. She taught him about perspective and negative space and contours and shading. She taught him the things he already knew so he'd understand what those things meant to another species, a species with the ability to see the world differently than it was.

They drew oranges for a week before his oranges began looking like her oranges, and not like photographs of oranges, and then for a week longer before his oranges stopped looking like her oranges, and started looking like oranges of his own.

On their sixth day, he did a painting of the violets on her windowsill that made her laugh: he'd drawn them so out of proportion that they looked like a child's art. It was the first time she'd laughed around him.

He threw himself away from her, his eyes huge, knocking over his easel, and ran from the room, slamming the door behind him.

"What's wrong, Spider?" she said through the door, and she listened to his breathing on the other side. "Are you okay?" She was surprised to discover that she cared if he was okay. He was a good man, even if he was an alien. He was trying so hard to learn. "Tell me you're okay."

"What was that noise?" he said after a long pause, and she said, "what noise?" and then realized and said, "I was laughing. Haven't you heard anybody laugh yet?" but it seemed he hadn't, and when she thought about it, she wondered why she'd expected anything different. He'd been kept in an official, officious cocoon since he got here. All the aliens had.

"It's a noise we make when we're happy," she said. "It's... an expression of delight. Of joy."

"Oh," he said.

"I'm sorry," she said through the door.

"Do not apologize for being joyful," he said, and he opened the door. "It is only that your laugh sounds like our war cries. I did not want to fight you."

She promised him she wouldn't laugh again, and he shook his head, and said, "Do not promise me that. I would like to delight you."

153

Sarah didn't know how to respond, so she just nodded, and that seemed to please him. He smiled at her, carefully not showing any teeth.

"Before I leave," he said. "I will give you more joy."

§

On their ninth day, she left him alone to get groceries. When she returned, a red sports car was taking up half of her driveway. It was Mark's car. She parked and let the engine idle for a moment, watching a squirrel standing on the telephone wire outside her house. It ran a few steps overhead, and then turned and ran back, and then stopped and looked back and forth. Sarah watched it dither. Finally it made a decision and ran to the other side of the road, dancing lightly over the surface of other people's conversations.

Mark was her husband. He had moved out six months before. They'd tried couples counseling, marijuana, antidepressants. He had suggested a second honeymoon but they hadn't been able to agree on a destination. Their shrink had suggested dating, so they'd eaten meals they didn't taste and sat on the sidelines at dance clubs and taken refuge in the enforced silence of movie theatres.

Finally, with a regret so subtle she still couldn't sense it, Mark had suggested separation. Just to get their heads together, and then they'd try again, he'd said. Sarah had agreed. Sarah had always agreed with him. After he'd left, she'd decided that was their problem: she gave him everything she had, even the things he'd never asked for, and then got angry when she felt empty. Well, whose fault was that?

She got the groceries out of the trunk and went inside. Mark was standing in her kitchen, holding a steaming mug of something in both hands, and Spider was sitting at the table, empty-handed. Sarah put the bags of groceries down on the floor.

"What are you doing here," she said to Mark. It came out a statement.

He said, "I can't believe you left a fucking alien alone in our house."

"Are you worried about the alien or the house," she said, still in that flat voice, and then she glanced apologetically at Spider, but he was staring at his hands and missed it. She stooped to pick up a bag. She put the milk and juice and carton of eggs in the fridge. Mark

Sarah's husband

said nothing. She stuck the jars of spaghetti sauce and the cavatappi noodles in the pantry. Mark shifted his weight, and took a sip from his mug. She emptied a bag of apples into the sink and washed the pesticide residue from their skins, pulled down a wooden bowl and put them, still dripping, inside, and set them on the table, where a shaft of sunlight lit them. It would make a good still life for Spider, she thought.

Mark cleared his throat.

Sarah said, "What do you want, Mark."

"I want a divorce," he said.

"Get out of my house."

"It's my house, Sarah. I paid for it."

"Funny how you saddled me with the mortgage."

"My lawyer gave me these for you," he said, and he bent to open a briefcase she hadn't noticed, and pull out a manila envelope, and hand it to her. She took it, and didn't say anything. She hoped he didn't notice the slight tremor in her hands. Somehow, despite everything, she hadn't expected this.

"You have a lawyer?" she said, and finally the question sounded like a question. At the up-turn in her voice, Spider's head came up, and he looked at her with what she thought might be pity, tumbling his hands over and over each other.

Mark laughed a little, and said, "Of course I have a lawyer. You should get one, too."

"I'm sorry you had to see that," she said to Spider when Mark had gone. "You can work on a new painting tonight. The apples. I'll be back down in a few hours. I'm sorry," and she went upstairs, but didn't cry. She laid on her bed—on her and Mark's bed—and watched the late afternoon light move across her ceiling, and thought about a world where laughter sounded like war.

The next day, Spider showed her his painting of the apples. They were too shiny, and their shadows housed little demons. The demons looked like Mark. She couldn't help laughing, and this time, Spider smiled at her.

"Everything reminds you," he said. "The apples remind you. Their empty bag reminds you. His scent waits for you in the kitchen. The kitchen itself reminds you. Just some of the hundreds of little ambushes this house has waiting for you."

"Why, Spider," she said, touching her upper lip with two fingers, "you're a poet."

155

§

Spider started to do self-portraits. She had shown him a succession of them: Albrecht Dürer, Sofonisba Anguissola, Frida Kahlo, Gustave Courbet, Jackson Pollack, Zhang Ji.

She told him that Rembrandt had probably done so many self-portraits so he could explore how to paint the expressions his wealthy clients wouldn't have wanted to see on their own faces, and showed him Rembrandt frowning, and Rembrandt grimacing, and Rembrandt sinking back into the shadows. She told him about Marc Chagall's childhood in Russia, and showed him *I And The Village.* "He wanted to know himself," Spider said, stroking the reproduction on her wall, and she said yes. She said she thought that was what self-portraits were for.

"May I see yours?" he asked, and she shook her head.

"I've never done a self-portrait I liked," she said.

§

The men from the exchange program came on at the end of the month: two humans and one alien, all dressed in sober suits, gray and black. Sarah couldn't tell if the alien was the same one who dropped off Spider's things when he'd arrived. The humans were different. They flanked the door while the alien carried out Spider's artwork, bundled in soft cloths and cardboard.

"Thank you," Spider said to her, and Sarah smiled and said, "Any time." He nodded, and then he left. She'd been told the aliens didn't believe in saying goodbye; their religion told them everybody meets again. One of the humans gave her an envelope with a check inside, and then they, too, left. Sarah stood at the door watching their car drive away, and then she just stood at the door.

The squirrel was back on the telephone wire outside her house. She watched it run toward her and stop. It sat back on its haunches and stared at her, chittering. She listened to the silence, and finally she went indoors. A painting was propped against the bowl of apples. The faces of the people in the painting were more beautiful than she could have drawn them. They were glowing with health and confidence, and something else, some kind of divinity that came through in the short strokes of the brush. Spider was a better painter than she was, she thought, and she reached out to touch it, and stopped short of the surface, worried it might still be wet.

There was her mother, and her first boyfriend, and her childhood friend Dale, and her current best friend Connie, and a host of others from her past. Everybody who had ever really mattered to her was in this painting. She wondered how Spider had known what they looked like. She wasn't one to keep photographs up in the house, and they hadn't discussed their lives. She wondered what else he'd found out about her without her knowing about it, but the thought held no terror.

Mark was there, at the edge of the crowd, his hands clasped behind his back, his face turned away from her. And there she was, the only human in the painting who wasn't glowingly gorgeous, her mouth pinched in a tight line and her eyes mere slits. Her hands were clenched into fists, one of them holding a paintbrush that dripped on the floor. Her cheekbones were slashes of tension across a stricken face.

Spider was in the painting, too, his overly large, awkward body partially hidden in a darkened corner. His feet stretched to touch hers, as though he were her shadow. His face was looking up, his chin jutting out with what would have been arrogance in a human, but which she'd learned to read as bewilderment. His strange hands hung at his sides, looking even stranger than they did in real life. All of the perfectly rendered people stood a little apart from them both.

Sarah picked up the phone and called the exchange program's office line. "Any complaints?" the admin officer asked, and Sarah said, "No, I want to participate again. Only I want to go to them." The admin officer said she'd see what she could do, her voice warm. There was a shortage of humans willing to exchange, she told Sarah. There should be no problem.

Sarah looked at the painting for a long time, until the sun was starting to set. She got a nail, and hung the painting in the kitchen above the table. She left the manila envelope below it, with the signed papers inside. Then she began to pack her things.

**ROSE LEMBERG**
# Three Immigrations

*First immigration: The Strangers of the Glass*
*in dress of handblown cinnamon and blue*
*and speaking speckled bubbles in the glass;*
*Their power is to come and pour a road—*
*to molt the land for us,*
*then leave*

**[The In-between]**
with luggage of caramel leather and brass locks—no,
there's no romance in this travel. Only a crumbled
book in Yiddish and a tin
of buttons *(remember the horn one from grandmother's*
*mustard dress she wore on the train to...)* cut from all the old
dresses, and grandmother's
death certificate is ten days old. A plastic bag
of photographs. A dry salami.
In Hungary, they put us behind bars.

**A Mini-Map**
There are two waters in my land
bridged by a road of molten glass
and if you step on it, you'll pass
outside of tenses:
neither past, nor present, nor a future, nor
(first, second, third) a person (singular or plural)
instead, a being on the road of glass

**[In Hungary, they put us behind bars]**
to wait for the plane. Like rats in a ca- /
people / sheep to the sla- / *(now you cross out)*
My grandmother's ghost
struggled to follow us, but lost her way
somewhere in the fields between point A
and the warehouse. They didn't
let us peek out. My father said
Budapest must be beautiful

*Second Immigration—The Strangers in Soldiers' Clothing*
*war-tossed in weeping ships*
*they arrive at Northwater. They left behind*
*everything,*
*even the ocean. Brought only the bell*
*forged by citymakers*
*by true voice-makers in the old country. The song*
*tolls the dead into their new earth. They build*
*a church at Graveyard Island, and hang*
*their voice there; then on*
*to the road of glass*

## [Arriving, the Gulf War]
is the first thing I remember. Bombs falling, and a gaping
hole in the wall. Sirens. A family of four,
we locked ourselves in the bathroom. The gas mask smelled
like gas, or burnt rubber,
or a language.
Cockroaches ate
my mother's salvaged wedding dress, and I learned
to speak; made up three languages to hide in

## Beginnings are endings
When they reached Southwater, the war clothing
seeped into their skins and they as speechless as fish
that clog the glassroad,
fish for the souls of the dead
scraped onto the glass.
They settled by the Southwater,
walled off a city there. Called her Bell,
or perhaps—
        nothing.

*Third Immigration—The Strangers with Animals*
*They come joyfully, bringing only*
*their most beloved ones—a small city*
*guarded by white beasts in the heart of one person; another*
*carries a snake abjad to spell the truth*
*in blunt consonants. Another's heart*
*protects the bird of vowels.*
*Shall they unlock*

*the larynx of love and longing, or shall they step*
*onto the road of molten glass?*

**[I was so terrified, I don't remember]**
a thing of that last journey. I'd packed
two changes of clothing (my mother had bought me
four-inch heels with her last money; I cannot
wear them, but have no other shoes).
Three books—
a battered copy
of the *Poetic Edda* in Old Norse, *Biblia*
*Hebraica Stuttgartensia,* and Ted Hughes' *Crow.*
I do not remember
how they stood—my father speaking
for the last time, or my mother—
before his stroke. I do not remember
how the plane smelled, or the long winding line
at immigration services.
Alone.
In the future of me, the San Francisco Bay Bridge
circles my head like a red dragon crown.

**Coda: I made three languages**
to hide in. Each within
the only land I've ever called my own
between the waters. I am still the same
or am I? How to know
if all my journeys are translated in the skin
or am I dithering
before the road of glass?

How to Live on Other Planets

# ZEN CHO
# The Four Generations of Chang E

## The First Generation

In the final days of Earth as we knew it, Chang E won the moon lottery. For Earthlings who were neither rich nor well-connected, the lottery was the only way to get on the Lunar Habitation Programme. (This was the Earthlings' name for it. The moon people said: "those fucking immigrants".)

Chang E sold everything she had: the car, the family heirloom enamel hairpin collection, her external brain. Humans were so much less intelligent than Moonites anyway. The extra brain would have made little difference.

She was entitled to the hairpins. Her grandmother had pressed them into Chang E's hands herself, her soft old hands folding over Chang E's.

"In the future it will be dangerous to be a woman," her grandmother had said. "Maybe even more dangerous than when my grandmother was a girl. You look after yourself, OK?"

It was not as if anyone else would. There was a row over the hairpins. Her parents had been saving them to pay for Elder Brother's education.

Hah! Education! Who had time for education in days like these? In these times you mated young before you died young, you plucked your roses before you came down with some hideous mutation or discovered one in your child, or else you did something crazy—like go to the moon. Like survive.

Chang E could see the signs. Her parents' eyes had started following her around hungrily, as if they were Bugs Bunny and she was a giant carrot. One night Chang E would wake up to find herself trussed up on the altar they had erected to Elder Brother.

Since the change Elder Brother had spent most of his time in his room, slumbering Kraken-like in the gloomful depths of his bed. But by the pricking of their thumbs, by the lengthening of his teeth, Mother and Father trusted that he was their way out of the last war, their guard against assault and cannibalism.

Offerings of oranges, watermelons and pink steamed rice cakes piled up around his bed. One day Chang E would join them. Everyone knew the new gods liked best the taste of the flesh of women.

So Chang E sold her last keepsake of her grandmother and pulled on her moon boots without regret.

On the moon Chang E floated free, untrammelled by the Earth's ponderous gravity, untroubled by that sticky thing called family. In the curious glances of the moon people, in their condescension ("your Lunarish is very good!") she was reinvented.

Away from home, you could be anything. Nobody knew who you'd been. Nobody cared.

She lived in one of the human ghettos, learnt to walk without needing the boots to tether her to the ground, married a human who chopped wood unceasingly to displace his intolerable homesickness.

One night she woke up and saw the light lying at the foot of her bed like snow on the grass. Lifting her head, she saw the weeping blue eye of home. The thought, exultant, thrilled through her: *I'm free! I'm free!*

## The Second Generation

Her mother had had a pet moon rabbit. This was before we found out they were sentient. She'd always treated it well, said Chang E. That was the irony: how well we had treated the rabbits! How little some of them deserved it!

Though if any rabbit had ever deserved good treatment, it was her mother's pet rabbit. When Chang E was little, it had made herbal tea for her when she was ill, and sung her nursery rhymes in its native moon rabbit tongue—little songs, simple and savage, but rather sweet. Of course Chang E wasn't able to sing them to you now. She'd forgotten.

But she was grateful to that rabbit. It had been like a second mother to her, said Chang E.

What Chang E didn't like was the rabbits claiming to be intelligent. It's one thing to cradle babies to your breast and sing them songs, stroking your silken paw across their foreheads. It's another to want the vote, demand entrance to schools, move in to the best part of town and start building warrens.

When Chang E went to university there was a rabbit living in her student hall. Imagine that. A rabbit sharing their kitchen, using their plates, filling the pantry with its food.

Chang E kept her chopsticks and bowls in her bedroom,

bringing them back from the kitchen every time she finished a meal. She was polite, in memory of her nanny, but it wasn't pleasant. The entire hall smelled of rabbit food. You worried other people would smell it on you.

Chang E was tired of smelling funny. She was tired of being ugly. She was tired of not fitting in. She'd learnt Lunarish from her immigrant mother, who'd made it sound like a song in a foreign language.

Her first day at school Chang E had sat on the floor, one of three humans among twenty children learning to add and subtract. When her teacher had asked what one and two made, her hand shot up.

"Tree!" she said.

Her teacher had smiled. She'd called up a tree on the holographic display.

"This is a tree." She called up the image of the number three. "Now, this is three."

She made the high-pitched clicking sound in the throat which is so difficult for humans to reproduce.

"Which is it, Changey?"

"Tree," Chang E had said stupidly. "Tree. Tree." Like a broken down robot.

In a month her Lunarish was perfect, accentless, and she rolled her eyes at her mother's singsong, "Chang E, you got listen or not?"

Chang E would have liked to be motherless, pastless, selfless. Why was her skin so yellow, her eyes so small, when she felt so green inside?

After she turned 16, Chang E begged the money off her dad, who was conveniently indulgent since the divorce, and went in secret for the surgery.

When she saw herself in the mirror for the first time after the operation she gasped.

Long ovoid eyes, the last word in Lunar beauty, all iris, no ugly inconvenient whites or dark browns to spoil that perfect reflective surface. The eyes took up half her face. They were like black eggs, like jewels.

Her mother screamed when she saw Chang E. Then she cried.

It was strange. Chang E had wanted this surgery with every fibre of her being—her nose hairs swooning with longing, her liver contracting with want.

Yet she would have cried too, seeing her mother so upset, if her new eyes had let her. But Moonite eyes didn't have tear ducts. No eyelids to cradle tears, no eyelashes to sweep them away. She stared unblinking and felt sorry for her mother, who was still alive, but locked in an inaccessible past.

## The Third Generation

Chang E met H'yi in the lab, on her first day at work. He was the only rabbit there and he had the wary, closed-off look so many rabbits had.

At Chang E's school the rabbit students had kept themselves to themselves. They had their own associations—the Rabbit Moonball Club, the Lapin Lacemaking Society—and sat in quiet groups at their own tables in the cafeteria.

Chang E had sat with her Moonite friends.

"There's only so much you can do," they'd said. "If they're not making any effort to integrate...."

But Chang E had wondered secretly if the rabbits had the right idea. When she met other Earthlings, each one alone in a group of Moonites, they'd exchange brief embarrassed glances before subsiding back into invisibility. The basic wrongness of being an Earthling was intensified in the presence of other Earthlings. When you were with normal people you could almost forget.

Around humans Chang E could feel her face become used to smiling and frowning, every emotion transmitted to her face with that flexibility of expression that was so distasteful to Moonites. As a child this had pained her, and she'd avoided it as much as possible—better the smoothness of surface that came to her when she was hidden among Moonites.

At 24, Chang E was coming to understand that this was no way to live. But it was a difficult business, this easing into being. She and H'yi did not speak to each other at first, though they were the only non-Moonites in the lab.

The first time she brought human food to work, filling the place with strange warm smells, she kept her head down over her lunch, shrinking from the Moonites' glances. H'yi looked over at her.

"Smells good," he said. "I love noodles."

"Have you had this before?" said Chang E. H'yi's ears twitched.

His face didn't change, but somehow Chang E knew he was laughing.

"I haven't spent my *entire* life in a warren," he said. "We do get out once in a while."

The first time Chang E slept over at his, she felt like she was coming home. The close dark warren was just big enough for her. It smelt of moon dust.

In H'yi's arms, her face buried in his fur, she felt as if the planet itself had caught her up in its embrace. She felt the wall vibrate: next door H'yi's mother was humming to her new litter. It was the moon's own lullaby.

Chang E's mother stopped speaking to her when she got married. It was rebellion, Ma said, but did she have to take it so far?

"I should have known when you changed your name," Ma wept. "After all the effort I went to, giving you a Moonite name. Having the throat operation so I could pronounce it. Sending you to all the best schools and making sure we lived in the right neighbourhoods. When will you grow up?"

Growing up meant wanting to be Moonite. Ma had always been disappointed by how bad Chang E was at this.

They only reconciled after Chang E had the baby. Her mother came to visit, sitting stiffly on the sofa. H'yi made himself invisible in the kitchen.

The carpet on the floor between Chang E and her mother might as well have been a maria. But the baby stirred and yawned in Chang E's arms—and stolen glance by jealous, stolen glance, her mother fell in love.

One day Chang E came home from the lab and heard her mother singing to the baby. She stopped outside the nursery and listened, her heart still.

Her mother was singing a rabbit song.

Creaky and true, the voice of an old peasant rabbit unwound from her mouth. The accent was flawless. Her face was innocent, wiped clean of murky passions, as if she'd gone back in time to a self that had not yet discovered its capacity for cruelty.

## The Fourth Generation

When Chang E was 16, her mother died. The next year Chang E left school and went to Earth, taking her mother's ashes with her in a brown ceramic urn.

The place her mother had chosen was on an island just above the equator, where, Ma had said, their Earthling ancestors had been buried. When Chang E came out of the environment-controlled port building, the air wrapped around her, sticky and close. It was like stepping into a god's mouth and being enclosed by his warm humid breath.

Even on Earth most people travelled by hovercraft, but on this remote outpost wheeled vehicles were still in use. The journey was bumpy—the wheels rendered them victim to every stray imperfection in the road. Chang E hugged the urn to her and stared out the window, trying to ignore her nausea.

It was strange to see so many humans around, and only humans. In the capital city you'd see plenty of Moonites, expats and tourists, but not in a small town like this.

Here, thought Chang E, was what her mother had dreamt of. Earthlings would not be like moon humans, always looking anxiously over their shoulder for the next way in which they would be found wanting.

And yet her mother had not chosen to come here in life. Only in death. Where would Chang E find the answer to that riddle?

Not in the graveyard. This was on an orange hill, studded with white and grey tombstones, the vermillion earth furred in places with scrubby grass.

The sun bore close to the Earth here. The sunshine was almost a tangible thing, the heat a repeated hammer's blow against the temple. The only shade was from the trees, starred with yellow-hearted white flowers. They smelled sweet when Chang E picked them up. She put one in her pocket.

The illness had been sudden, but they'd expected the death. Chang E's mother had arranged everything in advance, so that once Chang E arrived she did not have to do or understand anything. The nuns took over.

Following them, listening with only half her attention on their droning chant in a language she did not know to a god she did not recognise, she looked down on the town below. The air was thick with light over the stubby low buildings, crowded close together the way human habitations tended to be.

How godlike the Moonites must have felt when they entered these skies and saw such towns from above. To love a new world, you had to get close to the ground and listen.

You were not allowed to watch them lower the urn into the ground and cover it with soil. Chang E looked up obediently.

In the blue sky there was a dragon.

She blinked. It was a flock of birds, forming a long line against the sky. A cluster of birds at one end made it look like the dragon had turned its head. The sunlight glinting off their white bodies made it seem that the dragon looked straight at her with luminous eyes.

She stood and watched the sky, her hand shading her eyes, long after the dragon had left, until the urn was buried and her mother was back in the Earth.

What was the point of this funeral so far from home, a sky's worth of stars lying between Chang E's mother and everyone she had ever known? Had her mother wanted Chang E to stay? Had she hoped Chang E would fall in love with the home of her ancestors, find a human to marry, and by so doing somehow return them all to a place where they were known?

Chang E put her hand in her pocket and found the flower. The petals were waxen, the texture oddly plastic between her fingertips. They had none of the fragility she'd been taught to associate with flowers.

Here is a secret Chang E knew, though her mother didn't.

Past a certain point, you stop being able to go home. At this point, when you have got this far from where you were from, the thread snaps. The narrative breaks. And you are forced, pastless, motherless, selfless, to invent yourself anew.

At a certain point, this stops being sad—but who knows if any human has ever reached that point?

Chang E wiped her eyes and her streaming forehead, followed the nuns back to the temple, and knelt to pray to her nameless forebears.

She was at the exit when remembered the flower. The Lunar Border Agency got funny if you tried to bring Earth vegetation in. She left the flower on the steps to the temple.

Then Chang E flew back to the Moon.

**JULIE BLOSS KELSEY**
**two scifaiku**

tongue lashing
by galaxy border patrol...
barcodes on my teeth

anticipating
my next trip to Earth
—the itch of new skin

# TOM DOYLE
# The Floating Otherworld

## The Hell of Underwater Fire

Mid life's road, and it's August in Tokyo. But that isn't why you're sweating. You're alone with Kaguya-san, the night receptionist.

She looks younger than the other office ladies and damned younger than you. Instead of the formless office lady suit, she wears the latest Italian fashion. Japanese skirts are short, but hers is leather. Nothing improper, just enough difference to torment you.

The other employees have left promptly for the weekend O-Bon holiday. Japanese days of the dead. Late summer is the scary joyful season. Haunted houses, dancing, and fireworks. Fear helps people chill. It isn't helping you, maybe because you're a foreigner. *Gaijin.*

You ask, "Um, could you type this for me?"

She takes your scrawled notes. She doesn't smile. The other secretaries smile while they tell you they can't help you. No smile, but her face and eyes seem to shine with cool light.

"Your handwriting is difficult, Nolan-san. But I can manage."

You manage a *"domo arigato."*

"You're welcome. What are you doing tonight?"

You shrug. You say nothing. "I'll wait for the document" on a Friday seems too pathetic. You want to say, "Take a long bath with me, Kaguya-san, make me clean and Japanese and worthy." You say nothing.

"You should get out. To Roppongi. Lots of foreigners there."

Foreigners. You smile bitterly at another night of getting plastered and snogging with some expat from the British Commonwealth. "Maybe. Good night, Kaguya-san." You don't dare ask what she is doing later, even to be polite. Such questions are meaningless here, but not for you. You're too hungry to be trivial.

You take the train. You're pressed from all sides, but you're used to such meaningless contact.

"A young Japanese man was shot in your country." A poking finger punctuates the sentence; an unusually pointy nose threatens your chest. It's an old woman in a loud Tokyo Disney shirt and frameless plastic sunglasses, like she's just had eye surgery. That would explain the shirt. Her face is marked like she's been burned,

169

badly. So you're polite. "Yes, two of them in the last month. I'm sorry." Tourists in the wrong place at the wrong time.

No time for more. It's only one stop to your downtown apartment, three-bedroom by Tokyo standards, one-bedroom by yours. A view some have killed for—you overlook the Crown Prince's grounds, and Mt. Fuji is visible on the rare clear days. The folklore clowns say fire-and-snow Fuji is a woman. A distant volcano indeed.

Friday night, and your Tokyo gets dark early. Your lover in the States lasted only a sexless month before moving on. You aren't drunk (yet), so you will not call the home masseuse who gives special service. You will not call home. All your friends on the other side pretend you are dead.

She said "Roppongi." Where is Kaguya-san going tonight?

OK. Time for another Roppongi death march. No way to find her, no way to respect yourself, any way to forget yourself.

## Screaming Hell's Booze Hounds

Praise Buddha, you're already drunk and searching for a club called, appropriately enough, "The Gaijin Zone." You've been there before, but for some reason it eludes you now.

You turn left. You're on a quiet one-lane back street, with a few Cadillacs squeezed in and no people. The air is mistier, darker.

"Another Japanese student shot last year during Halloween."

Shit! You spin around. The voice belongs to an innocuous middle-aged man in a comfortable suit, non-salaryman issue. He's wearing wraparound shades at night, but his particularly prominent nose seems to have caught your scent. The heat doesn't seem to bother him in the least. Perhaps he wants to fuck you, but in Tokyo that's no reason to be rude in reply.

So again you're polite. "I'm very sorry about it. Do you know where the Gaijin Zone is?"

He steps uncomfortably closer. "America is a violent country."

This is annoying. You can't apologize for everything. "A woman was Cuisinarted in Kyoto last month." And bits of her flesh left all along the freeway. "Why did that only make page three of the papers here?"

"*So desu.* Very sad. What you are looking for is that way." He points further down the back street. "Say you are my guest. Oya's guest."

Fine. You'll go that way, but you're nobody's guest.

You go that way. The street and buildings get older, the lights get dimmer. The lane curves and comes to an end. Shit. You walk back the way you came. You've been orbiting around a fenced clearing. Peering through fence and darkness, you can see a ragged forest of headstones and monuments. A cemetery, old and unkempt. Not good, not good, not good.

You walk faster, but can't find your way back to the bright lights, away from the graves. A Shinto-Buddhist lesson: Tokyo's streets are non-Euclidean, its underworld non-Virgilian.

"Nolan-san." A familiar voice cuts through booze and mist. You turn and see Kaguya-san, dressed "body con"—a red form-hugging strapless one-piece, stiletto heels, fishnet stockings, definitely not office lady wear. She stands beneath a lone sign for a club, the full moonlight a faint spot on her face. Her red dress bleeds into the night. The sign says "Floating World Live House Four." Like the old art prints, she's very floating world right now.

"Hello." You're nervous—does she think you've been following her? You explain: "I'm looking for the Gaijin Zone."

"That will be difficult for you to find now. And to stay here would be, *eto,* difficult for you as well. Come to this club. It's better."

And she points to the open door. Stairs lead down towards the sound of music. A club next to the dead? Great. But she's here. You go in.

You stumble a bit on the stairs and apologize. "I'm feeling strange. *Hen desu.*"

"You are strange, Nolan-san." She laughs at you, and you're delighted—she never laughs at work.

At the bottom of the stairs, traditional lanterns reveal a Bon party in full throttle. Some have come as animals—foxes with sexy tails, badgers with big balls, catfish with legs. The musicians, cramped in a small corner, are birds with big beaks. Others are ghosts out of Clive Barker—Day-Glo disembowelments and worms that wriggle. You finally feel the chill. It's not as refreshing as you hoped.

A reality check is in order. "I didn't think people dressed up for the Bon festival."

She smiles. "This club is different."

"Is there going to be dancing later?"

"Yes, there is always dancing."

You might not be drunk enough for dancing or this club. "I'll get us some drinks."

"Are you sure?"

You're damned sure.

"You're very sweet. Ask him for two sakes in the box, special service. The special service is important." You think of the masseuse, and hope it's not the same thing.

As the band plays "Blue Suede Shoes," you cautiously approach the fragile looking Plexiglas bar—it doubles as an aquarium. Transparent channels carry water down the walls, through the floor, through the bar. Tiny fish swim about miniature kelp plants.

The bartender doesn't look fully Japanese; he's off-color and hairy. He balances a brimful tumbler on his head while he munches on some sushi rolls.

"Neat trick," you say. "Could I have two sakes in boxes, special service?"

"Just a minute, mate. I'm eating," he says in English, with a stuffed mouth and a slight Australian accent.

"Cucumber?"

"*Kappa maki,*" he says.

"'*Kappa*' is cucumber?"

He looks at you with clear disdain. "No, a *kappa* is a very noble, very maligned being, who happens to enjoy cucumbers."

You get it—he's supposed to be a *kappa,* whatever that is. "What else do you like?"

"Oh no you don't." He slams the bar with his hand, and the tumbler on his head wobbles. "It's all rubbish—ruptured rectums of livestock, my ass! Why would we want blood from a cow's rice hole—we're fucking vegetarians!"

He grips your shoulder, nails like claws, pulling you close. You stare at his pointy Japanese dentistry teeth. Whatever *kappas* want is fine with you.

"Peasants should ask their kids about the bloody livestock," he snarls. He slams the bar with his other hand. The tumbler on his head wobbles again, threatening to spill on you, so you grab it.

"*Shimatta,*" he cries in a breathless shout. He lets you go, feeling his head where the glass was. "OK, give it back, mate."

"Sure, but how about those drinks?"

He sighs. "Fine, it's a deal."

How to Live on Other Planets

You give him back the tumbler. He takes out a small dust-covered sake barrel and two ornately carved pine boxes. He sets the boxes on two burnt-green saucers, and mutters bits of Japanese as he fills the boxes to overflowing, then looks at you. "Who told you to ask for these?"

You point back to Kaguya-san, who has miraculously found a table.

"Well why didn't you just say so, mate? Tell her I've made them extra special. Oya-san is coming. Cheers."

You walk back towards your table, keeping the drinks as steady as you can in the crowd.

"For me?" A delicate white hand with fine blue veins reaches for a box. Yes, this is like Halloween.

"No, for my friend."

The hand belongs to a tall thin woman wearing a ski outfit in August. Her face is as pale as a winter's moon. "I am Yuki."

She's beautiful, so you decide to play along. "As in snow?"

"Yes, the same. Have you been to the mountains?"

You've been to Nagano.

"Nagano. The Olympics. Many tourists came, and some roamed far. Roam with me."

Ouch! The white hand grasps your arm. The sake boxes shudder. You feel her chill through your shirt, and suddenly you are hard for her, icy hard, and you want to shatter like a Creamsicle inside her.

A flash of red, and your arm is free. *"Dame!* Don't pay any attention to her, Nolan-san, she's frigid."

Kaguya-san has grabbed the boxes. You slouch into a seat at your table. You feel numb, and you're not sure what, if anything, just happened. The women exchange words through the music behind you, like "mine" and "guest."

Yuki says "Oya-san."

Kaguya-san says nothing. She returns, sets the boxes on the table and looks at you steadily.

You repeat, "Oya-san," but she shushes you. "First drink-up. *Kanpai."* She drinks, so you drink. She downs her whole box, so you do too. The sake tastes like an electrified mountain stream, with a hint of pine from the box. Your body aches as its warmth returns. She glances down into your empty box. *"Sugoi,* Nolan-san. Soon we'll sing karaoke, *ne,* when the band rests."

You need to know. "I've met Oya-san. He said I was his guest." Kaguya-san is silent. "Who is Oya-san?"

She sucks her breath. "Oya means landlord. And more. Like an uncle. I'm not sure what you would call him. We shouldn't disturb him, he's a busy man."

The band is rocking out with more Elvis. Kaguya-san brings her lips close to your ear to be heard. "Nolan-san, you know—"

But she doesn't finish. Before you see him, you see the reactions of those closer to the entrance. Everyone turns to look, and the band stops mid-song. You can hear the crowd whisper now, "Oya" over and over, like a chant.

Oya-san, the mild-mannered accuser from the street, has no Bon outfit and looks far too normal, too real for this party. He moves through the parting crowd. The ski woman strains her arm to touch him, but he just holds up a finger, *"Chotto matte,"* and she freezes.

The bandleader cranes his beak towards Oya's nose. "Roy Orbison, *ne?*"

Oya's finger again: *"Domo. Chotto."* Everyone, even the fish in the bar, follows his finger except Kaguya-san, who studies your table like a manuscript she must type.

Oya comes towards your table. You want to say "Yakuza." "Say nothing," Kaguya-san hisses.

Without asking, Oya sits at your table. He points at the band. They begin Orbison's "In Dreams." The bartender, tumbler back on his head, wordlessly brings Oya-san and the table drinks. Oya lights a cigarette. The spot of orange flame reflects on his dark glasses. His face and hands are the color of spent ash.

In the wrong place at the wrong time.

When the song ends, Oya says, "It's good no one will miss him."

Kaguya-san doesn't look up. "He's my guest now."

"Too late, once beloved. I've judged him."

Kaguya-san taps your empty sake box. "Careful. He's been drinking."

Oya's nostrils flare. *"Baka!* You can join him then." With his left hand, Oya seizes her perfect hair and pulls her face up, her eyes flashing.

Time telescopes to hold several things in a moment. The band commences Nirvana's "In Bloom." You say nothing. You swing your arm across the table and bring the edge of the sake box down into Oya's left shoulder.

Without expression, Oya lets go of Kaguya-san's hair. Kaguya-san says one word that sounds like *jazz* and *jism.*

Oya thrusts the palm of his right hand against your forehead.

Bam! The bartender screeches. The crowd howls. The bar shatters, and you feel the tingly spray of water, glass, and fish. The lanterns explode—your lights are going out. The drummer keeps thumping, afraid to stop.

Kaguya-san is pulling you in the dark. *"Ikimasho!"* You're going, going...

## Last Chance Hell

A gong sounds. The show begins. You don't remember how you got here—a combo casino and hostess bar. You are seated in a circular booth with a high back and a narrow opening. You can't see into the other booths, and they can't see you. Nearby, the floor show of comely women in lingerie parades mechanically to American pop songs. The recordings are sped up to sound like chipmunks on Ecstasy.

A corseted hostess comes to your table. You try to decline her company, but she just giggles in girlish style.

"House rules, dear. Every man must have a hostess."

That's OK. Hostesses just talk—they're chat whores. Not like you'd be doing anything wrong. Certainly nothing illegal.

The hostess starts right in on the chat, asking you about yourself. It feels wonderful, after being alone so long, to be listened to so raptly. You joke, she laughs. You rant, she justifies. You get maudlin, her eyes water. Lovely.

You feel relaxed. You think that maybe, if you talk cleverly enough, this woman will ask you to a private room and make painfully slow love to you, no charge. So you talk more, though you're getting sleepy. That's OK, it has been a long (endless) night, and then meeting Kaguya-san...

Say, where is Kaguya-san? She isn't next to you. You want to thank her for something, or show off how you're handling the hostess. Suddenly, the hostess's banter is tinny, mechanical. "You work so hard." Not really. "Nobody understands you." Should they? "You're such a real man." Then shouldn't you be with a real woman?

"Where's Kaguya-san?"

"Who?" Your hostess is sincerely dumbfounded.

"My friend." You want to talk with your friend.

"But I'm here to listen."

"We have talked enough. Where's my friend?"

"She'll be back. Please talk to me." She's desperate. Poor thing. You try another tack.

"Who are you?"

"Oh, I'm just a woman who enjoys your wonderful company."

"No, really, who are you? And why are you here? This is not a normal hostess bar."

"You really want to know. I can see that. I'll go now."

"No, please, first tell me."

"Those are the rules. If you honestly care enough to ask, I have to go." Before you can ask again, she's gone.

Kaguya-san comes tentatively to the table. She's wearing a modern kimono loosely over the body con, her dark hair pulled back with hair sticks. She holds a stack of casino chips in her hand. How long have you been here?

"Nolan-san, you're OK?"

You think so. "Let's go before another hostess comes."

You walk past the other booths. It's a Bon party at the hostess bar too. Table after table of ghastly, spectral women glare at their clients with raptor eyes. Their skin fluoresces in spots that are shapes—the shape of a hand where it slapped a cheek, the shape of a fist where it smacked an eye. And the men. They are emaciated gray or rotten purple-green. The women still speak to the rotted men, saying things like, "you should have gone home to your wife," "you should not have gone to Thailand," "now you will not leave here ever."

You're glad your hostess didn't look like these women. It's very kabuki or puppet play, unrequited love and *Twilight Zone* revenge. All you say is "ghost story."

Like the moon on a cloudy night, Kaguya-san avoids your eyes. "Something like that," she says. No laughter or smile. She's scared of something—is she afraid for you?

You look around again at the blurry, fearful room. Maybe this is really the otherworld, or maybe you're really dead. It doesn't matter. Drunk or dead, you'll stick with Kaguya-san. She at least seems to care what happens to you.

You follow her into the gaming room. It's more normal, comforting. There's a chaotic chime of pachinko machines playing themselves, balls falling into the random predestined paths. One of the gambling tables seems to be a Bon party special—some old guys in even older Imperial Navy uniforms playing poker. They bluff recklessly, they risk much early, and the chips go wildly back and forth across the table. They smile at you and ask if you'd like to join the game. Kaguya-san gives you some chips to bet with, but you politely decline. They nod, chuckling, and say it's just as well. They've played Americans before. "Let sleeping giants lie, *ne?*"

The rest of the club is empty now, chips left on the tables uncashed, roulette wheels still. In the long run, the house always wins.

An aria from *Madame Butterfly* replaces the pachinko chimes. "The American left her." Shit, now someone wants you to apologize for Italian opera. It's the most sensible thing you've heard all night. This time the accuser is a woman about your age. She wears the pointed sunglasses of a '50s movie starlet lightly on her beaklike nose—like she's Oya's sister or Oya in drag. She clenches a cigarette holder in her teeth as she rakes in the piles of spent chips.

Kaguya-san stands to the side, ready for a fight. "I want to speak to the manager," she says.

The accuser speaks to you instead. "I am the new manager of this club. From Kyoto. I heard you wanted to meet me."

This Oya offers you her hand to shake, western style. Her entire arm is crisscrossed with fine white scar lines, dotted like Morse code to invite scissors or knife to "cut here." A temporary costume? A permanent tattoo? Either way, this homage to the Kyoto butchery is both terrifying and in extremely poor taste. Your tolerance of the strange is worn out—you're pissed off. "Have you no fucking shame?"

Oya smiles with anger. "Ah, you see, but you do not yet understand. Here, a gift."

She flips you a chip, and you catch it and slap it into your left hand with your other chips. And you regret it. In fact, you regret everything. You regret the lost love and friends back home. You regret not making all the money that you could be making stateside. You regret things that haven't even happened yet: you are aware of *mono no aware*. Your parents are growing older, people are dying and you're not there. You're not really here either.

A tickling spider-web feeling distracts you from the abstract. Fine white lines have spread across your hand. Both hands. Your entire body. You know where you are going. Kyoto, with bits of your flesh left all along the freeway.

The white lines have turned crimson agony. You're coming undone. Soon, your fingers will fall to the ground, followed by everything else in small pieces.

The old men continue to play cards, unconcerned. Kaguya-san has not moved or spoken. She silently implores you to some action, but what can you do?

Your dissolution is taking an eternity. You sob at your own helpless pain. Oya, still smiling unhappily, offers you a dagger. You know what the knife is for; you've seen it in the movies. You suppose it's the Japanese thing to do.

No. Stake it all, while you still can. That's the Tokyo way. You're still gripping your chips in a left hand that's useless with fraying tendons. But now you've got a blade in your right. You chop through the hanging threads of your left wrist with indifferent pain, and toss your hand on a roulette table. Red four.

Oya is not smiling now, but she spins. The wheel spins, the ball spins. You're spinning.

"*Ikimasho,* Nolan-san." Kaguya-san wraps her kimono around you, containing your fractures for another moment, and you fall into the red.

## The Hell Spa-ed

You're standing, barefoot and in a *yukata* robe. You might as well be naked. You rub the old scar on your left wrist that you don't like people to see. The décor is cave—sometimes faux, sometimes rocky real. You smell the lightest hint of sulfur and minerals. The sign says "World Famous Hells." A hot spring spa. Heavenly.

A woman in a white robe brings you another box of sake. You take a sip. You won't make the same mistake twice, so you immediately ask, "Where is Kaguya-san?"

"Oya-san?" she asks. Definitely not. But she points towards the rear of the cave, and that's the way you go.

On the walls of the cave are traditional sliding doors, with nothing indicating where they may lead. You walk further down the hall. One set of three sliding doors is different from the others. The middle door is a mirror, and the doors on either side feature lovely, simple paintings. To the left, a dragon holds a sword blade. To the right, a dragon clutches jewels.

You open the mirror door. Kaguya-san is there in her loose robe with no body con beneath. "Welcome to my spa, Nolan-san. Time to take the bath with me. But first, get clean."

She directs you to the left. You go, trying not to appear as anxious as you feel. It's a locker room of sorts, with a shower and a heated toilet that makes noises to mask your biological functions. You get clean.

Beyond the shower is another door, the entrance to the central chamber and hot spring bath. You enter—it's dim, wet, and warm. The pool glows and steams, crater-like, a comfortable fit for two.

Kaguya-san leaves her robe by the water's edge, and slides into the pool with effortless grace. You try to avoid staring—naked is your problem, not theirs—but you sense the smallness of her curves, and find with relief and expectation that small is beautiful.

You test the water with the ball of your foot. Goddamn, the water is painfully hot. They threw Christians into boiling springs, didn't they? But Kaguya-san got in, so you have to follow.

As you slowly lower yourself into the pool, the water moves up your body as a line of fire. Below the water, your legs are a fun house of melted plastic. Then, you're all the way in, except for your head, the last bit of dissolving ice. All the years of bad booze and bad food are steaming out of you.

Kaguya-san rubs your neck and shoulders with a cloth. You keep your eyes focused above the waterline. "That's nice," you say.

She smiles at you. "Nolan-san, you know I like you."

"No, I mean, well, I like you too." You still aren't sure what she means; you've crossed your cultural signals before.

She puts her arms around your neck. Her skin feels different, Japanese. You can't believe this is happening.

It isn't. With shocking force, she pulls your head underwater.

The water stings your eyes. Your need for air becomes pressing, but the force holding you under does not relent. Drowning? Maybe. So it goes.

Then, just as forcefully, she lifts your head up. "I think you're done." She laughs.

*Some joke,* you think, but the Japanese don't like sarcasm, so you keep silent for a moment. You look at your hands. There's been no change of color, she hasn't made you Japanese, your dream has not come true.

"Time's up. We need to get out."

You get out of the pool, and the warm air feels cool. You go towards the way you came in.

"No, not that way, this way."

You follow her into the right-hand room. With every step, your plastic-like body cools and firms into shape.

She helps you dress. Her kimono. Strange. It fits all right, but gives you the appearance, the feeling of breasts. She wears your *yukata,* and it's hard to see any curve to her at all.

"Now we are ready for karaoke?" You exit the jewel door, and cross the hall. It's a private karaoke room, with an enormous video screen and a comfortable sofa, and a phone for ordering drinks and food.

There are three other, older women there. In greeting, they say "Oya-san." You jump, and Kaguya-san notices.

"Don't worry, Nolan-san, the other Oya will not come here."

You think the other Oya may be everywhere, but you say, "Your beloved?"

"That was long ago. Let's sing."

You let them select your songs. You sing "Crazy for You" by Madonna in duet with Kaguya-san. You're not bad. You sing a Japanese song of spring in autumn for the winter people, and though you mangle some words, your feeling is pure. You sing "Stairway to Heaven" and "Hotel California," and they go very wrong, but no one seems to mind. Harmony of feeling is more important than technique here.

The older women sing together, something about "three more for every two lost," and seem very amused by you and Kaguya-san. The music is now mostly percussion in irregular rhythm. *ICHI, ni, san, shi. Ichi, NI, san, shi. Ichi, ni, SAN, shi. Ichi, NI, san, shi. Ichi.* In out in, ah. Ah, out in out. The drums sound live, not karaoke machine.

The satellite feed for the karaoke glitches for a moment, and suddenly, Oya's on the video, dressed like a schnozzy Elvis gone Eastern and sexually ambiguous, shades to match. He roars like he's live at Budokan the words to Neil Sedaka's "Oh Carol," substituting your name for the woman's. "Oh Noran-san, I'm soo in rooove with yoouuuuu!"

Kaguya-san looks over at you, blushing, and almost sings, "Are you ready?" She points to the door.

The sound of ocean surf pounds at the door to the room, punctuating the drum rhythm with power and threat. Steamy water dribbles down the door cracks. Your heart drums in your head—*ichi, ni, san, SHI*. You nod. Whatever it is, even drowning, you're ready.

She motions you to the door, and places your hand on the handle. "On the count of four, *ikimasho! Ichi, ni, san…*"

## The Hell of No Interval

*"SHI!"*

The drums outside and inside you have stopped. The stars and the full moon do not move. And that is how you know that it is always a particular day and hour here. The hour is *shi* o'clock in the morning. Said that way, four o'clock is death o'clock.

The day, or night, is August 15. Bon time, and the end of the last war.

The place is a memorial shrine that doesn't exist except in the death o'clock world. It's a shrine composed of other shrines, ashes upon ashes. It's a shrine stripped of the inessentials, death's place, simple and austere. Yasakuni Shrine to the War Dead unadorned with false glory, Hiroshima Peace Park without the peace platitudes.

The air is cold, you're cold. You touch Kaguya-san's hand. She's cold, shivering in your thin robe. No light in her eyes—she's crying. Whoever else she's been for you tonight, now she's just the night receptionist again. Shitty timing, cause there's no time left here.

There's a smell of incense, and a smell of smoke that the incense is trying to cover. You've got company.

All the dead of Japan's last war are here. The soldiers of the War Shrine have come, ordered here by a nationalist spirit that has never completely died, enshrined whether they want to be or not—a forced internment of interment. The burned women and children of Tokyo, the melted fleshlings of Hiroshima and Nagasaki, they have come too. So many years ago, and yet always here.

The scale is too vast, so you focus on particulars you recognize. The card players stand in the front rank, forgoing their game to return to this place, smiling still, but without humor. You see that some of these dead are of more recent vintage—murdered Japanese tourists, irradiated and drowned fishermen. You get it. These dead are here for you.

Flickering like a flame between Yakuza/old woman/dead woman/Elvis is the Oya of death o'clock, executioner, accuser, judge, eyes shielded from a world that is always too bright. He takes off his shades, and his eyes are all-devouring like cremation fires, like hungry ghosts. All is ash, firebomb, nuke. "This is the end, *gaijin*. You don't belong here. Go." Then the all-Oya screams at the dead in an old Japanese that you can't follow at all—archaic and best forgotten.

Their accusations hit like a rainstorm, first a drop, then three drops, then a deluge. You interned us in camps, you bombed us conventionally and obscenely. You can never understand. You are not Japanese.

So here it is, the longest divide. It's old and easily dismissed in daylight, yet it's too much for you to cross now. A chasm of sadness and pain bottled away for decades. Any words seem foolish. You can't apologize. It's not your place, nor could you be sincere. You would not have wanted that war to have been fought a day longer. And it's not even mostly an American guilt, though you'll hear no apology from those here for anything. You cannot condemn. Those here have already paid for the sins of war and aggression, apologies be damned.

Behind you, just over your shoulder (they have a Protestant shyness about manifesting), you hear the voices of your own dead murmur in agreement with the Oya. What the hell are you doing here? Get home, boy. Your family is and will be there.

Instead of listening, you turn to face Kaguya-san. Her arms are stretched out towards two sets of elderly couples, imploring, but they're having none of it. You reach out a hand for her, but she's having none of that. You're not going to be able to negotiate this agreement, counselor, not in English or Japanese.

So, broken tired guilty wronged, you take a step away. And then you take a step towards. And then you take a step away. And then a step towards. Step away, step towards, and you circle around and start again.

Start again. The drum inside you starts again. Kaguya-san stares at you, caught between amazement and dismay. Her expression says, *You're doing it all wrong.* You shake your head. Oh no, you're not. There's always only been one solution. Shut up and dance. Do ya, do ya wanna dance with me?

Your dancing becomes more expansive, outrageous. She joins you, if only to slow you, to show you.

Kaguya-san moves in front of you, the start of a ritual conga line. *Laissez les bon temps rouler.* The drums outside start again, thrumming from all directions, telling you you're not dancing alone, the whole country is dancing this sex-death life-reaping. And you hear the dead lining up behind like guests at a wedding reception, swaying solemnly, some speaking English and damned surprised to be there. And in front you hear those who are to come, and some of them speak Japanese.

Oya's gotta dance too, like he does in the pictures. His incendiary heat eases to autumn. You and she and he are part of a wave that rocks the globe, season to season, hemisphere to hemisphere.

Kaguya-san turns and takes your hand, and dances slowly with you, against you. The shrine fades into the view of Mt. Fuji in moonlight from your balcony, robes become suit and body con. Nobody is watching you and everybody is watching you.

You think this isn't happening. It is.

And you're still dancing, and she rolls her thin red dress up over her hips, and you're turning Japanese you really think so.

You're dancing still.

## The Hell of a Day

Sunday. Time moves ahead again, though slowly. You're on a picnic near a shrine, in a sunlit park, bento boxes for two, jeans and Tokyo Disney T-shirts. Heavy metal bands line the park road at every fifty feet, a cacophonous whole more intriguing than its parts. Everyone is smiling at you, because you need no help. Even Mt. Fuji smiles and winks—you're going to do just fine here.

Kaguya-san's orange-brown eyes are lowered. "Thank you for celebrating the Bon holiday with me, Nolan-san."

Even now, you are still Nolan-san to her in public. It's still a strange place here, *ne?* Can you live with such distance, such formality? You don't have to. She places her hands on your face and bends you towards her to kiss your forehead, your lips. Her lips are like the flutter of a moth.

You stare at Kaguya-san. You could stare for hours. She's more and less luminescent than before, sun lit instead of moon glowing. Everything in its season. Autumn is coming, there will be more moon viewings. By then, your apartment might really be both one and three bedrooms, and Kaguya-san (unilluminated, un-Bon-ified but bona fide) might fit there.

Underworld lord and party animal Oya will come back every

year, and one year you'll not dance away. That's OK. You know how to be a polite host now. You can share tea, and discuss the new hanging scroll that your girlfriend has found for you before you drum him along. *Kappas* will party with Mickey and Bugs, Marley's ghost will throw beans at a snow woman, Jesus and Buddha will be bouncers at the door.

One day, some way, you both must leave, but you're here now. So *ikimasho,* Nolan-san. Doesn't matter where. You will not be going home, you're already there.

Translation: *Nihon ga daisuki desu.* You love Japan.

# DANIEL JOSÉ OLDER
## Phantom Overload

I'm late to a meeting with The New York Council of the Dead so I swing by my favorite Dominican spot for a ferocious coffee. It's kind of on the way, but mostly I do it to bother my icy, irritating superiors. I'll roll up twenty minutes in, smug, caffeinated and palpably disinterested. I linger even longer than I have to, partially because I'm in a good mood but mostly because the counter honey's strapless shirt keeps slipping up like a curtain from her paunchy little tummy. Every time it happens my meeting with the Council becomes less and less important.

The spot's called EL MAR. It's one of those over-decorated 24-hour joints that always has dim lights and a disco ball. Corny papier-mâché coral reefs dangle off all the walls and there's usually a lively crowd of stubby little middle age couples and taxi drivers.

"My friend Gordo's playing here Friday," I say, aiming for casual chitchat but achieving only uninvited randomness. The counter honey raises two well-threaded eyebrows and pouts her lips—which I roughly translate to mean *"Whoopdeedoo, jackass."* But it's spring outside, a warm and breezy afternoon, and my good mood has granted me temporary invincibility. Besides, I like a girl that can say a lot without even opening her mouth. "The big Cuban guy?" I offer. "I've never seen him play before but I hear it's amazing."

She softens some, leans back against the liquor cabinet and exhales. "Gordo's a friend of my tío. He alright." The shadow of a smile is fluttering around her face, threatening to show up at any moment. I try not to stare. "Brings a weirdo crowd though," she adds.

Here's the part where I'm supposed to hand her the dollar, letting the touch linger just a fleeting moment longer than it has to so my fingers can tell her fingers about all the rambunctious lovemaking I have planned for us. But my skin is inhumanly cold; my pulse a mere whisper. I am barely alive at all, a botched resurrection, trapped in perpetual ambiguity with not even so much as a flicker of what life was like before my violent death. Surely, whatever flutterings of passion trickle through my veins wouldn't make the jump from one body to the next. Plus I'd probably ick her out. I put the money on the counter and walk out the door.

§

185

The New York Council of the Dead holds court in a warehouse in the industrial wastelands of Sunset Park, Brooklyn. The outside is nondescript: Another towering, dull monstrosity clustered between the highway and the harbor. Inside, a whole restless bureaucracy of afterlife turns eternal circles like a cursed carnival ride. Mostly dead though I may be, it's here that I always remember how alive I really am. Everyone else in the place is a shroud, a shimmering, translucent version of the person they once were. The glowing shadows spin and buzz about their business in the misty air around me. After five years of showing up here every couple weeks for a new assignment, the presence of this walking anomaly doesn't even warrant a sidewise glance.

I stroll through chilly little crowds of ghosts and into the back offices. I'm a good half-hour late and still murkily ecstatic from the nascent spring and my non-conversation with Bonita Applebum. Unfortunately, they seem to have been waiting up for me.

Chairman Botus's hulking form rises like a burst of steam from behind his magnificent desk. He's the only one of the seven Council Chairmen that anyone's ever seen; the rest lurk in some secret lair, supposedly for security purposes. "Ah, Carlos, wonderful you're here!" Something is definitely very wrong—the Chairman is never happy to see anybody. Botus smiling means someone, somewhere is suffering. I grunt unintelligibly and sip at my lukewarm coffee. There's two other ghosts in the room: A tall, impish character that I figure for some kind of personal assistant or secretary and a very sullen looking Mexican.

"Carlos," Botus grins, "this is Silvan García, spokesman for our friends out in the Remote District 17." The Mexican squints suspiciously at me, nodding a slight acknowledgment. His carefully trimmed goatee accentuates a severe frown. "Silvan, Agent Delacruz here is our leading soulcatcher prime. An investigator of the highest spiritual order. He's done terrific work in the Hispanic communities."

I don't believe in animal spirit guides, but if I had one it just curled up and died. Nothing marginalizes marginalized people like a dead white guy talking sympathetically.

Plus he's managed to deflate my rare bout of perkiness. The secretary, apparently unworthy of any introduction, just stares at me.

"It seems Mr. García's community is experiencing some, er, turmoil," Botus grins hideously down at Silvan. "Is that the word you would use, Sil? Turmoil? Anyway, in short, they're in Phantom

Overload and need our," another smirking pause, false searching for the right word, "assistance."

It's a tense moment. The Remote Districts are a few scattered neighborhoods around New York that unanimously reject any interference from the all powerful Council. Instead, they deal with their own dead however they see fit. I believe 17 is the strip of East New York surrounding the above ground train tracks on Fulton Street, but either way, for them to ask help from the NYCOD means something's really messed up over there. Unfortunately, I haven't peeked at my terminology manual, well, ever, so I just nod my head with concern and mutter, "Phantom Overload, mmm."

The meeting wraps up quickly after that: Many nods and smiles from Botus and grimaces from Silvan García.

"The fuck is Phantom Overload?" I say once the curt spokesman has floated briskly away. Shockingly, Botus's smile hasn't evaporated along with his guest. He appears to be genuinely happy. It's a terrifying thought.

"Oh, Carlos Carlos Carlos," he mutters, letting his long cloudy form recline luxuriously behind his desk. "You're weird and of questionable allegiance, but you're the best we got and I like you."

"You're sinister and untrustworthy," I say, "and I can't stand to be around you. What's Phantom Overload?"

"It means our good friends at RA 17 can't handle their business. No surprise there of course. Seems they have a bus that makes a routine drive through the area picking up souls, collecting the dead, you know—it's all very quaint."

"Until?"

"Until the motherfucker disappears!" Botus lets out a belly laugh.

"The ghost bus disappeared?"

"Can you imagine the irony? Is there anywhere Mexicans *don't* go stuffed into buses? Man!"

I have this blade that I carry concealed inside my walking stick. It's specially designed and spiritually charged to obliterate even the toughest afterlifer. In moments like these that I have to work very hard not to use it.

"Anyway," Botus continues once he's collected himself, "yeah, the ghost bus gone and disappeared, or ain't showing up for whatever reason and so yeah, of course," he rolls his eyes and makes an exaggerated shoulder shrug, "they're gonna go into Overload.

Phoebus, tell him what Overload is."

The slender secretary ghost, who had become so inconsequential that I'd actually forgotten he was there, suddenly leaps into action. "It means, sirs, that the souls are all hanging around and can't be carted off to the Underworld and instead congeal and cause havoc and generally make nuisances of themselves. The situation can be exacerbated by high murder or infant mortality rates and can reach a critical point in as few as 72 hours."

"Critical point?"

"Would be classified as an utterly overwhelming level of chaos derived from the overcrowding and massive spiritual collisions."

"A fucking disaster," Botus puts in. "A Mexican clusterfuck of the highest order. Trust me. You don't wanna see it. It'd be like 9/11 for the dead, but worse. Or like that other thing that happened, the one with the levees and whatever."

"So they sent an emissary?"

"To beg for help. Cocksuckers refuse and refuse and refuse assistance from the Council for decades. No, it'll compromise our autonomy, it'll create dependency on the COD. Blah blah blah. You know the whine. What can you do? Wait around 'til some shit pops off they can't handle. Fine. Here we are. Took a little longer than expected, but no matter. We'll move ahead as planned."

"As planned?"

"Like I said, we all knew this was gonna happen. It was only a matter of when. So did we have a plan in place for when the inevitable occurred? Of course we did, Carlos, that's what the NYCOD does: It prepares. That's how these things work. Stay ahead of the game and you rule the planet. Come unprepared and the world will fuck your face and shit in your soul."

"Is that what it says on your gravestone?" Botus chuckles mildly and I start getting antsy. "So you want me to..."

"Set up in RD 17 and lay some preliminary groundwork for an incoming squadron of soulcatchers. It's gonna be a hazy mess in there, kid, and I'd like things to be a little ready for our boys when they show up. Minimize damages, if you know what I mean. You start tomorrow. Phoebus here will be your partner."

My what? I gape at Botus for a full three seconds before recovering. "My what?"

But the matter's closed. The Chairman has already immersed

himself in some other paperwork and Phoebus is hovering eagerly beside me.

§

I'm heading back towards Bushwick, running through all the reasons why the Phoebus thing is a wack disaster. Number one on the list is Jimmy. Jimmy's a high school kid, my friend Victor's cousin. A freakish incident with a granny and some soul-eating porcelain dolls a couple months back left him able to see afterlifers. He's not half-dead like me but he's definitely another uneasy interloper between two worlds and I've taken him under my wing to thank him for making my unusual status that much less lonely.

But with winky little Phoebus tagging along, I'll have to explain why I'm bringing a live teenager around in flagrant disregard for the most basic NYCOD protocol: Stay the fuck away from the living. Whatever, I'll figure it out.

I find Jimmy playing checkers on a little sidestreet off Myrtle Ave. Even sitting down, the kid towers over the table and has to squint through his librarian/Nation of Islam glasses to see the board. He's playing against Gordo, a great big Cubano cat who's down with the living, the dead and probably a whole slew of saints and demons that no one's even heard of yet. Says it has something to do with the music he writes. He plays a mean game of checkers too, and from the look of it he's hammering Jimmy something fierce.

"If this were a real game, like chess," Jimmy is saying when I walk up, "you'd be on the floor beggin' me for mercy."

Gordo is tapping away on a cell phone, which is a startling new addition for him. Whatever it is he's doing must be fascinating, because his eyes are wide and he's grinning like a school kid. When Jimmy prods him, Gordo looks up and triple jumps across the board.

"How is it," I say, pulling up a chair, "that you can be such a freaking wizard at a game as complex as chess and get your ass handed to you in a glorified Connect-4?"

"Who asked you?"

I gank one of Gordo's Malagueñas and light it up. "I need you both tomorrow." Gordo raises an eyebrow but keeps his concentration on the board.

"What you got?" Jimmy asks.

I explain more-or-less the situation, eliminating the part

where I had to ask what Phantom Overload is.

Gordo's looking interested when I finish. "This ghost bus—she just disappeared? She estopped coming completely?"

"Apparently. Maybe it's on strike. The little irate Mexican Silvan said he'd try to arrange a meeting for us tomorrow with the ghost bus driver but it wasn't a guarantee."

"Silvan García?" Gordo says. "He's Ecuadorian."

Figures my oversized living friend would know more about my assignment than I do. "Either way," I say, "he's already given me the dirty eye 'cause Botus did his poor Hispanic communities routine and now I look like Malinche again."

Gordo lets out a long sigh. "One day, Carlos, I am going to kill your boss." It's not an idle threat but he'll probably have to wait in line.

"Who's Malinche?" Jimmy asks.

"The chick that helped a couple white guys on horses take down the whole Aztec empire," I say. Jimmy looks crestfallen. "Or got kidnapped and forced into being a historical scapegoat, more than likely."

Gordo looks very sad all the sudden. "It is always easier to blame one of our own."

"Oh and there's more," I say. "They stuck me with a partner. Some doofy little guy named Phoebe or something."

"Phoebe's a girl's name," Jimmy informs me.

"Either way, I want you to tag along. Should be an interesting mess. We'll work it out with the partner. Gordo, can you mingle around Fulton while we meet with Silvan, see what you can find out?"

Gordo nods and then jumps Jimmy's last two checkers.

"Fuckassshit."

Gordo just chuckles: "Should've stuck with basketball."

§

"Who's that?" Phoebus wants to know when I show up to meet him with Jimmy in tow. It's the beginning of a beautiful breezy spring night. The whole world seems to be milling pleasantly about under the Fulton Street train tracks. It's gametime and gossip hour outside the bakeries, dollar stores and beauty salons of East New York. I'm in another weirdly chipper mood but I don't let it show; instead I get up in Phoebus's face.

"Listen, partner," I say real slow and menacing, "I'm glad you have the protocol book memorized and got good grades in the academy, but now you're in the streets and it's a different game." Okay, I got the speech from a cop flick I was watching the night before, but it translates pretty well. "Now we gonna play by my rules. Got it?"

"Got it," Phoebus mumbles. "But who's that?"

"That's Jimmy," I say. "He's my trainee. And he's coming with us."

"Nice to meet you," Jimmy says, smiling down at Phoebus.

"He can see me?" The new guy is scandalized.

I'm about to spit out some other slick line I had memorized when I notice it: With the coming dusk, the ghosts have floated gradually out into the streets and there's hundreds and hundreds of them. More ghosts than people. Phantom Overload. What's more, they're bustling about and interacting with the living like it's just the way things are supposed to be. I'm rendered speechless for a few seconds. It's disturbing but strangely beautiful too. My first instinct is to leave Phoebus and Jimmy behind and go for a jaunty stroll down a street where for once, the two disparate halves of me happily cohabitate.

"This is all highly irregular," Phoebus sputters. I can tell from Jimmy's awed face he's as entranced as I am. But there's business to be taken care of. Several battalions of soulcatchers are gearing themselves up and will soon be on the way to wreak havoc on this quiet intermingling. And we still have no idea what's going on.

"Phoebe," I say.

"Phoebus."

"Phoebus, keep an eye on things over here. I'm going to meet Silvan and the bus driver at the abandoned lot."

"We're not—uh—we're not supposed to split up."

"And yet: Off I go."

"Oh."

I almost feel bad, but then I remember that Phoebus is just a feeble extension of Botus. Sympathy dissolves into disdain. Much better. Jimmy and I walk off towards the lot.

§

"Turns out you're not Mexican," I tell Silvan when we reach the top of the trash-strewn hill where he's waiting for us. "You're Ecuadorian."

"I know," says Silvan. "But you fucking Dominicans can't tell the difference."

"I'm fucking Puerto Rican."

"I know that too."

So a little Latin to Latin humor is not the way to start things out. Live and learn. The bus driver and Jimmy are looking uncomfortably back and forth between me and Silvan.

"Um—con permiso," The bus driver ventures timidly. He's a tall, round ghost with big bulgy eyes and three days of stubble. His beat up old van idles a few feet away. "You think we could get down to business? I can't stay long."

"I'll be brief," I say. "I don't know what the problem is, sir—"

"Esteban Morales, from Michoacán." The bus driver's wide eyes dance across the abandoned lot like shivering searchlights.

"Señor Morales, The New York Council of the Dead has been anxious for any excuse to kick some Remote District ass. Now, I for one, don't want that to happen, and I don't think Mr. Silvan here does either, ornery bastard though he might be, but believe me when I tell you they are on their way and it won't be pretty. So, Esteban, please, tell us what it will take to get you to start collecting the dead again."

"No," Esteban says. "No se puede."

"What do you mean, 'no se puede?'"

"It means it can't be done," Silvan says.

"I know that," I growl. "I mean why not?"

"It's that the dead won't let me take them because they aren't from my jurisdiction. They're not from here. They're our people but they're from faraway."

Immigrant dead? That in its own right isn't so unusual—when you die and get carted off you can turn up any damn place or nowhere at all. Thing is, it's really not up to you and you certainly can't go moving from place to place in packs. You're basically stuck in whatever city or township you pop up in. At least, in the States that how it works...

"It seems," Silvan says, "that several communities around Latin America have figured out how to travel in the afterlife."

"And they've come to be with their families?" Jimmy blurts out. "That's sweet!"

"It is sweet," Silvan nods, "but unfortunately it is also an untenable situation. Resources are running dry. Overcrowding has become the constant state. We are quickly approaching critical point."

All this terminology is getting on my nerves. I'm about to say something slick about it when I notice a rustling motion at the foot of our trashy hill. A crowd of ghosts is waiting down there, glaring icily towards us. Their wraith clouds wave gently like drying laundry in the evening breeze. They look pissed.

"We're not leaving," a tall gangly ghost calls out from the crowd. "Never leaving. Not by force and not by choice. And not in the damn bus."

Esteban takes his cue and makes himself scarce. The ghost bus leaves a puff of exhaust behind as it sputters off into the night. Jimmy is suddenly very anxious. I can feel his jitters sparkling around him like eager fireflies. The crowd of ghosts hovers up the hill.

I take a step towards them. "Look, I'm from the Council but I hear where you're coming from. I don't want this to get messy."

"Then get out of here, güey, and take your Council goons. We've come this far to be with our families. We're not going nowhere." A general hoorah goes up. As the ghost mob starts to clutter closer around us I notice most of them are carrying chains and clubs.

"The Council goons are coming regardless of what I tell them to do," I say. As if to prove my point, the mournful battle howl of the approaching soulcatchers rings out in the night air. It's not a comforting sound. "They wanted an excuse to get in this place and you've all given them one. I know you want to be with your people, but all you're doing is putting the ones you love in danger."

"You really believe that mierda, compadre?" the tall gangly one demands. He steps a few feet out of the crowd. He has a scraggily black beard and eyes that keep rolling in different directions. An epic adventure is scrawled in tatts over his translucent skin. Jimmy takes a step behind me, but surely his skinny-ass moose head is poking out well above mine.

"We are happy here!" gangly says, to more uproarious applause.

"Tell 'em, Moco! ¡Dile la verdad!" someone yells. "¡Sí se puede!"

"No," I say. "No se puede. Something must not've been working out because..." I have to stop mid-sentence. My mind is suddenly too busy working things out to bother making my mouth move. "Silvan!" I say quietly. "Jimmy, where's Silvan?"

"Dunno, Carlos."

I whirl around but the slippery instigator has vanished. And here I was thinking I was the Malinche.

"Your representative is the one you need to talk to, people," I announce. "García went to the Council begging for help. Probably received a pretty payoff from it too. The wheels are in motion now though, there's no stopping it. You have to clear out."

"We'll crush the Council!" Moco yells, his eyes boggling wildly. Another hoorah goes up.

It's getting to be time to leave. I back up a few steps to position myself behind a rusted-out refrigerator. At the edge of the field I see my new partner Phoebus at the head of a group of armored soulcatchers. He looks different, Phoebus. His whole demeanor has changed—he's floating upright instead of in the usual cowering posture. Also, he's yelling out orders. But I don't even get a chance to think it all through because then Moco spots the soldiers.

"¡Compadres!" he hollers. "Let's kill the insolent pigfuckers!" Doesn't take much poetry to rile up a bloodthirsty crowd. The angry ghosts rush towards the edge of the lot, chains and clubs swinging wildly above their heads. At a command from the newly non-doofy Phoebus, the soulcatchers jump into a defensive position: a solid wall of impenetrable supernatural armor. It looks fierce, but some of those boys are pissing themselves with fear. The mob moves as one—they surge suddenly up into the air above the lot and come crashing down on the heads of the waiting soulcatchers like a damn tsunami wave.

You can see right off the bat it's not going well for the COD boys. Armed with the superior numbers, the fury of the righteous and those nasty clubs and chains, the mob is laying a solid beating on the dozen or so soulcatchers. Three fellows in straw hats have cornered a soldier and are laying into him with their clubs—I hear him screaming in agony as the blows pierce through his armor and shred his translucent cloud. Moco storms through the melee, his chain whipping in a vicious circle above his head. The thrill of victory is in his stride, a casual overconfidence that I know well.

"What you wanna do?" Jimmy says behind me.

"This whole damn situation is starting to feel like one big setup, kid."

"Silvan?"

"Definitely in on it, somehow. I don't like it. Feel like a damn pawn and I'm not even sure whose."

"Can we go?"

I realize Jimmy's trembling. It wasn't so long ago he was having his living soul torn out by those American Girl dolls, so I can see where he'd be a little hesitant about the vicious battle raging a few feet away. "You go head, kid. I have to see this one through."

"'salright," he says, fixing his mouth into a determined frown. "You stay I stay." Not bad. "You got a plan?"

"Nope. Gotta see what happens next."

§

The fighting has scattered out into the streets now and it sends a vicious whirlwind of combat swirling beneath the tracks. The few living folks walking by recognize something wrong and take cover in shops and behind cars. Seems the soulcatchers have rallied some: They've slashed a few mob members into tattered ghost shards that lie motionless on the pavement. Suddenly Phoebus rears up above the fighting. I'm still stunned by his transformation from dweeb to superghost. "If you won't heed the Council," he calls out over the din of battle, "perhaps you haven't fully understood what is at risk to you and your loved ones." Jeering and shouts from the crowd as a few objects fly up towards him. Undeterred, my deceptive partner nods at four of his men and they immediately detach from their adversaries and bee-line it into one of the storefront churches.

"Stop them!" Moco hollers. But the soulcatchers have already returned out onto the street, each wrapped around a living, breathing, screaming person. The fighting, the yelling, the sound of weapons tearing into dead flesh: Everything stops. The angry mob is suddenly very quiet as they turn and stare at the hostages—two middle-aged women, a guy in his twenties and a fourteen year old girl...

"That's my granddaughter!" an aging guajiro ghost yells, throwing down his club and stepping forward.

"And my nephew, Alex!" calls out another.

"¡Mi hija!" screams a middle-aged ghost as she rushes forward.

"I thought the NYCOD wasn't supposed to fuck with the living!" Jimmy whispers.

"They're—we're not." I realize now I'm trembling. For all the chaos, everything's still feeling like it's playing out according to some heinous plan. "Someone high up must've given them the authority to…" Nothing is what it seems. I already knew that but apparenly I have to learn again and again. I'm getting ready to hole up for an extended hostage negotiation when the four soulcatchers wrap their arms around their hostages' faces like cellophane. I think the crowd is just too stunned to react in time: After about five seconds of squirming each living human goes limp and then sprawls out lifelessly on the pavement.

The crowd surges forward en masse, toppling the four soulcatchers and instantly tearing two of them to shreds. I hear Jimmy throwing up behind me. In the chaos of it all though, I notice the remaining COD soldiers jump into motion and sprint away from the fray. "Now that you see what we will do to your beloved families," Phoebus yells at the crowd, "maybe you'll rethink sticking around. We're pulling back, but not for long. Regroup yourselves and come to your senses, rebels!" The soulcatchers pour out of the shops and salons, each wrapped around a struggling human, and fall back towards the abandoned lot that Jimmy and I are hiding in.

"Get out of here, now!" I whispershout at Jimmy, who's trying to spit the last bits of vomit out of his mouth. He stands but just stares past me, eyes wide. "Go!" I say. "Not the time to be all heroic, kid, just get out!" He's still not moving, just staring. Finally, I turn around to see what he's looking at.

"They've got Gordo," he says. And it's true.

§

The Council soulcatchers are all in a tizzy as they retreat up the hill towards us. They're young, barely older than Jimmy, and by the look of their crisp, unstained uniforms and shiny helmets, brand new recruits. A few of them are injured, limbs hanging useless at their sides. Whatever plan is in place, these kids were clearly kept far out of the loop. Gordo walks calmly along with his fatigued captor. He's trying to appear unimpressed but is probably terrified. Or maybe I'm projecting.

I grab Jimmy roughly around the neck and throw him on the ground as they walk up. A couple of the boys I've seen before come running up to me. "Where you been, Carlos?" a kid named Dennis asks.

"Yes, Agent Delacruz," Phoebus says, eyeing Jimmy. "Where have you been?"

"Infiltrated the rebel mob," I say. "And I took a hostage of my own while I was at it."

"We're not really gonna kill these ones too, are we?" Dennis says. You can hear a quiver of fear in his voice. A few of the hostages are sobbing.

"We can't!" another one yells. "The mob'll tear us to pieces! This is crazy!"

"Everyone shut up," Phoebus snaps. "You're soldiers, soulcatchers. You will not show fear. You will not retreat or give up, ever. Understand?"

"But you knew they would rush in on our guys when you had them kill those hostages, didn't you?" Dennis demands. "You did that on purpose."

"It's not for you to question my decisions," Phoebus says. He's seething with restrained rage. "Now, everyone fall into line and shut up." There's a few murmurs of frustration and the soldiers fall into a tense kind of quiet. Shouldn't take much to rile 'em back up though.

"I heard the mob is planning an ambush," I say. "There was a few lurking around here I had to deal with before you guys showed up, but a couple got away. They're probably crawling all over this place by now."

"Oh shit oh shit oh shit," one of the soulcatchers starts chanting.

"What's the matter, Tyler?"

"I thought I saw something move over there by that old car!"

"Where?"

"By the car, asshole, by the fucking car!"

"Wait!" I yell pointing at some random spot in the dark lot. "What's that over there?" Everyone turns and gapes into the emptiness.

"This is fucked up," someone says.

"Calm down!" Phoebus yells. "Everyone calm the fuck down!" I suppress a chuckle.

"Listen," I say. "I have orders from Botus. Everyone is to remain here with the prisoners. Phoebus and I are gonna go politick with the rebels and see what we can work out to end this mess peacefully." A general murmur of approval rises from the soldiers.

"Now now," Phoebus stutters, "let's not be rash. Let the fools have a moment to discuss..."

"Every moment more we give them is a moment they have to

plan another attack," I say. "Rebels love ambushes."

"He's right!" Tyler declares. "Go now!"

"It's true," says Dennis. "Wrap this shit up quick."

I start walking down the hill. "You coming?" I can feel Phoebus's furious glare on the back of my head as I hobble down the hill on my cane. He growls and then floats after me, frowning.

"How quickly your young friend went from student to hostage," Phoebus muses when we round a corner onto a quiet residential block. By way of an answer I pull the blade out of my cane and swipe at him. He hurls himself away just a split second too late and I hack a sliver of cold cloud off him. Before I can swing again, he's on me, icy hands wrapped around my neck, cool breath on my face. I push forward against him, throwing us into a brick wall. Phoebus loosens his grip just long enough for me to shove him off and stumble backwards a few steps. I raise my blade. "Alright, Phoebus—or should I say Chairman Phoebus?"

He pulls his own blade out and grunts with irritation.

"You can act, I'll give you that," I say. "Definitely had me convinced you were just a sniveling little new guy. But why bother? You could've just waltzed in as is and torn shit up."

"But you see, we don't trust you, Carlos." His voice seethes with hatred. "We wanted to see what you'd do. Keep an eye on you. For the plan to proceed, it had to be kept completely secret."

"Even from the youngins you got doing the dirty work."

He lunges forward, blade first, and I parry off the attack and sidestep out of the way. The Chairman is panting heavily now.

"What I want to know," he says, "is are you just a renegade dickhead or are you working for someone?"

"Too many questions," I say, making like I'm going to swipe at him again. When he goes to block I stab forward instead, catching him right in the core of his long silvery body. Chairman Phoebus howls and stumbles, forcing the blade deeper into himself and pinning us both back against the brick wall. Higher ups are usually crap at one-on-one combat.

"You can't...kill me," he gasps and for a second I'm afraid he might mean that literally. Did the bastard figure out some slick supernatural way not to die again? But then he finishes his thought: "...I'm a Chairman..."

"Guess now there's only six," I say, pulling out my blade. He's oozing out all over, his flickering corpse now a dead weight draped over me. Don't know if I'll ever be able to shower enough to get that feeling away. I heave him off me as his whole body sheds itself into a mess of tattered ghost flesh.

The angry mob has transformed itself into a confused support group when I find them huddled in a storefront church. A few of the ghosts are sobbing inconsolably while others pat them on their heaving backs. Moco is walking in anxious circles, trying to rile folks up again.

"Listen up," I say, walking into the dusty church, "we can end this now. It's only gonna get worse if we don't." I send Moco a piercing stare, which isn't easy the way his damn eyes keep boggling, but he seems to take my point and stays quiet. "I can tell you that any battle that comes after this won't go well for you, and it'll go even worse for your loved ones. It's not a threat—I didn't know it was going to go down like that tonight, and I'm sorry it did." Ghosts are looking up at me with sorrow and fear in their eyes. "I know you just came here to be with your families, to carry on in an afterlife that's harmonious with the living. And believe me," I had been in let's-clean-this-mess-up mode but I'm suddenly choking over my words, "I want as much as any of you to see that happen, here in New York." They believe me. Even I believe me. I guess it's 'cause it's true, but still—I'm startled. "But it's not time yet. There's more work to be done. Foundations to be laid. I dealt with the dickhead that ordered your living relatives to be murdered." A cautious hurrah rises from the mourning ghosts, startling me again. "But I'm going to have to say that you did it so I can keep working things from the inside." That seems to be alright with everyone.

"You can't stay here in RA 17 though, you have to scatter." More nods and whispers. "Moco and I are going to go back to the Council soulcatchers and work out the arrangements."

§

"What do you mean they killed Phoebus?" Botus is livid, which means somewhere an angel is getting head. "I don't understand. Which one of them? We have to exact revenge!"

"Well, that won't actually be so easy. He was kind of torn up in the mob, it wasn't like one or the other. And they're all gone now anyway. Scattered."

"What do you mean they're all gone?"

"Isn't that what we wanted?" I'm trying so hard not to smile that it actually hurts. "Phantom Overload no more. Situation remedied. Voilà. A few of them lit out for Mexico I think. Shame about Phoebe though."

"I don't understand," Botus says again.

I light a Malagueña and exhale thick plumes of smoke into his office. "My full report's on your desk, sir. Just had one more question."

Botus barely looks up. "Eh?"

"Where might I find Silvan García?"

§

It's another beautiful afternoon. My mark is hovering in a quiet reverie on the walking path that winds alongside the Belt Parkway, not far from the Verazzano Bridge to Staten Island. Perhaps he's contemplating the sun sparkling on the water or the way the lapping of waves contrasts with the rushing traffic. Either way, he's about to get sliced.

I come up quietly, trying but failing, always failing, not to look too sketchy. Standing by a tree on this twinkly spring day with my long trench coat and walking stick. There's something definitely off about that guy, the joggers are thinking, where's his spandex and toothy grin? Why no headband or fanny pack?

I'm just biding my time, waiting for a break in the constant stream of exercise dorks so I can make my move. When it comes I take one step forward before a thick, warm hand wraps around my arm. It's Gordo, looking cheery as always but a little worse the wear after his harrowing hostage experience. I already apologized too many times to him for that and he's already swatted away each one jauntily, so I just nod at him. "What are you doing here, papa?"

"I am estopping you."

"What you mean?"

"Not this one. This one is not for you."

"Gordo, if it wasn't for this asshole…"

"Yo sé lo que hizo. And it doesn't matter." His hand is extremely strong and me tussling with a fat old guy would not be a good look right now. "It's not right and you know it's not right."

I'm about to argue with him when I realize he has a point. Ending García gets us nowhere and risks blowing my cover. It was Botus, after all, that told me where to find him. The trail would lead right back to me. All I'm left with is 'but I want to' and that's obviously not going to get me anywhere. "It is always easier," Gordo says, "to blame one of our own."

I shrug my acceptance and Gordo cautiously releases his hold on my arm. We turn together, away from the water, away from Silvan and my useless vengeance schemes, and begin walking back into Brooklyn. "You are coming tonight?" Gordo wants to know.

"Wouldn't miss it."

§

Six mojitos deep, I stumble towards the counter honey. Around me, the living and the dead are bopping up and down together to the sacred and sexy rhythms coming from Gordo's motley crew of musicians. Even a few of the soulcatchers showed up, including Dennis and Tyler, which I found kinda touching once I was drunk enough not to be eeked out by it. Moco is dancing up a storm towards the front, apparently in a world all to himself. The music is pounding and relentlessly beautiful. It strips us, if only for this night, of all inhibitions and traumas.

The counter honey's making eyes at me. I think. She's smiling even. Maybe at me. I'm not so sloppy yet, just have a little extra swing to me. I've been watching her and she's not fazed by the ghosts. The bar must be its own little Remote District—outside the Council's grasp, free of the fears and taboos of the living.

"What's your name?" I say, careful not to slur.

"Melissa." It's a little plain for how pretty she is, but I don't mind.

"It's a little plain for how pretty you are." Oops. She looks me dead in the eye and then laughs.

"You don't like to touch people?" she says, still burrowing her gaze right through me. "We're Latin, man. We touch. Get with it."

"I know, I know," I say, putting a hand to my face. "It's that, I'm...I'm like them." I nod at the ceiling, where a few adolescent ghosts are grinding their crotches into each other in anxious imitation of adulthood.

"What, a horny teenager?"

"No!" Ah, she's laughing again. She also touches her hair, which my best friend Riley once told me means she wants me to eat her ass. I manage to keep that insight to myself though. "No, I'm partially slightly dead. I died. But I came back."

"Ah." She nods knowledgably, like customers tell her that all the time. "That's cool."

It is? I mean, I knew it was, to me anyway, and to my dead friends, and to Jimmy, who's gawking at me rudely from a few barstools away, but I never thought it was alright to someone like Melissa. Someone pretty. "I don't know how I died though. Or how old I am." I put my hand on the bar and squint up at nothing in particular, trying to look thoughtful.

Melissa reaches over, in this room full of stunning music and the pulsating, celebrating bodies of the living and the dead, and puts her hand on mine.

# BRYAN THAO WORRA
## Dead End in December

When you leave me, don't think
You've truly gone.
You're fastened to too many gluons
And neurons, anchored to this gray
Beneath bone between wood and wave.

Don't believe you're some seagull.
You haven't wings.

Sitting by the seaside, these planks
Of ancient piers,
Let those ships sail on without you.
You try to live like everyone else.
You try to mind your business.
You get married; you have your children.
But you will return.
Whether from Yoharneth-Lahai,
Antarctica, Pakse, some Plutonian bay,
The call is deep, relentless,
Your true fate an old cobblestone
Set in place, long ago,
When we first began to howl together,
Pledging faith from the same shadows.

## The Deep Ones

From the sea we come,
From the sea we come,
Our mouths the inns of the world.
The salt of the earth unwelcome
At the tables and charts of
Explorers who expect:
Commodity and pliant territory.
Kingdoms, not wisdom.
Blood, not heaven's children.
We grow with uncertain immortality
At the edge not made for man,

Bending, curving, humming cosmic.
Awake and alien.

Our mass a dark and foaming mask,
A bed of enigma to certain eyes,

One with the moon,
One with the stars,
One with the ash that whispers history.

In the same breath as myth and gods
Whose great backs yawn before us,

As we change with a growing tongue,
Growling amid the dreamlands
We built one blade, one leaf, one golden wall at a time.

# INDRAPRAMIT DAS
# muo-ka's Child

Ziara watched her parent, muo-ka, curl up and die, like an insect might on Earth.

muo-ka was a giant of a thing, no insect. Ziara was the one who'd always felt like an insect around it. Its curled body pushed against the death shroud it had excreted in its dying hours, the membrane stretched taut against rigid limbs. She touched the shroud. It felt smooth but sticky. Her fingertips stuck lightly to it, leaving prints. It felt different from her clothes. muo-ka had excreted the ones she wore a month ago. They smelled softer than the death shroud, flowers from Earth on a distant, cosmic breeze. She raised her fingers to her face, touching them with her tongue. So salty and pungent it burned. She gagged instantly, coughing to stop herself retching.

"muo-ka," she said, throat thick. "You are my life." Ziara thought about this. "You *are* my life, here." She meant these words, but felt a hollow, aching relief that muo-ka's presence was gone.

She closed her eyes to remember the blue rind of Earth, furred with clouds, receding behind the glass as she drifted into amniotic sleep. Orphan. Volunteer. Voyager. A mere twenty years on that planet. When she had opened her eyes after the primordial dream of that year of folding space, the first thing she saw and felt was muo-ka pulling her from the coma, breaking open the steaming pod with predatory lurches. Its threaded knot of limbs rippling like a shredded banner in the sweltering light, stuck on the leviathan swell of its dark shape. She had opened her mouth, spraying vomit into the air, lazy spurts that moved differently than on Earth. muo-ka had pulled her out of the pod and towards it, its limbs sometimes whiplashes, sometimes articulated arms, flickering between stiffness and liquid softness so quickly it hurt her eyes to see that tangled embrace. Stray barbed limbs tugged and snapped at the rubbery coil of her umbilicus, ripping it off so pale shreds clung to the valve above her navel.

muo-ka had grasped at Ziara's strange, small, alien body, making her float in the singing air as she tried and tried to scream.

§

Ziara watched the shroud settle over muo-ka. Already the corpse had shrunk considerably as air and water left it. Its body whistled softly. A quiet song for coming evening. With a bone knife, she cut small slits into the shroud to let the gas escape more freely, even though the membrane was porous. The little rents fluttered. A breeze ruffled the flat waters of the eya-rith basin into undulations that lapped across muo-ka's islet, washing Ziara's bare feet and wetting the weedy edges of the stone deathbed. The water sloshed in the ruined shell of the pod at the edge of the islet, its sleek surfaces cracked and scabbed with mossy growth. Inside was a small surveying and recording kit. She had discovered the kit, sprung free of its wall compartment, shattered and drowned from the rough landing. Even if it had worked, it seemed a useless thing to her now.

When the pod had once threatened to float away, Ziara had clung to it, trying to pull it back with her tiny human arms, heaving with frantic effort. muo-ka had lunged, sealed the wreck to the islet with secretions. Now it stood in a grassy thatch of fungal filaments, a relic from another planet.

muo-ka had no spoken words. Yet, its islet felt quieter than it had ever been. Ziara had learned its name, and some of its words, by becoming its mouth, speaking aloud the language that hummed in a part of its body that she had to touch. It had been shockingly easy to do this. What secret part of her had muo-ka unlocked, or taught to wake? muo-ka's skin had always felt febrile when she touched it, and when it spoke through her she felt hot as well.

The first thing it had said through her mouth was "muo-ka," and she had known that was its name. "Ziara," she had said, still touching it. "Jih-ara," it had said in her mouth, exuding a humid heat, a taste of blood and berries in her head. Ziara had disengaged her palm with a smack, making it shiver violently. Clammy with panic, she had walked away. It had felt too strange, too much like becoming a part of muo-ka, becoming an organ of its own.

Ziara rarely spoke to muo-ka in the time that followed. When she got an urge to communicate, she'd often stifle it. And she did get the urge, again and again. In those moments she'd hide in the broken pod on the islet's shore. She'd curl into its clammy, broken womb and think of the grassy earth of the hostel playground, of playing catch with her friends until the trees darkened, of being reprimanded by the wardens, and smoking cigarettes by the barred moonlight of the cavernous bathrooms, stifling coughs into silent giggles when patrols came by. Daydreams of their passing footsteps would become apocalyptic with the siren wail of muo-ka's cries. It never could smell or detect her in the strange machinery of the wrecked pod. She assumed the screams were ones of alarm.

"You've fed me," Ziara said to the corpse. "And clothed me. And taught me to leap across the sky." Those stiffened limbs that its shroud now clung to had snatched her from the air if she leaped too high, almost twisting her shoulders out of their sockets once. She'd landed on the mud of the islet safe, alive. In the shadow of muo-ka she'd whispered "Fuck you. Just, fuck you. Fuck you, muo-ka."

She had tasted the sourness of boiled fruit at the back of her throat. muo-ka covered the sky above her, and offered one of its orifices. Gushing with the steam of regurgitate cooked inside it. She'd reached inside and took the scorching gumbo in her hands. The protein from dredged sea and air animals tasted like spongy fish. It was spiced with what might have been fear.

§

Ziara didn't have an exact idea of how long it had been since muo-ka had pulled her into the air of this world from the pod. She had marked weeks, months and years on a rock slick with colonies of luminescent bacteria. Left a calendar of glowing fingerprints that she had smeared clean and then restarted at the end of every twelve months, marking the passing years with long lines at the top. She had three lines now. They glowed strongest at dusk. If they were right, they told her she was twenty-four years old now. muo-ka had been her parent for three years.

Not that the number mattered. Days and years were shorter here. muo-ka had always lingered by that rocky calendar of fingerprints, hovering over it in quiet observation when it thought she wasn't looking, when she was off swimming in the shallows. Watching from afar in the water, she could always taste an ethanol bitterness at the back of her throat and sinuses. A taste she came to associate with sadness, or whatever muo-ka would call sadness.

muo-ka had never washed the calendar clean. It had never touched it. It had only ever looked at that glimmering imprint of time mapped according to a distant world invisible in the night sky. The dancing fingertips of its incredible child.

§

The evening began to cast shadows across the shallow seas. Across the horizon, uong-i was setting into mountains taller than Everest and Olympus Mons. uong-i at this time was the blue of a gas flame on a stove, though hot and bright. Sometimes the atmosphere would tint it green at dawn and dusk, and during the day it was the white of daylit snow. But now it was blue.

Ziara touched muo-ka's shroud again. It was drier, slightly more tough as it wrapped around the contours of the moaning, rattling body. She lit the flares by scratching them on the mossed rocks. The two stalks arced hot across the water, sparks dancing across her skin. She plunged them into the soil by the deathbed.

Her eyes ached with the new light. Again, she remembered her first moment with muo-ka, remembered her panic at the thing ensnaring her in blinding daylight. The savagery with which it severed her umbilicus, the painful spasming of its limbs around her. She remembered these things, and knew muo-ka had been in as much panic as she had. She had long since realized this, even if she hadn't let it sink in.

From her first moment here, muo-ka remained a giant, terrifying thing. The days of recovery in the chrysalid blanket it wove around her. She'd been trapped while it smothered her with boiling food from its belly, trying and failing to be gentle. Fevers raging from nanite vaccines recalibrating her system, to digest what her parent was feeding her and breathe the different air, the new soup of microbes. "Stop," she would tell muo-ka. "Please stop. I can't eat your food. I'm dying." But it would only clutch her cocooned body and tilt her so she could vomit, the ends of its limbs sharp against her back. It would continue feeding her, keep letting her shit and piss and vomit in that cocoon, which only digested it all, preventing any infections.

Sure enough, the fevers faded away and one day the cocoon came off in gummy strips. Ziara could move again, could move like she had on Earth. At first it was an aching crawl, leaving troughs in the rich mud of the islet. But she'd balled that mud in her fists and growled, standing on shaking legs. She watched her human shadow unfurl long across the silty islet, right under the eclipsing shape of muo-ka above her, its limbs whipping around her, supporting her until she shrugged them off.

How to Live on Other Planets

Ziara had laughed and laughed, to be able to stand again, until phlegm had gathered in her throat and she had to spit in joy. So she walked, walked over this human stain she had left on the ground, walked over the wet warmth of muo-ka's land. She walked until she could run. She was so euphoric that she could only dance and leap across the basin, flexing her muscles, testing her augmented metal bones in this low gravity. Sick with adrenalin, she soared through the air, watching the horizon expand and expand, bounding from rock to rock, whipping past exoskeletal flying creatures that flashed in the sun. muo-ka watched, its leviathan darkness suddenly iridescent. Then Ziara stood in one place panting, and she screamed, emptied her lungs of that year of deep sleep through a pierced universe. She screamed goodbye to the planet of her first birth. As this unknown sound swept across the basin, muo-ka's limbs glittered with barbs that it flung into itself.

Ziara nodded at this memory. "muo-ka. Leaping? You taught me to walk," she said with a smile.

§

She had avoided muo-ka's oppressive presence by hiding in the pod. She would shit and piss, too, under the shade of the tilted wreck, in its rain of re-leaked tidal water. When she didn't want the smallness of the pod, she slipped into the basin's seas, walked across the landbridges and glittering sandbars to swirling landscapes of rock and mud fronded with life-colonies that clung like oversized froth. But always her parent would be looming on the horizon, its hovering shape bobbing over the water, limbs alternating in a flicker over the surface as it dredged for food. Sometimes it would soar over her in the evening, its blinking night eyes flickering lights, stars or aircraft from the striated skies of Earthly dusks. With those guiding lights it would lead her back to the islet. Her throat would throb in anger and frustration, at the miles of watery, rocky, mountainous horizon she couldn't escape, but she'd know that straying far would likely mean she'd be killed by something on land or sea that was deadlier than her.

It took her a while to have her first period on the planet, because of the nanite vaccine calibrations and the shock of acclimatisation. All things considered, it hadn't been her worst. But she had recognized the leaden pain of cramps immediately, swallowed the salty spit of nausea and gone to the pod again. She'd squatted under it and bled into the unearthly sea.

Looking at that, she'd wondered what she was doing. Whether she was seeding something, whether she was changing the ecosystem. She'd felt like an irresponsible teenager. But looking at those crimson blossoms in the waves, she'd also felt a sudden, overwhelming longing. She'd become breathless at the thought that there was nobody else in the world. Not a single human beyond that horizon of seas and mountains and mudflats. Only the unbelievably remote promise that the mission would continue if the unmanned ship that had ejected her pod managed to return to Earth, with the news that the visitation had been successful. Another human might be sent, years later, maybe two if they could manage, hurtling down somewhere on the world with no means of communicating with her. Or a robot probe sent to scour the planet until it found and recorded her impact, just like the first probes that had seeded messages and artifacts to indicate Ziara's arrival.

But at that moment, she was as alone as any human could be. It was conceivable that she might never see a human again. Her eyelids had swollen with tears, and she'd watched her blood fall into the sea. She hadn't been able to see muo-ka from under the pod then. But she'd heard it secreting something, with loud rattling coughs. She'd sat and waited until her legs ached, until the rising tide lapped at her thighs.

Later she'd found fresh, coarse membranes strewn across the ground next to her rock calendar. They were waterproof.

New clothes.

Ziara had wrapped the membranes around herself like a saree, not knowing how else to wear them. She became light-headed when she caught the scent of flowers in them. It was a shocking sensation, a smell she'd never encountered on this world before.

muo-ka had been absent that whole day. When it returned, lights flickering in sunset, she held out her hand. It lurched gracelessly through the air as if caught in turbulence, before hovering down to her, curtaining her in softened limbs. Her palm fell against the familiar spot behind the limbs. She flinched at the heat.

"Thank you," Ziara said.

It said nothing through her, only unfurling, drowning the back of her throat in bloody sweetness.

§

muo-ka had been dying for months. It had told Ziara, in its sparse way, a cloying thick taste of both sweet berried blood and bitterness in her head.

"Sick?" she had asked.

"Sh-ikh," it had said in her mouth. "Ii-sey-na," it said, and when the word formed in her throat she knew it meant "death."

"Sorry," she had whispered.

"Euh-i," it had said. No. Not sorry.

Ziara had let it talk for longer than ever before. For hours, her hand flushed red from its heat. It had told her several words, sentences, that made up an idea of what to do with its dead body. Then it went on, forming concepts, ideas, lengthier than ever before. muo-ka told her many things.

§

Ziara thought about her relief, now, looking at dead muo-ka. It disturbed her, but it was the truth. There was a clarity to her world now. To this world. She would move along the mudflats and sandbridges and mountains. She would make blades of her parent's bones, as it had told her, and explore the world. She would finally go beyond that horizon, which now flared and dimmed with the setting of uong-i.

She was an alien, and the world would kill her, sooner rather than later. Even if by some miracle the second human arrived in the coming months, he'd be too weak to help. If one of the leviathans adopted him—and it would be a man that fell this time—it might even violently keep Ziara away from him as its own child, and she had no chance of fighting that. She knew nothing about the dynamics of this adoption. She was the first, after all. They had come into this without much knowledge, except their curiosity and gentle handling of the initial probes.

Until and unless Earth sent an actual colonization team that could touch down a vessel with equipment and tools on the surface, humans wouldn't be able to survive here without the help of muo-ka's kind. As muo-ka's child, she wondered if she might be able to befriend one of them, or whether she'd be killed in an instant.

Ziara shook her head. It was no point overthinking. She would walk this world, and see what came. She had chosen this, after all. She hadn't chosen her parent, but there it was, in front of her, dead as she was alive. And she was alive because of it.

The blue dome of the gas giant appeared over the horizon, filling the seas with reflections. In the sparking light of the flares, Ziara waited. The shroud had fossilized into a flexible papyrus, with an organic pattern that looked like writing, symbols. The shrunken behemoth finally vented its innards as the stars and far moons appeared in the night sky, behind streaks of radiant aurora. Ziara clenched her jaw and began to scoop the entrails up to give to the sea, as was dignified. For a moment, she wondered what the deaths of these solitary creatures were normally like. She had seen others on the horizons, but always so far they seemed mirages. They lived their lives alone on this world, severed from each other. It had to be the child that conducted the death rites, once it was ready to move on. Perhaps they induced death in themselves once their child was mature enough.

She stopped, recoiling from the mess.

In the reeking slop of its guts, she saw muo-ka replicated. A small muo-ka. But not muo-ka. A nameless one, budded in its leviathan body. It was dead. The child's limbs were tangled in the oily foam of its parent's death. The body was crushed. Her hands slid over its cold, broken form.

muo-ka had budded a child. A child that would have done muo-ka's death rites once it had matured, ready to go on its own.

"Oh," she said, fingers squelching in the translucent mud seeping out of muo-ka's child. "Oh, no. My muo-ka. My dear muo-ka," she whispered, to both corpses.

muo-ka had budded a child, and finding a mature child already ready to venture out into the world, it had crushed the one growing inside it. Only ziara was muo-ka's child.

"You brought me to life," ziara said, leaning in her parent's guts, holding her dead sibling, wrapped in clothes her parent had made. Her face crumpled as she buried it in the remains of muo-ka's life, her body shaking.

§

ziara left her sibling in the sea with muo-ka's guts. Using the bone-knife, she cut away the death shroud carefully and wore it around her shoulders. One day, ziara swore to herself, she would translate the symbols it had excreted on it. Her parent's death letter. She sliced off a part of the deflated hide, scrubbed it in the sea, and wore it as a cowl to keep her head warm during nights. The flares had smoked out. She looked at muo-ka curled dead. It had told her the creatures of the air would come and consume it, slowly, as it should be. She felt bad leaving it there on that stony deathbed, but that was what it had told her to do. She wiped her eyes and face. A bone knife and a whole world she didn't belong in, except right here on this islet.

A fiery line streaked across the sky. A human vessel. Or a shooting star. ziara gazed at its afterimage for a moment, and walked off the islet and across the shallows and mudflats of the basin. She had named that basin once, or muo-ka had, with her mouth.

eya-rith. Earth, so she would not be homesick.

# TINA CONNOLLY
## Turning the Apples

"Getcher cells," says Szo to the streaming tourists. "New world, need a cell, get 'em here."

"Not interested."

"Bought one on the ship."

Szo opens his jacket, reveals a wall of buttons, cornrowed phones. "Come in handy if you get in trouble, mister."

Some local shoves him; fast pecker his age in shiny shoes. "Why doncha leave with the other tourists, foreigner."

Szo can't afford trouble so he ducks his head smiling. When the local goes by he nabs his cashflap. Swore to Mack that he wouldn't, maybe, but that was before six months of taunts. Before it was driven home that honest hawking is a recipe for no food, no cash.

No ticket off.

Hand on his sleeve and he whirls, cell that ain't a cell slicking out a blade, ready to take the thug if he has to. But it ain't no regular thug, it's double-job Jonny and that's bad because the only time Jonny comes to see him nowadays is for Hawk.

"Whazzup?" Szo says, all cool. His hand retracts to his pocket. A likely mark walks by but he can't go, not with Jonny draped and breathing hot on his collar.

"I've got apples in the stockyard," says Jonny. "Fresh."

Apples is code for comabodies, that one percent of off-world tourists that get the infection. They disappear, if Hawk is fast and the crematory's slow. Stockyard is the freight shipyard, that's easy. But he's blocked out what fresh is.

"Got a good gig now," Szo mumbles.

Jonny flicks a cashflap out and it's Szo's. Jonny always was better at lifting than Szo, even back when they were scrawny jerky kids, back before Jonny turned tricks and Szo was just learning to turn minds. "Eighteen bucks offa tourists?" Jonny says. "You know Hawk'll give you two thou for an hour at the stockyard."

"Cells," says Szo to a fat tourist. "Getcher cells."

Jonny slams his hand into Szo's shoulder and there's no knife there but the force of what Jonny holds on Szo. "This ain't a negotiation, boyo," says Jonny. "They're fresh and Hawk's in a lather, he needs what you do. You're the only survivor in the city right now. Stockyard. 3:30."

Then Jonny is gone and Szo is sick to his knees because he's just remembered that fresh means awake and screaming.

§

"The fuck you been?" says Hawk.

It's 3:31, after Szo spent the last hour looking for them. In the moonlight the shipyard is a mountainous dark, the whir of generators vibrates in his ears. It might cover the sound of fresh apples. He tries not to listen.

"Listen, boyo. Turn them for us fast, just like the old days. Jonny says you need the cash."

The problem is Szo's jonesing now. The touch of his mind into the comabodies is something he's tried like hell to forget, but they press into his grey folds like a million firsts with a million new girls, touching his mind with vibrations hot and sweet and fleeting.

He's been clean nearly half a year. So long, too long. The comabodies always come in waves, the wave of tourist season, the wave of Hawk finding new suppliers. There are five propped sitting against a hangar wall, leaning on each other.

They *are* screaming. The worst kind. Hawk's got dirty rags in their mouths, but their cheeks are taut around it. At least someone's closed their eyes, probably Jonny.

"What do you want them for?"

"Never mind that."

Szo shoves hands in pockets. Hawk goes cagey when it's a new venture, never mind that he knows the drill, never mind that he knows he's got Szo over a barrel. "You know fuckall, Hawk. Are they for the waste, the minefield, what? I can't code them right if I don't know what you want them to do."

"Fine," Hawk says. "I need swimmers. I need them to seek out pearls in the sulfur pits where the heat blisters your arms and the gasses belly out your lungs. Rose-colored pearls, each coiled like the belly button of a giant."

Jonny rolls his eyes at Hawk's purple words and the boys grin. For a minute it ain't tight-pants Jonny and weary Szo, for a moment they're two kids playing pickpocket for Hawk and life is sometimes okay. At least they're alive, you know?

That's what Szo always thinks when he first touches the comabodies. At least *I'm* alive. He closes his eyes, savoring the last moment before he gives in. Jonny and Hawk walk away, fade away, and Szo touches the first one on the head and *reaches.*

Szo doesn't think of much while turning; he can't. But in that first moment he thinks of palm trees.

Szo barely remembers his home planet. He and his mom came here when he was four. Despite what she claimed, it wasn't a vacation to the fabled water parks half-a-day south of here, the hot springs and waterfalls that kept tourists coming back. His mom was fleeing her old life. That's something he only pieced together a decade later, he and Jonny flopped on Hawk's couch, high on greensmack.

He doesn't know which planet it was, or what the whole of it was like. All he remembers is a swatch of green grass with a palm tree. Occasionally other things float back; words or faces or sayings. The image of the palm tree is what he calls home, though for all he knows it wasn't even on his planet. Maybe it was something he saw on the ship over. Maybe it was a cardboard palm tree, a carpet of plastic grass and maybe he sat there and waited for his mom to come out of the ship's bar.

He tries all these images on till the palm trees disintegrate in swimming and pearls and pure white nothing, and he still doesn't know.

Last comabody turned and now the five are all turned, ready to dive for pearls for Hawk. Szo's full of buzzing aftermath, his mind panting like he's jizzed all over them. Hawk drops a wad of cash that thunks his shoulder. Sure he grabs it, but it's nothing compared to the fierce relief that floods his brain.

He limps down the long road from the shipyard, blood dripping from a bitten tongue. He thinks he'll avoid the street for a few days, lie low, score some greensmack, anything to take the edge offa wanting to do more apples. Maybe two thou is enough to get him on a ship himself, get him off the planet. If it weren't for Hawk, his past, Szo could stay clean.

It's cold out here in the early morning. The greensmack is quick to come by. The pee stink outside his squats hardly bugs, not while he's all strung on comabodies. If he had another fifty in the alley he'd do them all, but instead he rolls up the greensmack under his tongue and flops on the mattress.

The greensmack makes him sad; it always does. It ain't most punks' drug of choice, but it's Szo's. This time on the greensmack he remembers how he and his mom got infected. The first he knew something was wrong was his mother asleep standing up, pouring whiskey over a mug and onto her hand. She woke up once, and then she fell into a coma. He remembers toddling around the hotel room, before he fell asleep too. His dreams were beautiful, dreams of something orgasmic that was a new sensation at four. Gorgeousness lush and happy, and when he woke, he was sweaty and starving and his mother was flopped on the hotel bed.

Szo can't forgive himself for toddling out to find food, for inadvertently reporting her. Because white blurs of grownups and cots took her away. He traded her for a ham sandwich, that's how he feels, and here and now on the greensmack he cries snot and spits more blood.

That's when the poli comes to his crappy squats, and hauls Szo himself away, still crying like a four-year-old.

They don't even give him a ham sandwich.

At the brick station, Mack stretches and sighs. "Give us the details, Szo. You might as well."

"You already know what's up, why do you want me?" Szo hunches around his knees. There's bits of glass on his pant leg from the shipyard tarmac. He flicks it onto Mack's desk, which Mack ignores.

"We know it's Hawk, we know this supplier. We know it's five or six bodies. We don't know where they're going and jesus Szo, we'd like to track them down. Don't you think your mother would've liked that?"

"Keep talking about her and I won't tell you anything." Truth is, he hates to disappoint Mack. Mack picked him up the first time he was caught. Eight years old and he'd already turned fifty-three bodies for Hawk. Fifty-three because he remembers each one. Mack cleaned him up and got him in a foster home, a decent one where they didn't hit you, but when Hawk came to him with more apples, Szo went straight back.

"I know you've been clean half a year, Szo," says Mack. "I was rooting for you. What's Hawk got on ya that you can't resist?"

"Just the money," Szo lies. "I need to eat, don't I?"

"Join up with us," Mack says. "Help us hunt down the guys like Hawk, rescue other tourist kids who survived and got caught up in this. Don't you wish you'd never known what it was like to touch their minds?"

Of course he does, but so what? "If I worked for you, they wouldn't tell me what they were up to, duh," he says.

Mack rises and cracks his back. Looks out the window at a grungy building a meter away. It's painted red brick like so much of this port city, like a fleeting bright color will slick over decay. "There's a rumor," Mack says, "that a kid like you—except better than you, a fighter—has managed to undo the damage."

Szo's heart pounds so hard he thinks he can't hear Mack. "A-all?"

"All. Wakes them up." Mack's voice does that measured thing. "She says it hurts a bit, but the rush comes later. Like a stalling afore the pleasure." He twirls a pen. "Too bad she's in East Enland—they ain't letting her past their borders for cash nor love. It'd have to be the guy we know here trying it." His eyes catch Szo's.

"To heal them...."

"There'd be cash for each one you turn. From the general missing persons stockpile."

Awake. Alive. Okay.

Szo can't breathe, can't think. Because the hold that Hawk's got on him is his mom, coma-cold and alone and digging waste out in the desert.

§

He hadn't known that Hawk had his mother for a long time. Hawk had been using another kid back in those days. A girl, stranded here. Her parents had been cremated quick; Hawk hadn't gotten them. The girl lasted a few years. Then she tried to wean herself from comabodies with street drugs and lost. That's when Jonny found Szo, his hair and skin a dead alien giveaway.

Getting infected makes your brain rewriteable. Surviving makes you able to rewrite. Not everyone gets it; most natives are immune and even many tourists are. One percent is a low enough number that tourists flock in by the thousands, through the major port city and down south to the waters. The adults that get it are in a coma within 24 hours.

It's only kids who sometimes survive.

By the time Szo saw his mother, he'd turned nineteen minds for Hawk. He remembers the first one particularly, like you remember a first girl or first trick. But he remembers all the others, too. "Don't know why you would," says Jonny. "I don't remember all the men." But Szo does, and he clings to each one, proof that somehow he is not like Jonny, not like Hawk, not like himself. This is all temporary and therefore changeable, rewriteable.

Szo doesn't know if he recognized his mother the moment he saw her. He wants to say yes, but the truth is there was this moment when he saw this smelly, skin-rashed woman and a moment when he saw his mother, and the two seem to be laid on top of each other, vibrating.

§

Five whole days on the streetcorner, and Szo's only made twelve bucks and two fistfights before Jonny comes back.

"Apples at the cellar," says Jonny.

"*In* the cellar," says Szo.

"Fancy words, Hawk," mocks Jonny.

"A cellar is a basement, so if cellar's your code you should say in, not at." He's too eager, and strange words, strange memories, spill forth as he tries to hide his jittery hands. "Cells, getcher cells," he says, turning, aping his former self.

Jonny slugs his ribs, bruising him via the phones in his jacket. "We don't talk about codes," he says, and his breath is sweet with cherrymint. "Midnight." He's gone, whistling through the crowd and Szo pats Mack's wire in his sleeve, pats his ribs. When neither is broken he says "Getcher cells" until Jonny is vanished.

Cherrymint's nice, it floods your mind with sweet and your breath with sugar. But it ain't touching the hot rush of comabodies. It's the drug of choice for people like Jonny, who spend their nights getting it up.

That's a fucked-up job, Szo thinks. Maybe his life sucks sometimes, but he ain't Jonny. Szo's had sex exactly twice, and he doesn't seem to be cut out for it. If he could meet that girl from East Enland he'd ask her what she thinks. Cause for him this thing that everyone wants ain't so great, it's a millionth of what it is to be hot inside the comabodies. It's pale and localized and hardly worth the anxiety. Maybe that girl would know what he means. Maybe the two of them could figure it out together, could trick out their own substitution for the drug they can't resist.

For now it's just one more thing that makes him feel alien and alone on this planet, as much as the grey tint of his skin, the silky texture of hair. He wants a jolt no one else can do or understand, and he doesn't want a joy that fills everyone else.

It touches on his own work, sure. There ain't a big trade in comapussy but there's some, like there is for anything. Szo saw one alone once, a young girl with hair like a cottonball and lipstick smearing off. She was sat down at the corner by some local who teared off in a hurry. She was probably tracked by the pimp; he probably had a detector set to send someone out for her. Too witless to run, and her brains were coded by Szo or someone like Szo.

Szo crept along the alley. She was crooning. Not rocking, not coiled. Limp against the building, singing a song about a sparrow.

He didn't recognize her face. But, checking, slipped his mind in and then was sure he didn't know her, hadn't done her. He was doing her now though, her brain hot against his, slipping through the vibrating folds. She rocked her head back, still singing, staring at the moons.

Szo recoiled then. There was an instant of pause and then he rewrote her. Rewrote her to walk down to the shipyard and stand under a shuttle.

Now, thinking back, he thinks—could I have saved her? Woke her up? No matter how much life sucks sometimes, Szo likes it better than the reverse. He'd a granted that to the woman, too, only back then everyone *knew* comabodies were dead in all but their meat.

At midnight, Szo pats his wire and drops into the cellar. It really is underground—Hawk packs in and out every time he uses it, slipping in and out by dawn. The wire is for Hawk's sake. Hawk knows he's been with Mack a lot, and Szo has never been good at hiding jitters. It's why Jonny is a better pickpocket than he is, and a better trick.

Hawk pulls the wire out of Szo's jacket with a snap, laughs at Szo's expression, and tosses it on the ground. "I'd be mad but you're too lame," he says, and grinds it flat. "Come on, there's apples. Code them for waste."

Szo reaches in and when he touches the first there's all that mad rush of vibrating brain. All that buzzing that usually makes it so easy to code the apple to do what Hawk wants. But now, following Mack's instructions he's going to take out the buzzing.

It takes fumbling. It isn't natural; it's like swimming upstream. Until it clicks, and then every place he feels the buzz that lets him hook in, he reverses it, until the apple drains. The infection he's cutting out, it seems to fill him. It's a horrid *wrong* and he twitches with it, trying to dispel the notion. At last the hook is less and less and Szo has next to nothing to hook into, then nothing and he's locked outside. The apple's eyelids flutter and Szo quick leans down and whispers "Play dead."

The man seems to obey, and Szo quick tries the same reversal on the second, the third, slogging through as his brain tells him it's stuffed with the comabodies' infection. It does hurt, he does want release, but he keeps going. Holding back seems a deserved punishment, Szo almost feels holy with it, which is another word from the past. But before Szo can start the fourth, number two spasms.

"I remember, I remember, I know —" he screams, and Hawk and Jonny come running. Jonny's belt's undone, Szo realizes later. But right now it's all the stupid fat number two, and number three's too twitchy to play dead next to that. Number two runs on shaky legs, yelling for the poli and his wife and Hawk shoots him. Number one stays stiff, but number three bolts and is shot.

"What the hell did you do to them?"

"I dunno, I dunno," whimpers Szo, like he's four again and piss-scared.

Hawk's eyeing Szo, but what distracts him is Jonny says "I know he did it, he did it somehow."

"And how the hell would he do that, huh?" says Hawk and he smacks Jonny upside the head. "Just cause you wish you could do his job instead of your little pervy one. It must be a mutation. You —" and he points into Szo's face—"Figure out how to adapt to this, or you're dead."

He stalks off, and Jonny with a crumpled face hurries after.

Number one's eyes go to him. Szo doesn't know if it's like looking at someone he killed or birthed, but either way he can't stand the intimate touch of the man's eyes. "Back door's past the stairs," he says, and then he hurries out before he can be any more responsible, for anyone.

At the red brick station Szo says: "Two were shot, but. I saved one. It worked," and Mack believes him and hands him cash, just like that. Mack doesn't ask the awkward questions, like what the man's eyes were like or how Szo feels now, stuffed taut and bursting with a mind full of infection. Szo squirrels the cash away with the rest of

Hawk's money.

"Ready to try it again? I've got a lead on four prostitutes we haven't rounded up yet."

"Any time," says Szo, and the thought is fine. If this keeps working, maybe he doesn't have to flee the planet like he longs to. Maybe he could play both sides and come out smelling clean. The thought's a relief, here with his mind still thick with the swarming of the comabodies' infection. There must be some way to let that go, but it hasn't drained yet. But he'll figure that out, he's sure, here with bright hope flickering.

"No time like the present," says Mack, and he shoves his chair back. "Unless you know somewhere else we should go."

Hope floods a crowded brain. "Hawk's taking one to the desert," says Szo.

After Szo found his mom, he started sneaking back to be with her. Not right after a comabodies rush, but two, three days later, when the high had worn off. Then he watched his mother trundle over buried nuclear waste, and didn't know what to feel.

He hated the idea but he tried it anyway: if he can rewrite comabodies, why not rewrite his mom? And so he laid his brain alongside hers though the vibrations were awesome and disgusting. He overlaid her with ideas of mother and son and hugs and palm trees. And when he backed out she bent down and gave his exhausted body a hug. Then trundled back into the waste, scanning with her monitors and smiling on one side of her face. Most miserable thing ever, sent him running straight for Jonny's couch and the greensmack.

But today, he doesn't have to run. Szo says desert and Mack knows right where to go. Waste cleanup is one of the uses for comabodies that the poli don't do anything about; officially it doesn't happen. Few minutes out here isn't going to hurt anyone, and Mack and Szo thread through the few lone figures, past the red-painted bunkhouse, until Szo says "That one."

"Your mother?" says Mack, and Szo stunned, nods.

Mack knows, then. Szo had thought he might, but that Mack hasn't done anything with this knowledge opens up a black wedge between them.

Szo tumbles out of the car, backs away from Mack and towards his mom.

"Don't do it," says Mack. "It's been thirteen years, mate. She's gone."

"How do you know?" says Szo.

"Rumor. That girl like you in East Enland, she couldn't wake 'em up right beyond three years. Their minds were too dead."

"I don't believe you." Maybe this girl is a fantasy, he thinks, a made-up ideal for Mack to prod Szo one way or another.

"I've got the file with her notes. Let me grab it," says Mack, and Szo watches his mother pace the site. She's in that same brown shift and her arms and hands are cracked and red and white. Her bare legs are brown and green. It's like any other day out here, except this day has a different ending.

But there's a whistle behind him, Jonny's. From the bunkhouse.

Szo idles that way, on guard. "What are you doing here?"

"You're in trouble, boyo," says Jonny. "I told Hawk he should punish you but he says you're worth even more to him if you just come back. Or something." He studies Szo and sighs, all the air whooshing from his thin frame. "Is it true you can wake 'em up now?"

Szo nods, and Jonny kind of pats his shoulder, doesn't slug him or arm burn him.

Then Hawk's behind Jonny and he says, "Get your poli back here and I'll kneecap him." He's got a rusting iron bar that he draws up. "We'll take you back, don't worry." There are two comabodies wandering around the bunkhouse, both in those brown shifts. One is so diseased looking Szo assumes he's too far gone to wander around with a monitor, even for an apple. Hawk practice swings. "Is he coming?"

"You're small-time, aren't you?" Szo says. He hadn't realized it, growing up in it, but the constantly shifting locations, the raising young boys like Jonny....

Hawk swings at him, but he jumps back.

"You don't own me," says Szo. "Not like Jonny. You never did."

Hawk swings again, slashing wildly at Szo, but Mack's there behind him. He tasers Hawk and throws the handcuffs on him.

Jonny backs away. "I ain't done nothin, nothin."

Mack breathes. "Honest, Szo, I wouldn't try waking your mother." She's there behind them, trying to hug Jonny.

"You knew she was here."

"What could I do about it?"

But that floods Szo's mind with the image of the young comabody whore with hair like a dandelion. He grabs his mother's blotchy wrist, holds it tight tighter and leans in. Then he's gone, in this strange new method of pulling things out and into himself. Pulling in the rotted bits, pulling in the mechanical bits, taking them into his own self. It hurts, yes, but when he's done there's that *holiness* in it too, and he sags onto the ground, painful in every bone, on edge.

His mother doesn't move.

"I'm sorry, Szo," said Mack, but then her eyes open.

Her eyes are lopsided and she looks at him, her rat's nest of hair falling over and like a lightning burst she croaks, "Boy." Then she collapses, falling limb by limb to the whitened ground. Her eyes whiten, and her pitted hands search aimlessly for her monitor. Slower they search, and slower. Her nose presses into dirt.

Szo can't look at Mack, knows the pity on Mack's face. "I'm sure it'll get better," Mack says, and this is the first time Mack's lied *directly* to him. Mack knows it too, and he flinches, burly shoulders twitching.

"Loser," rasps Hawk. His shoulder twitches from the tase. "Shoulda woke her up when you were four. Course then you wouldn't a got to fuck them all, which *I* let you do. Wouldn't got to spend your life making cash for screwing them over...."

Szo hurls himself at Hawk, knocking the manacled man backwards, and before Mack can pull him off Szo punches out at Hawk, not with his fists but his infected mind. It sears out, taut and bursting, it's all been waiting to be released and all four infections he's scored pour into Hawk and knock him cold. Cold, but screaming; Hawk's fresh all right, unawake and crying on the ground.

They are all stunned, all but Szo's silent-still mother.

Szo's shocked and twitching and he runs, lopsided, stumbling with the spent energy. Full of strange highs and horrible thoughts, he takes Hawk's car through the desert and back to the city. Mack doesn't come after him, nor Jonny, not in the next twelve hours, which is what it takes to come down from the high and the shock and count his cash from comabodies.

He can get to palm trees, he thinks. If he knew where they was and if he should go.

Cause there's East Enland too, and maybe it seems to him that a tourist is a guy who never interacts with his own life. Never slips into the deep.

Szo runs hard to the port, where he breathes hard and fast. He watches the heat waves of the shuttles, ships in flight.

## MARY BUCHINGER
## Transplanted

All my life I lived on a hard red slope
along the bony ridge near ivory cliffs
until, one morning in May
at nine-thirty-five precisely,
I left.

The hole my leaving made
gaped for days, tender,
watched for weeping,
probed for all its strangeness.
But it was said, over time,
the gap would grow over—

In the moments between places,
I was stretched out, pink and quivering,
naked on a white, folded field
spotted with my blood. Nothing,
nothing to cling to,
spread and measured
in cold and open air.

Then finally, I was moved
to the front where all things enter,
where the principal work is carried out,
and where, once I am established,
I will neither rest nor hide again.
Brought here to add my bulk,
to lift up and help hold in place,
with no guarantee that I will take,
that any of this will work out—

How to Live on Other Planets

# ALEX DALLY MACFARLANE
# Found

## Star anise

Star anise was the contents of one drawer in my spice cabinet: was worth one good energy cell—or three not-so-good ones, or six bad ones, or eight that provided barely any power at all.

I had never traded for just one energy cell. None remained.

At this last asteroid, I had not traded for any. I had found its interior spaces open and airless, blast-marked, most of its equipment broken or gone, debris—shards of metal, rock, old synth materials, blackened bits of bone—still lodged in some deep crannies. In such a small asteroid, a sudden equipment failure could be unsurvivable. I knew this.

It shook me to see it true, after the changes and losses and accidents we had adapted to.

As I confirmed my trajectory and fired my small thrusters two times, once to get clear from the asteroid and once to push me to the next asteroid—just a bright dot in the distance, lost among the stars like another granule of salt—I couldn't stop myself thinking: *What if Aagot had lived there?*

## Bay

I placed a bay leaf on my tongue.

I manoeuvred my craft carefully into the landing crater: a process as natural, as easy as an asteroid's spin. Still, I sighed with relief when my craft hooked into place. It wouldn't survive a crash.

After triple-checking the integrity of my suit, I drifted out onto the asteroid's surface with my spice cabinet.

Cut into another part of the asteroid was a landing bay built for spacecraft far bigger than mine: craft that would have arrived to collect platinum and iron and enough liquid hydrogen to fuel their onward journeys. A story. A dream of the past. If I could land in the landing bay, I wouldn't have to go outside for the metres it took to reach the small airlock—outside, where the stars waited like teeth for my suit to fail—but its use required too much energy.

When the people from Cai Nu arrived, would they be welcomed into the asteroids' landing bays?

I winced. I wanted to think of something else.

I pressed the bay leaf to the roof of my mouth.

The people of this asteroid had barely opened their mouths before the words 'Cai Nu' fell out. They gathered around me in the small communal room, wanting my words even more than my spices. "I have cardamom," I said. "We managed to get it growing again." And a few people sighed longingly, before one of them asked what people were saying privately, face-to-face—instead of on the inter-asteroid comms—about the impending arrival of the Cai Nu people. Almost everyone who lived in the asteroid was holding onto the poles running along the room's rock walls. I counted over twenty people. Though I recognised many of the faces, not one was Aagot's. "I don't know much more than what's on the comms," I said, reluctant to admit that I rarely listened to the messages my craft picked up between the asteroids. I knew that the Cai Nu people would arrive in less than a year. I knew that our lives in the asteroids would end.

The questions continued to come.

Eventually they realised that I could tell them nothing. Disappointed, a few people drifted away. Others spoke: explaining how many energy cells they could give me, asking what spices that was worth.

"What would you like?" I asked, touching the grey drawers of my cabinet. Etched into the iron were the names of the spices: star anise, cardamom pods, cloves, chillis, cinnamon bark, peppercorns, fennel seeds, coriander seeds, dried coriander leaves, dried sage leaves, juniper berries, lemongrass, dried makrut leaves, cumin seeds, dried mint leaves, dried bay leaves, sprigs of thyme and rosemary, flakes of galangal, flakes of turmeric. Flavour. Some people said that word like a plea at a shrine. Spices made our food— synthetic, completely nourishing, completely tasteless—alive, made it something we wanted to share with each other. Chewing a cardamom pod brought tears to people's eyes. A sage leaf provoked joyous laughter.

Nouf Kassem, who did most of this asteroid's trade, began to point to drawers. I opened them one by one, withdrawing pouches. The items of our trade hung in the air between us. When I had given ten bad energy cells' worth, Nouf didn't release the handle of her box.

"You trade as if you'll be able to reach all the asteroids before the Cai Nu people arrive," she said. "As if you've got a whole year. I hear that on Cai Nu the strips of cinnamon are as tall as the tallest woman, that they grow parsley and rose and sumac. I hear there are mounds of spices in powders. Are your family saving these spices for then?"

Silence surrounded us, sharp as space.

I wanted to say: *What makes you think everyone's leaving the asteroids?*

I wanted to say: *Why?*

I hadn't thought of trading all our stock, I hadn't thought of sending a message to my mothers asking whether I should make more generous offers. I hadn't—

"Just a few more pouches of cumin and mint," Nouf said.

I gave them to her.

In past visits, I had spent time with the people of the asteroid. I had invented stories with them. I had kissed a man called Ammar, laughed when he shrieked with joy at the bay leaf on my tongue—I had, years ago, chosen a spice per asteroid and placed that same spice on my tongue at every visit—and then I had kissed him again, shared the flavour between us. I had listened to the elders of the asteroid and played with the children and eaten turmeric-soaked food. How bright! How bitter!

How soon until these memories would not be renewed.

I slipped away, outside, into my craft and the space between the asteroids. The bay leaf's taste lingered. We would not.

## Juniper berries

The first story Aagot gave me, with juniper berries crushed on our tongues, was one created by Aagot as a child. I couldn't linger on that asteroid. I met Aagot there—one conversation on my trade visit, three hours of stories more precious than fuel cells.

Aagot told me of a child who needed a name: a new name, not the birth-name that lingered at their ears like the whine of a faulty air processor, as ill-fitting as 'girl,' as 'boy.'

I remembered Aagot's voice, saying: *When the spice trader comes, they bring flavours and news and new people from other asteroids. But there's one thing they don't bring: new names. There's no drawer in the spice trader's cabinet for that. For one child, this meant never finding one that fit.* But the spice trader in the story— like spice traders in many stories—took the child as an apprentice between the asteroids and there the child found their name: in the herb they most loved handling, crushing, coating their fingers with its scent. Thyme.

I remembered Aagot's voice, full of longing like a drawer of thyme.

I left.

## Thyme

I finally realised, two years later, chewing thyme on an outlying asteroid where six people stubbornly survived, that I was like Thyme: ill-suited to 'boy' or 'girl.'

## Juniper berries

When I returned to the juniper berry asteroid—when I realised how much I needed to speak to Aagot again—Aagot had left, bought passage a year after my visit on one of the rare other craft that still functioned. There were only nineteen asteroids—eighteen, now, with the disaster in the star anise asteroid—but I didn't visit every one annually, I didn't undertake every one of my family's trade journeys, I didn't see Aagot again.

I retold Aagot's story to myself between the asteroids.

## Cinnamon

One of the earliest messages sent to us by the Cai Nu people had explained our abandonment: *Two hundred years ago we were too ambitious. We overextended ourselves. We should have focused on our settlements on Cai Nu, but we wanted the asteroids, we wanted the other habitable planets and moons of this solar system. So we established settlements in the Liu Yang asteroid family. Then, almost immediately, a health crisis struck and led to widespread social upheaval, in which much was lost, including knowledge of your continued survival. Now that we have recovered and grown our population, and rediscovered you, we can't leave you living in such poor conditions.*

## Cumin

I approached the next asteroid on my trade journey. Plans travelled faster: communications sent between the asteroids. Questions. Debates. My name was mentioned often. "Lo Yiying can help bring people here." "What's the maximum amount of passengers and cargo that Lo Yiying's craft carries?" "Lo Yiying, how long until you reach Iskander? Can you collect us all?" "Aside from Lo Yiying, who can fly a craft to bring people to the Lo family's asteroid?"

I heard, for the first time, a firm date for the Cai Nu people's arrival: twenty-two weeks.

I would not have my spacecraft, I would not fly spices between the asteroids, I would not drift through the corridors of asteroids with my cabinet behind me and the taste of bay or cumin or thyme in my mouth.

Everyone would gather at my family's asteroid. A message was sent to the Cai Nu craft, telling them the asteroid's current co-ordinates so they could track it and adjust their approach accordingly. They confirmed its convenience for their current trajectory and fuel supplies.

My purpose changed: to reach the next asteroid—Iskander, cumin—and collect its inhabitants and turn, like a crooked stem, back to my family's asteroid. Sissel Haugli, who lived on the outermost asteroid at this end of the group, had already begun her journey towards the centre, gathering the families I would not reach. Two people at other points in the asteroid group were also underway.

Trade was no longer important. My cabinet's drawers would remain unopened.

Still I journeyed, the next asteroid gradually growing from a mote to a seed—comm-conversations not once suggesting that anyone would remain behind after the Cai Nu people arrived, very few people discussing the difficulties we would face on Cai Nu—and then, the asteroid a spinning, dark rock, I concentrated on landing.

The landing bay door slowly opened. I carefully manoeuvred my shuttle into the bay, where multiple lights shone: a brightness I rarely saw in any asteroid. The bay door closed. The unit on one wall restored air.

It was unusual, to arrive like this.

I instinctively went to my spice cabinet and picked up its harness.

I entered the asteroid without it, feeling not myself—though people greeted me, entering the landing bay in family-clusters, towing their possessions, saying "Lo Yiying!" and "Thank you for coming here!" as if I brought spices and news. "Do you think you'll be able to fit all of these boxes on your shuttle?" asked Inas Kassem, who had done most of the talking for this asteroid. "We've packed only important things: all of our fuel cells, the racks of moss so we can help keep your shuttle's air fresh. We've got food and water tanks. And some small things. Qurans, small shrine statues, old family journals, a few personal ornaments."

No one else came through the small door from the asteroid. Everyone hung in front of me, looking at me, at my shuttle, at the walls—the last part of their home they would see.

No Aagot.

"Shall we begin loading?" asked Inas.

"Yes."

I had crunched cumin seeds between my teeth before leaving my shuttle. The taste faded as we worked: arranging boxes in the cargo area of my shuttle, setting up the moss racks, deciding how people would sleep. Then we were ready. No one spoke as I closed my shuttle's door, as Inas showed me what signal to send to open the landing bay door. It creaked, in the moment before sound was lost. Beyond, the stars gleamed—and the ones that were not stars: asteroids, Cai Nu's planet, Cai Nu itself, smaller than a fragment of peppercorn. I didn't know what to say. Nor did anyone. So I began our journey.

Several people started to cry. Others talked, others remained silent, others sang: a braid of emotions in three languages, passed from mouth to mouth, lasting hours.

I cooked.

From the spice cabinet, secured beside my chair, I took cumin seeds and sprigs of thyme and peppercorns and cardamom pods and makrut leaves and lemongrass stalks and galangal. I cooked pot after pot, sometimes mixing spices, sometimes using just one, and passed carved chunks of the finished meal around the cargo area of my shuttle, where the people of the cumin asteroid had tethered themselves to the walls and their boxes.

On Cai Nu we would eat food we only knew from stories: rice, noodles, dumplings, bread, meat, vegetables, sweets. Spices wouldn't be the only flavours.

When people started discussing this, I retreated to my seat.

Two women followed. I knew Ma Wanlu, Inas' daughter. The

other was introduced as her wife, Bilge Yılmaz, who wanted to see Cai Nu.

"It's nothing," I said. "A small dot."

"Our home," Bilge murmured, rapt at the sight: as if I'd offered her a handful of cumin seeds.

I looked away.

"What troubles you?" Ma Wanlu asked.

"We won't be able to go outside. We won't be able to work. We'll die in that place they're building for us, forgotten by our children, useless. Who will we be?"

Ma Wanlu frowned. "Well, what are we now?"

"We work—your family works on the fuel cells."

"Work!" Ma Wanlu almost choked on the word. "Work. Oh, we work. We desperately work to get a little more life from our dwindling resources."

"We are all trapped in our asteroids," Bilge said, "working every day to ensure our habitat is still intact, that our oxygen-exchange mosses aren't dying, that our fuel cells haven't stopped. When my cousin's pregnancy went wrong, what could we do? When my father got cancer, what could we do? Who will we be on Cai Nu? Not dying like this." Bilge's voice shook; she looked out of my craft, out at the stars and the bright dot of Cai Nu's planet. "And we try to move between asteroids, to keep from inbreeding, and people like my mother never see their parents and siblings and aunts and uncles and grandparents again, only hear them, just hundreds of thousands of kilometres away but it's as if they're on a rock around that star, or that one."

I thought of Aagot, lost among just eighteen asteroids.

"Here," Ma Wanlu said, "our children will die, gasping for air."

"When the Cai Nu people talk about never having to worry about energy supplies," Bilge said, "or medicine or food, I think of... I..."

Silence drifted between us like dust.

"I don't know if I want to go," I murmured: an admission I'd made only to my spice cabinet, to the stars.

Ma Wanlu and Bilge stared.

Finally Ma Wanlu said, "Your family's asteroid really must be better than all the others. I thought that was just a story." She manoeuvred herself back into the cargo area. Bilge followed. I sat alone, staring at that small dot.

## Cinnamon

I remembered the Cai Nu people's first message, sent in ten languages. I remembered shock and wonder. Questions. Possibilities. To know that there were people beyond the asteroids!

I had never believed those stories.

I had joined, as a child, in a ten-year Sending: a message flung towards the bright light we knew to be a planet and the smaller light of its moon. We had eaten cinnamon-flavoured food and stayed awake for four hours, eight hours, long past the time when a reply could have come.

*We live on the moon Cai Nu,* the reply had come, six years after the most recent Sending. *We received your messages. Do you truly live in the asteroids?*

Somewhere on my latest trade journey, the possibilities had drifted away like carelessly handled cloves.

They had started with questions.

*How many people live in each asteroid? How do you ensure a supply of fresh air and water? How do you celebrate New Year? What do you eat? What languages do you speak? Have you built shrines inside the asteroids? Mosques? Temples? What is your life expectancy? Your infant mortality rate? How has your bone density withstood little or no exposure to gravity? How has—*

I had tried not to think about the questions, I had tried not to think about what I knew: that our ancestors' genes had been modified for low-gravity habitats, that it hadn't been enough, that the people of Cai Nu were far healthier than us.

That we wouldn't adapt well to the 0.8G of Cai Nu.

*We have reviewed the information you've given us,* one of their messages had said, just sixteen weeks ago. Team Leader Hu Leyi, whose voice we knew the best, had sent it: her speech carefully crafted to convey sorrow and hope. *We agree that you cannot survive in the asteroids much longer. We cannot, at this point, invest in improved infrastructure in the asteroids, which means that we must bring you to Cai Nu and from there decide how and where you will live.* Reassurances had followed. *When you reach Cai Nu, we will ensure that there are doctors who speak all of your languages. We will build a place where you can live comfortably while we find ways for you to adapt to life on Cai Nu. We will also find ways for you to use your current skills and gain new ones. We want your futures to be prosperous.*

Reactions had fallen from my craft's comm panel: loud, tearful, questioning, accepting.

And there were other conversations, a mass of them like a drawer of star anise and fennel seeds.

Team Leader Hu Leyi had asked, before their decision about our futures: *Our records indicate that an experiment in agricultural production was established in the asteroid XI-258. Is that experiment on-going?*

To that, Jidarat Chanprasert—the family head of one asteroid, where I placed a sliver of galangal on my tongue—had replied: *The Lo family inhabit an asteroid where spices are grown.*

*How interesting! Several people here are very excited to hear this and would very much like to know more about what species have proved successful.* Later, Team Leader Hu Leyi had talked of samples to be brought to Cai Nu.

Jidarat had replied: *Perhaps one of the Lo family would like to talk to Team Leader Hu Leyi about this.*

Later, I had heard Older Mother's voice take over, giving Team Leader Hu Leyi the full history of our fields, our production methods, our trade with the other asteroids. I imagined Older Mother walking among the fields inside our asteroid with Younger Mother at her side, talking as they worked.

Sometimes individuals—not heads of an asteroid's family, not important, knowledgeable people—got onto one of the comm units. One child asked: *How many classes are there at your schools?*

Team Leader Hu Leyi—or one of her colleagues—replied to every question. *There are many classes: mathematics, science, agriculture, history, literature, music, many different types of engineering, many languages.*

A day later, the girl said: *I want to make plants!*

A colleague replied: *We have a great interest in bioengineering at the moment, as we progress with the terraforming of the still-unnamed third planet in the system. It is a very exciting field.*

*Can I do that?*

*Of course! We will provide an education for all of the children and any adults who want it. We want you to do work that fulfils you, whether it is in bioengineering or finance or poetic composition.*

The Cai Nu person sounded delighted by the girl's interest, but the conversation did not turn to our adaptation. Perhaps it would be easier for children. Perhaps the Cai Nu people didn't know how much could be achieved with their technology.

In my comm's chiming I had heard excitement. I had heard joy: to listen to stories of millions of people, stories of great temples and mosques, stories of New Year celebrations that filled thousands of streets with food and colour and people, and religious festivities and Landing, the anniversary of arriving on Cai Nu from a different star system, and birthdays in families of over a hundred relations—to listen to this was to marvel, to disbelieve, to hope.

Two days before my arrival at the cumin asteroid, Team Leader Hu Leyi had finally admitted what I had feared: *It will be very difficult for you. Your bodies have adapted to the absence of gravity. You will not be able to step from the landing craft onto the surface of our world, but we are building you a zero-gravity habitat, we are already researching the possibilities of technologically-assisted adaptation. However you are able to live here, we will strive to ensure comfort. You will never hunger, never lack medicine, never lack people to talk to. And your children will have every possibility laid out before them.*

I had replayed this message until I knew it as well as Aagot's story.

## Thyme

I feared many things, but this was what stuck in me like a blockage in an air supply pipe, like a star anise's point in a throat: what if people didn't understand me. I imagined people like Thyme being so rare that they laughed. I imagined the people whose languages used gendered pronouns insisting that I choose male or female. I imagined every one of these one million people needing to be told that I was un-gendered, a different gender—if I didn't even know what to call myself, how could I expect to be taken seriously?—the way I had needed to tell everyone I knew in the asteroids when I was younger. I imagined giving up.

I told myself to stop being foolish. How could one million people have only two fixed genders?

But the only other person like me in all the asteroids was Aagot, who I couldn't find.

## Fields

It was not quite the last time I would approach my family's asteroid: that pitted, dark peppercorn-shape, orbited by a moon only three kilometres in diameter, that landscape at the heart of my personal stories. Home. No, it was not quite the last time I would approach it, but I hurt enough to believe it was.

"Big Cousin!" my youngest cousin's voice came in over the comm. "We're opening the smaller landing bay for you. Bring everyone in!"

A hole slowly opened in the asteroid's side.

I wordlessly landed my craft, waited for the bay doors to close and the air to return, waited for the signal to unlock my craft's door. Unloading began. My family emerged from the corridors to help: to organise the storage of possessions, to lead people to places they could sleep and spend time until the Cai Nu people arrived.

I slipped away to the fields.

They filled four vast rooms: stacked shelves holding soil and spice-plants. I drifted above them, perpendicular to their ends, looking along each shelf at sage bushes, carefully stunted cinnamon trees, red-fruited chillis, long fennel stalks fronded with white flowers, clusters of bay and berry-heavy juniper and green-leafed plants hung with the star-seeds of anise. So many smells: green and sharp and sweet. Home-smells.

Many plants had been recently harvested: leaves thinned out—taken for drying—and seeds picked. Others soon would be. Our last harvest.

I went to a cluster of star anise plants.

The light gravity generator in the shelf pulled me to the soil. Clods between my toes. Glossy leaves against my legs. The weight of my body startled me, pulled me to my knees. I steadied myself. It was always uncomfortable, returning to the fields after a long journey. Soon— no. I sat. I placed an unripe seed—green, eight-pointed—on my tongue, I dug my fingers into the soil. My skin already smelled of the fields: green, earthy. Home.

Would I ever work in a field on Cai Nu? Would I ever adjust to that much gravity?

I wanted to think of nothing but star anise against my tongue, against my skin.

Younger Mother's voice cut through the air. "Oldest Child? Is that you?"

"Yes."

Boots clanged on metal: she climbed down from far above me, shelf to shelf, until she appeared at the end of mine and swung herself onto the soil with an ease I lacked. A bag of cinnamon hung from her shoulder. She walked towards me with bark-stained fingers and bare feet—and the way she walked, straight-backed and sturdy, reminded me suddenly of the pictures of the Cai Nu people.

"I didn't hear you working," I said.

"I was thinking about, well, a lot of things." She crouched at my side, smiling. "Why are you in here?"

"I wanted to sit in the fields, as we'll be abandoning them soon." My voice was as brittle as a dried cardamom pod.

Younger Mother's smile faded.

I looked away, at the soil, at the star anise, as my mother quietly said, "It will be better. For everyone. Just— just imagine the fields there! Real fields, laid flat across the ground not stacked like this, like *shelves* because we don't have to room to do it any other way—and *sunshine!*"

"I see the sun regularly," I murmured.

Above our heads, the underside of the next shelf held UV lights that replicated the sun for the plants: a constellation of hundreds across the fields.

"I've read about rain and snow in a thousand poems," Younger Mother said, "but to see them! To feel them on my skin!"

We—I—wouldn't. I had grown up in the fields, gravity on my bones, but I had spent so much of the past ten years among the asteroids. I loved it: the cumin or clove or galangal on my tongue, the spice cabinet doors sliding open, the happiness I brought, the stories shared. But I doubted my body was much healthier than those of the people I traded with.

Would my field-working family adapt quickly? Would they work in real fields?

"And they will have new spices there," Younger Mother said, running her fingers over the star anise's leaves. "New flavours. New— so much."

New spices.

"It will be better."

"And difficult," I said. "No one seems to want to talk about that."

"What else can we do? You know this, you see the other asteroids and everything that's broken and old in them."

I remembered the star anise asteroid, broken open like a seed casing, all its contents—its people, who I had once known—spilled out.

"I need to get back to harvesting," Younger Mother said. "I know there won't be much need for all this on Cai Nu, but it would be a shame for it to go to waste."

"I'll eat it."

She smiled, then left me among the star anise plants, their seeds hanging around me like the view from an asteroid's surface. I couldn't imagine any other view.

I returned to my craft, to my journey—not a trade journey, any more.

## Cinnamon, Turmeric, Rosemary, Cloves, Galangal, Sage

I started to forget to place spices on my tongue as I arrived at each asteroid, collecting its people—bringing them closer to the Cai Nu people's arrival. I started—slowly, reluctantly—to think of the ways life on Cai Nu would be better for them, for me.

## Found

Everyone gathered. Everyone. Who had ever imagined such a sight? So many people holding onto the walls or drifting carefully, so many bags and boxes tethered with them, so many voices all at once—people who had never seen each other, only spoken over the comms, suddenly able to talk unending, to shyly smile and embrace and unhesitatingly kiss. A wonder. A hundred people, another hundred, another. A community, not stretched out like sparse flowers on an ill chilli plant but here, together, one. Everyone.

I couldn't deny my excitement. I couldn't subdue my fear.

I looked and looked for Aagot.

Older Mother had set up comm units throughout the large loading bay, so that her voice could be heard everywhere in that vast space, among so many people. Periodically she said, "The Cai Nu craft is now two hours away!" and, "The Cai Nu craft is continuing its steady course, only an hour away!" until, suddenly, too soon, "The Cai Nu craft will enter the landing bay in ten minutes." I drifted through the loading bay. Around me, people drew in breath together, a long silence before new conversations streamed out like air into space.

Then—so soon—we heard the grinding as the landing bay

doors opened for the first time in over a hundred years. We heard nothing, nothing, noise lost in vacuum—then a gentle set of metal-on-metal sounds. The Cai Nu craft landing. I drifted, unseeing. I only knew sounds. Arrival. The landing bay doors closing again. The first set of airlock doors between the two bays opening. I didn't breathe, I didn't speak—no one did. I reached a wall. I held.

The second set of airlock doors opened.

The people—five of them—wore dark blue suits and helmets with clear visors, but I was too far away to see their faces. Into our silence they slowly entered, using the handrails that spread across the wall like roots. They removed their helmets. They looked at us with cautious smiles. One said in Mandarin, "I am Team Leader Hu Leyi. It is a pleasure to finally be here and meeting you all."

Older Mother drifted forward, saying, "I am Lo Minyu. On behalf of everyone: welcome. You are very welcome here."

The other four Cai Nu people looked around the loading bay, as if trying to match faces to the voices they had heard over the comms.

"Are you all here?" Hu Leyi asked.

What did they think of us? What did they—

I saw, then, a long, thin braid of hair with a circular metal ornament fixed to its end.

I remembered: etched with a person crouched inside the shape of a bear.

"Aagot!" Then fear reached my tongue and I couldn't talk. Was this Aagot? Was this some other person, who did not know me, did not want to talk to me—

The person turned.

"Aagot," I managed.

A slight frown. "Ecralali, now."

Now. A name-change—a reason I hadn't been able to find Aagot Fossen, who no longer existed.

"Did we meet when I was younger?" Ecralali asked.

"Yes. Yes. I am Lo Yiying."

Quietly, Ecralali said, "I know you."

"Years ago, we talked about—" One or two people were interested in our conversation. I wanted privacy. I wanted no one to judge our words unimportant, irrelevant. Most of all, I wanted Ecralali to remember me. "We talked about Thyme and gender and—" I might as well have bared my skin in the space between the asteroids. "It was the most important conversation I've ever had."

Ecralali's face changed: astonishment and delight. Unless I interpreted wrongly, unless I imagined—

"I remember," Ecralali said, "I remember telling you about ungendered Houyi—"

"I'd only ever known Houyi as a woman before then," I said, as full of wonder as if I was hearing the tale of Chang E and Houyi for the first time. "That's how my mothers always tell the story."

"—and the story of the stars, whose lives are not measured in gender."

"Thyme," I said, fennel-foliage soft, "who is like me."

"Yes."

Hu Leyi and her colleagues were still talking: moving among us, taking names, inventorying possessions, dividing us into groups.

"I know more stories now," Ecralali said.

"I— I would like to hear them."

"I know about Cai Nu—the founder, not the moon—I've read everything in our records, listened to every story. A lot of them tell that Cai Nu was fluidly gendered."

"The founder was..."

Ecralali's smile was as rich as a whole cabinet of spices.

I half-heard announcements. We would have a room for each family on the Cai Nu people's spacecraft, as well as several communal spaces, connected by a long corridor. I thought of stems. I thought of floating above the spices still growing on the shelves of my family's fields. They would shrivel and die and I would never again be Lo Yiying the spice trader. I would be far from my home. Then we would reach Cai Nu. Gleaming. Strange. Skied.

Storied.

"I want to know what stories are told there," Ecralali said.

"I would listen to every one."

It hadn't occurred to me—

I had needed to explain myself to my family, to people among the asteroids. Before that—to myself. That had taken almost twenty years. I had only found myself in the stories that fell from Ecralali's—once-Aagot's—mouth like star anise. To even imagine that I might be found in other stories—

I hadn't.

"My favourite stories," Ecralali said, "are those that say 'Cai Nu' is a chosen name."

One of Hu Leyi's colleagues reached us. As Ecralali said, "Ecralali Fos," and pointed to just one small bag, I thought of my own name: a gift from my mothers. Could I— No. I still wanted it. It had clung to me, all these years, like a grain of soil under a fingernail: a welcome reminder of my family on the long journeys between the asteroids. It fit me.

Below us, the first group passed through the airlock doors to the spacecraft.

"Lo Yiying," I said, and my voice was almost steady. "My possessions are with my family—Lo Minyu and Xu Weina are my mothers." I didn't think I needed to list the rest of my family— brother, cousins, aunts, uncles, a single grandfather. They all waited together, with the spice cabinet—full of the final harvest—between them.

The man made a note on the translucent screen that hovered in front of him, then moved on.

"I should go to my family," I said, though I couldn't imagine moving, couldn't imagine any of what would happen next.

"We have months of journeying ahead of us," Ecralali said. "Plenty of time for telling stories."

## Thyme

The fourth story Ecralali gave me, with thyme on our tongues, was of Cai Nu: working on a team of scientists identifying planets and moons suitable for human settlement, finding the moon that would eventually bear their name, spending decades preparing the team for the long journey and the tireless tasks at the other end—then, being invited to join the team despite their advanced age.

*Cai Nu lived a year on the moon before finally dying. They are remembered forever: their vision of people living on this moon, their hard work making it more than a story.*

*Their name, chosen in the same year that they first saw a promising moon in their data.*

I pressed the thyme to the roof of my mouth.

I was not alone.

# NICK WOOD
## Azania

I'd never been very cold before—not until I headed into space. Deep space I'm talking, not a joyride to the moon. So deep, we go on and on, past suns and planets, moons and nebulae—deep, deep space, through the coldest of empty places that hang between the stars.

So cold, it penetrates our star-ship TaNK, infiltrating the dreams of my long sleep; for I see nothing of all we pass.

Instead, I lie encased in ice, too cold to scream.

For twelve years...

And still more.

*It is time for the last lesson but thunder rumbles over the sound of the bell. I laugh and run, finding myself in a strange field, far from home and school. The ground is bitten red-rock dry and marked only by redder crumbling fragments of dried out anthills. No trees, no grass, no houses or sounds. Above me, the sky roils in with darkness and lightning sheets that spark my blood. I laugh and tilt my head backwards, flicking my hair so that it tumbles down my back. I close my eyes, opening my mouth as the wind sweeps in great water blasts that sting my face and lips. I suck greedily, as the dust churns to muddy rivulets beneath me, shifting my footing, muddying my feet. The warm water slakes my throat, turning cold and then, to ice. I choke, mouth frozen open, unable to breathe. I am pinned tight in a latticed cage of ice. I open my eyes. There is nothing else around me; nothing, till a flash in the darkness. I turn, but too late. The arrow pierces my right ear and bores into my brain. I can only gag on ice.*

I wake shivering.

Above me, there is a large overhanging tree trunk. Frosty edges of the dream-cage melt around me and I track the blurred branch to the huge trunk and overhanging canopy.

Muuyo—the African baobab. The soft green leaves swirl and shake, always just out of my frozen reach. I struggle to stretch out painful fingers, searching for warmth in the green. But the organic patterns shift and reform, distant as stars, untouchable.

*She* watches me through the leaves, wearing the face of Wangari Maathai. Is it in identification with me that *She* is mostly female?

I sigh. So...

Not my Copperbelt home then, nor my old school.

Not even Earth.

Planet XA- I've lost the numbers in my cold, waking head-fog—or, as we prefer to call it, Azania. (A planet partially mapped by the African Union Robotic Missions with (just) breathable air and water and no known advanced life forms—a veritable waiting Eden).

The baobab branch bending and swaying above me, however, is but a digital shadow on our domed roof—a shape without texture, form without life.

Wangari, *She* smiles, with richly red lips: <Mangwanani, Aneni.>

"Morning," I grunt, sitting up and casting a glance at grandfather's rough, reddish-brown stone sculpture, dimly but decoratively placed near the screened window, as if keeping alien forces at bay.

Besides me, Ezi stirs.

I sign to *She* to keep quiet and swivel clumsily out of bed; bracing my stomach muscles for the pull of serious gravity. The room spins beneath the canopy of faux leaves and my feet fail to find floor.

Instead, my face, fists, and breasts do, hands barely in place quick enough to protect my teeth.

I spit blood from a cut lip, concerned about one thing.

There is something in my ear.

It's a faint tickle in the right ear, deep inside, but followed by a sputtering burst of popping noises, as if my ear is protesting and trying to expel something. Then a pain lances through the right side of my face and I grunt and clasp my ear.

I sway.

Ezi is starting to snore, low and rasping, as she has rolled onto her back. I watch her for the barest of moments, sealing the pain within me so that I don't wake her, reacquainting myself with my old adversary.

It's been many, many years—but, almost without thinking, I rate the pain five out of ten and akin to a bright blue candle burning inside my ear. I close my eyes to pour cooling imaginary water onto it, but it continues to burn just as brightly, just as painfully.

I'm out of practice, my spine now comfortably straight, even stiffened and dulled by the passing years. Pain pulls me back to thirteen again, my last spinal surgery sharpened by anxiety around my first period.

This time, though, there is no mother to hold me.

Instead, I need to see *She* in the Core Room.

Firstly though, I cover Ezi with the scrambled thermo-sheet to keep her warm. (Always, she kicks herself bare).

I manage the corridor with my left hand braced against the wall, following etched tendril roots, past the men's door and on into the heart of our Base, where *She* sits.

Or squats—her heavy casing hides her Quantum core, scored with bright geometric Sotho art—her flickering holographic face above the casing is now the usual generic wise elder woman, grandmother of all.

*She* straddles the centre of the circular room, like a Spider vibrating the Info-Web.

*She* smiles again, but this time with pale and uncertain lips.

"I need help," I say, "A full medical scan. My ear feels painful and my balance has gone."

<A *full* scan?>

I swallow, appreciating the caution in her emphasis, but strip off my night suit with a shaky but firm certitude: "Yes."

And so I am needled, weighed, poked, sampled, scraped, and gouged, until I shrink with exhaustion from the battery of bots *She* has whizzing around me. I finally take refuge in a chair near the door and gulp a cup of my pleasure, neuro-enhanced South Sudanese coffee.

*She* calls off her bots and they swing back into fixed brown brackets raised around the edge of the room, as if pots on shelves in an ancient traditional rondavel. *She* has her eyes closed, soaking in the analysis.

I finish the cup and rub my stinging lip where it's cut.

*She* speaks: <Not detecting any pathogen nor otological dysfunction, but I do see diffuse activated pain perception across your somato-sensory cortex.>

"Show me." I am a doctor after all, even if many years a psychiatrist now, specialised in space psychosis and zero-G neurosurgery.

I watch my rotating holographic brain in bright blue, with red traces glowing in the anterior insula and cingulate cortex—sensory, motor, and cognitive components, involved then: a dull, all-encompassing pain, no identifiable specificities tracing a direct neural link to the ear. There's new pain merged and mixed with old memories perhaps, fudging and blurring my experiential pathways? I scan the data that *She* scrolls condescendingly before me—no, there are no clear signs of dysfunction clearly emanating from my inner ear that I can see either.

I stand and sway. Surely it can't all be in my head?

"Aneni?" It's Ezi on our room screen, frowning from the bed, thermo-sheet clutched to her chin. "There's something sore in my right ear."

Dhodhi! As always, I keep the expletive hidden inside me. "I'm on my way, Ezi."

I lurch back down the corridor, just as the men's door slides open. Petrus is on his hands and knees and startles as I stop and lean against the wall opposite him. I watch the corridor light bounce off his brightly tattooed scalp as he bends his head to look up at me.

"Sorry Cap'n," he says. "Can't seem to stand upright anymore... and my ear's *fokkin'* sore."

I'm always cold, whatever temperature we set here, but now this coldness bites almost as deeply as my pain.

§

We meet where we eat, genetically diverse, even though we number just four. It is dull but honest food, the cassava and eddoes Anwar had saved on arrival, holding starvation at bay on this alien planet.

I nibble and long for a pineapple or banana.

Finishing up quickly, the others look shaken, unwell, with little appetite.

*She* has sprinkled the table and walls with swathes of savannah grass and shimmering pools of blue water. They bleed into my vertigo. I ask her for plain reality. *She* gives us a brown table, flanked by opposing brown seat-bunks, ergo-green kitchen neatly splayed behind with heaters and processors. *She* has the windows sealed white against the planet's night, keeping the focus on our preparatory tasks within.

I steady myself with a firm grip on the table—tension is building—I don't need my psychiatric training to tell me that. The men sit opposite us. Ezi and I exchange the briefest of encouraging glances and brace ourselves. At least some vestibular stability has returned for us all.

Sure enough, it's Petrus who sits opposite me; brown head and hairless, smooth face lined by late middle age and constant earnestness. "So… *Captain,* what is responsible for our ear pain and dizziness?"

He has not used my name nor looked at me directly since three Earth days after we arrived; certainly not since I moved in with Ezi. That's six weeks and rising now, in Earth time.

Azanian time, though, it's been just four days.

I shrug and gesture to the ceiling, where leaves still hang heavily over us: "*She* doesn't know."

Anwar chuckles at me; his white teeth sharply offset against his trimmed black beard and moustache, his ashen grey skin obviously short of sunlight. His teeth look sharp, conveying little of his humour; but perhaps it's just my mood.

"*She* is not omniscient though, am I correct, Aneni?"

I nod and smile: "*She* wants to check all of us thoroughly. *She*'s learned literally nothing from me."

All three of them groan and I let slip a smile.

"Is it the same ear for all of us?" asks Ezi. Both men turn to look at her; Petrus gesturing right, Anwar left.

"Random, then?"

Ezi ignores me. "Mine's the right ear like Aneni and Petrus," she says, leaning forward, right hand grasping the cream, circular utilities remote. With a flick of her wrist, she sends it straight towards Anwar's midriff. He stops it with his left hand.

"Maybe your dominant ear is left," says Ezi, "but then, what do I know? I'm only the engineer." (Why does she look at me? We all know she is a special engineer, simply the best on antimatter rockets. More to the point now, her genius resides in having gotten our waste recycling going again, such a welcome respite for our noses.)

"Neurologically targeted?" I ask.

Ezi shrugs, coiled corn-plats flicking across her shoulders. "What do you think, *She?*"

<I cannot speculate without sufficient evidence, but I can confirm a full physical is needed for all of you.>

They eye each other with reluctance; the full physical on waking from years of enforced hibernation six weeks earlier no doubt still fresh in mind. A rigorous exam followed by even more rigorous exercises to recondition our severely weakened bodies— we still struggle against the pull of this planet, even though it is barely five percent more than full Earth gee.

I smile again, despite the ear-pain, having done my time. "We'll stay here until we've all been assessed. Alphabetical order, first name."

Anwar scowls at me as he gets up to go through to the Core-Room.

Petrus looks at the cup of coffee in front of me. "So, what do you suspect, Captain?"

I look at his scalp, feeling inexplicably sad. Two human figures are etched in sub-dermal nano-ink on his skull. They've not moved since we've woken from our Star-Sleep, their micro-programmed motility messages seemingly degraded and destroyed by his prolonged, lowered neural activity. His head used to show the Mandelas walking endlessly free from prison in the late twentieth century—now; it's just two faded humanoid shapes frozen together, smeared like an ancient Rorschach blot across his scalp. I can't explain it, but the still and fading images continue to cool my early desires for him.

"Aneni?" Petrus is looking at me, green eyes fierce and I am reminded of his rough Cape Town Flats roots.

"At this point I can't say, but there has to be some foreign pathogen, despite all our precautions. We can't all be ill with the same symptoms simultaneously."

He raises his eyebrows and leans forward, "Foreign?"

For some reason, I can't take my eyes off the Mandelas on his head, "From Azania perhaps, although we can't rule out a hidden, mutated infectious agent from Earth."

Anwar stomps in and Ezi sighs as she stands up.

It's strange to sit alone again with the two men, both who appear to keep smouldering with residual resentment at my authority and unexpected relationship with Ezi. Strange too, to think it's a full sixty years now since the African Gender and Sexuality Equality Act. Laws we were all born with—but still for some, slow to shape trans-generational attitudes around queer sexuality—despite credible arguments they are internalised residues of negative colonial views. (In the end though, nothing is so neatly separated, unless you're an exceptional surgeon. As for me, my words are my customary tools, blunter than any scalpel, so I keep my thoughts private.)

The men mutter briefly and inaudibly to each other. I smile behind my hands, for I am used to masculine silence; fifteen years in the Zambian army is preparation enough.

Ezi comes back and Petrus leaves. We stare with discomfort at the table; we have silently avoided this threesome.

I am startled when Anwar breaks it. "I've made a holo-disk of Yakubu Chukwu."

It's Ezi's favourite West African Federation footballer. "Really?" she smiles.

I stand to halt a surge of emotions. Ridiculous really, as if physical actions can stop feelings—I should indeed know better. Walking over to the blinds that hide this planet from us, I grasp their metal slats, ready to claw them away.

*This* is why we are here.

*This* is where we need to survive.

But Ezi's eyes do not follow me, so I hesitate.

Ezi's from South of the Tenth Parallel, an old fracture line Anwar may not find so easy to cross—Africa harbours exacting fault lines, both ancient and modern.

Still, the AU is—was?—a powerful, if fragile and fast ripening fruit of i-networked Lion economies, ready to burst across the burnt out husk of the Earth—if it survives the gathering heat. We are indeed the first of its more ambitious and widely dispersed seeds...

A further ten missions have been planned, but spread across a number of promising solar systems. None follow us here. We will remain alone.

I look at the others and suddenly begrudge them nothing. This will be a hard place to survive.

As if on cue, Petrus returns. He looks at me and I turn away to the window—thinking of seeds, I thumb the shutter button.

The slats rise on darkness. An almost impenetrable blackness, with both moons yet to rise. I press my nose against the cold-treated quartz—against the faint starlight and the reflected light from within; I make out huge trunked shapes swaying in a light nocturnal breeze.

It's *always* windy here; circulating air continuously ensuring temperatures are not excessively varying across the long days and nights.

In the reflected window, I can see Petrus is standing quietly behind me. He glances up.

*She* is back amongst the canopy of leaves over our heads: <There are no clear biological markers I can identify as yet, I'm afraid—but I can offer you all a blunt neural painkiller. Our

scheduled venture onto the planet surface will be set back indefinitely. We are, in effect, quarantined. I will also ask Kwame Nkrumah for His thoughts.>

Ah, Kwame Nkrumah, the Father-ship that circles above our head, He who watches from above.

More waiting, more cages, quarantine shuts me in, like the ice cage of my dream.

So many people left behind too, of whom I miss my daughter the most. Anashe, she was barely twenty-three when we launched from Kinshasa. As a child, she had loved to sit under the baobab.

I look up at *She's* swaying branches and *'tccchhh!'* with irritation, "I am tired of baobabs, *She,* give me a fever tree."

Above us, a yellowish tree with fern like leaves billows, photosynthesising through the pale bark—an odd tree indeed, but somehow more suitable for this strange planet we still try to hold at bay with walls and shutters.

I stare into the darkness again, no longer hungry.

§

I wake.

It is worse.

*Much* worse.

I look pleadingly at *She* but there is nothing for my gaze to hold onto, just a rumbling, tumbling vertiginous splash of browns and greens and yellows. I sway and spin even though I am lying still and wait quietly for the vomit urge to die, sweating out my fear.

Blurred colours sharpen and take shape.

Chinanga—the fever tree.

Cautiously, I lift my head.

Chikala! Of course, my bed is empty too.

Slowly, I swing my legs out of the bunk and anchor them on ground. I sit and earth my feet on synthi-steel, one by one.

The pain shreds my ear.

I close my eyes and isolate it. There is only one arrow. It is nine out of ten and ice cold, bright blue-white. I send my spirit to stroke it, warm it, but it cuts at my hands. I blow my warm breath onto it, steaming it red in my mind. My breath runs out. Blue it burns again.

I ask for help from grandfather, holding his rough-hewn

sculpture, warm Shona stone, but all I hear is silence—the silence that leaks from vast and cold interstellar distances. We are alone here. Only the wind speaks, but in what a strange and empty tongue.

I stand and move before the pain burns too brightly, eyes open, anchoring my swaying body and shaking ankles with step-by-step focused visual cues, to help stabilise my proprioceptors.

There, door button, now press... root tendril designs, pick one, follow along the hall to *She's* heart; ow, get up, get up, focus, follow and lean on that root, don't lose sight, don't think ahead, not of *She*; get up, damn it, again, same root, that's it, ow, that's it, up again, the root's thickening, approaching CR, door button, press, collapse...

The floor is cold beneath my back.

I look upwards, feeling sick as my ear burns more and more. What on Earth is happening? No, *not* Earth; is that indeed the point?

Don't fight it; it's just one Buddhist arrow. No thoughts and emotions to make a second arrow, a second and deeper wound. Examine it; inspect it. This arrow is seven out of ten—steel grey, but pulsing blue. It's only pain. It will shift; it will change. Everything does.

Eventually.

Above me, *She's* face is a familiar old bald white man in a white coat. He's got a stethoscope draped around his neck. I remember him, old Doctor Botha from my childhood. He'd been one of the South African émigrés, moving north for new opportunities, new challenges. Why has *She* become him?

*She* speaks slowly, words pulsing with warmth: <You seem ill Aneni, what can I do?>

I cough, but my throat is clear, I am not choking. "Make it go away *She*... please!"

The old man shakes his head. <I still don't know the cause, although I can maybe dull the pain.>

Yes... and no. Fuck it; I don't want to just *ease* things. There's a job to do. There's always a job; but how can we live and work if this world is somehow poisoning us, sickening us? I lever myself slowly into a sitting position and slide against the wall. "Open all room channels, *She.*"

Two screens flicker on as the wake-alarm sounds.

Ezi is hanging head down, retching over the side of her mattress, now stacked on top of a black bench-press in our tiny Gym-room. Every day, she must pack her bed away, for all of us still need

251

to bulk up our bodies with exercise there, ever-fighting against this planet's enervating pull.

Petrus is lying in his bunk, body still, limbs twitching and eyes open. Anwar is strapped to a Smart-chair facing skywards, a chair that constantly cranks itself towards our solar system. He must have been praying, even though Mecca itself is too blunt a target at this distance.

"Aneni here, how are you all doing?"

Ezi is in no state to talk and the men can only groan, although Petrus makes a fist of it. *"Kak!"* is all he says.

I look at my old Doctor, whose face is now filling the room with concern. "Is this terminal?" I ask.

*She* looks at me long and hard before shrugging: <I'm afraid I don't know, Aneni.>

I sigh, gathering in strength for more words, hard words, "I'm taking a vote on Procedure F76."

*She's* eyes widen with simulated shock: <That would breach our Primary Mission Goal.>

"If we're going to die, we should at least have the choice of *where* that is."

Silence.

I look down. The arrow is eight and rising; purple now, steady and aching. Wrap it tight with the words you must say. "All in favour of F76, special emergency protocol I am empowered to authorise, just say 'me'; voice recognition certification on full, *She.*"

The old man looks disappointed and puts on a pair of glasses, black horn-rimmed archaic ones. I don't remember *those.*

"This is to return to Earth, no?"

It takes me some moments to realise it is Petrus speaking, his body twitching but stilling in his bunk.

I nod, suddenly feeling cowardly.

"I think Allah has brought us safely here for a reason."

Confused momentarily, I suddenly realise Anwar has followed up on Petrus's question. (His face averted skywards; I had not seen his lips move.)

The old man *She* looks up at me, smiling.

"And...," continues Anwar, panting after each brief rush of words: "Do we really want to... to bring back with us... dare I say it... a plague of... of possibly Biblical proportions?"

His words shame me and remind me of time, both ancient and

future. "If we do leave, *She,* when will we arrive back on Earth?"

*She* is no longer my doctor, but has morphed into a small, elderly and sharp featured brown woman in a bright orange sari. I immediately recognise Indira Moodley, my teacher, the great Kenyan psychiatrist who revised Fanon, integrating his theory with genetic neuro-physiology into a marvellous psychiatric Theory of Everything. (From the mindfulness of cells to the Minds within politico-cultural events and back down again.)

<It'll be 2190 when we get back.>

I realise I'm looking at a long dead woman.

*Seventy* years gone! I'm freezing fast on this icy surface. I close my eyes. The arrow is Ten and vivid fucking violet. Out of the darkness I see the second arrow coming, but I am too cold to move, ice forming around me like a casket.

There is no way home. There never was. I'd known that in my head when we'd left—we all had, but not to the core of our cells and selves.

There is nothing else to do but whisper goodbye to my family, to Earth, although my voice is broken: *"Sarai zvakanaka."*

Anashe will be dead too—perhaps *long* dead, my beloved daughter. My eyes sting, so I close them, coughing out words I hope can be heard. "Shall we vote?"

I knuckle my eyes and open them, but *She* doesn't even bother to wait for us—swelling, shifting, and swaying... Finally bursting into a huge windstalk above us, a thick-stalked purple plant with splayed giant leaves hanging from the apex—but swirling to the sound of alien winds we cannot hear.

As for the arrow of pain, now drilling through my head and into my left ear, there is only one thing left I can do.

I hold it, my fingers cupping my ears, burning and melting into the white-hot shaft of pain. I hold and don't let go, as if my hands have fused across my ears.

Tonight, please let me dream of the Copperbelt again, even just fleeting fragments of places I don't recognise. (Huge rainy season droplets on my tongue will be enough, toes curled into reddish-brown earth. No, *anything* will do...)

Later on, though, I dream of nothing.

§

We gather for the Sun-Show meal, warming up first with my Zambo-Chinese tai chi lessons—short form, the long form can come later. Petrus has proved himself a natural master in waiting, moving with a slow grace. So too have I taught them to harness their visual attention and their muscle proprioception, in order to compensate for now periodic vestibular disturbance.

*She* opens the blinds as daylight gathers above the rocking purple windstalks, standing ten to twenty metres tall. We watch them sway as we eat, our balance strangely bolstered in the pending dawn. Anwar has prepared a glorious meal indeed—tested on the five mice that survived the trip—spliced and pummelled purple cereal lifted from 'bot samples, with a sharp, but curiously pleasant tang.

At the end, we all look at him and he smiles: "It is our first safe combination of Earth and exo-plants." (He'd been thrilled to find a workable genetic compatibility, Allah seeding the Universe.)

So. We will greet the new day with a hope of real sustainability—perhaps we shall not starve, nor die, anytime soon. As for our ear pain, it both fluctuates and hovers, like a random and ghostly wasp who has been angered.

Perhaps it is here to warn us, that here too, we also need to bend our ways of working to survive? I have banned religion from the table—Western tables must be really dull without politics as well—but for once I relent.

It is that afterwards, with thanks, I hold a truncated ceremony of *kurova guva*—welcoming the spirits of the deceased, although Anwar leaves to say his own prayers. I know remembrance rituals differ across the continent, so I keep it brief and generic. "We leave a bowl for those who travel to new places and hunger in the holes between. May you all find your way to new joys… and just perhaps a few of you may even make it here."

Ezi has no belief, but still she cries, quietly. (Hers was a close family indeed, her grandmother a Hero of the Oil Wars; the start of Africa reclaiming her resources.)

The sky is paling fast, the windstalks bending before the heat of this sun's heralding winds. We stay quarantined; the First planned Walk is no longer taking place.

But I am tired of waiting. Still the pain bites deep in my ear, but I feel there are no answers here.

I bow to the others and leave the room, making my way to the airlock. (We're just about breathing native air by now anyway, sterilised and incrementally added into our closeted atmosphere.)

I pick up a head-suit with visor; there is no reason to take unnecessary risks on the eyes. The scalp cap peels on with a sticky tightness and I flip the visor down, the small room darkening instantly. Flicking a switch, an inner door seals the small room, lined with built-in benches in case of prolonged emergency use. I pick up a walking rod too.

<Is this wise, Aneni?> *She* warbles into the ear-speaker.

"Since when have I been wise, *She?* Open the external door please."

<And if I deem this a breach of safety protocol, given our quarantined status?>

"We're humans. We *do* things. I am tired of cowering from this place."

The door remains shut. I turn and lever the walking rod through the handles of the inner door, effectively locking it.

<*What* are you doing, Aneni?>

I sit. "Just waiting for you to open the external door."

<We don't know enough yet about the biological risks.>

"Perhaps we never will," I say. "Life is a biological risk. Open the door."

<You're not ready for all possible challenges that may arise, in your physically compromised state.>

"I am a woman."

The external door light glows green, but it remains shut. I make a note to ask Petrus whether quantum *She* can have two different minds at the same time.

"I am an *African* woman!"

A green light flickers on and I hear a hiss from the ceiling as odourless but penetrating and sterilising nanoparticles descend, seeping through my overalls, cleansing me in readiness for a new place. Slowly, the door grinds open and I gasp and cough at the acrid, burning air. Gradually my breathing eases and I'm able to raise my head. The ground outside our Base is rough, uneven, with tightly latticed blue grass of sorts.

As my gaze lifts, I sweep past the Lander-Plane that spring-loaded our base, down a rough, uneven slope towards indigo reeds lining a patch of dark water. The water is partially obscured by towering windstalks that seem to be circling the small lake, like giants rearing above us and emitting a stench that seems part sulphur, part acid. My eyes stream under the visor and I cough again, but pull the walking rod free and step forward, moving slowly around our circular base.

The others are pressed against the wide kitchen window and wave, but I'm too engrossed with the sparkle of orange-red rays amongst heavy grey clouds overhead.

"Azania," I breathe.

*She* must have patched the suit-speaker into the kitchen.

I recognize Ezi's voice, groaning: "Ahhhh, mmmmm!"

"What?" I turn to the shadowed shapes behind the window; Ezi is etched thinner and taller than the men.

"Ahhhhh, mmmmmm," she repeats. "The sound of this place. We're not going to repeat the same shit that happened to us, we're not going to do a Shell Oil or Cecil Rhodes on this place!"

I laugh, coughing at the burning, almost peppery air. "Good point, although if we're going to change the name of this planet, wouldn't 'Euromerica' be a more easily pronounceable name?"

"Look," says Petrus, and I see him pointing high behind me.

The first rays of the young new sun are flashing through the windstalks, now shimmering a deep violet. Below them, the ground sways with rustling purple reed ferns. Shadows shrink, hiding nothing but vivid variegations of purple and movement—as well as purpose? Have our projections onto the landscape begun? Or are there some things or beings hidden and active amongst the vegetation? TaNK has seen nothing so far, but He is not God.

Still, could there be things so small they invade our ears undetected—even now, the pain is five and... I forget the numbers, there are too many beautiful colours flowing down the groaning windstalks as I brace myself against a blast of hot and pungent air.

And then it comes again. A high-pitched keening sound, but more modulated, subtler.

"Ahhhhhh, mmmm," Ezi repeats in my painful ears, but she's not even close.

The atmospherics amplify and fracture the sound, enhancing into a multitude of varying tones, polyphony of sounds and calls. It's as if the windstalks are talking.

<Aneni,> I know from the intimacy of her tone, *She* has secured this communication just for me. <I'm picking up a slight neuronal rewiring throughout your auditory cortex, a hint of

neurogenesis.>

"Ah!" I say. So it's my brain, not my ear. Have we been colonised so deeply too, from within? Or is this the consciousness of cells responding to a new and alien call?

I take grandfather's sculpture out of my baggy jacket pocket, stoop with bended knees and braced back, placing it carefully on the ground. It's not a spirit or a person, not a totem or God—Grandfather Mapfumo prided himself on being a modern man—his grandfather before him driving regime change in Zimbabwe with Chimurenga music. Instead, it's a Zanoosi, Zimbabwe's first Eco-car, running on degraded organic waste, not someone else's food, like maize. The car he helped design, which powers the Southern African Federation lion economy. This sculpture was of the same car he drove us all up to Mufulira in, where he traded with the Chinese and we settled, establishing new factories. (And it was he alone who never laughed at me, when I spoke of going into space as a little girl.)

I straighten, stiffening my spine against the pull of the planet. I taste the sour but balmy breeze on my tongue, knotted, blue grass closing around the sculpted stone, sealing it from view.

I believe the rain here is a little heavier, a little saltier.

Out of Africa and now out of Earth...

No, not Earth, but a new... place. Home is a hard word. Why couldn't I have just gone back some several hundred k's to my old familial roots in Mutare, instead of trillions of miles here? Of course, the signs were closing in, as Earth heated up and disasters grew worse and I'd never been able to convince myself, unlike mother, that it all meant the Rapture was indeed near.

So, here we are, with biological seeds from Earth, including a frozen egg from my very own daughter. It is here we must make our heaven.

I stand stiffly, locked into the planet in a left bow stance, as the bright new sun burns its heat into me. 'This is the same sun imbued with illusions/the same sky disguising hidden presences'— words from an old Leopold Senghor poem that circulate my head.

But—this is a *new* sun and I have no idea what lies beneath it; whether voices or spirits, plants or animals.

"Salaam Aleichem."

Behind me there are racking coughs. I turn—all three have followed me out, arms around shoulders as they walk, bracing themselves against the whipping wind. Ezi, thin, but as strong as rope, is in the middle.

"Don't tell me you want to hog this planet's air all to yourself, Aneni?" she chides me: "Wasn't stealing my sheets bad enough?"

An old joke, but who knows the barb beneath? The English have a saying about dirty laundry—but as for us, all is public, all is shared.

I smile; the new Sun shines on Petrus' scalp; almost making the Mandelas dance. He gestures at me to join them. I smile at him again but move next to Anwar, who stiffens at my touch.

We can't afford to lapse too quickly into neat and convenient relationships, however fecund. Not yet. This world has hurt and shaken us, perhaps for a reason, perhaps not. But for now, we must stay on our toes and learn new things, new ways of being.

At the end of the line, Petrus breaks into a slow tai chi stepping motion, moving from a left bow stance. But his left arm is still anchored around Ezi. Down the line, we echo and ripple his motions, the line dipping and rising with the flow of movement.

So it is, we dance African tai chi in our first real alien dawn. As we move, I note the pain—neither an adversary, nor a friend. Like rain and bananas, mice and joy, it just is.

We move slowly in a clumsy, lurching and stumbling dance—I laugh as Ezi bursts into a song, in words I don't understand.

Finally, I am warm again.

## PEG DUTHIE
## With Light-Years Come Heaviness

My brother
turning away
from the can of pickles
brought by the latest messenger,
jarred by its new logo,
childhood over
in a blink.

# DEAN FRANCIS ALFAR
## Ohkti

My big sister hooked up with a heza boy with the most ridiculous fringe around his neck. Zemi, this is Dusi, the bitch said, pointing to the short-legged myconid that gently swayed next to her. So I said hey, whatever, and looked back down at the old vids I watching on my tab, and swallowed what I really wanted to say.

Which was how could you do this again after what happened with Chiso, the other heza boy? Wasn't it just seven or so months ago? Haven't you learned anything, you ignorant bitch? Heza change, they can change just like that, any moment any time, like Chiso did, despite the promises he made to you, promises you repeated over and over again to me while I tried to sleep on the lino floor. Oh, Zemi, you'd say, listen to what Chiso told me today, I'm so happy. Or, oh, ohkti, this is the plan for next year when Chiso and I get out of this place, inshallah. And then you'd tell me the same story: how Chiso and you would save up for your fare—he with his job at the air scrubbery, you with yours selling comestibles to miners—and smuggle him up the Luna elevator then across the void on a shuttle and then down the Terra elevator where, like a pair of loveable scoundrels in a vid, you'd work your way to a better tomorrow, trusting in fortune or in a benevolent universe to bring things your way, as if the old world would not detect his illegal alien ass, until your wished-for future finally arrived and you could mix spore and eggs how exactly I don't want to know and produce a brood of sprouts that you'd both watch over until they'd grown, hand in stalk, weathering time until you died in each other's embrace etcetera etcetera.

I'm so familiar with the story, so bored with it, that I've spun my own versions, like: how you and Chiso somehow scrape together enough credit for a one-way elevator ride down and he dumps you as soon as his heza roots touch the old world, because you're just flesh to him and he's a myconid, you dumb bitch, and that's why they're haram on Terra, and you cry in shock and beg him to take you back, you remind him while sobbing how you've uprooted yourself from Luna and that the deal was for both of you to take root together, that all the carnal premature celebrations you both engaged in resulted in a zygote in your fleshy belly, again how I don't want to know, and he's the parent like you're the parent and oh what happens now and oh think of the sprout etcetera etcetera, but the heza bastard is already in green sleep, communing with their viridian space gods and has forgotten you, and you feel used because you were used, spored to be precise, reduced to the hand that moved a heza to a better place, except that you wanted to stay but you can't because flesh needs to move, so you do, you move on, as far as your feet can take you, as far as your ass can buy you, turning tricks for as long the sprout stays secret and small inside you, and inevitably you fall again, for another illegal heza of course, because you never learn, you cannot learn, and you mix it up and inhale his pollen and you are spored again, until you wake up with another heza's sprout joining sprout number one in your belly, and so on etcetera etcetera. I haven't decided the ending of that one, except that it has to be tragic because that's how all stories end.

Hey, ohkti, she said through a forced smile, I said this is Dusi. Isn't he just the thing? Come over here, Zemi. The last part is almost a shout and I imagined for a moment what she'd have done if I didn't get up, didn't come over, and instead hurled my tab at her or, even better, at her new heza boyfriend. But she knew me well enough and I did not like to provoke her unnecessarily, not more than usual, so I dragged my ass off the mat on the floor and skipped to where they stood, put on my biggest grin and said kamusta mustasa to the heza. For a moment I thought Zara would explode but instead she let out a huge laugh, the reckless kind which involved spittle flying all over the place, and I didn't bother to shield myself because, despite everything, I loved the bitch with all my heart. She just made really senseless choices most of the time.

Dusi, the new heza, did not understand what I said, so Zara translated for him, rubbing a bit of oil from her nose onto his splayed head. Soon the heza boy was soundlessly rocking back and forth in place and that's when I decided that Dusi wasn't so bad, for a mindbending sporesending myconid. We spent the rest of the day watching vids on my battered tab, well actually they did, as I couldn't concentrate and found myself looking at them, mostly. Dusi's fringe was splotched red and gold with tiny beads of moisture that my sister popped between her thumb and little finger while she kept her eyes on the flickering screen. It was a Pinoy comedy that played, the usual talking animals in entangled relationships voiced by withered ex-child stars on Terra, a zoological love pentad, that tired old trope. Dusi seemed to enjoy it, ensuring in my mind that he was the only heza I ever met with a sense of humor. Or irony.

Jealous, Zara mouthed to me. I just rolled my eyes at her and made a face. I'd never fall for a heza. I am nothing like the bitch.

They went out for the rest of the season and I'd see Zara only in the late evenings long after I'd returned from madrasa. If I were already asleep, she'd position her foot on my ribcage and make me squeal as I rolled around the floor, as if we were kids again, saying stupid things while invisible stars sparkled in her eyes. Zemi, she'd say, wake up, I want to tell you a story, about what Dusi and I did tonight. Or, bitch, have you been to the Gruithuisen Domes—oh, of course you haven't but you should someday. Or, ohkti, do they still teach you in madrasa that Luna is the coldest place in the solar system? Because it's not true when Dusi is with me. I would groan or throw something at her, but the bitch would continue her dual-pronged combination assault of foot and naïve romantic vignettes and the floor is a terrible field of battle. So I resigned myself to my inevitable force-fed diet of stories.

I was twelve years old, almost thirteen then, which made Zara nineteen. Our ummi passed when I was six, leaving my big sister to function as the mother—which, I must point out, I needed only for a short amount of time. Not that the bitch didn't do her best, she did, within her means. But Zara was a teenager who had to leave the madrasa to work so we would both have something in addition to the small pension our ummi left behind. Leaving school was something she used to remind me of whenever I did something that made her angry. I sacrificed a bit of my life for you, ohkti, the bitch would say. The least you could do be grateful etcetera etcetera.

We rarely talked about our ummi. The truth is that I barely remembered her despite the number of vids we have of her. Before her bones were powdered and interred with the rest of the dust outside, she prepared a series of vids of her talking, telling stories about how she got to Luna, interspersed with lectures on how to keep our bayt clean and crap like that. When I was young, the woman in the vids was a stranger, no different from any of the women in the feeds my tab could access given enough credit. Zara was even more dismissive. We don't need her anymore, the bitch told me. She's gone and there's only you and me and I promise you we'll make it because we'll always have each other and I'll never leave you, inshallah etcetera etcetera. Which was all true for the most part as she rebuffed all efforts to separate us, giving the men of the PopCon the runaround in a way only the most creative or desperate can. It's only until I'm legal, Zara told me when she moved us to the slums of Mons Shithole, where many migrant Filipino miners lived and worked. As a little girl, I really had no choice but to believe her and hold on for dear life, adjusting to the small space with no beds no furniture no nothing that would be our home for years. It was during those early years of hiding from the men in the moon that I rediscovered our ummi. In one vid, she tells her love story, one that I seared into my brain because of sheer repetition brought about by lack of anything better to do, which I only understood years later.

This is a love story but it has nothing to do with a man. You had no father, because a father means someone who stays to be a father, and the man who helped make you was anything but that. He was a berdugo, useless in every way except that he made me happy. And it was because of happiness that I believed every word he said and allowed myself to be fooled into his arms, not once but twice. First was with you, Zara, and I thought I had it made, that I had the meaning of life with you in my arms and him by my side one two three, but he left soon after you were born and I had to find my own meaning. Later, we met again, and once more happiness bloomed despite my caution and precautions and we had you, Zemi. And I thought that he would stay, that this time he would say Mahal, I will stay forever, but of course he didn't and I had the two of you to think of. So do not mistake happiness for love or hope for reality because neither is worth living for. What matters is what matters and what matters is you and you and our life on Luna. We will thrive here, I promise, inshallah.

One time, Zara came home early and found me watching our ummi telling the same story. You should stop watching that, the bitch said with a sad smile. It's no good listening to other people's stories, always looking to the past. Which was completely and utterly hypocritical of her obviously but at that time she was the universe to me. But she's our mother, I said. Oh, ohkti, that's true, but she's gone and we both need to keep looking forward. Far better to work and save credits, or in your case, finish madrasa because you still can while I have sacrificed everything for you. You don't want to be like me, unfinished, no prospects. You have all the tomorrows I'll never have, inshallah. The bitch always knew how to turn any conversation about anything to something about her.

I hated every minute that I spent in school, with all the other poor children of the miners and junkers. But I especially hated how we'd all have to crane our necks and look up to Terra when it was time to pray. Mecca the homeland is there, our teacher told us, and we respect and remember. I do not know why I don't have faith or what happened to it if I ever had it. At that time what mattered more to me was that the bitch didn't have to go to madrasa anymore and I still had to. I spent long hours imagining ways to get out, to escape, to run from the endless lessons that I didn't see sense in—dome maintenance, mineral chemistry, atmospheric gradations etcetera etcetera interspersed with prayers aimed at the unfathomably holy place I'd never see anyway on a world that wanted none of us. I was so obsessed with schemes and plans that I didn't realize that a new boy had taken to sitting next to me.

Oh, Huddin, source of temptation and confusion and unexpected life. If I could go back in time I'd strangle you to prevent those words from escaping your lips. I think you're beautiful, yes, those particular words, the very first ones you whispered to me, provoking me to look at you. If, back in time, I fail to prevent you from speaking, then I will gouge out your eyes, yes, those eyes that met mine and captured them with the mere hint of a promise of something else something new something exciting. But you know I mean none of that.

Fuck off, I told you.

Shouldn't talk like that, you laughed. It upsets the fucking teachers.

And with that I was doomed, charmed by a boy a year older than me with the barest of beginnings of a moustache, with the uneven jaw you told me later was broken when you resisted your brother's fist, with well-muscled arms that were so strange so hard so real to me, Huddin of the fucking words and stories.

The heza aren't all that bad, you told me one time when we both crept out of madrasa to look at the Luna elevator, watching its slow ascent to the platform high above. At least we have a home, a real home here and an old one spinning above us. They don't have anything.

They floated in space until they got here, I replied. They can just float away as far as I'm concerned. No one wants them.

But everyone needs a home, you told me, leaning in for what would be the first kiss of many. Even if no one wants them.

Especially so.

That kiss, that kiss I remember the most, because it took away my capacity for words, and unable to argue about the unwanted proliferation of heza, all I could do was respond to the softness of your lips and the taste of your tongue. And I think you knew, obviously you did, that I knew nothing, which just heightened the forbidden act. But even now I know I'm being unjust because I was not completely void of reason. But you represented another universe, someone something that wasn't Zara.

I'm afraid, I told you as I brought your hand to the space between my trembling legs. Be gentle.

You withdrew your hand so quickly that it startled me. No, Zemi, you said, red in face. We are too young.

I could say nothing and said nothing, the shame inside me almost bursting out from my skin. When I made to run, you held my hand.

Don't go, you said. So I stayed and when it became comfortable for words to surface again, we told each other stories beginning that day and for many days after. I told you about Zara.

You should be kinder to her, you told me much later. And don't call her a bitch.

But I am and she is, I told you, tracing the contour of your thick arms while you held me. Besides, what is it to you?

If my brothers and I had the kind of thing you have with your sister—

Then they would be bitches. Or bastards.

Zara, of course, took to Huddin instantly, responding to his well-placed words and miner's son's charm. Oh, ohkti, you are so lucky someone wants you in the first place. First love is wonderful if you can hold on to it, inshallah. Under other circumstances I would have said something or at the very least made a face, but like our ummi I was happy so I didn't. Sure, sure, was all the acid I could muster.

So then the four of us began to have dinner together, with the bitch and her heza boyfriend foregoing some of their jaunts around Luna after their work cycles just to be with us. Because I like seeing you happy, Zara told me, and Dusi likes Huddin very much. After eating, we would play games or watch vids until it was time for the boys to go home. But mostly we told stories to each other, not that I had much to tell at that time. That's when I learned of Dusi's long journey out in the void, part of a whole group of spores that do not remember where they came from. That's when I learned of Huddin's ambition to one day manage the mine where his older brothers worked. And that's when I learned that Zara was pregnant with Dusi's sprout.

She just came out and told all of us. And I, she said right after one of Huddin's stupid jokes, am carrying his sprout. Her fingers caressed Dusi's fringe. I remember raining a litany of abuse on the bitch, restrained only by Huddin, exacerbated by the way the guilty myconid just rocked back and forth on the floor. It's true, Dusi, she told him, you're going to be a father. When the heza stopped rocking I knew that it was news to him as well.

How could you, Zara? How could you be so stupid? I always knew you were a dumb bitch but held hope that you'd somehow know better. Zara simply asked the boys to leave us alone, telling Dusi that they'd talk some more later and how everything would work out in the end, inshallah. When they did, when it was just her and me and my arsenal of shocked recriminations, she cried.

Tell me it will all be all right, ohkti.

I can't, you stupid bitch. I can't.

Dusi vanished. Of course he did. Because our ummi had tried to warn us and only I remembered her love story. Huddin and his brothers looked everywhere, asked other heza but could not find him. The myconid had dissolved into the air of the scubbery or floated up past the dome of Mons Shithole back into the void that spawned him to find some other person to ruin.

Zara wept until she had nothing left but what he left inside her belly and surrendered to her fate. It is what it is and I just hope to live through it, inshallah. Those were her last words before she turned inward and journeyed to a place in her head so deep and so far I could no longer reach her.

Huddin moved in and slept on the floor with us, helping me keep the bitch I loved alive, even as her flesh changed color, even as the sprout began to consume her.

Huddin, this was the time that I was more than unjust to you. Save her, I commanded. Find a way. You talk so much and know so much, so do something, I demanded. And when you could not, when all you offer was empty hands and your strong arms and your soft kisses, I told you to fuck off. Because my sister was dying and since you were useless to her you were useless to me.

How to Live on Other Planets

I will stay outside, you told me, after everything I screamed at you. And you did, for the next several months, sleeping outside, bringing us food, while I festered with anger and helplessness and watched Zara deteriorate. It was you who brought the mine's doctor, convincing your brothers to spend much of their hardwon credits. And it was your doctor who told us that there was really nothing to be done, repeating the terrible fact that women could not bear heza offspring. That human flesh was like a field where sprouts could take root. That she would either survive or not, inshallah. So I spat at your expensive doctor and told you again to fuck off.

I will stay outside, you said again. And you did until the time that I came outside because Zara, my okhti, my bitch, was gone, lost somewhere in the grey ravaged body she left behind. I tore the sprout the killed her apart and I tore at you, went mad and shouted and wept and called you everything horrible I could and you took it all until I was spent and trembling in your arms.

You knew better than to say anything. It will be all right would be met by an explosion of rage. You will survive this would be met by unmitigated venom. I'll be here for you would be met by complete and utter disbelief. So you said nothing and I said nothing. You and your brothers took her remains away. I swept the bayt clean like my ummi taught me in one of her vids.

You gave me time to grieve for her.

I want you to go away.

I want to stay.

No, I told you. Go away.

I won't be far.

Go away.

I finished madrasa and found work with the dome and convinced myself that everything that was in the past meant nothing, did not mean a thing. I put you and Zara aside.

But I couldn't, really.

And years later, when I was ready to live again, I knew where to find you.

Will you come with me to visit the old world, I asked you.

Of course, you said, and we traced the path of my sister's longing, went up and across and down elevators to Terra, to the Philippines, where my ummi's dreams began. After everything you took me in your arms and said it's time to go home.

And so we did, back to the moon.

When I look at our children now, I remember my sister, and when I tell them about her, I don't call her a bitch. I tell them about her sacrifice and her laughter and how she dreamed of one day going up the elevator to the platform, then riding a shuttle, then landing on the Terra platform, then taking that elevator down to the old world where the oldest and most beautiful hopes have a chance of coming true. I tell them how love is important and how I know that to be true because you are still here, Huddin. No longer waiting outside, always beside me. And I tell them that while most stories are sad, what matters, what really matters is what happens afterwards, that for as long as we have each other we will be fine, inshallah, and then I tell them my about sister, and I give them all my memories.

I tell them to remember.

# LEWIS SHINER
# Primes

## 1.

For nearly an hour Nick had been stuck on Interstate 40, surrounded by the worst traffic he'd ever seen. He'd watched the last heat of the sun set fire to the horizon and burn out, and now the first stars were tunneling through the haze. He had one arm out the open window in the unnatural 60-degree heat of the desiccated January evening. In the better parts of his brain, to keep himself amused, he was revising the code for his new graphics driver project.

Once past the Durham Freeway, I-40 had narrowed to a two-lane bottleneck. Traffic seemed to have doubled since that morning, with two cars trying to squeeze onto the road for every one that crawled off in defeat.

He was wearing a black T-shirt from the 544 club in New Orleans, where he and Angela had danced on their honeymoon two years before. A huge diesel rig inched past him on the right. The trailer was stark white except for the rear panel, where the number 544 stood out in stark black numerals. Nick glanced down at the dashboard clock. It was 5:44. For an instant he felt an abyss of inexplicability open under him, and then he shook it off. It was a bizarre coincidence, nothing more, something to tell Angela about, if he ever made it home.

By six he was close enough to the Lake Jordan exit that he could pull onto the shoulder and ease around the motionless right hand lane. It took fifteen minutes more to cover the remaining mile and a half to his driveway, and by then he was too tired to think much about the Cadillac parked where Angela's gold Acura should have been. Her battery had been acting up, he knew, and she'd probably gotten a ride home with somebody from Duke Hospital, where she was on the faculty.

In truth, for most of that particular day, Nick had been consciously happy. Despite the endless commute, despite approaching deadlines on his driver, the components of his life were laid out in what seemed a comfortable and sustainable order. He and Angela had no debts except the house, and they'd nearly paid that off. They'd both weathered the latest flu epidemic and were back to full health. And Thursday was Nick's night to cook. His attention was already shifting from traffic and programming to the free-range chicken and sour cream and tortillas waiting in the refrigerator to be transformed into *enchiladas suizas.*

The fear didn't fully hit him until he climbed out of the truck and saw the color of the door that he was about to slam shut.

His beautiful white pickup truck was bright red, red as a stoplight, red as blood.

He'd been driving that pickup for four years, from the time before he'd moved to North Carolina and met and married Angela. He'd bought it back in Austin, where a white paint job could make the difference of a few crucial degrees in the inside temperature under the Texas sun. It had been white when he'd gotten into it in the office parking lot at a quarter to five. He knew himself to be sober, drug-free, and possessed of a clean bill of psychiatric health. It was simply not possible that the truck was red.

He tried to remember if he'd noticed the hood of the truck while he was driving home. It had been dark and he hadn't been paying attention. He looked at the key in his hand. It was the wrong size and shape and there were no other keys with it. His hand lunged reflexively for his pocket and found nothing there. All of his pockets were empty: no wallet, no checkbook, no change.

He searched the red truck. It too was empty except for a jack behind the seat and an owner's manual in the glove compartment. It could be a rental, he thought. Maybe he'd been in an accident that damaged his short term memory, and nobody had realized it. Maybe he'd absentmindedly left his wallet somewhere.

He started to run for the house, his shoes slapping awkwardly at the sidewalk. The front door was locked and he pounded on it with the flat of his hand until he heard the lock click and felt the door swing inward.

The man who opened it was in his thirties, tall and fit looking, with an angular face and fair receding hair. He wore a long-sleeved blue oxford-cloth shirt, crisply pressed khakis, tasseled loafers. He had a drink in his left hand. He looked Nick over and stepped aside to let him in. "Angela?" the man said, looking behind him, "I believe Nick has arrived."

The accent, as Nick knew it would be, was cultivated British. Nick had seen the man's photo in one of Angela's albums that dated back to before Nick's time with her. His name, Nick knew, was David. He was Angela's first husband, and he'd died in 1995.

## 2.

"David Graham," David said, extending his hand. "I expect you're a little surprised to see me here."

"I thought you were dead," Nick told him, looking down to find he'd gripped David's hand by sheer reflex.

"Ah. Angela said much the same thing."

Nick backed into the living room and sat on the couch to ease the trembling in his legs. "What are you doing here?"

"I'm afraid I live here, actually."

Angela appeared in the doorway that led into the kitchen and leaned against the jamb, arms folded. She was still in her hospital scrubs and Nick couldn't help noticing, as he always did, how that shade of green set off the red-gold in her hair. A little mascara and eyebrow pencil would have made her conventionally beautiful, but she disdained makeup and so instead her appeal was more subtle. It had taken Nick all of a minute and a half—the interval between the first time he met her and the first time he managed to make her laugh—to be overwhelmed by it.

Nick tried and failed to read her mood through the barricade of her posture. David, on the other hand, was as transparent as glass. He looked at Angela with wonder, longing, and a fading glow of residual despair.

"Is anybody going to tell me what the hell is going on here?" Nick heard his voice go shrill in the particular way that inspired him to self-loathing.

"It's not just here," Angela said. "It's all over the news."

"So you just, what, came home, saw David, and turned on CNN for an explanation?" In fact it wouldn't have surprised him. She found her stability in the calm urgency of the newscasters, in the way they stood between mere mortals and the avalanche of information that threatened to bury all of civilization.

"I got home at four-thirty. About an hour later I went out to get something from my car and it was gone, and there was some strange car in the driveway instead. I got freaked and came in and tried to call the police, but all the lines were tied up. That's when David walked in on me." She stopped for a second, and Nick could see her fast-forward through her emotions. "At that point we knew something big was happening." She turned away. "Come on in and see."

Nick followed them meekly into the den and sat on the sofa between them. He was just in time for a recap of the day's top story.

Between five and six in the afternoon, eastern time, the population of the east coast of North America had doubled, as had the population of the western bulge of South America, which lay along the same longitude. The phenomenon seemed to be spreading westward at the same rate the Earth revolved.

Nick understood that what he was hearing was true, believed it on a cellular level, but he couldn't find a handle for his emotions. The scale of the disaster seemed to overshadow his own confusion and panic.

"I've checked the other stations," Angela said, answering a question he hadn't needed to ask. "If it's a hoax, they're all in on it."

"It's not a hoax," Nick said. He glanced at David. "You know it's not a hoax."

"With some significant exceptions," said CNN anchor Judy Woodruff, "every human being in the affected area—which now includes Chicago, Memphis, and eastern edge of New Orleans—now seems to have an exact double." The camera panned to a duplicate Judy Woodruff in a canvas chair at the edge of the set, patting nervously at her shoulder-length blonde hair.

The scene shifted to Bernard Shaw interviewing his double on a Washington DC street corner that was sliding into chaos. In the background, abandoned cars stood with their doors open as pedestrians swarmed without apparent purpose between them. Half of the people in the crowd had twins standing somewhere near them. What struck Nick was that not all the pairs wore the same clothes, and some had radically different outfits or hair styles. The picture jumped periodically as someone from the alarmed, but not yet hysterical, mob collided with the camera operator.

"So what are these 'significant exceptions' she was talking about?" Nick asked Angela. "Is that us? And where did David come from?"

"David lives here," David said.

"They don't know yet," Angela said. "Shhhhh."

The street scene ended abruptly, and during a second or so of on-screen darkness Nick heard the ambient noise of an impending press conference: chairs shifting, throats clearing. "We're live," somebody said, and then the screen cleared to show a generic wood-grain folding table under harsh fluorescent lights. Two identical men sat at the table, each with long dark hair and a single diamond stud in his left ear. A young woman reporter Nick didn't recognize said, "We're here at MIT with the Doctors Jason Berlin of the theoretical physics department. Gentlemen, I understand you have a theory to explain the bizarre events we've seen tonight."

"Merely a hypothesis," said the Dr. Berlin on Nick's left. "Have you ever heard of something called the 'Many Worlds' interpretation of quantum physics?"

"I'm not sure," the reporter said. "Was it ever on *Star Trek?*"

"Frequently, as a matter of fact," said the Dr. Berlin on the right. "It's a sort of thought experiment that postulates an infinite number of universes parallel to our own, in which all possibilities are real."

The other Dr. Berlin nodded. "Exactly. And every possibility splits off a new world. For instance, you might have a world where the Axis Powers won the Second World War. Or where Fidel Castro played major league baseball."

The reporter said, "What does that have to do with what we're seeing tonight?"

The first doctor leaned forward. "Picture our Earth, and then a second Earth that's almost identical, but not quite. Call it, I don't know, call it Earth Prime. In one of them Bill Clinton is President, in the other it's Dan Quayle."

"Dan Quayle?" Nick asked. "Is he kidding?"

Angela shushed him again.

"There'll be other differences," the second doctor said. "Some people will have died in one world and not in the other. Two otherwise identical people will have different jobs, different spouses. Now suppose these two universes, that had split off at some point in the past, merged together again."

"How could that happen?" the reporter asked.

"I have no idea. Maybe the universe is downsizing." The crowd, which had been buzzing with low conversation, now erupted in nervous laughter. "But you'd see what we're seeing—most people would be duplicated, though with all kinds of subtle variations."

"Why isn't it happening all at once?" the reporter asked. "Why only people? Why no trees or cats or skyscrapers?"

The first doctor shrugged and the second said, "Frankly, we're at a bit of a loss to explain that just yet."

"Back to you, Judy," the reporter said. "Or is that Judy Prime?"

Angela hit the mute button and sat for a moment, as if gathering herself. Then she looked past Nick to David and said, "Tell me. How did I die?"

## 3.

David got up and refilled his glass from the liquor cabinet under the TV. Then he sat down again and said, "Car crash. The brakes were bad on the Mazda, and you insisted on going out in the rain to rent a film. We had a bit of a row about it, actually, and I only gave in because I felt like I was coming down with something and I wasn't up to getting wet. You...you slid through a stop sign." He took a drink. "A sixteen-year-old girl hit you broadside. They pronounced you dead at the scene."

"In my world," Angela said, "you went out for the movie. A movie you didn't even want."

The rising tide of emotion threatened to wash Nick out to sea. "Excuse me," he said, and went to the kitchen.

There he discovered that the refrigerator was wrong. No orange juice, no 7-Up, no raw materials for enchiladas. Instead he found two six packs of Heineken, a pizza box, some leftover Chinese takeout, a few half-pint bottles of Perrier. Over the hum of the refrigerator he heard David, his voice choked with emotion, say, "My life ended that night."

Nick closed the refrigerator and stared at his reflection in the window above the kitchen sink. "'My life ended that night,'" he mouthed, and watched himself mime putting a finger down his throat. Then he washed his face in the sink, trying to scrub away the fear and jealousy and despair.

As he turned from the sink, looking for someplace to throw his paper towels, he saw that morning's *News and Observer* on the butcher block table. The headline read, "Quayle apologizes for State of Union blunder."

"Oh my God," Nick said.

It was not, then, a merger of two worlds. It was a hostile takeover where one world vanished and one remained. The trees and cats and skyscrapers the reporter had been talking about belonged to someone other than Nick. David was not the intruder; like he'd been saying all along, David lived here.

Nick looked at Angela where she sat in highly-charged

conversation with David on the couch and did the math. Angela was not an intruder here either, world of origin notwithstanding. There was only one person who didn't fit in the equation, and Nick had been staring at his reflection only moments before.

## 5.

Nick had caught Angela on the rebound, and he knew he'd never have had a chance with her otherwise. He'd still been in Austin when David died, still been married to his first wife, still involved in an affair that was about to turn publicly sour in a narrow circle of acquaintance. He was writing code then for a small software house called Computics and thinking more and more about North Carolina.

Computics had a customer named Richard who sold medical information systems in the Raleigh area. On a business trip in 1995 Richard had shown Nick around the Triangle and Nick had been impressed with how green everything was, how it rained even in August. Summer rain in Texas was only a distant memory. When everything fell apart in Austin the next year—divorce, threats of more layoffs at Computics, another summer of rationed water and parched brown lawns—Nick packed it in and headed east. Richard helped him find a job and an apartment, and at his New Year's party four months later he introduced Nick to Angela.

Nick was graceful for a man his size, and he'd taken the trouble to dress well that night: charcoal suit, silk tie, cufflinks. Somehow he summoned the nerve to ask Angela to dance. She'd been drinking for the first time since David's funeral that June and it was the champagne that said yes.

A year and a half into the marriage Nick insisted on therapy, where Angela complained that Nick was too much in control, that he wanted her but didn't need her, that he didn't truly need anyone. In the third week she admitted that she loved Nick, but not in the way she'd loved David. She was afraid to love anyone that much again.

Nick slept in the guest house for a month or so after that, wanting to leave but imprisoned by his desire for her. Finally that desire became stronger than his anger and they began to make love again. He moved back into the bedroom and their attempt at therapy became, like David, one more thing they didn't discuss. Life was good again, or at least comfortable, until one day he came home and his pickup was red and David was waiting for him in the living room.

## 7.

David fixed mushroom omelets and they ate on TV trays in the den. Nick suppressed the thought that this was how the world ended, with neither bang nor whimper, but with CNN analyzing it to death.

After dinner Nick did the dishes and then took the portable phone into the darkened formal living room. The lines were jammed, but after half an hour he managed to reach his mother in San Antonio. She was fine, she said, but this duplicate version of herself kept following her around and talking incessantly. Nick nodded silently; his father was dead, then, in this world too. His mother supposed she would just have to put up with the inconvenience. Then the duplicate got on the phone and seemed unable to understand why he wasn't calling from Austin.

After he hung up he sat in the darkness for a long time. Eventually he switched the phone on again, and after a dozen attempts got through to directory assistance. He tried Raleigh, Durham, and Chapel Hill without finding a listing for his name. He tried again in Austin and this time the computer-generated voice recited a phone number—not his old one, but an exchange that Nick recognized as West Lake Hills, a big step up from his old neighborhood east of I-35.

That knowledge made it even harder to call. He could hear a voice saying, "I wondered when I'd hear from you," a tired and put-upon voice that Nick suddenly realized was that of his father, the fat, balding, sweaty and selfish man Nick had spent his whole life trying not to turn into.

If it had been the other way around, if Nick had been flush and his other self in Austin broke and desperate, Nick would have reached out to him in a heartbeat. But this way, to have to call from a position of weakness, even with no intent of asking for help, was more than he could bring himself to do.

He put the phone down, an immense sense of loss flowering slowly in his mind. He went out the sliding glass door at the back of the kitchen and crossed the patio to the guest apartment, a free-standing building that in Texas he would have called an *abuelita*, a grandmother's house. It was unlocked. He switched on the light to face what his logical mind had assured him he would find there: all of his books gone, all his vinyl albums and CDs, the bookshelves he'd put together and stained by hand, the Heathkit amp he'd built in college, his Math Cup from high school, all gone.

David's guest house instead contained a chair, a double bed with a white chambray spread and no headboard, a pair of framed Impressionist prints on the walls. A green banker's lamp bowed over the night stand, resting on top of a 1997 almanac and a John Grisham novel.

Nick sat on the bed and closed his eyes. When he opened them again, the room hadn't changed. It was full of absence. No favorite T-shirts, no photos of old girlfriends, no plastic model of the Space Shuttle from eighth grade. Every physical object that meant anything to him was gone.

## 11.

By the time Nick got back to the den, the many-worlds theory of the Doctors Berlin had expanded to fill the gap left by any other rational explanation. CNN now referred to the crisis as the "Prime Event" and their art department had produced a graphic showing twin Earths just touching edges inside an infinity symbol.

At seven p.m. eastern time, CNN estimated the population of Mexico City at 60 million, a figure Nick could not meaningfully comprehend. Much of the city was on fire by 8:00 and the smoke, on top of the already lethal pollution, quickly sent population estimates downward. The sidewalks were choked with corpses of the very young and very old, and the reporters began to speak in hushed voices about typhus and cholera.

Despite warnings, LA drivers began to head out into the worst traffic jam in California history. Meanwhile, gang members cruised the fringes of enemy turf, waiting to mow down newly arrived doubles of rival gang members as they appeared. "Too many f*cking Crips already, man," a young Blood told reporters, his "fuck" censored by a faint beep. "I ain't sharing with no f*cking Primes."

Airline traffic had come to a complete halt as nearly empty planes disappeared from airport gates and hangers, only to land minutes later fully laden with Primes. There were no rental cars, hotel rooms, or clean public rest rooms to be found in North America. Restaurants were out of food, service stations out of gas, ATMs out of money.

Eight o'clock Thursday night in Durham was 3 a.m. Friday in Moscow and along the Palestinian border; 5 a.m. in Sarajevo; ten in the morning in Beijing. Around the world everyone was poised for 5 p.m. ethnic cleansing time, taking an example from the LA gangs, or more likely not needing one.

At nine Angela switched to a local channel and learned that banks were limiting withdrawals to $100 per day per account, and holding all checks until the federal government told them exactly what their exposure was. Meanwhile local police departments asked all off-duty officers—prime or otherwise—to show up for night duty at banks, groceries, convenience stores, malls, and emergency rooms.

At ten o'clock Nick stood up. "Look, I can't just sit here and watch this any more."

Angela stared at him as if he'd lost his mind. "This is only the most devastating event since, what, the extinction of the dinosaurs?"

"At least the dinosaurs didn't sit around watching comet reports on CNN," Nick said. "I can't do anything about what's happening, and I can't just sit here and passively soak up any more second-hand pain and suffering. I'm full up."

Nick saw he was keeping Angela from the next round of disasters. He turned to David and said, "I know I don't have any right to ask this..."

"Of course you'll stay here," David said. "Take the guest house for as long as you need. I should think you already know where everything is."

"Yes. Thank you." The less charitable part of Nick's personality knew David wouldn't think of turning them out, not while Angela was part of the equation.

He picked up a handful of newspapers and magazines in the living room and went back outside.

## 13.

He was exhausted, and he badly wanted Angela to find him asleep if she did happen to look in. Two troubled marriages had taught him that sleeping well could indeed be the best revenge, but that night his twitchy nerves made it hopeless. After half an hour of flinging himself from one side of the bed to the other he switched on the banker's lamp and reached for the almanac.

He verified that Dan Quayle was President, impossible as it had seemed at first. In this universe—David's World, as he'd come to think of it, not without bitterness—Clinton had been caught *en flagrante* two days before the 1992 election and the press had crucified him. Bush had not only won, but solidified a new era of conservatism. Quayle rode the rising backlash against affirmative action, foreigners, feminism, and welfare straight into the White House.

What surprised Nick was how little difference it had made in the end. *Time* magazine featured Saddam, Tony Blair, and Nelson Mandella cheek to jowl with faces Nick had never seen before: a Father Dominguez who was leading an armed insurrection in the Yucatan; Selma Jones, US ambassador to China, who was urging favored nation status for the totalitarian regime; Davy Davis, teen heartthrob, who had the Ricky Nelson role in the upcoming feature film version of *Ozzie and Harriet.* But for all he knew, Selma Jones had been ambassador to China is his world as well, and Nick had never kept up with matinee idols.

The thing that really seized his attention was a three-page spread on the man who'd just been anointed the richest in the world: Harvey Chambers, CEO of the Computics empire headquartered in Austin, Texas.

Nick, like everyone else in the business, had many times heard the story of the Xerox Palo Alto Research Center and the point-and-click interface they'd invented for one of their pipe-dream projects. In Nick's World, Steve Jobs saw a demo and went home to build the first Macintosh. Bill Gates saw the Mac, and then there was Windows.

In David's World Harvey Chambers saw the demo first. He was a comics fan, so instead of windows his operating system had "panels," and instead of dialog boxes it had "captions" and "balloons." Parents didn't get it, but kids did, and the first computer-savvy generation grew up on Computics. Chambers avoided Apple's fatal error and licensed out his hardware designs to third party vendors, concentrating his own efforts on software—first games, then study aids, then office suites, growing up with his customers. Jobs and Gates never had a chance.

Like Gates in the world Nick came from, Chambers was locked in a battle with the Department of Justice. With a Republican that Chambers had helped elect in the White House, presiding over a Republican Congress, Justice never had a chance.

In Nick's World, Computics had never pioneered anything. Chambers had sold the struggling company in the late eighties and retired to Mexico to do some serious drinking. The people who'd known him said he'd had too much ambition and too little luck, a combination they thought would kill him in the end.

Nick's rich double in Austin no doubt worked for this gleaming, world-beating Computics, pickup long ago traded for a hunter green sport utility, the *Wall Street Journal* delivered every morning so he could check his stocks as he sat in his overstuffed leather armchair, careful to avoid wrinkling his Brooks Brothers suit. It was a scab Nick should have been able to pick at successfully for quite a while, but instead his attention kept drifting to more fundamental questions.

Like how he was going to live, for one. Angela would have work—it didn't take a Nostradamus to predict a shortage of doctors. The computer industry, however, looked like it could be in a serious recession as people concentrated on the basics of food, shelter, and transportation. All the things Nick no longer had.

The thought of the Angela-shaped hole in this world brought him to the toughest question of all. He and Angela. Angela and David.

He woke at some point before dawn with Angela curled into his back, holding him. The knowledge of something terribly wrong nagged at his memory, just within reach, but he shied away from it and dove back into sleep.

## 17.

David was the perfect gentleman. He made breakfast for Nick in the morning while Angela slept in, and gave him a robe to put on after his shower. He even found a couple of old T-shirts and a pair of sweat pants that Nick was able to fit into. While Nick tried to wake up, David went about his business, making reassuring noises on the phone to his most important clients without communicating any real data. He seemed to function in some gray area between the law and finance, and Nick was content not to know any more than that. "It's too early to tell," David said into the phone, to one client after another. "We'll just have to see how this all falls out."

On the news that morning they had an explanation, of sorts, for the red pickup. The two Doctors Berlin, now instant celebrities, were explaining the situation in terms of conservation of angular momentum (the primes who appeared in cars or planes were already moving at a high rate of speed) and conservation of mass and energy in a closed system (twice as many people, but only the same number of cars, planes, bicycles, and so on). Anyone who'd been driving at the time of the Prime Event had ended up in a car from David's World that wasn't in use at the time. Cars had disappeared from dealerships and rental agencies and even locked garages, then turned up on the highway with people like Nick behind the wheel.

"Improbable as this sounds," one of the doctors said on the TV in the next room, "there's a precedent for matter relocating itself like this. All the way back in 1964, Bell's Theorem projected this kind of behavior from subatomic particles into the macrocosmic world."

Meanwhile, repo agents were already out in force, and the reporters expected steady growth in that sector of the economy for at least the next few weeks.

The news didn't help the clenched feeling in the pit of Nick's stomach. He watched Angela stumble in and sit at the kitchen table with a cup of coffee and knew he had to get moving. If he went back to bed and pulled the covers over his head like he wanted to, he might never come out. The next time David was between calls, Nick said, "I'm going in to work."

"Why?" Angela said.

"Because I have to at least try. I can't just keep sitting here."

"Be careful," David said. "They say traffic is even worse today than last night."

Nick bent over to kiss Angela goodbye and she turned away at the last second, putting one arm around his neck and squeezing briefly. Her self-consciousness was palpable and Nick attributed it to David being there in the room, watching. Nothing had happened between Angela and David yet, Nick was sure, but he knew he was an idiot to walk out and leave them alone there together.

Nonetheless he turned away and started toward the door, and David followed him. "Listen," David said, and Nick turned to see him holding out two twenty-dollar bills. "Think of it as a loan, if you must. You can't go out there with empty pockets."

He was right, of course. Nick had no idea how much gas there was in the truck, and he had nothing to take for lunch. "Thanks," he said, the word leaving a numb spot on his tongue.

He turned the red pickup around and waited at the head of the driveway until, with a resigned nod and a flick of the hand, a middle-aged man finally let him join the slow parade of cars. On the commercial stations the drive-to-work crews hashed over the news with morbid humor, inviting people to call in with their most humiliating prime story. Nick escaped to a university station playing Mozart.

What most surprised him were the numbers of people on foot. Most were men, some with their thumbs out, some just walking with their heads down, postures closed against the morning chill. There was menace in the hard metal of the other cars, and Nick kept turning the radio down because he thought he heard something: a collision, a scream.

Just before the 54/55 exit, he saw a late model Honda and a Ford Explorer pulled over on the shoulder and two men, one black, one white, shoving and grabbing at each other beside the cars. As Nick slowly rolled past he could see the tight, weary expressions on their faces. Two miles later he saw a squad car stopped on the westbound side, and a cop forcing someone face down onto the hood.

For minutes at a time, one or another of the walking men would keep pace with Nick's truck as it inched forward. Once Nick turned his head and found one of the men staring in at him through the passenger window. The man's gaze was flat, empty of emotion. As if, Nick thought, the absence of hope had stranded him in an eternal present, without envy or expectation. Nick averted his eyes, his desire to offer a ride utterly quashed by the images of violence he'd seen throughout the long night on the television screen, and by the ugliness he'd already witnessed that morning through the windscreen of his truck.

He made it to the office in just under two hours. The front desk was deserted when he first walked in, then John, the slight, middle-aged receptionist, ducked out of the conference room and looked at him blankly. "Can I...help you with something?"

"Is Lisa in?" Lisa was the owner, and Richard had introduced her to Nick on his first trip to North Carolina. There was a chance she might remember him.

"Everyone's in a company meeting now," he said.

"Is this about the prime business? Because until yesterday I worked here. Your name is John Fanthorpe and your father was a logger in Oregon. Lisa's kids are named Spike and Janet. The alarm on the back door goes off every morning at 8:31 and nobody will drink the coffee when Dave Lee makes it."

John thought it over while Nick counted silently to five. "You might as well come in," he said at last.

Nick stood against one wall and scanned the room. He knew all but two of the fifty or so people there. Almost all of them were sitting in pairs, and some of the ones from Nick's world met his eyes and nodded. Both Dave Lees, Nick noticed, had on identical black jeans, black running shoes, and black 3dfx T-shirts.

One Lisa sat in the audience. The other Lisa stood at the front of the room and said, "You have to keep in mind that we're a small company, and a lot of federal guidelines don't apply here. Hell, you know as well as I do there aren't any federal regulations to cover this kind of mess. So what it comes down to is, I'm going to do whatever I think is best for the company, because in the long run that's going to do the most good for the greatest number of you all.

"I've got to sit down and crunch some numbers and make some decisions. So what I want everybody to do is to go on home." There were groans from the audience. "I know, it took you hours to get here. But you should all be home with your families right now. I will call each and every one of you before five o'clock today, Bell South and GTE willing, so that means any of you primes that aren't staying with your originals, come up here and give me a number where I can get hold of you."

Nick had heard the TV reporters distinguish between "primes" and "originals" but it sounded different when it was his job on the line. It sounded like there was no point in signing up.

"That's it," Lisa said. "Everybody go home, try and be cool, wait for this thing to shake itself out. I'm not even going to ask for questions because there aren't enough answers to go around right now."

Hands went up anyway and one or two people started sentences with "What about..."

Lisa shook her head decisively. "I'm serious, people. I'll talk to you all one-on-one later today." She held up one placating hand and left the room.

Nick forced himself to get in line and put his name and David's phone number on the legal pad. The Lisa who'd been sitting in the audience came up behind him. "Hey, Nick. I looked over the employee list and didn't see your name."

"Apparently I'm still in Texas," Nick told her. Lisa had been all right for an owner. She didn't pretend to be one of the gang, but she didn't distance herself either. Her office door was open most of the time, which meant on bad days Nick had been able to hear her yelling into the phone all the way back to his office. She was about fifty, with purplish-black skin and the first traces of gray in her short, stiff hair.

"Uh oh," she said sympathetically.

"Yeah. Kind of takes a bite out of my seniority."

"You want some coffee or anything? It's not bad, Dave Lee didn't make it."

"No thanks. I got a long drive coming up."

They sat on two of the folding chairs and Lisa said, "I'll tell you what. I don't think seniority or equal opportunity or even friendship is going to matter much. I know what I'd do in her place. If I could have two Dave Lees and lose a few entry-level programmers to do it, I wouldn't hesitate. Especially since I could probably get the second Dave dirt cheap."

"And let's face it, who would know better than you what she'd do?"

"Indeed."

"So what happens to you?"

"Lisa's putting me and the kids up for the time being. My guess is she's going to offer me some kind of a buyout. The thing is, the old definitions of wealth are probably going to cease to matter much. Don't get me wrong—I'm sure the same people are going to be on top, probably by a greater margin than ever, but the units of measure are going to change. Nobody knows yet what that measure is going to be, but the more liquid it is, the more likely it is to carry the day. So if she offers me a big wad of stock, it's probably not going to hurt her much to do it. She can salve her conscience on the cheap, and I'll have to take it, because what choice do I have? Which means I have to find a way to turn that stock into something to eat and a place to sleep." She drained her coffee cup, which featured Gary Larson cartoon dinosaurs. "What about you?"

"My situation is a bit complicated. Angela's ex-husband is alive here and her double isn't. I think she's going to have to make a choice, and...let's just say my seniority isn't looking that good anywhere."

"Maybe seniority won't matter there, either."

"Yeah. We can always hope, right?"

And hope did, in fact, die hard, Nick realized, as he found himself headed toward his old office as if he would find some trace of himself there. Instead he found a fierce-looking young woman with black hair and a thin face, staring at the computer screen and typing with blinding speed. She had her own posters on the wall, no plants, no stereo. There would be no email for Nick on her machine, no code for his new graphics driver.

On the way out he ran into Tom, his project leader. Tom was heavy and graying, with a bristling white mustache. He and Nick had been friends, but never particularly close.

"Hey, Nick," he said.

"Thereby identifying yourself," Nick said, "as the Prime Tom."

Tom nodded. "A bunch of us fifth wheels are talking about having a picnic tomorrow over at Lake Crabtree. Start around noon or so, go on all day. Everybody bring what they can. Maybe take our minds off things for a little while."

"I'll just have to see," Nick told him. "Tomorrow seems like a million years away right now."

## 19.

It took Nick less than an hour and a half to get back to Hope Valley Road. As he idled past the bank which no longer held any of his money, he watched a National Guardsman in full riot gear turn people away from the cash machine, which bore a hand-lettered sign reading "Out of Service."

"It's a fucking lie!" a woman was screaming. Tears were running down her face and she was waving her ATM card in the Guardsman's face. "There's nothing wrong with that machine except the greedy bastards who shut it down!" The Guardsman was faceless behind his Plexiglas mask, but Nick could read the nervousness in his posture.

Nick looked away. The two twenties in his pants pockets had a palpable weight. The urge to drive to Food Lion and squander the entire forty dollars on candy bars and balloons and toys almost overwhelmed him. Being an adult was more of a burden than he could carry. He wanted someone to take him by the hand and either beat hell out of him or tell him everything was going to be all right.

Instead he drove back to David's house and the chilly comfort of CNN.

On Headline News, the world's religious leaders stepped up for their share of the limelight. "If God had no hand in this," Pat Robertson asked, "then who put these drivers into automobiles to guard their safety? Who put these passengers into airplanes? Science can't explain what's happened to us in the last twenty-four hours. Life is a miracle, and we've just seen six billion miracles in a single day."

Anchor Lynne Russell noted, without comment, that the whereabouts of only one Pat Robertson was known. Whether the one who addressed the nation was original or prime was likewise a mystery.

Twin Dalai Lamas, from separate encampments, each declared the other to be but *maya*, illusion, a physical manifestation of earthly greed. The Pope, meanwhile, had gone into seclusion with his prime, intimating that they might be a while.

On the scientific side of the fence, the EPA issued a statement pointing out that the simple body heat of an additional six billion people, not to mention the carbon dioxide they exhaled, could escalate global warming catastrophically. One source speculated that the entire land surface of the planet could be desert within ten years.

The global population continued to drop rapidly, however. The combined overnight death toll from Bosnia, Khazakhstan, Jordan, Somalia, and Mexico was already estimated in the tens of millions, with no end in sight. Large portions of LA, London, and Moscow were on fire, while Mexico City had burned out from lack of oxygen. Australia and New Zealand had both closed their borders, turning back all incoming sea and air traffic while ferrying foreign tourists out of both countries on nationalized Qantas planes.

President Quayle, not knowing what else to do with him, had appointed the Bill Clinton from Nick's world as Special Advisor on Prime Affairs. The "Affairs" part had commentators sniggering. The two emerged at 5:00 eastern time to announce the formation of the US Peacekeeping Force, a new organization that would incorporate existing members of the Army, National Guard, and local police forces, plus anyone else who wanted to volunteer. The government promised all recruits three meals a day, a place to sleep, their nation's gratitude, and pay in the form of government scrip to be redeemed when the crisis was over.

"That's it," David said. "They just flushed the dollar down the loo."

At the inevitable press conference, with a freshly minted USPF logo on a banner behind him, Quayle said, "The mission of this force is to protect private property, safeguard human life, and provide an orderly." He squinted at his TelePrompTer. "Transition."

"Property first, of course," David said, and Nick felt a surge of warmth toward him.

"Transition to what?" Angela asked.

"Martial law," Nick said. "God help us all."

Helicopter footage showed an unbroken line of the desperate and homeless that stretched from Mexico City to the Texas border—cars, bicycles, pedestrians, wagons, horses. Somebody had blown up the International Bridge at Laredo in the early morning hours. The US Border Patrol blamed right-wing extremists and the Governor of Tamulipas blamed the US Border Patrol. The loss of the bridge made no perceptible difference. The tidal wave of humanity rolled across the Rio Grande like it was a mud puddle, and refugees simply swarmed over the few cops who were willing to open fire.

"In Austin, Texas," Russell said, "billionaire Harvey Chambers has become a one-man Works Progress Administration." Nick had been drifting into his own alarming fantasies of Quayle's personal New World Order, but the mention of Austin brought him back. The screen showed what seemed to be thousands of workers outside a huge complex of steel and glass towers. As one crew cleared live oaks and mesquite bushes in a long straight line, a second crew came behind them, digging a shallow trench. In the background still more workers unloaded massive blocks of stone from flatbed trucks.

In the foreground, a young male reporter in khakis and a polo shirt turned to the camera and said, "Offering good pay, hot food, and accommodations at a Tent City of his own creation, Chambers has commissioned a large-scale building project on his Computics campus. Though Chambers hasn't released any details of what he's up to, it doesn't take one of his resident geniuses to make an informed guess. It looks to be a very high, very thick wall, and with the visitors headed his way from south of the border, he may need it."

An hour later, as Nick was washing the dinner dishes, the phone rang. David didn't answer so Nick let the machine take it. "This is a message for Nick," Lisa's voice said. "I'm sorry, but we're not going to be able to find a place for you. I'm sure you appreciate the situation." Nick could hear her relief that she didn't have to break the news to him directly. "If you haven't heard, though, the government is going to have jobs for anybody who needs one."

## 23.

Nick woke at seven the next morning, cranky and sullen. He'd been dreaming about deserts and sandstorms, and in the middle of it all a pyramid with Computics logos carved into its sides.

Angela murmured something unintelligible and turned her back to him as he got out of bed. He dressed and went over to the main house, shivering a little in the distinctly colder morning air. David was still not up, so Nick made coffee and brought in the paper. Enjoy this, he told himself. Solitude is now the most precious commodity on Earth.

The front page told him that the USPF was an instant hit. The government, cleverly anticipating that they wouldn't have enough guns or uniforms to go around, had declared that volunteers were to provide their own uniforms of blue jeans and white shirts. Their commanders would issue them red bandannas. They were encouraged to bring along their own personal weapons.

In separate, but nearly identical statements, two Ralph Naders warned that there was little difference between the USPF and licensed vigilantism. Any unstable person with a piece of red cloth and a gun could wreak unchallenged havoc. The reporter covering the story dismissed him as a harmless crank.

Saturday had always been Nick's favorite day of the week. Just seven days ago he'd cooked his strawberry mint crepes in his special pan and sat on the patio in the sun to eat them. This Saturday he spread the classifieds—reduced to eight pages from the usual two dozen—across the dining room table and looked for work.

There were personal ads, mostly from primes looking for missing persons. Auto dealers were looking for temporary repossession specialists and drivers. And there was still plenty of work for telemarketers. The rest of world seemed to be holding its breath.

David eventually wandered in and logged on to his Internet provider so Nick could check job listings on the Web. The Web seemed largely unfazed by the Prime Event. And why not? Nick thought. There was no shortage of room in cyberspace. Ads for electronic stock trading services still popped up everywhere. On ZDNet, Jesse Berst—now with two photos of himself at the head of his column—asked his readers if it was the end of life as they knew it or simply the biggest stunt yet by Harvey Chambers and Computics to stall the Justice Department. The AltaVista search engine invited Nick to ask a question like, "Where did all these people come from?"

How to Live on Other Planets

He found half a dozen openings for C++ developers in the area, though he suspected most of them were no longer viable. He switched over to the Computics Writer program, figured out the slightly cheesy interface, and put together a quick resume. If he had to fill out a job application, he wondered, would there be a box to check if you were a Prime?

By the time he'd emailed the copies of his resume it was after noon. Angela, puffy and uncommunicative, was watching CNN with David. Special Presidential Advisor Bill Clinton was addressing protesters at the Washington Mall. "I'm a Prime just as many of you are," he said. "I know your sense of dislocation and anxiety."

The crowd jeered and shouted insults.

Clinton raised his hands. "I urge you to return to your homes. This disruption is only delaying our efforts to bring help to those of you who need it the most." Clinton's words disappeared under a chorus of heckling, and finally he shrugged and walked away with his head down, surrounded by bodyguards in dark suits.

Voices began to chant, "No justice, no peace," over and over. Nick could hear growing alarm in the voices of the CNN reporters, and then, moments later, the crowd seemed to buck, like a single organism reacting to a shock. The camera swung wildly around to show a wedge of USPF recruits in white shirts and red bandannas, swinging clubs and baseball bats and firing something into the air. The screen filled with smoke from pepper spray and tear gas, leaving sound as the only evidence of what was happening: screams, grunts, the sound of wood impacting flesh, the muted thunder of running feet. Nick, horrified, covered his ears and went into the bathroom, running water in the sink to mask the noise of the TV.

When he came out he had decided to go to the picnic at Lake Crabtree. He had real friends there, and friendship seemed less contingent than everything else in his life at that moment. He got all the way to the hall closet, looking for his softball and glove, before he remembered that he wouldn't find them there.

He stuck his head back into the den, where CNN had moved on to the next atrocity and David and Angela were in the midst of a heated discussion. "...has nothing of real value to back it up," David was saying. "There's no disincentive to inflation."

"Where have you been for the last thirty years?" Angela was leaning forward aggressively, but Nick could see she was enjoying herself. "Money isn't real. It's a necessary fiction that everybody's bought into for the sake of the game. There's nothing to back it up but good intentions anyway."

"There's your, what do you call it, Federal Reserve System."

"It's the Emperor's New Money, except the emperor is naked now. So people will transfer all their leftover hope and need to this government scrip. It's Tinkerbell money, but people will clap for it. Wait and see."

Why can't I look up from people being beaten and debate economic theory? Nick wondered. If I could have fought with her like that, over something other than wounded feelings, then maybe she could have loved me too.

"Listen," he said. "There's a company picnic thing at work, and I think I want to go." Too late, and with too little enthusiasm, he added, "You guys can come along if you like."

David looked at Angela, who was already shaking her head. "I'll pass," she said.

"I think there's some veggie dogs in the freezer," David said, "if you don't want to go empty handed."

## 29.

The crowding was less severe on I-40, but there was still insufficient room for Nick to shake off the restlessness that gripped him, to push the accelerator to the floor and watch the landscape come hurtling at him. He knew it was just another misguided impulse, like the one that had sent him to the closet for his baseball glove.

He got to Lake Crabtree by two and parked at the edge of the entrance road. Groups of families seemed to be living in the open-walled picnic structures and in camper trucks in the parking lots. Long lines waited outside both restrooms. It took Nick twenty minutes to find Tom and the others where they'd built a fire in the center of a soccer field and ringed it with Styrofoam coolers. The wall reminded Nick of Harvey Chambers' macroengineering in Austin, and that in turn reminded him of his dream.

Nick offered his veggie dogs and half a loaf of oat bread. "Is it okay to just build a fire like this?"

"You're kidding, right?" Tom said. "What exactly are you worried about? Pollution from the smoke? Using up precious natural resources? Park rangers busting us for not having a permit?" He waved an arm at the crowds that surrounded them. "All that stuff is over. Moot. Finito."

They sat down together and roasted a couple of hot dogs while Tom told his story. Everybody had a story now, though Nick considered his own rather pedestrian.

"I was working late," Tom said, "so I wasn't on the highway when it happened. Sometime before six I got up and went to the bathroom, and when I came back this other guy who looked just like me was sitting in my chair, typing on my computer. It was the single weirdest moment of my entire life. That feeling, to be looking at something for which you know there cannot ever be a rational explanation. I just turned around and went back into the hall and pictured that kid in the *Little Nemo* comic strip. You're too young to know what I'm talking about. Anyway, he had this hat with a sign on it that said 'Wake Up!' Flip, his name was. I tried everything I could think of to wake up—looking at my hands, pinching myself, holding my breath.

"About that time the two Lisas came by and rounded everybody up who was still in the building and took us into the conference room. We borrowed John's boom box and listened to the news, and of course once we understood what was happening we all wanted to go home, make sure our wives and husbands and kids were okay.

"There was only one car between me and the other Tom, and by this point we'd figured out whose world this was. I mean, he had the keys and my pockets were empty. So he gave me a ride home and put me and my Suzie up in his and his Suzie's guest room. I guess I can't really complain, but…you can't tell the difference between us by looking. Only I'm in the guest room and he's in the whole rest of the house. He drives and I have to ask if I can ride along. And he always makes me ask. He hasn't refused me anything, but he always makes me ask."

They both looked at the fire for a minute, and then Tom said, "Doesn't it bother you? Them calling us 'primes'?"

"What do you mean?"

"You're a math person, like me. What's the definition of a prime number?"

"Divisible only by one and itself."

"Doesn't that seem lonely to you? Do you remember what they call numbers that aren't 1 or a prime?"

Nick shrugged. "I forget."

"Composites. Because they're made up of other numbers. But the primes are all alone."

"Maybe they're just self-sufficient," Nick said, in an attempt to lighten him up.

"You think?" Tom asked, staring with an intensity that made Nick look away.

After another brief silence Tom said, "You know what's really weird? The other Tom, he doesn't have any trains." In Nick's world, Tom didn't actually have a guest room because it was completely given over to his model railroad. "When I asked him about it, it was the first time he showed any real interest in me. 'I always thought about doing that,' he says. 'I had this Lionel set I really loved when I was kid.' And I go, 'Yeah, I know. I was there.'

"But they're all gone, all those trains I put together by hand. The Texas Eagle. Southern Pacific Number One. Wiped out." He snapped his fingers. "Just like that. I mean, you have to wonder what exactly is the point, when you can lose everything, just like that."

Although sympathetic, Nick hadn't lost sight of the fact that he'd come to the park to get cheered up. He ate two hot dogs and drank a Coke, then extricated himself to join the softball game starting nearby. Other than having to play barehanded, it was the best he'd felt in two days, running, chasing fly balls, swinging a big stick at something.

Darkness ended the game by five o'clock, and even with the night turning rapidly cold, the beer started to flow. Nick was not much of a drinker, and without physical exertion to distract him his thoughts kept stumbling over Angela, Angela and David, alone together back at David's house.

"Hey," a voice yelled. "Anybody here speak Spanish?"

At the edge of the fire Nick saw John the receptionist next to a slight man in black jeans, denim jacket, and a battered straw cowboy hat.

Nick walked over. "A little," he told John, and nodded to the other man. *"Que tal?"*

*"Es mi esposa,"* the stranger said. *"Ayudame, por favor."*

"Okay," Nick said, and asked him what the trouble was with his wife.

"She's having a baby," the man said. "But it's too soon." His Spanish came fast and slurred, the way Nick was used to hearing it in Texas. "I need the hospital, but I can't take her because somebody stole my car."

Nick looked back at the fire, thought briefly about Angela again, and then remembered all the men he'd passed on the road in the last two days. Guilt welled up inside him.

"Okay," he said. "I'll take you."

*"Gracias, muchas gracias. Dios te paje."*

The man's gratitude made Nick even more uncomfortable. As they started across the field he said, "My name's Nick. Where are you from?"

"I'm Carlos." He shook Nick's hand. "I come from Vera Cruz, originally. Just now from San Antonio."

Nick said that he used to live in Austin.

"I know Austin," Carlos said. "There is supposed to be much work there." He was nervous and sweating, and it was getting very dark. Nick heard voices nearby and couldn't pinpoint where they came from. Suddenly he felt vulnerable and a little foolish.

*"Aqui es,"* Carlos said abruptly.

Someone shone a flashlight in Nick's eyes and he had to fight the urge to turn and run. After a few seconds his eyes cleared enough to see a middle-aged woman in a black mantilla sitting on the grass. A girl who didn't seem older than her late teens had her head on the woman's lap. Two or three other men, one of them now holding the flashlight on the girl, stood in the shadows.

Nick asked if she could walk.

"I don't know," Carlos said.

They were only a hundred yards or so from one of the parking lots. "I'll go get my truck," Nick said, realizing, once the words were out, that they might think he was running away. "Carlos, you want to come with me?"

Nick half-ran, half-walked toward the spot where he'd left his truck. Carlos jogged beside him, thanking him again. "It's the red one, there," Nick said, then pulled up short. A man in jeans and a white sweatshirt was sliding a flat piece of metal into the window on the driver's side.

"Hey," Nick said in English. "Hey, what're you doing?"

The man glanced at Nick with apparent disinterest and went back to work. In the glow of a nearby streetlight Nick could see the man's dirty blond hair and narrow eyes.

"That's my truck!" Nick said, his voice cracking as the humiliations of the last two days reached critical mass. He ran at the man, grabbing for the hand with the jimmy. The man spun away, leaving the jimmy in the truck door and pulling something out of his waistband.

It was a .38 revolver. For a second, as the muzzle swung in front of his face and the hole in the barrel filled the world, Nick considered that he was about to die. He reacted to the thought with sadness and a flash of self-pity.

"Correction, mother*fucker,*" said the man with the gun. "According to the VIN, this here truck's the property of University Ford in Chapel Hill." There was something red around his neck. Nick realized that this was one of the new vigilantes, whatever it was they were calling themselves.

"Look," Nick said, "this man's wife is sick. We need to get her to the hospital."

"I don't see nobody." Nick looked back and saw that Carlos had disappeared. "Now," the man said, "you got the key to this thing?"

Nick could hear the pulse in his neck as his T-shirt scraped against it. It seemed oddly slow, but so was everything compared to the speed of his thoughts. He went through several possibilities before he finally said, "Yes."

"Hand that son of a bitch over."

Nick took the truck key out of his pocket. His hand trembled and he stood looking at it for what seemed like a long time.

"You scared, motherfucker? You got every reason to be."

In fact Nick felt enraged and helpless, which was something altogether different. It made him want to cry. As he held out the key it shook loose from his fingers and clanged on the asphalt.

"You clumsy piece of shit! God dammit!" The man took one step back and waved the pistol toward the weeds by the side of the road. "Get over there and get on your God damn knees."

"No," Nick said, listening to his voice squirm out of control again. Self-loathing washed over him. "You've got the key, you've got the truck, you probably just killed that poor guy's wife and child. If that's not enough, go ahead and kill me too."

"You prime fuck. You think if I did kill you, anybody would give a God damn?" Nick saw then that the man was more afraid than Nick was, that Nick had caught him off guard by showing up so unexpectedly, that the man had failed to think through what it would mean to point his gun at someone. Nick still wanted to smash his ugly head with a baseball bat, but he no longer believed the man was ready to shoot him.

"You've got the truck," Nick said again, to remind the man that he had, after all, won. Then he turned and walked away, wondering if he'd misjudged and if the man would shoot him after all.

He walked into a clump of trees and pissed against one of them. It wasn't as private as he would have liked, but at that point he was beyond caring. It felt like hot blood draining out of him, and he was weak and shaky when he finished.

Carlos and the others were gone. Nick made a half-hearted attempt to look for them, then went back to the company fire. He thrust his hands nearly into the flames and there still was not enough heat to warm him.

Tom and Lisa materialized on either side of him. "Are you okay?" Lisa asked. "What happened?"

Nick could only shake his head. "What's going to become of us?"

## 31.

Lisa gave him a ride home. "It's only a couple hours out of my way," she said.

"He had a Palm Pilot," Nick said. He couldn't seem to stop rehashing the incident in his head. "I didn't really register that until just now. It was in a little holster thing on his belt. He was using it to run the Vehicle ID Numbers. Crackers with guns and hand-held computers."

"Now that's really scary," Lisa agreed.

"He called me a 'fucking prime.' No, wait. He said, 'you prime fuck.' There was this absolute hatred in his voice."

Lisa glanced at him just long enough to make him wish he'd kept his childlike discoveries to himself. "Yeah, okay," he said. "Nice weather we're having."

Lisa laughed. "Not for long. They say it may freeze tonight."

She let him out in his driveway and he walked around to the driver's side. "You want to come in or anything? David's being pretty accommodating, I'm sure he wouldn't mind my asking."

"It's late."

Nick nodded. "Thanks for the ride."

She put a hand lightly on his arm. "Take care of yourself, all right? Just take everything slow and easy. You'll be surprised what you can learn to live with."

She turned around in the driveway and Nick saw her hand come up over the roof of the car in a final salute before she pulled onto Hope Valley Road and was gone. Was that the goal, then? he wondered. To find out exactly how much he could in fact put up with? Until he too was shambling along the roadside on sheer inertia, eyes glazed, with nothing behind him and nothing in front of him?

The house was dark except for a single light over the kitchen counter. Nick stopped there to scrub his face with dishwashing liquid and water as hot as he could stand. His fingers still twitched slightly, as if he'd had too much coffee.

He went on through into the den. The TV was off for once and the house was deathly silent. Nick knew something was wrong, but he couldn't say what it was. The night's violence had left him thinking murder and mayhem, and that was the only reason he went into David's bedroom.

Before he could speak he heard the rustling of covers followed by Angela's voice saying, "Nick?"

He froze.

"Oh my god," she said. "Oh my god. We fell asleep."

Nick switched on the light. Angela was holding the sheet up over her bare breasts. David was blinking, pushing himself up on one elbow.

Nick turned the light off again.

"Nick?" Angela said. "Nick, wait. Oh, Christ, Nick, I'm so sorry..."

What Nick really wanted was a long, hot shower. He knew, though, that it would be some time before he got one. "When you're dressed, David," he said, "I need to talk to you for a minute." He went back to the den and sat on the couch.

The two of them came out together a few seconds later. David was in pants and shirt, Angela in a terrycloth robe. Angela was crying silently.

"Just David," Nick said.

She looked at David, then at Nick, and thought better of whatever she'd been about to say. She went through the kitchen and the sliding glass doors to the guest house.

"I'll need a few things," Nick said. "Some sweat clothes, or some drawstring pants, maybe a jacket. Whatever you have that might fit me. A sleeping bag if you've got one."

"Look here, I'm really sorry about this. We didn't either of us mean for it to happen—"

"I don't want to talk about it. Could you see if you could find those clothes?"

David nodded and left the room. Nick leaned his head back and closed his eyes. He couldn't remember ever being so exhausted. Part of it, he knew, was the anticipation of fatigue to come.

"Nick?"

He started awake, amazed to realize that he'd actually drifted off for a few seconds. David was holding out a soft-side flight bag. Inside Nick found clothes, a tightly rolled sleeping bag, a Swiss Army knife, a couple of towels, a first-aid kit, some toilet paper. At the bottom was something metallic that Nick fished out and set on the couch beside him. It was a .22 target pistol.

David laughed nervously. "I expect some might think me a bit mad to offer you that in the circumstances. But I thought you might—"

"No, thanks," Nick said. "Just put it away somewhere, will you?"

David stashed it in one of the built-in drawers next to the TV, and when he came back he had money in his hand. "I've only got a couple of hundred here at the house. If you want to wait till tomorrow I could sort you out some more."

"No," Nick said. "This will do." The money only made Nick more resentful. The business with Angela was a separate issue, something he'd known would happen sooner or later. At that moment he hated David because David had everything to give and because Nick had nothing to do but take it. It made Nick careless of what David thought of him, made him greedy and arrogant and willing to push for more.

Instead he zipped the bag and stood up. Then he followed David's gaze and saw Angela in the kitchen doorway. Her cheeks were still wet. "You're not going...?" she said. "Please, please don't go. Wait until morning. Let us talk about it, at least."

"I'm just going over to Richard's house." David didn't flinch, willingly complicit in the lie. Nick felt the chill he'd known once when he'd cut himself badly in the kitchen. The knife had gone much too deeply into his flesh, but there was no true sensation at first. "I'll call you," he said, in a hurry to get outside before the pain hit.

"Be careful," Angela said, with a catch in her voice that Nick knew he would remember later.

He hefted the bag and walked outside.

# 37.

The night was clear and cold and he stopped to put on David's jacket. Once he got moving he was actually making better time than the cars on Hope Valley, and there was satisfaction in that. It took him only half an hour to get to I-40, where he turned right and headed west along the access road.

Fragments of his dream flashed through his mind, overlaying the reality of the stalled and abandoned cars beside the road, the smell of exhaust fumes, the trash tangled in the thick, brown grass of the hillsides. It was easy to imagine the drought never ending, the trees withering, falling, decaying into dust, while the privileged few huddled in their pyramids. But who would actually choose the desert, given the choice? Who would not walk, head down, putting one foot in front of the other, for hundreds and hundreds of miles toward whatever hope was left?

He'd been walking for an hour when he heard voices speaking Spanish beside him. He looked up, in the space of a second imagining that it might be Carlos, somehow with his wife and a healthy, if slightly premature, baby, and that they would offer him a ride because he had at least tried to help.

Instead it was a battered pickup that coasted along beside him, three men in the cabin. They all wore baseball caps and work clothes. One of them saw Nick's searching look and nodded stiffly.

Nick nodded back and said, *"Buenas noches."*

*"Buenas,"* the man said. *"A donde vas?"*

*"Tejas,"* Nick said, giving in the Mexican pronunciation. "Austin."

"Us too," the man said in Spanish. "I hear there's much work there."

"It's true," Nick said, also in Spanish. "I saw it on the television."

Work, he thought, and more. For Nick it meant the only person in the world who would have to take him in, no matter what. Because how could you look into someone's face, knowing they were just the same as you, and turn them away?

The man smiled and jerked his head at the bed of the pickup truck, cluttered with tools and folded plastic and canvas tarps. "You want a ride?"

*"Gracias,"* Nick said. *"Muchas gracias."*

The truck paused momentarily and Nick vaulted over the side.

How to Live on Other Planets

He propped his duffel against the back of the cab and in minutes he was asleep.

**MINAL HAJRATWALA**
## The Unicorn at the Racetrack

### I. In It To Win It

look at the shining one, she
is not one of us, she mimics
hummingbirds not hooves, not
whole hound hurdle-halvers, *who
the hell let that in here?* my small man says *And right
before the race! concentrate!* but how
to un-see
hubris of luminous mane, lustrous
sparkle like cool trough at track's tail—oh
how many rounds must i lap for the juice,
apple lust dribbling my lips, whose
hay will i huddle in tonight? & this boy-man
with the sharp feet, hard tensing thighs & short
bright whip! running i am nothing
but running
run
run
faster
ugh please
faster not the
oh running
fast as fast can i
NO not the whip
faster
nose forward
nose
slow
stop
stand

pant

breathe

where

is she

where is her

blaze?


## II. Out While You Can

O my half-
brothers, your
persistent
gleaming
thighs!

O stallions
drumming power—
what flanks!
Thunder on,
yes, but

not for this sham
ecosystem of turf & scam,
not for the hurt or the sweet
steel-cut hay or the taste
of the bit.

    Won't you,
my tame trained kin,
mahogany muscles
insurrectionary
royal

scatter the men from their grand stands,
refute that green ellipse,
break your false orbit,

fly?

# RJ ASTRUC
# A Believer's Guide to Azagarth

If you visit the planet Azagarth, bring warm clothes. Most of the year it's under five degrees celsius, and even colder in the valleys, around which the ice—which is orange here, not white, due to some strange refraction of the dual, distant suns—rises like the mouth of a volcano. But this is where the *hikhik,* the indigenous tribes of Azargarth, choose to live. Their stout, square homes sit within the great circles of ice in a way that reminds me of the ancient walled cities of Europe's middle ages.

"It's not a welcoming planet," says Sister Therese, when I arrive at the mission. "You don't see the resort companies queuing up for space. No one wants to come here. Too flat for the skiing crowd, and summer's too short to melt the ice. We get tourists, sometimes, and other missionaries... and *journalists,* of course."

Her tone slips from friendly to testy, and I realise she's still suspicious of me. As she has every right to be, given the situation. Journalists are far from uncommon on Azagarth. Tourists may not like the weather or the scenery, but journalists—especially photo journalists—love the hikhik, a race of plasmoid mimics. There's been a recent fancy for earth's tabloids to print pictures of hikhiks masquerading as celebrities, with one particular attribute grossly exaggerated—a chubby Pinky Bryant with breasts like torpedoes, a Jim Vagner with oversized lips that dangle to his collarbones.

I am not a photo journalist, I explain to Sister Therese, but a staff writer for *HeLives* magazine, a monthly Christian digest with a solid publishing record (40 years with Christ, as it says on the cover). "I'm here to tell your story," I reassure her. "This is an amazing moment in history, not only for the church but for the entire human race—our first dealings with an alien race significantly less advanced than our own."

She smiles in a faint, restrained way and shows me to my room, a small cell—although despite its name, it is quite a cosy place. I have a bed, a desk, and a shelf on which to stick my clothes. My window, which is wide and covers almost the entire eastern wall, looks down upon the hikhik settlement. I can't see them as the light outside is too dim, but I can hear them chattering to each other in their slow, monotonous voices. Speech and language itself is new to the hikhik—the first gifts of the human missionaries. They have been taught English, Sister Therese tells me, and some Latin, so as to better understand the Catholic mass.

When the sister leaves me I begin a rough draft of my article's outline (a misguided, optimistic early version of the article you now read). I check my notes on the mission's history—eighteen months now in hikhik country—and the history of the planet itself. First discovered twenty years ago, Azagarth has been settled and resettled numerous times, but no one has ever stayed. The Christian missions, known here collectively as the St Christopher's movement, are the longest settlement of humans on the planet.

As I turn in for the night I notice something strange about my room. Two glowing red heater-beams hang ominously above the bed; on the wall directly opposite is a simple crucifix. There is something childishly terrible about this: I am to sleep between my God and a warm place.

§

I meet the hikhik the next day. A younger sister, who insists I call her plain Paul instead of *Sister* Paul, leads me from the mission building to the school. The school is a rough, square building, clearly built by the hikhik themselves, and one side leans heavily against the mission's solid, human-made wall. It is about as big as a tennis court, and painted with surprisingly realistic murals of Biblical scenes.

"The hikhik reproduced them perfectly from the movies and books we gave them," says Paul. "They're amazingly talented."

Inside the school lesson is in progress. Half the room is simple plastic desks, while the rest of the class—the younger children, I assume—sit on the floor at the teacher's feet. The teacher is an elderly nun with fine dark features and an animated way of moving her hands. She is teaching them about the story of Noah, from what I can tell. Her image and voice are projected as a hologram at the room's midpoint, so every student is able to hear and see her. I expect that sort of tricky software was financed by one of the St Christopher movement's rich backers—Sister Therese has been guarded when I ask her questions about money, but I've done enough research to know that there's a lot of people back home determined that this mission will prove a success.

But of course it isn't the nun or the holograph I really notice first, but the hikhiks themselves.

There are perhaps a hundred and fifty of them squashed into the room. Most of them have taken on semi-human forms, replicas (I assume) of past tourists and travellers to Azagarth, but others are 2D cartoon characters and trees and icicles and countless other things that they've mimicked since their first interactions with humans. An empty argyle-patterned coat scribbles industriously on its pad; a Siamese cat raises its hand to answer a question; a computer takes down the lesson by pressing its own keys. The letter E—the actual *letter*—is sitting on my far right, its lowest branch tucked under the desk, the middle one clutching a pencil, while the topmost looks toward the teacher, a flat face straining on a hideously long neck.

"It's okay if you want to take a minute," says Paul. "People usually do when they see them. I expect if you're not used to it, this can all seem a little strange."

"It's like a Mary Poppins fantasy," I say—too loudly, because instantly the two hikhiks sitting nearby have turned into perfect simulacra of Dick Van Dyke. One of them begins to rise toward the ceiling, his mouth opening and closing in silent laughter.

"Oh, you've distracted them," says Paul, sighing, and ushers me out.

As I go I see something I wish I hadn't; one of the hikhik has assumed the form of—terribly—a tortured Jesus on the cross. It's just a brief flash, before it syncs its amorphous body into some other weird mutation, but it's definitely Jesus. The sight fills me with horror, but when I tell Paul about it, she smiles and shakes her head.

"They're funny things, aren't they? They don't really know what they're doing. Obviously when we catch them at it we tell them off, but I don't think they all understand blasphemy yet. You can't really be annoyed at them, it'd be getting cross at a small child."

My next visit today is to a young family who are proud members of the St Christopher movement. At the door I am warmly received by the lady of the house, who after clasping my hand and performing a small hikhik ceremony of whistles and smiles, leads me to the kitchen, where her husband is cooking a meal for their four children.

"Meat vegetable meat horse," the husband says, also smiling, his green teeth sparkling. "Bowl soup fork vegetable fork."

"On earth as it is in heaven," says the wife, somewhat apropos.

We eat the food—which is good, delicious even—and make stilted conversation. The hikhik can't talk, not really; they suffer a strange echolia that allows them to repeat back anything they've ever heard, and when they don't have an appropriate answer in their phrase-bank, they subside into nonsense. For example, when I ask them how many children they have, they say, "four"; when I ask them their jobs and they chant, delightedly, "A farmer wants a wife, a farmer wants a wife," but when I bring up the missions, and what they think about them—a question that requires a personal opinion—the wife can only manage a few stilted passages from Genesis before giving up. Her husband doesn't even try.

I remember reading stories about feral children, brought back from the wild, who grew up to understand words but not *language*. They were literalists of the purist sense—they saw only the nouns and verbs of this world. The hikhiks' whole-hearted embracing of Christianity confuses me because Christianity is not a literal religion—its books are contradictory, its timelines and lineages conflicting, and its passages have been interpreted, and reinterpreted, to mean different things at different points in history. Is it a wise idea to give a book such as the Bible to a people who are unable to differentiate between spiritual guidance and spiritual dictate?

"Well you know what happened in Kenya back in the 'zeros," says Paul later, when I breach the subject. "We taught them about God and Jesus and then a few years later we came back to find they were burning people as witches and casting the devils out of small children for exorbitant fees."

"How do you know that won't happen here?"

"Don't tell anyone I told you this, but humans at heart are wicked things. Sometimes I think they're out looking to find temptations. While the hikhik, they're true innocents. True children of God. They could never do anything terrible or wish ill upon another."

"They like to please people," I say. "They like to please the missions."

Paul nods. "They want to know God. We can show them the way."

§

A moment of truth: I am a Christian of the forever-lapsing sort. I fight my faith and my faith fights back and my infrequent truces with God are as uneasy and uncertain as my convictions. It is my own fault I am this way; I did not go peaceably into the bright light of salvation. In school I chose to study biology, which was, in its substance, silently disproving of God; in college I took an elective course in abiogenesis, which was worse. I had hoped learning about science would strengthen my faith, but instead I felt it slipping, as if I were emerging from a cocoon and would soon be exposed, painfully, to the terrible darkness of a Godless life.

And yet somehow my belief, although damaged, did not die. In desperation I read the works of the apologetics, and was reassured. Now I think of my religion as one would a job—I work at it, it exhausts and perplexes me, but it is occasionally rewarding. At this point in my life, occasional rewards are enough to satisfy me. Perhaps in the future this will change, but I doubt it. I am a simple-living man.

The editors of *HeLives* won't like me saying this, but the idea of bringing a new religion to a non-human country disturbs me on some level. I won't be the first to point out that the Bible never mentions aliens—really, do they even have souls? And did Jesus, who died for all *man*kind, die for their sins too? I have always thought of Christianity (and I suppose other religions too) as an evidence of our humanity. No other alien race has a religion, at least as we understand it, although a few revere their ancestors in a similar way to some Asian and Pacific Island cultures. Mission work with aliens, especially the more advanced cultures, has been embarrassingly fruitless. Only the hikhik have shown any sign of interest in faith—any faith—and I'm starting to think that the St Christopher movement may have mistaken a genuine desire to know God for the hikhiks' innate ability to show people what they ask for.

On my third day on Azagarth I am left to my own devices; Paul, who was a triage nurse before getting the call, has been called away to attend to a sick priest. I take the time to walk around the settlement, which is perhaps three kilometres wide. I am the only human on the gravelled streets, and on spotting me the hikhik children come whooping down from doorsteps and swings and chase after me in a myriad of different forms. In a group they seem to have a fondness for copying each other—it is a sort of game amongst them, I think. At one point I am being followed by a veritable forest of limber-rooted eucalypts; at another I lead a pack of furiously waddling daschunds.

How to Live on Other Planets

After a time I get used to them, and ignore them—believe it or not, there is only so much hikhik weirdness that a person can take before they tune it out. Instead of watching the children, my mind drifts to thoughts of home and of the church my wife and I attend. We are members of a tiny Unitarian congregation—the Unitarians forgive my struggles with faith more than the Baptist church we left some years ago (there, they always considered me a backslider, and a seemingly unrepentant one at that). Our pastor is an older man who gets on well with my wife, who is often as inquisitive of her faith as I am. I expect that while I am away she will be spending most of her time in his company; and it is with these things in mind that I turn around to check, absently, on the activities of the children behind me.

They are doing an awful thing.

I am sorry to write this; trust me when I say that I do not *want* to write this, that the very idea of putting it down on paper upsets me. But I am a journalist—I have always believed (perhaps blasphemously) that journalism, too, is a calling to truth—and I must chronicle without judgement, without bias. So here it is: the children have assumed the naked forms of my wife and my priest, and they are fornicating.

I think I must have screamed or shouted because instantly the children, seeing my distress, turn into other things, into pretty, silly, inconsequential things, like teddy bears and fruit and balloons and books. It's so fast, so *harmless,* like a kid pulling a face behind a teacher's back. Except that what they've shown me is not harmless, and it shakes me to my root. I am not easily enraged—and, please understand, I have never before yelled at a child—and yet I rush at them, at their balloons and toys, bowling them over and sending them yelping and scattering back to their homes. Some hikhik adults exit their homes to stare at me, this shaking, sweating, *shamed* human in their midst.

"There but for the grace of God," says one, and vanishes back into his house.

As I walk back to the mission building I see Mary Magdalene cuddling a boil-encrusted Job in a thin alley between two streets. Three lepers, one with no arms, are licking their feet with forked tongues. I know who they are because I've seen the movies; they are appearing in the same guises as actors in a recent series of Bible movies produced by Word, a Christian company that also owns

*HeLives* magazine. Needless to say, this debauched scene does not appear in *any* of Word's productions.

"They can read minds, sometimes. Or read feelings," says Paul later, scrunching up her face. I've told her *something* happened in the village, but not the precise details. Still, she seems to have guessed some of it, if not the particulars. "I'm not sure how it works, but if you're thinking of something, they can replicate it."

"I wasn't thinking about *that.*"

"They just get the images, the shapes. They put them together in whatever way they feel is right. I know, I know, they're difficult and alien but at base they have good hearts. I'm sure they didn't mean to offend you. In fact they were probably trying to impress you."

I wish I had words to explain what I fear about the hikhik. At base I suppose it is that they are not *human*—which sounds bad, in this multi-species world, where aliens are our friends, our co-workers. So perhaps I should say that they are *in*human, they do not possess any of the traits our intergalactic colleagues do: they do not understand empathy, or speech, or opinions, or that doing what they *did* went beyond a simple childish prank into something truly twisted, wicked, and perhaps, evil.

There's an article I did for *HeLives* last winter about a mission in Sudan. I wrote dispassionately and faithfully about the deaths of starving children and adults; my friend the photographer Joe Halliewell took pictures of bodies ravaged by poverty, people reduced to little more than walking skeletons. It upset me, but it did not unhinge me. There was an evil in Sudan, but it was a natural, human evil; it was containable and understandable. The evil of the hikhiks is a truly alien thing, it is an evil of miscommunication and, in fact, a complete *lack* of communication. It chills me because I know, with a strange certainty that I've never felt about any other alien race, that these are truly soulless things.

"Pray with me," says Paul, taking my hand. "Please?"

We pray together in the mission's chapel. There are no hikhiks here, and it makes me feel better—until I realise that there *may* in fact be hikhiks in the building, hundreds of them, and I will never be able to distinguish them from the humans, or other inanimate objects, unless they change shape in front of my eyes.

§

On day four (I have only five to spend in Azagarth, before *HeLives* propels me on to the Hi'iknthis cluster and a story on a congregation of earth migrants) I leave Paul behind and seek out a hikhik interviewee. I do not want to, I would far prefer to sit in my cell until my shuttle leaves the following night, but I have an article—this article—to write.

I walk out amongst the hikhiks. Once I am well away from the mission, they start to taunt me. There are more images of my wife, and more images of things I choose, as a Christian, writing for a Christian audience, not to describe. There are Biblical scenes, perverted beyond recognition, in which the wise men eviscerate a limpid-eyed Mary, the shepherds have the heads of their sheep, and the holy child rides a three-headed goat. There are nuns, nuns I recognise (the stony-faced Sister Therese is amongst them) in various states of undress. And yet at the same time there are other banal images, there are playful monkeys and bunches of flowers and smiling clouds and a lamp post that gleams with a real and near-phosphorescent green light.

Have the nuns never seen them do this? I wonder. Is this a performance for me alone? Or—and this is the worst possibility, the one I hate to consider—are the nuns so pure that such things would never enter their minds? I cannot see any connection between my thoughts and the most horrible of the images, and yet some of them—I won't say which ones—seem strangely familiar, as if they have been plucked from a distant nightmare. Have the hikhik plumbed the depths of my sub-conscious for material?

"What are you?" I ask them. "Why are you doing this?"

"Hikhik," offers a toy train that moves awkwardly along a wooden track.

"We are legion," says another, ominously, but it's only reciting words it has heard before in the mission's classrooms.

"Why are you doing this? Why are you doing this? Why are you doing this?" a child chants, caught in an echoliac loop like a Tourettes sufferer.

"Please," I say, gesturing to the twisted nativity. I am slowly (impossibly) regaining my self-control. "Stop this. It's blasphemous. It's horrible. Surely the nuns have told you that."

"God loved the world so much he gave us his only son," says the three-headed goat in an agreeable tone, and reverts into the shape of a single, flailing bulrush. Others repeat the famous passage after it; the words tumble through the nativity's members like a virus, spreading, until they are all bulrushes and my wife has become the brown path of the Nile through a muddy delta made of refashioned nuns. A single hikhik, as a basket, floats along their backs, but never reaches the shore.

"Do you even understand what religion is?" I ask. "Do you understand Christ's message? Yes, I know, you can paint pictures of Bible scenes, you can even *become* them, but there's no point unless you understand their meaning. The nuns here are very wonderful, and it would hurt them to know they had wasted their time with you all. If you can't *feel*, if you can't grasp what it means to be saved, then there's no point in them continuing with the mission."

"We like nuns," says the basket. Around it the Nile peels back and becomes the Red Sea; the basket swells and becomes an ark; the Red Sea converges into flood waters. "We like nuns," it says again. "They show us. What we can be."

I cover my face with my hands. "They aren't here to show you new shapes to form. They're here with a genuine desire to help you find God through his son, Jesus Christ. They're here to help you form a spiritual relationship with our Lord. This isn't a game to them. And if it's a game to you, you need to stop. It's unfair, it's horrible."

At the word horrible images of my wife and my priest reoccur. I see flashes of flesh between my shaking fingers. It is cold out here, freezing, but my anger, my frustration, keeps me warm. "Stop it," I say again. "What you're doing is not appropriate; it is rude and offensive. Do you understand?"

The ark reappears. Animals approach it two-by-two. I recognise this scene from a Word documentary on the flood; the animals have a false, computer-generated quality about them.

"Christ suffered," I tell them. In all my years I have never had this conversation; I have never had to explain my faith to another, although many have helped confirm mine. "Christ, the son of God, died for your sins. It is the greatest act of kindness and sacrifice the world has known. And even if you do not believe in what he did, at least show some empathy and respect. What you are doing here, with your images, with your perversions, is denigrating our faith."

"Sorry," says a giraffe. Its mouth is pulled down dramatically at the corners. "We are sorry."

"Forgive us," says a hippo. "We seek forgiveness."

"We will be Christ-like," promises its mate. "We will be as little children."

"Please," I say. It's hard to tell if I've gotten through to them—their faces, no matter their form, are always completely impassive and mask-like. I wonder if this is because they are hiding their feelings, or if they have no real feelings at all. *The devil,* I remember my priest once saying, *has only the face men make for him.* "For the sake of the mission. A lot of people are counting on you to be our first shining example of an alien race who has found Christ."

"Shining example of an alien race," they chant. "Found Christ."

It sounds like more echolia, but there's a different note to it—their voices have become reedy in rejoicing. They swarm to me and press their hands, their tentacles, their branches, against me in a way that suggests they desire to be absolved, to be forgiven for their wickedness. I touch them; their flesh is soft and pliant, like the skin of a newborn.

"Thank you," I say, choked with a sudden emotion. "Thank you."

I return to the mission feeling pleased with myself, and not, I suppose, without warrant; I believe I have communicated myself adequately to a race without true speech, and that they, in turn, have spoken back in confirmation, even if it is with my own recycled words. At dinner Paul asks me if I feel better and I nod. I am already revising this article in my head, working out a new conclusion that casts the *HeLives* magazine *itself* as a character in the story, an important cog in this great societal change. I go to bed filled with joy for the future, but my dreams are plagued by the spectre of the three-headed goat.

§

The nuns accompany me to the space pod—a small grey transporter platform set against the western ice ridge. Struggling through the orange snow in their warm black robes they do look, I have to admit, a little like the waddling penguins they're often compared to. It is a testament to their kindness that they have come here to see me off; they know that my time here has been difficult, more difficult than I or my editors anticipated. Their presence on the edge of the space pod is a show of moral support.

"Did you get enough material for your article?" Paul wants to know, as she helps me fasten myself into the transporter. It is a two-man vessel, a simple port that will bring me onward to my next assignment. The Hi'iknthis cluster and its human migrants await. "I'm sorry I couldn't be more helpful. I'm new, I'm not really sure what journalists want to see."

"You were great," I reassure her. "You're doing great work here, all of you."

"Bless you," says Paul, ducking her head and blushing.

Even Sister Therese comes to say her good-byes. Paul has evidently worked hard to convince her that I am not just another tabloid photo-monkey. She leads the nuns in a short, simple prayer for my safe passage through the universe. The wind whips over their bowed heads and sends the loose smocks of their habits waving and diving like pennants. It is a wonderful thing to be prayed over by nuns; I close my eyes and feel a great calmness pass over me.

Then there is a shout. I open my eyes to see that one nun (I do not know her name, we have never been introduced) has broken away from the others and is pointing toward a distant hikhik house. There, on the clumsily cobbled garden, is a human form, a stooped man dragging something behind him, and dragging it toward us. As he draws closer it is clear that he has been hurt, badly; there are bloodstains on his ragged clothes, on his head and hands. Where has he come from? To my knowledge I am the only tourist currently at the settlement. It is only when he is within a few metres of the nuns that I recognise his face, and realise why they are shrieking.

The man is Jesus.

He's not the Jesus of any Word documentary I've ever seen, but he is still *a* Jesus: his hair is long and fair, his beard full, and his eyes are a bright and heavenly blue. He wears a pale Hessian-cloth robe, butchered around the left elbow, with bloodstains across the chest and stomach. Thorns circle his head like a fallen halo. The thing he drags behind him is the broken intersection of a cross. He drops it now, reaching his bleeding hands toward the nuns, and cries out, in a voice high with religious euphoria: "Forsake me! Forgive me! Forsake me!"

It becomes a chant; and other voices are soon raised to join his. From the village's alleys, from doorways, from out of gardens and behind drifts of snow, come the hikhiks in the thousand faces of Christ. There is the crawling child-Christ; there is the Christ who spoke to the snake in the desert; there is a naked, bloody Christ-of-the-crucifixion, whose cross hops toward us in ungainly and comical strides. Some lumber along as if they are zombies, others run, their robes snapping about their ankles. Others crawl on their bellies as if struggling beneath the weight of the sins of the world. And they are all screaming out their forsake-forgive-forsake mantra, their heads thrown back, their mouths curved terribly into identical rictus. As promised, they have become Christ-like, and they are seeking absolution for the sins they, I admit now, likely do not even understand. They have taken my suggestions, my deepest thoughts, and perverted them into this farce.

The nuns are surrounded, and are forced to cower around the pod's grey platform. There are so many of them, the Christs, the Christi; they are suddenly a seething mass of blood and redemption. It is one thing I expect to teach a group of obedience hikhik in the quiet of the mission schoolhouse, but another to see them mobilised, and bleeding, and tortured, and screaming. I catch sight of Paul's face, just once, as she turns to look up at me—her expression is a sort of plaintive surprise, a desperate *why* glimmering in her eyes. My heart is beating so fast I hear it in my ears, in the tremble of my spine. The Christi hordes advance, so close that we—I, and those nuns brave enough to look up from their shaking hands—can see the incredible details of their wounds, their upturned hands, the deep gashes from the thorns at their brows. It is an *orgy* (I use the term in a descriptive form) of pain, of suffering; it is the kind of human torment you see only in the goriest of medieval paintings. And yet they are child-like too, presenting these gashes to the nuns like small ones showing a cut knee to mother. *Look, see, what I have done to myself. Look, see, what you have made me do.*

After a time they start to eat each other, and the nuns start to scream. From my high platform I watch this all play out, frozen in the pod's metallic throne like a statue. It is my fault, and I cannot stop it; nor can I bear it. So I do what it is that all cowards must; I run. I press in my transport codes, I fix my trajectory, I shoot myself across the universe in a spray of atoms and at once force my mind away from the hikhik and their horrible mimicry to a calmer, sweeter place— where my Christ is a Lord unseen, who is *coming* but not yet come, and whose sacrifice was pure and distant, not visceral and *here.*

§

I have no neat conclusion for this article, if it is indeed an article at all. I'm sure the editors of *HeLives* will consider it unfit for print, but perhaps some sanitised version will appear in the pages, one that spares our gentle-minded readers from the worst terrors of this place. A short note, maybe along the lines of: *The missions have encountered a problem; the hikhik are too enthusiastic in their adoption of Christianity.* Or they may simply send a different journalist to cover—to *re*cover the story.

I do not want to talk of the repercussions my trip to Azagarth has had on my personal life, but I will say that my faith since that day has been a steady, solid thing, a rock against which even the greatest tribulations founder. My priest says that when faith is tested, it becomes stronger; and so it has, and so I am.

The St Christopher movement continues on Azagarth. The things I witnessed there were, according to Sister Therese, a small hiccup in the process of the hikhiks' conversion. A mistake, a misinterpretation. I wish the nuns there the very best in continuing their work.

May God bless you and keep you.

# ELYSS G. PUNSALAN
## Ashland

You'll get used to it, they said to her. And it's only a couple of weeks. The task is simple enough. Think of it as a holiday—it'll be good for you.

Those were the last words she heard, before plunging into the quiet. Ashland was reclaimed terrain, beyond the fringes of the colony. The ash fall was heavier there, and of a different sort.

The ash were sound-eaters. They gnawed on creaks made by metal hinges, and devoured radio frequencies. They swirled and danced in the atmosphere, feeding silently on bits of electric cackle. It was a mystery, to the scientists at the research center where she worked. She was an inventory clerk; what would she know?

A world without sound isn't safe, they said. It'll take time to make it habitable, but the government isn't sending enough people for scouts. Damn budget cuts. We have to do it ourselves.

Her name came out in the February draft.

The month-long assignment is mandatory, the memo said. She'll be stationed at the Ashland Wave Hub, one of the oldest facilities on the M3. She's guaranteed full audibility inside the Hub, courtesy of an acoustech, as well as a fully-stocked pantry and endless hours of classic movies, right at her fingertips. Every other hour she's to visit each of the akitometers in the vicinity of the Hub. Jot down readings. Check calibration. Trouble-shoot. Repeat. She'll be trained for the work, just like the others. She's to work alone, just like the others, too. Damn budget cuts, the memo seemed to say.

She was transported using the Leviathan Terrestrial Craft, which was a joke to her, really. It was too small to be 'leviathan,' and the descriptor 'terrestrial' made it an oxymoron. The only thing that held true was the word 'craft,' because it looked like a school project, made of titanium and dirt. The Leviathan traveled on autodrive, the coordinates of Ashland scribed into its circuitry.

The blue lamp near you will light up when you're there, they said.

They didn't have to tell her. When she couldn't hear the chain wheels crushing against gravel, she knew she had reached the place.

§

She wakes up before the alarm goes off. Today is Thursday, her inner clock says. It's been a week. She drags herself out of bed, and turns on the music to full blast. She hates jazz because of how dated it sounds, but plays it anyway. It's the only thing on the Hub playlist that doesn't remind her of anything. She's pleased that the acoustech is working, even after her failed experiments to make it work outside.

She chucks a foil bag of yang chow into the heater. When it's done she doesn't bother using a bowl, but instead tears the pack open and spoons the contents into her mouth. Post-ablutions, she dons her work gear, which is almost like a space suit except that it has a lighter head bubble and sleeker insulation. There are also no comm devices, which is a relief to her; the ones she used at the center had an energy pack that weighed a ton.

She looks at herself in the bathroom mirror; a picture of her departed husband is stuck between the glass and the mirror frame. She waves her arms like a bird, then strikes a ninja pose. He isn't impressed. He's frozen in that silly expression she can't describe. She ditches the gloves and the head bubble, and puts on a fresh layer of lipstick. She decides to replace the bubble with a head mask. Before leaving the bathroom, she kisses her fingers and touches the picture with them.

She peers out the window, and outside, the akitometers stand like short red sentinels. They surround the Hub, equidistant from each other, and there are yellow pinlights shining on their heads. She finds them adorable now, even giving each a name, but in the beginning she loathed them.

Little devils, she used to say, maybe they're hiding little tridents too.

She knew, of course, that it wasn't the machines that scared her. More than anything, she was terrified of the quiet.

§

The first day didn't start out well. After the double Hub doors had slid open, she treaded out slowly, her legs sinking into the soft ash. The gray matter billowed around her like fine snow, muffling the sound of the doors as they closed.

She walked further on, toward the first red machine, but felt the air thickening, smothering her face like a pillow. It was suffocating, and when she couldn't hear herself gasping, couldn't hear her heart racing, she panicked even more. She ran and stumbled back toward the Hub.

Once shielded from the ash, the acoustech kicked in, and the sound of her shrieking startled her. It took a while to calm down. The light outside had already changed, and her work gear had been strewn on the floor like entrails.

She cried in the bathroom, until her eyes hurt and her throat was sore. She had not cried as much since the funeral. Her sobs bounced back from the tiles. The picture of her husband fell, and drifted to where she sat. She held his face in her hands for a moment, then stuck it right back onto the mirror.

She picked up her suit and put it back on. When the doors opened, she didn't come back until she had read every one of the akitometers.

She's not afraid of the quiet anymore, and finds it rather comforting nowadays, the way even her thoughts are silenced, at the right moments. Today, after going through half of the machines, she is inspired to run naked among them and let the ash touch her. She lets the sound-eaters work their way into her head, where memories of friends come unbidden. 'We're so sorry about your loss' becomes 'We're so sor—' then turns into '—.'

§

Hello, Scarlet, she tells an akitometer.

She doesn't hear herself say it, but she imagines that Scarlet can lip-read. The metrics are spelled out clearly on the dial, and she replicates the reading into her handheld. Seeing nothing unusual, she slogs to the next machine and greets it with the same fervor.

Hello, Redmond.

She looks at the dial, and sees it is way above the average reading. It is as expected. Redmond is farthest from the Hub, and stands at what trainers at the center called a 'rabbit hole,' a shifting pocket in the atmosphere where remnants of uneaten sound take their last shimmy in the universe, then die.

It's quite scarce in Ashland, they said, only one in eight hundred thousand square miles.

Static crackles, and she hears "Hello, Redmond," through her thin mask.

We can't fit a whole new colony into a tiny rabbit hole, she mock-telepaths to Redmond.

She removes her mask and sings the first lines of a folk song. The rabbit hole echoes, *"O, naraniag a bulan, un-unnoyko indengam..."* The words warble through bits of faded grating, jarring, burring, jangling, clicking and clanging. Ghosts of the Hub doors closing, the windows relenting, the Leviathan pushing, her heart pulsing, her lungs expanding, her mouth screaming. The song thins and wears out, and the rabbit hole empties itself of her voice.

She thinks about the sounds she misses, and tries to conjure them in her mind. A brown sparrow chirps the morning in through their window, and her husband grunts about having breakfast in bed. His breath touches her cheek. He sucks her tongue. He moans softly when she touches him there. He compliments the way her hair falls on her shoulders. He says her name. The phone rings and she is back at the hospital, waiting for the surgeon's news.

That last one, I don't miss that at all, she protests.

She dismisses the memory by checking Redmond again. She turns the power off, and sees the pointer a few lines off the zero mark. It needs to be recalibrated. She reaches for tools in her belt bag.

The rabbit hole opens, and a sigh escapes.

It is a human sigh, she is sure of it. Is it hers? She stands very still, her hand clutching the metal tools, to keep them from moving. She moves her ear closer to the rabbit hole.

A voice floats in the pocket. The words are faint, jumbled in an illogical sequence, thrown about by the ash, their beginnings and ends cut off. The timbre is liquid and deep. The timbre is a man's.

§

There is nothing else to think of, when she is back at the Hub. The memory of the voice needles its way to her and touches her temples. Another jazz singer croons from the speakers. The playlist is killing her.

She shuts the music down, and listens to her self exhale. The voice from the rabbit hole evokes a silhouette unlike the picture in the bathroom. It speaks nonsense, "—eyde— ... —rik—...—hosth—..." but she recognizes them as words. Though broken, they were once part of a thought that meant something, to someone.

The last scout was a man, they said.

Is that all?

We can't tell you anything more.

The last scout must be back at the colony, she thinks, back on Earth, even. Has a wife, kids, and a mistress. Runs every morning. Speaks seven languages.

Before going home, he must have said "Fuck you, Ashland. Thanks for the memories," then left the Hub with a crappy playlist. It's a wonder his voice has lasted this long. The ash must have hated the words. They must have tasted of bile.

She remembers the sigh. It licks the space between her legs, and her breasts swell beneath her shirt. The bed sheets rustle as she stirs.

§

She wonders if the akitometers notice that she is ignoring the one with the rabbit hole. Her guilt instructs her to take her time with each machine, to calibrate when there isn't any need.

Finally, at dusk, she sets aside her childishness and attends to Redmond. As she draws nearer, however, she notices a spinning sphere above it. Frayed sheets of ash glide on the surface, like storm clouds in a small globe. The moving ash traverses to one side, and shoots an endless silver thread into the air, past the secure vicinity of the Hub.

Its appearance troubles her, and leads her to question her sanity. This is probably what grief does, her fear answers her. But her mind persists on trying to produce an explanation. She is deaf outside the Hub, and the absence of sound amplifies the strength of other senses, like how the absence of sight intensifies one's ability to hear.

§

The numbers on the dial are higher than usual. She pulls out the handheld to check for similar readings in the past, and the screen flashes a graph taken a month ago. A spike cuts the metric graph at the center, and mirrors the numbers she sees.

Help me here, Redmond.

She hears the voice again and, for a second, thinks it is Redmond answering back. The words tumble from the rabbit hole in the same chaotic fashion, but are sharper by several degrees.

"—ment—... mayd—...—shland..."

"Mayd—"

The silver tail has grown in thickness, has reached further out. It is wider and longer, and cannot be missed.

"Mayda—..."

"Mayday..."

The call is weak and desperate. Her heart aches, when she realizes that the hopelessness she hears is similar to her husband's when he was racked with cancer, before he wasted away.

She runs, and follows the path of the suspended tail. It goes over a hill and a shallow basin where more ash had gathered, taking on the appearance of a powdered-sugar lake. She looks back at the roof of the Hub, before it disappears from view. From hereon, only the tail connects her from where she was to where she is.

She hears nothing still, but the quiet has become denser, and solidifies like ice in her ears. Her chest pounds with the pain of breathing; the back of her leg threatens to tear itself apart.

The run progresses longer than she had expected. When she cannot go any farther, she stops to look at the tail above her, and sees the ash swirling continuously around it. She glances back in the direction of the Hub, and is alarmed by what she sees at a distance. The end of the tail unravels, then consumes itself quickly, as if it were a charged wick.

Her panic swells from within her, and erupts into a soundless scream.

§

She scampers after the tail's end, as it passes by her. Her hands reach into the air to grasp it, to keep it from snuffing out, but the tail zips ahead faster than she can run. In mere seconds, it terminates into a white point in space, then dies out.

The darkness has settled in completely. She reaches for the photowafer on her head mask, and activates it with a tap of her finger. The light beam hits the place where the tail had ended, and it illuminates a fallen craft, buried halfway in the ash beside a cliff.

It is a Leviathan, with its legs smashed against a rock bed. She guesses that the positioning system must have gone haywire before it stepped off the ledge.

She finds the door lock jutting out from the side, and she twists it with both hands. The metal door disengages and lifts upward. The scent of decay pushes out forcefully, as the crown of a bloodied head peeks out. Her eyes water, and she doesn't understand her tears.

Fuck you, Ashland, she tries to say for him. The falling ash eats the words anyway.

She closes the door gently and sits down next to the Leviathan. She wraps her arms around her knees, and takes in the land around her. Everything looks the same. She can't remember where she came from. She had been too focused following the tail.

The cold begins to seep through her suit. Her eyes don't dry up as the ash around her grows thicker.

She thinks about the sounds she misses the most. Rain pelting against pavement. Her mother making dinner in the kitchen. Her friends clinking glasses for a birthday toast. The delivery truck horns at work. Jazz. Yes, even jazz.

She studies the descending ash and ponders where they have been. As she does this she notices the ash parting, yielding to an invisible shape, which grows as it approaches her. The ash trickles along the figure's surface, and forms begin to emerge and distinguish themselves—first a head, then shoulders, then arms and legs. The cinders cling to its body thickly and completely. An ash face smiles at her.

Hello, he says. It is his voice, and her voice too, fused together.

She stands up to see him clearly. You are a walking, talking, human-like rabbit hole, she mouths.

She is crushed when her spoken wit disintegrates in the air. The ash man takes her hand, and she hears her reply reverberate in his fingers. His hand is warm, and feels like skin against hers.

§

Are you okay? he asks.

I miss listening to Billie Holiday, she says.

The corners of his ash eyes crinkle with laughter. Let's get you home, he says to her.

They walk hand in hand through ash-covered hills and valleys, through columns of ash-crusted rock that spiral upward and disappear into ash-heavy clouds. Their walk is long and full of conversation, of song and memory, and she almost forgets that she spent a year as widow, had they not talked about their grief.

This is where we say goodbye, he says.

Beyond him, the akitometers all stand at attention, with Redmond exhibiting the proudest salute.

I don't understand, she says.

You're already doing so well. I'll only make things worse for you if I stay, he says.

She nods her head meekly, and takes his hand to touch her face. Thank you, she says.

He moves his fingers from her cheek to close her eyes. She does not hear his voice, nor see his face, but as she breathed she felt lips press against her own, as tender as sunlight. She does not need to open her eyes to know he is gone.

**LISA BAO**
# like father like daughter

you were born in the colony
first of three sons
learning to read by
guttering halolight

I was birthed in organic linen
longed-for precious child
under a single moon
reading novels about home

you got up at sunrise
to find the cheapest green
-house bok choy
raised from real seed

I never got raw milk
or nitrogen ice cream
but as many fresh
mangoes as I liked

now you wear an ironed collar
and light-faded sweaters
save up for a cherry table
and six matching oak chairs

I save my first paycheck
towards a spidersilk dress
the colors of dragonfruit
as bright as your silence now

# PINCKNEY BENEDICT
## Zog-19

Zog-19 is learning to drive a stick shift. He backs up, judders to a stop, and stalls. It's a big Ford F-250 diesel that he is driving, and it's got a hinky clutch. The two shovel-headed dogs in the bed of the truck bark hysterically. On Zog-19's planet, there are no cars and trucks with manual transmissions. There are no motor vehicles at all. Zog-19 shakes his head, flaps his hands, stomps in on the hinky clutch, and twists the ignition key. The Ford rattles back into life. Zog-19 decides that he will sell the Ford at the first opportunity and replace it with a vehicle that has an automatic transmission. In his short time here on Earth, Zog-19 has had about all he can stand of stick shifts.

A woman watches Zog-19's struggles with the truck. She squints her eyes worriedly. She thinks she's watching Donny McGinty fighting the hinky clutch. She is Missus McGinty, she is Donny McGinty's wife. Zog-19 is not in fact young McGinty, but he resembles McGinty down to the most minute detail. Even McGinty's dogs believe that Zog-19 is McGinty. The problem is, Zog-19 does not know how to drive a stick shift, and McGinty does, McGinty *did*.

McGinty knew how to do a blue million things that Zog-19 has never even so much as heard of on his own planet.

The Ford leaps forward several feet, stops, lurches forward again, dies. Missus McGinty shakes her head in disbelief. McGinty has never before, to her knowledge, had a bit of trouble with the truck, though that clutch often defies her. She is a small woman, and her legs aren't long enough or strong enough to manipulate the truck's pedals. Around her, around Missus McGinty and Zog-19, McGinty's little dairy operation—a hundred acres of decent land in the river bottom, inherited upon the death of McGinty's old man, and twenty-five complacent cows—is going to wrack and ruin. In the days when McGinty's old man ran the place, it gleamed, it glistened. No more, though. There are so many things that Zog-19 doesn't know how to accomplish.

Zog-19 waves to Missus McGinty from the truck. He wants badly to allay her apprehensions about him. "Toot toot," he says.

§

On Zog-19's planet, no one communicates by talking. All of Zog-19's people are equipped with powerful steam whistles. Well, not steam whistles exactly, because they sound using sentient gases rather than steam. The Zogs use their whistles to talk back and forth, using a system not unlike Morse code. On Zog-19's planet, "Toot toot" means "Don't worry." It also means "I love you" and "Everything is A-okay, everything is just peachy keen."

§

Zog-19 frets that McGinty's best friend, Angstrom, will notice the substitution. Zog-19 is not so good at imitating McGinty yet, but he is working hard to get better. Zog-19 is a diligent worker, even though he is not entirely sure what it is that he's supposed to accomplish here on Earth, in the guise of the farmer McGinty. He does know that he's supposed to act just the same as McGinty, and so for the moment he's working like heck at being McGinty.

"Goddamn it hurts," Angstrom says. He's got his arms wrapped around his middle, sways back and forth. He looks like a gargoyle, he looks like he should be a downspout on some French cathedral. Angstrom's belly hurts all the time. Maybe it's cancer, maybe it's an ulcer, maybe it's something else. Whatever it is, Angstrom can feel the blackness growing within him. At night, his hands and feet are cold as blocks of ice. The only thing that scares him more than whatever's going on inside him is how bad the cure for it might be.

Doctors killed Angstrom's old man. Angstrom's old man, strong as a bull, went to the doctors about a painful black dot on the skin of his back. The doctors hollowed him out, and he died. So now Angstrom sits on a hard chair in his kitchen and rocks back and forth, looking like a gargoyle.

"Toot toot," says Zog-19. He likes Angstrom. He's glad McGinty had Angstrom for a friend, that Angstrom is by default Zog-19's friend now, but he wishes that Angstrom felt better. He worries that Angstrom will notice that he isn't McGinty. He wishes that he knew just a bit more clearly what his mission might be. He wishes that, whatever it is, someone else, someone more suitable, had been chosen for it.

§

Zog-19's planet is made of iron. From space, Zog-19's planet looks just like a giant steelie marble. The planet is called Zog. Zog-19's people are called the Zogs. Donny McGinty had a magnificent steelie marble when he was a little boy. He adored the slick, cool feel of the steelie in his hand, he loved the look of it, he loved the click it made when he flicked it against other marbles. He loved the rich tautness in the pit of his stomach when he sent his beloved steelie into battle, when he played marbles with other kids. When he was using that steelie as his striker, he simply could not be beaten. He was the marbles champion of his grammar school up in the highlands of Seneca County.

Those were good days for McGinty. McGinty's old man was alive, Angstrom's old man was alive, the little dairy farm shone like a jewel at a bend in the Seneca River, and Angstrom's belly didn't hurt all the time. It seemed, when McGinty held that heavy, dully gleaming steelie in his hand, like they might all manage to live forever.

Zog-19's planet is a great hollow iron ball, filled with sentient gas. Zog-19's people are also made of iron, and they are also filled with sentient gas. When they walk, their iron feet strike the iron surface of the planet, and the whole thing rings just like a giant bell. With all the ringing, and all the tooting, Zog-19's planet can get very noisy.

§

Missus McGinty talks. She talks and talks. She keeps on talking about Angstrom, how she wishes that Angstrom would go to the doctor. He should go to the doctor, she says, or he should quit complaining. One or the other. She talks about Angstrom to avoid talking about McGinty. She has noticed all the changes in him lately—how could she not?—but she doesn't know that he's been replaced by Zog-19. She just thinks he's very, very sad about the death of his old man.

She has a great deal to say on the subject of Angstrom. He should wash more frequently, for one thing. It worries Zog-19 when she talks so much. On his planet, every time you talk through your whistle, you use up a little of your sentient gas. You've got a lot to start off with, so it doesn't seem to be a big deal at first; but little by little, you use it up, sure as shooting. When all the sentient gas is gone, that's it. Zog-19 watches Missus McGinty's mouth for telltale signs of the gas. He watches to see whether it's escaping. He thinks maybe it is. He does not want Missus McGinty to run out of sentient gas.

"You should wash more, too," Missus McGinty tells him. "You're getting to be just like old dirty Angstrom." It's true, Zog-19 does not wash himself frequently. He is used to being made of iron. Washing frightens him. He has only recently been made into a creature of flesh, a creature that resembles McGinty down to the last detail, a creature that can pass muster with McGinty's dogs, and he has trouble recalling that he's no longer iron. Do you know what happens when you wash iron? It *corrodes.*

"You smell like a boar hog," says Missus McGinty. "I don't even like to be in the same bed with you anymore." Zog-19 knows that she's only saying these things because she loves him. On his planet, no one talks about anyone they don't love. They can't afford to waste the sentient gas. She loves him, and she loves Angstrom too, she loves him like a brother. She and McGinty have known Angstrom all their lives. Zog-19 imagines that, once he is better able to imitate McGinty, once he forgets that he used to be made out of iron, he'll be able to love her as well.

But here's another thing that scares him: when people on Earth touch a piece of iron, he has noticed, they leave behind prints, they leave behind fingerprints. No two people on Earth, he has heard it said, have the same fingerprints. All those fingerprints, and every one different! No one on Zog-19's planet has any fingerprints at all. And these human fingerprints are composed of body oils, they are acid in their content. Unless they are swiftly scrubbed away, they oxidize the iron, they eat into it, they etch its surface with little ridges and valleys and hollows, they make smooth pristine iron into a rough red landscape of rust. Almost nothing could be worse for someone from the planet Zog than the touch of a human hand.

§

In the year 2347, space explorers from Earth will discover Zog-19's planet. The space explorers will leave their rusting fingerprints all over the iron surface of Zog. During their visit, the space explorers will discover that the sentient gas which fills the planet, and which coincidentally fills and animates the Zogs themselves, makes the space explorers' ships go very, very fast. Because they like to go very, very fast, they will ask the Zogs for the gas. They will ask politely at first.

Because the gas makes their planet ring so nicely under their iron feet, the Zogs will refuse it to them. The space explorers will ask again, less politely this time, more pointedly, and the Zogs will explain, with their thundering whistles, their immutable position on the matter.

War. At first, it looks as though the Zogs will easily win. They are numerous and powerful, and the space explorers are few and a long way from home. The Zogs are made of iron (to the space explorers, they look like great foundry boilers with arms and legs and heads), and the space explorers are made of water and soft meat. Their bones are brittle and break easily. "Toot toot," the Zogs will reassuringly say to one another as they prepare for battle. "Toot toot!"

But one of the space explorers will think of a thing: he will think of a way to magnetize the whole iron planet. He will think of a way to use vast dynamos to turn the entire planet into a gigantic electromagnet. He will get the idea from watching a TV show, one where a big electromagnet-equipped crane picks up a car, a huge old Hudson Terraplane, and drops it into a hydraulic crusher.

McGinty used to see this show in reruns every now and again, before he got replaced by Zog-19, and he was always amazed by what happened to that car. Every time the show played, the crusher mashed the car down into a manageable cube, not much larger than a coffee table.

"Look at that," McGinty would say to Angstrom whenever the show was on. "That's my old man's car that's getting crushed."

§

McGinty's old man used to have a car just like that one when he was young, when he was McGinty's age, and he and McGinty's mother (though McGinty had not been born yet) would run around the county in that big old powerhouse of a car, blowing the horn in a friendly way and waving to everybody they knew, which was pretty much everybody they saw. McGinty does not know it, but he was conceived in the backseat of that Hudson Terraplane.

His old man wanted to sire a child, he wanted a son, and McGinty's mother was only too happy to oblige. While they were making love in the backseat of the Hudson, McGinty's mother's left heel caught the hornring on the steering wheel a pretty blow, and the horn sounded, just as McGinty's old man and his mother were making McGinty. And the sound it made? *Toot toot.*

§

"We don't make love anymore," says Missus McGinty, "not since your father died." Zog-19 has never made love to anyone.

On his planet, they do not have sex. They do not have babies. When a Zog runs out of sentient gas, it is simply replaced by another full-grown Zog more or less like it. Where do these new Zogs come from? No one knows. Perhaps the planet makes them. Once, the best thinkers on the planet Zog gathered together for a summit on the matter. They thought that they'd put their heads together and figure the thing out—where do new Zogs come from?—once and for all. But once they were all together, they got worried about losing all their sentient gas in the course of the palaver. They worried that they themselves would have to be replaced by the as-yet-unfathomed process of Zog regeneration. And so they figured, "What the heck?" and they went home again.

Missus McGinty leads Zog-19 into the cool bedroom of their farmhouse. She draws the shades. She does not ask him to speak. She undresses him and sponges him off with cool water. He does not corrode. She undresses herself. She is not built like a foundry boiler. Her pale, naked skin is luminous in the darkened room. She has a slender waist and a darling little dimple above each buttock. When he sees those dimples, Zog-19 says, "Toot toot."

Because she is only made of water and soft meat, Zog-19 is afraid that he will hurt her when he touches her. He is afraid that his dense, tremendous bulk will crush her, like the Hudson Terraplane on the TV show. He is afraid that his iron claws will puncture her skin. When she draws him to her, and when he enters her, he becomes momentarily convinced that he has injured her, and he tries to lift himself away. But she pulls him back again, with surprising strength, and he concedes, for a time, that he too is only made of water and meat.

§

So the space explorers will magnetize the planet, and the feet of the

Zogs will stick to it like glue. Think of it! Poor Zogs. All they will be able to do is look up at the sky as the Earth ships descend. They will look up at the sky, and they will hoot at one another with their whistles. They will not say, "Toot toot," because things will not be A-okay, things will not be hunky-dory. Instead, as the space explorers land and rig up a great sharpened molybdenum straw that will penetrate the surface of Zog and siphon off the sentient gas, the Zogs will whistle, "Hoot hoot hoot," all over the planet.

To the Earthmen who are setting up the molybdenum straw, it will seem a very sad sound. It will also seem very loud, and every Earth space explorer will be issued a set of sturdy earmuffs to prevent damage to sensitive human eardrums. And the sound will mean this: it will mean "I'm sad" and "The end is near" and "We are most definitely screwed."

§

The loafers that hang out at the Modern Barbershop in Mount Nebo, where McGinty used to get his hair cut, and where Zog-19 goes now in imitation of McGinty, are convinced that the death of McGinty's old man has driven McGinty around the bend. They chuckle when McGinty says to them, "Toot toot." They try to jolly him out of the funk he is in.

They are by and large elderly fellows, the loafers, and they tell McGinty stories about his old man when his old man was young. They tell him stories about his old man roaring around the county in his big old Hudson Terraplane, a car so well made that, if McGinty's old man hadn't smashed it into a tree one drunken night, that car would still be out on the road today. All the loafers agree that nobody makes cars anymore that are anywhere near as good as that faithful Hudson.

They tell him other stories too. They tell him how, when he was a little boy, he and his old man used to sing a song, to the delight of everybody in the barbershop. McGinty's old man would set young McGinty up in the barber's chair, and the barber would drape a sheet around young McGinty's neck and set to work with his comb and his flashing silver scissors and his long cutthroat razor, and McGinty's old man would stand before the chair, his arms spread like an orchestra conductor's, and he and young McGinty would sing. And the song they sang went like this: it went, "Well, McGinty is dead and

McCarty don't know it, McCarty is dead and McGinty don't know it, and they're both of them dead, and they're in the same bed, and neither one knows that the other is dead."

There was a fellow named McCarty who always loafed at the Modern Barbershop, a tough old guy who had been a frogman in the Second World War, so it was like the McGintys were singing a song about themselves and about McCarty. The loafers at the barbershop loved the song when McGinty was a little boy, and remembering it now they love it all over again. They love it so much that they laugh, laugh really hard, laugh themselves breathless, and pretty soon it is hard to tell if it's a barbershop full of laughing old men or weeping old men.

Of course, when McGinty's old man sang the song, back in McGinty's childhood, both McGinty and McCarty were alive, even though the song said they were dead, and that made it all the funnier. But now McGinty really *is* dead, and McCarty really is dead too, carried off by a wandering blood clot a decade before, and they are both buried out in the graveyard of the Evangelical Church of the New Remnant north of town, which is kind of like being in the same bed. None of the song was true before, and now a lot of it is true, and so it isn't all that funny.

"Poor McGinty," says one of the loafers, when they have all thought of how the song is true and not so funny anymore. And nobody knows whether he's talking about McGinty, or McGinty's old man.

§

Before long, the Earth spacemen, with their very, very fast spaceships, will manage to conquer the entire universe. Everywhere they go, the people who live there will ask them, "How in the heck do you make your spaceships go so darned fast?" The space explorers will be tempted to tell them, because they will want to boast about the clever way in which they defeated the Zogs, but they will play it cagey. They will keep their traps closed. They won't want anybody getting any ideas about using the sentient gas themselves.

Before long, also, the sentient gas that fills the planet of the Zogs will begin to run out. There will be that many Earth spaceships! And the space explorers will become very worried, because, even though they will have conquered the entire universe, they will nonetheless continue to think that there might be something beyond that which they might like to conquer as well.

§

McGinty and Angstrom also used to sing a song. They used to sing it when they got drunk. They used to sing it back in the days when McGinty's old man was alive, when Angstrom's old man was alive, back in the days when even McCarty, the tough old frogman, was alive. They would sing it while they played card games, Deuces and Beggar Your Neighbor.

They used to sing it to girls, too, because it was a slightly naughty song. They used to love singing it to girls. And the song they sang went like this: it went, "Roll me over in the clover. Roll me over and do it again."

It was a simple, silly song, but it seemed to be about sex, and that was unusual in a place where almost nothing was about sex. So little was about sex in the Seneca Valley in the days when McGinty's old man and Angstrom's old man were alive that, weirdly, almost everything seemed to be about sex. Anything could make you think about sex in those days, even a silly little song, even a silly little song about clover. Clover is a kind of fodder that cows and sheep especially like. A clover with four leaves is said on Earth to be particularly lucky.

In addition to the hundred acres of decent bottomland, McGinty's old man also accumulated a little highland pasturage to the north of the valley, where he kept a few fat, lazy sheep. These mountain pastures were almost completely grown over in sweet clover. When McGinty and Angstrom sang the song, when they sang, "Roll me over in the clover," McGinty was always thinking about those pastures. He was thinking about rolling over a girl in the mountain pastures. He was thinking about rolling over a girl he knew who had sweet dimples above her buttocks. He was thinking about rolling her over in the cool mountain pastures.

And now Angstrom tries to teach the song to Zog-19. He cannot believe that McGinty has forgotten the song. Zog-19 understands that it's a song that he's supposed to know, supposed to like, and so he makes a diligent effort to learn it, for Angstrom's sake. Angstrom has been drinking, an activity that sometimes eases the pain in his belly and sometimes exacerbates it. For the moment, drinking seems to have eased the pain.

"Roll me over," sings Angstrom in his scratchy baritone voice.

"Over," sings Zog-19, in McGinty's pleasant, clear tenor.

"In the clover," sings Angstrom, waving a bottle.

"Clover," answers Zog-19. He does not know yet what clover is, but he likes the sound of it. He hopes that someone will teach him about clover, about which McGinty doubtless knew volumes, about which McGinty doubtless knew every little thing. He hopes that someone will teach him soon.

§

All this time, while they will have been out conquering the width and breadth of the universe, the space explorers will have kept the planet of Zog magnetized, with the poor old Zogs stuck to its surface like flies stuck to a strip of flypaper.

The Zogs will still manage to talk back and forth among themselves. Mostly, what they will say is "Hoot hoot hoot." Sometimes one among them, a Zog optimist, will venture a "Toot toot," but he will inevitably be shouted down by a chorus of hooting.

§

Zog-19 wants the spinning radiator fan of the Ford F-250 to stop spinning, and so he simply reaches out a hand to stop it. On Zog, this would not have been a problem. The spinning steel fan blades might have struck a spark or two from his hard iron claws, and then the fan would have been stilled in his mighty grip.

On Earth, though, it is a big problem. On Earth, Zog-19 is only made of water and soft meat. The radiator fan slices easily through the water and meat of his fingers. It sends the tips of two of the fingers cartwheeling off, sailing away to land God knows where, slashes tendons in the other fingers, cross-hatches his palms with bleeding gashes. Zog-19 holds his ruined hand up before his face, stares at it in horror. He knows that he has made a terrible mistake, a mistake of ignorance, and one that it won't be possible to remedy. He wants to shout for Missus McGinty, whose name he has only just mastered. He struggles to come up with her name, but the pain and terror of his hand have driven it from his memory. All that he can come up with is this: he calls out, "Hoot hoot hoot," in a pitiful voice, and then he collapses.

§

Probably by this point you have questions. How is it possible to know what will happen to the Zogs in the year 2347? That might be one of the questions. Easy. The Zogs have seen the future. They have seen the past, too. They watch it the way we watch television. Zog science makes it possible. They have seen what happened on the iron planet a million years ago, and what happened five minutes ago, and what will happen in the year 2347. They can watch the present, too, but they don't.

They have seen the space explorers from Earth. They have seen the depopulation of their planet, they have seen it emptied of its precious sentient gas. In fact, that episode of their history—a holocaust of such indescribable proportions that most Zogs can be brought to tears merely by the mention of it—is by far the most popular program on Zog. Every Zog watches it again and again, backward and forward. Every Zog knows by heart all its images—the Zogs stuck helplessly to the planet's iron surface, the molybdenum straw, the descent of the Earth ships on tongues of fire—and all its dialogue. They are obsessed with their own doom.

Another question: What is Zog-19 doing on Earth, in McGinty's exact form, with McGinty's wife and McGinty's dogs, and with McGinty's best friend, Angstrom? And: How was the switch accomplished? And what the heck happened to the real McGinty?

In a nutshell: Zog-19 was sent to Earth by a Zog scientist who was not enamored of the program, who hated what Fate held in store for Zog. His name was Zog-One-Billion, and he was a very important fellow. He was also brilliant. Being brilliant, he was able to invent a device that allowed him to send one of his own people to Earth in the guise of a human being. The device allowed him to examine Earth at his leisure, and to pick one of its citizens—the most likely of them, as he saw it, to be able to put a stop to the upcoming extermination of the Zogs—as a target for Zog replacement.

Zog-19 didn't go willingly. He had to do what Zog-One-Billion said because he had a lower number, a *much* lower number. The higher numbers tell the lower numbers what to do, and the lower numbers do it. It makes sense to the Zogs, and so that's how Zog society is arranged. Zog-19 couldn't even complain. Zog-One-Billion wanted him to be some unknown thing, a farmer named McGinty a galaxy away, and so Zog-19 had to be that thing that Zog-One-Billion wanted.

In all the excitement, the selection of McGinty and the sending of Zog-19 across the galaxy, Zog-One-Billion failed to explain to Zog-19 what precisely he was to undertake in order to avert the Zog apocalypse. It's possible that he didn't really have many firm ideas in that direction himself. There's no way of knowing because, as he sent Zog-19 on his long sojourn, he gave a last great toot of triumph and went still. His sentient gas was depleted.

What is known is this: it's known that, during his surveillance of Earth, Zog-One-Billion came particularly to like and admire human farmers. He saw them, for some reason, as the possible salvation of Zog. It is believed that he regarded farmers thus because many farmers own cows. Cows were particularly impressive to Zog-One-Billion, especially the big black-and-white ones that give milk. These cows are called Holstein-Friesians, for a region in Europe; or just Holsteins for short.

There are no cows on Zog. There are no animals whatsoever. Cows burp and fart when they're relaxed. That's why it's a terrific compliment when a cow burps in your face, or if it farts when you're around. It means you don't make the cow nervous. You don't make all its innards tighten up.

McGinty didn't make his cows nervous. McGinty's cows were always terrifically relaxed around McGinty, as they always had been around McGinty's old man, and it's believed that this reaction in some way influenced the brilliant scientist Zog-One-Billion, that this lack of nerves on the part of the cows of McGinty attracted the attention of Zog-One-Billion from across the galaxy.

Perhaps the great Holstein-Friesians fascinated Zog-One-Billion because they reminded him of Zogs, because they reminded him of himself, with their great barrel bodies and their hard, blunt heads. Perhaps the burps and farts of the Holsteins reminded him of the sentient gas within himself, the sentient gas within every Zog, the sentient gas within the planet of Zog, the gas that made the iron planet ring in such an exotic and charming way. And yet—this would have been particularly impressive to Zog-One-Billion—cows never run out of gas, no matter how much of it they release. They manufacture the stuff! They are like gas factories made from water and soft meat.

And what happened to poor McGinty, the good-looking young dairy farmer with the beloved shovel-headed dogs and the beloved dimpled wife? Sad to say. Like the released sentient gas of Zog-One-Billion, McGinty simply... went away when Zog-19 replaced him. Drifted off. Dispersed. Vanished. Zog-One-Billion believed that McGinty's vanishment was the only way to save his beloved planet. If Zog-One-Billion, a very important Zog, was willing to make the ultimate sacrifice for the salvation of his planet and race, perhaps he reasoned, who was McGinty to object to making the same sacrifice? Of course, it wasn't McGinty's race or McGinty's planet, but there was no good way, given the enormous distances that separated them, for Zog-One-Billion to ask him.

§

Oh, McGinty is dead and McCarty don't know it. McCarty is dead and McGinty don't know it. They're both of them dead and they're in the same bed, and neither one knows that the other is dead.

§

Just when it looks like the ships of the space explorers will run out of sentient gas, the planet of the Zogs having been utterly depleted in this respect; just when it looks like the space explorers will have to stop going very, very fast, one of their number (he was the same one who thought of magnetizing the iron planet of the Zogs) will remember a thing: he will remember that the Zogs themselves are filled with the selfsame sentient gas. That gas is what makes the Zogs the Zogs, and each Zog is filled with quite a quantity of the stuff. He will remember it just in time!

§

Zog-19 cradles his wrecked hand against his chest. The hand is wrapped in a thick webbing of bandages. Zog-19 works hard to forget what the hand looked like after he stuck it into the blades of the radiator fan. He tries to think about what the hand looked like before that, the instant before, when the hand was reaching, and the hand was whole. Angstrom has just been by, and he brought the

How to Live on Other Planets

greetings of all the loafers down at the Modern Barbershop, who shook their heads sagely when they heard the news about the hand. Angstrom tried to interest Zog-19 in a rousing chorus of "Roll Me Over in the Clover," but Zog-19 couldn't forget about the hand long enough to sing. It did not take Angstrom long to leave.

Now Missus McGinty is with Zog-19. She holds his head cradled against her breasts. Zog-19's hand stings and throbs too much for him to take interest in the breasts, either. He does not know about healing. On Zog, no one heals. They are a hardy bunch, the Zogs, and usually last for thousands of years before all their gas is gone and they settle into de-animation. And all that time, all that time, the scars that life inflicts upon them gather on their great iron bodies, until, near the end, most Zogs come to look like rusted, pockmarked, ding-riddled caricatures of themselves. Zog-19 has no idea that his hand will not always hurt.

He is working very hard to listen to what Missus McGinty is telling him. She says it to him over and over, the same five words. And what she says is this: Missus McGinty, lovely dimpled Missus McGinty says, "Everything will be all right. Everything will be all right." Zog-19 knows what that phrase means. It means "Toot toot." He wants to believe it. He wants very badly to believe that everything will be all right.

Zog-19 is also working very hard to forget that he is Zog-19. He's not worried about the Zog extinction now. Right now he's worried about Zog-19, and about making Zog-19 believe that he is not made of iron, that he is made of water and soft meat. He is concerned with making Zog-19 believe that he is actually McGinty. He understands that, if he cannot forget that he is Zog-19, if he cannot come to believe that he is in fact what he seems to be, which is McGinty, he will—by accident, of course, by doing something that water and meat should never do—kill himself dead.

§

And so the intrepid space explorers will begin sticking sharpened molybdenum straws straight into the Zogs and drawing out their sentient gas. The Zogs will make a very good source of the gas, and the space explorers will be able to keep on going very, very fast. There is nothing beyond the universe they have conquered, they will discover that disheartening fact after a while, but they sure as heck won't waste any time getting there.

Drawing out the gas will de-animate the Zogs, of course. Magnetized as they are, the emptied iron Zogs won't seem to the space explorers much different from the full Zogs, except that they will be quiet, which won't be a problem. It will be, in fact, a decided benefit. Once they have de-animated many of the Zogs, the space explorers will find that they can take their earmuffs off. It will be more comfortable to work without the earmuffs, and so productivity and efficiency will both rise. They will go on sticking molybdenum straws into Zog after Zog and drawing out the sentient gas, until there will be only one unemptied Zog left.

This depletion will happen quickly, because once a space explorer hears about Zog and what the sentient gas can do, he will go there as quickly as possible (of course, he will leave much, much more quickly, thanks to the properties of the sentient gas when combined with Earth spaceships) in order to get his share. Most of the space explorers who come to Zog will never have seen the Zogs before they were magnetized, and so they won't be able to imagine why it might be a problem to empty a Zog of his gas. Except for the Zog's subsequent silence, it will seem the same afterward as it did before.

Everyone knows that the gas will run out—how could it not? And how could they not know?—but this knowledge will just make them swarm to Zog faster and faster, in ever-increasing numbers, because they won't want the gas to run out before they get there. What a dilemma.

§

Zog-19 rounds up his cows in the early morning for milking. It's still dark when he does so. Missus McGinty stays in bed while Zog-19 gathers the cows. Later, she will rise and make him breakfast, she will make him some pancakes. But now she is warm in bed, and dawn will brighten the sky soon, and she can hear Zog-19's voice out in the pasture, calling in the cows. He whoops and hollers, he sings out, and sometimes his voice sounds to her like a whistle, and sometimes it sounds like a regular voice.

The cows come trotting eagerly up to Zog-19. They follow him into the milking parlor. They are ready to be milked.

The cows are not nervous around Zog-19. Zog-19 is not nervous around the cows. The cows are large and black-and-white, they are noble Holstein-Friesians, and some of them weigh nearly a ton. If they wanted to, they could rampage and smash up the barn and smash up Zog-19 and smash up any of the water and meat people who got in their way, even though they themselves, the cows, are made only of water-and-meat, and not iron. Lucky for Zog-19—lucky for all of us!—that they never care to rampage.

Zog-19's favorite cow burps directly into his face. This is, as previously mentioned, high praise from a cow. A tag in the cow's ear reads 127. On Zog's planet, that number would make the cow the boss of Zog-19, since it is a higher number than nineteen. She would be able to tell him what to do, and he would have to do it, whether he wanted to or not. She would be able to tell him to go to some other planet for some half-understood reason, and replace some poor sap who lived there with his wife and his dogs, and Zog-19 would have to do just what she said.

Here, though, that number doesn't make the cow the boss of Zog-19. It doesn't make her the boss of anything, not even of the other cows with lower numbers. It's just a number. Cows never want to rampage, and they never want to be the boss.

When the cow burps in Zog-19's face, her breath is fragrant with the scent of masticated clover.

§

The last surviving Zog will be named Zog-1049. That is not a very impressive name for a Zog. Zog-1049 will only be more important than a thousand or so other Zogs, and he will be less important than many other Zogs. He will be much less important, for instance, than Zog-One-Billion, the Zog who sent Zog-19 to Earth to take McGinty's shape. Zog-One-Billion had a very impressive name, even though he didn't really know what he was doing. Zog-1049 will be, as you can see, more important than Zog-19, though not by much.

The space explorer's hand will rest on the big red button that will plunge the molybdenum straw into Zog-1049. He will wonder how much sentient gas the last Zog contains. He will wonder how far his ship will be able to go on that amount of gas, and how fast it will be able to get there.

Zog-1049 will say to the explorer, "Toot toot?" The space explorer will have heard it a million times, from a million Zogs, and still he won't know what it means. He won't know that it means "Don't you love me? I love you. Everything is hunky-dory."

When Zog-1049 realizes that the space explorer means to empty his sentient gas through the molybdenum straw no matter what he says, he will begin to hoot. "Hoot hoot hoot," he will say. He will hoot so long and so hard that he will expend a lot of his own gas this way. The space explorer will hate to hear Zog-1049 hoot so. He will know that it means the supply of sentient gas inside Zog-1049— and thus the supply of sentient gas in the entire universe—is dwindling ever faster. He will decide to stop contemplating Zog-1049 and go ahead and empty him.

The space explorer—whose name, by a vast coincidence that you have perhaps already intuited, will be Spaceman McGinty; he will be the great-great-great-however-many-greats-grandson of Missus McGinty and Zog-19—will take a final glance at this last of all the Zogs. He will take in the great iron foundry-boiler body, the sad, wagging head, the iron feet pinioned to the planet's surface by surging electromagnetic energy. He will take it all in, this pathetic, trapped creature, this iron being completely alien to him and useful to him only as fuel. And he will think he hears, as though they come to him from some realm far beyond his own, the lyrics of a silly song. They will ring in his head.

*Roll me over in the clover.*

Clover? Spaceman McGinty will never have seen clover. He will have heard of it, though, a family legend, passed down through the generations. Certainly there is no clover on Zog.

*Roll me over and do it again.*

The song will be a happy one. Looking at Zog-1049, and hearing the clover song in his head, Spaceman McGinty will feel unaccountably joyful. Looking at Zog-1049, Spaceman McGinty will think of cows, another family legend, great wide-bodied Holstein-Friesians, and he will think of clover, of a single lucky four-leaf clover, and of crickets hidden within the clover, and of sheep trit-trotting across mountain pastures, and of dogs at his heel. He will think of a little farm in a bend of the Seneca River, now lost forever. He will think—unreasonably, he will admit, but still he will think it—of McGinty his distant forebear, who for a time could say nothing but "toot toot" and "hoot hoot hoot," but who finally regained the power of human speech.

He will not know why he thinks of these things, but he will think of them. He will feel the joy of reunion, he will feel his family stretching out for hundreds of years behind him, and before him too, a long line of honorable men and women, almost all farmers but for him, but for Spaceman McGinty. And his family, somehow, impossibly, will encompass poor old Zog-1049. What a peculiar family, these McGintys!

And remembering the cows, and the clover, and the farm, and the family, and the happy song, Spaceman McGinty will stay his hand.

Without the sentient gas that resides within Zog-1049, he will think, he will at last be able to settle down, this formerly peripatetic Spaceman McGinty, he will put down roots, perhaps he will find a planet somewhere that will accommodate him, where he can bust the sod like his ancestors and build a little house and even—dare he think it?—have a few cows, maybe some sheep, maybe some dogs. His blood will call him to it. And on this farm he will have the time he needs to think about the dark ringing hollowness at the core of him, the hollowness that has driven him out into the universe to discover and to conquer. And perhaps by its contemplation, he will be able to understand that hollowness, and even to fill it up, just a bit.

§

Zog-19 has discovered McGinty's sheep pastures, high up on the ridges at the northern end of the county. He has driven the Ford F-250 up there. He no longer wants to sell the Ford, because he has mastered the stick shift. He drives the truck as well as McGinty ever did, even though he is missing the tips of a couple of fingers from his right hand, his shifting hand. A lot of other things are coming along as well, but the farm still looks like hell, it still looks like an amateur's running it. McGinty's old man would have a fit if he were to rise up from the grave and have a look at it. Rust everywhere. Busted machinery. Still, progress is progress.

The hand is healing up all right, but at night the thick scar tissue across the palm itches like hell (it's a sign of healing, so Missus McGinty says, and she does not complain about the scar tissue or the missing tips of the fingers when Zog-19 comes to her in their bed), and he can sometimes feel the amputated finger joints tingling and aching. Sometimes, quite unexpectedly, he can feel McGinty in that same way, poor vanished McGinty, he can feel the pull of the man when he is performing some chore, when he's hooking Number 127 up to the milking machine, when McGinty's dogs come dashing up to him, when he runs the wrecked hand over Missus McGinty's dimples.

Sometimes Zog-19 feels as though McGinty is standing just behind him, as though McGinty is looking out through his eyes. Is there any way that McGinty could come back from the void? Zog-19 does not know. Zog-One-Billion didn't mention the possibility, but then of course there are a blue million things that Zog-One-Billion never mentioned, including stick shift automobiles and spinning radiator fan blades.

McGinty's dogs are with Zog-19 now, scrambling and scrabbling across the metal bed of the truck as it rumbles along the rutted mountain road, their nails scraping and scratching, in a fever of excitement as they recognize the way up to the sheep pastures, as they recognize the pastures themselves. It is lonely up here. It makes Zog-19 feel like he's the last creature on the planet when he comes up here.

He parks the truck, and the dogs are over the side of the truck bed and away; they are across the field before he can climb down from the cab. They swim through the clover like seals. Zog-19 shouts after them, he has learned their names, but they ignore him. Zog-19 doesn't mind. If he were having as much fun as they are, leaping out at each other in mock battle, rolling over and over in the lush, crisp grass, growling playfully, he would ignore him too.

He strolls over to a sagging line of woven-wire fence, leans against it, breathes in, breathes out. He watches the sheep that drift across the field like small clouds heavy with snow. He has learned that he will have to shear them before long, that is part of his job, that is part of McGinty's job. He thinks that probably he can get one of the loafers down at the Modern Barbershop in Mount Nebo to tell him how to do such a thing. They seem to know pretty much everything that a man who wanted to imitate McGinty might care to know, and they're always happy to share. Needless to say, nothing on Zog ever needed shearing. Still, he imagines that he can handle it.

He whistles for the dogs, and they perk up their ears at the summons, then go back to playing. He smiles. He knows. After a while, they will tire. After a while, McGinty's dogs will run out of steam, and they will return to him on their own.

§

Spaceman McGinty—the only space explorer still on Zog—will shut down the great dynamos. It will be his final act before leaving the planet behind forever.

And the last Zog, unimportant Zog-1049, the final, last, and only Zog, will find himself his own master again. But how Zog has changed during his captivity! He knew something bad was happening, but trapped as he was, he could not imagine the scope of it, the impossible magnitude of the disaster. He will take up wandering the planet, he will pass through the rows upon rows of deanimated Zogs, empty, inert Zogs in their ranked, silent billions. He will use his whistle, he will release his sentient gas, the last to be found anywhere, in copious, even reckless, amounts, calling out across the dead echoing iron planet for any compatriot, for any other Zog who is still living. "Toot toot," he will call. He will call, and he will call, and he will call.

§

Zog-19 enjoys a hearty breakfast. He's eating a tall stack of buckwheat pancakes just dripping with melted creamery butter and warm blackstrap molasses. He's never eaten anything that made him happier. He cleans his plate and offers it to Missus McGinty, who refills it with pleasure. McGinty always liked his pancakes and molasses, and to Missus McGinty this healthy appetite, this love for something from his past, a forgotten favorite, is a sure sign of McGinty's return.

He's been gone from her a long time, someplace in his head, gone from her in a way that she can't imagine, and she's awfully happy to have him back. What brought him back? She does not know. She cannot venture a guess, and she does not care. She has wept many bitter tears over his absence, over his apparent madness, the amnesia, the peculiarity (small word for it!), but she thinks that maybe she won't be crying quite so much in the days to come. Watching Zog-19 with his handsome young head low over his plate, tucking into the pancakes with vigor, his injured hand working the fork as of old, working it up and down and up again like the restless bucket of a steam shovel, she can believe this absolutely.

And what of the planet Zog? Depopulated, hollow Zog? Well, the space explorers, once they have finished with the sentient gas, the space explorers will feel just terrible about what they have done. They will be determined to make amends. And so they will do what Earth people can always be expected to do in a pinch: they will go to work with a great goodwill.

They will send all kinds of heavy moving equipment, bulldozers and end-loaders and cranes and trucks and forklifts, to Zog. They will work, and they will work, and they will work. They will raise up a great monument. They will move the bodies around, they will use the inanimate husks of the Zogs in building their monument (the materials being so close to hand, and free), they will pile them atop one another in great stacks that will stretch up and up into the Zog sky. They will use every deanimated Zog to make the memorial, every single one.

Zog-1049 will almost get swept up and used too, but he will hoot desperately at the last minute, just as the blade of the snorting bulldozer is about to propel him into the mounting pile of the dead. The good-natured fellow who is driving the bulldozer will climb down, laughing with relief at the mistake he's nearly made, almost shoving the last living Zog into the memorial to the Zog dead, and he will brush Zog-1049 off, leaving some acid oil on Zog-1049's sleek iron body, and he will direct Zog-1049 to a safe spot from which to watch the goings-on without getting into any more trouble. The bulldozer operator will shake his head as Zog-1049 totters off across the empty landscape, hooting and tooting. Poor old thing, the bulldozer man will say to himself. He's gone out of his mind. And who can blame him!

Soon enough, the memorial will be finished. And it will be, all will agree, a magnificent testament to the remorse of mankind at their shocking treatment of the Zogs.

The memorial will be this: it will be a single word, a single two-syllable word, written in letters (and one mark of punctuation) tens of miles tall, the word itself hundreds of miles across. It will be a huge sign, the biggest sign ever made, a record-breaking sign in iron bodies, across the face of the iron planet, and, when the planet revolves on its axis so that the sign lies in daylight, so that the fierce sun of that system strikes lurid fire from the skins of the defunct

Zogs, it will be visible from far out in space. It will be a word written across the sterile face of the steelie, the face occupied now only by eternally wandering Zog-1049, and the word will be this: the word will be *SORRY!*

§

Spaceman McGinty will, in the end, find himself on a sweet grass planet (plenty of clover there! and the breeze always blowing out of the east, blowing clover ripples across the face of the grass) far out at the raggedy edge of the universe. No one will live on the planet but McGinty and a primitive race of cricket people who communicate solely by rubbing their back legs together. The cricket people will live hidden in the tall grass, and McGinty will never so much as glimpse one of them, not in his whole life on their world. He will hear them though. He will hear them always. Their stridulation will make a soft, whispering, breezy music to which, at night, former Spaceman McGinty will sometimes sing.

And what will he sing?

Sometimes he will sing, "McCarty is dead and McGinty don't know it. McGinty is dead and McCarty don't know it."

And other times he will sing, "Roll me over in the clover."

And still other times he won't sing at all, but will simply dance, naked and sweating and all alone; former spaceman McGinty will dance along on the balls of his bare feet in the soft rustling waist-high grass of that lonely place.

All that, of course, is in the very far-off future.

§

Zog-19 is back in the sheep pastures. He feels relaxed, and he burps. A crisp breeze has sprung up, and he watches it play over the surface of the pastures; he enjoys the waves that the breeze sends shivering across the tops of the sweet clover. So much like water. Water used to frighten him, but he doesn't worry about it now.

McGinty is dead. McCarty is dead. Angstrom is dead.

The dogs are chivying the sheep over in the far part of the pasture. They are pretending that something, some fox or coyote or wolf or catamount, threatens the sheep, and they must keep the sheep tightly packed together, must keep them moving in a tightly knit body, in order to save their lives. The dogs love this game. The sheep aren't smart enough to know that there's no real danger, and they're bleating with worry.

"Hi," Zog-19 calls out to the dogs. More and more these days, he sounds like McGinty without even thinking about it. "Hi, you dogs! Get away from them woollies!" The dogs ignore him.

Let the dead bury their dead. That is what Missus McGinty tells him. There are so many dead. There is McGinty's old man, there is McCarty, there is Angstrom's old man, there is Angstrom, there is McGinty (though more and more these days, Zog-19 feels McGinty in the room with him, McGinty behind his eyes), there are the Zogs. What could Zog-19 do to prevent the tragedies that have unfolded, to prevent the tragedies that will continue to unfold in the world, across the galaxy? He's only a dairy farmer, he's a man who lives among the grasses. His cows like him. They are relaxed around him. They burp in his face to show their affection. What is there that a man can do?

"Toot toot," says Zog-19, experimentally, but it sounds like an expression from an unknown foreign language to him now.

Let the dead bury their dead.

Missus McGinty has come with him to the sheep pastures. Later in the day, they will shear the sheep together. It turns out that Missus McGinty is a champion sheep shearer, Seneca County Four-H, Heart Head Hands and Health, three years running. They'll have the sheep done in no time. Right now, though, they're in the act of finishing up a delicious picnic lunch. They're sitting together on a cheery red-and-white-checked picnic blanket, sitting in the wealth of the wind-rippled field of clover, Zog-19 and Missus McGinty. Around them are the remains of their meal: a thermos still half full of good, cold raw milk, the gnawed bones of Missus McGinty's wonderful Southern-fried chicken, a couple of crisp Granny Smith apples. Yum.

McGinty would have given the dogs the chicken bones, but Zog-19 will not. He worries that they will crack the bones with their teeth, leaving razor-sharp ends exposed, and that they will then swallow the bones. He is afraid that the bones would lacerate their innards. That's one difference between Zog-19 and McGinty.

"Roll me over in the clover," Missus McGinty sings in her frothy alto voice. She's lying on the checked picnic blanket, and she plucks at Zog-19's sleeve. Her expression is cheerful but serious. She's fiddling with the buttons of her blouse. She takes Zog-19's hand

and places it where her hand was, on the buttons. Zog-19 knows that it's now his turn to fiddle with the buttons.

The dogs are barking. The sheep are bleating. The buttons are beneath Zog-19's hand. Missus McGinty is beneath the buttons. The crickets are chirring loudly, hidden deep within the clover. McGinty is standing behind Zog-19 somewhere. The sun is hot on Zog-19's head. There is a four-leaf clover in this pasture, he knows. Somewhere, in among all the regular clover, there must be at least one. His head is swimming with the sun. He feels as though, if he does not move, if he does not speak, if he doesn't do something, something, something, and pretty damned quick, he is going to burst into flame.

Zog-19 can't know it, but it is time for him to resume the line that will lead to that far-off Spaceman McGinty, the one who will spare Zog-1049. It is time for him to sire a brand-new McGinty.

"Roll me over and do it again," Missus McGinty sings. The button comes off in Zog-19's hand. It is small in his scarred palm, like a hard, smooth little pill. He tosses it over his shoulder, laughing. He tosses it in McGinty's direction. He tugs at the next button down. He wants that one too. He wants the one after that one. He wants them all. He wants them all.

The wind ripples the clover, the wind ripples Missus McGinty's chestnut hair.

# BENJAMIN S. GROSSBERG
# The Space Traveler's Husband

In terms of location, all I can say is
"back there," and point
to a patch of sky: a place no thicker
or thinner in stars. In terms
of the quality of life, the color
and heat of its sun, atmospheric
feel on the skin, I can say
nothing. And yet nights—my ship
in the yard—I lay, a guest,
in one of their frame structures.
He was not the most acute
of their species; he failed to notice
that I needed a helmet to breathe or
that my limbs did not unfold (enfold)
like his own. Maybe he noticed
and didn't care. He brought bowls
of a limp green vegetable and we
ate beside each other in silence.
This was always in winter, always
with blankets he drew around us.
There was a moment before I left,
standing on the ship's retractable stairs,
back to the arched door: I saw him
watch me through the kitchen window.
It was night and the darkness of space
pressed right down against his lawn.
Well, it's years since that moment.
I have grown old in this ship, balled
like a worm in its silver pods.
And because I have been traveling
faster than light, nearly fifty
generations have slid between us.
(I am in fact the only living thing
that knows he existed.) But
it's also possible that I am caught
in that moment right now: still
seeing careworn eyes through a pane

How to Live on Other Planets

of glass. A yellow incandescence
burns behind him, and both of us
wonder if I'm really going to leave.

## The Space Traveler and Boston

I once walked the streets with a native.
Beside me, he gesticulated, smiled,
pointed out bits of local color: here
a senator's house; there a high-rise
breezeway that led to the water front.
His hands conducted the city into place,
seemed to materialize the structures
he gestured toward. (I recognize
this is not a power humans possess.)
For a while, all was going so well.
My rocket ship hidden beneath
an overpass, my human suit fitting
snug, without the sort of bunchings
or gaps that would've given me away.
It seemed entirely likely he would
invite me to observe up close a few
more unusual aspects of human
interface. But then we stopped
in a store and I emerged with half
a watermelon, and proceeded to
unmask myself in a pink dripping mess.
So hard to stay contained in the filling
of desire: the fingernail scraping
of its green rind. *No, no, you're not
supposed to eat that part,* he said
slowly backing away, his palms
held out in front of his chest.
I looked up from the raw shell,
and it's then I fear my eyes began to
dilate differently: a split completely
wrong for one of your species.
O he still showed me what he had
to show, no less sloppy than myself
in the plying of his satisfactions.
But by morning, I had slunk back
to the overpass, to where my ship
lodged on its side amid wrappers,

rags, and old cardboard, its perfect
chrome now sullied by car exhaust.

# The Space Traveler and the Promised Planet

All right, no one promised. And yet
my very medium seemed to tingle
with the likelihood, as if suffused
with silver filings that captured the light.
Or maybe the odds just felt with me—
so many worlds, so many strains
of evolution, surely no biosphere
predicted the shape of any other.
One it seemed would have to meet
even those desires I hadn't yet
formulated, the latent tastes, needs
about to bloom in petals much larger,
more saturated than I had expected—
a vine unknown to itself, its own
tendrils and traveling, how its stamen
would center, the shape of its flower.
Once I observed such a vine
up close, the hollow green flutes—
saw that it produced blanched nubs,
blunt fingers poking toward
the soil of its world. I wondered
how it knew, how it decided when
and where to put forth those nubs, if
it could sense in the undersoil some
needed liquid or element. And if so,
perhaps I too could do that: could be
my own divining rod—bare forked
stick that trembled at discovery.
You understand, it felt possible
then. So world after world passed
underneath me. Each time
I checked myself for trembling.

# ABBEY MEI OTIS
# Blood Blood

I'm sixteen when George and I figure out the aliens will pay to watch us fight. We're leaning against milk crates in the alley behind the library and he's giving me shit about losing my waitressing job. To shut him up I bring my fist back in slow motion and plow my knuckles into the side of his mouth. He does an exaggerated, drawn-out reaction, flapping his lips out and staggering into the cinderblock. Then at the last moment he spins, catches me around my waist and pulls me in to him. My foot snags the milk crates and the stack comes clattering down.

A group of aliens are leaving the library—a family, maybe, if families are something they have. They catch sight of us—smell us, sense us, whatever—and drift over to the mouth of the alley. I feel George tense as the aliens say, What are you doing? What does this mean?

His face is drawing tight with irritation when I reach back and tickle him. My fingers dig into the softness between his ribs hard enough—maybe—to leave bruises. We topple to the pavement. He lands on top of me. His elbow jams my boob. Or, as my mom would say, the place where my boob ought to be.

"Shit, *ow.*"

"So says the weaker sex."

"I hate you."

His whisper hums against my neck. "I know."

I flip out of his grasp and my knee drags along pavement, leaving a stain of capillary blood on the faded asphalt and the tufts of grass that break through.

How thrilling, the aliens murmur. How visceral.

A moment later George lies on his stomach. His feet kick feebly, like a turtle. "Mercy, fair lady!"

Sitting on his back, I inspect my nails. Each capped with a rind of black grime. Sweat, his and mine, soaks through my Stray Cat Diner polo.

"Mercy!"

When I let him up, he picks his messenger cap off the pavement. Dusts it off. Drops his card in, and waves it toward the cluster of aliens. "Donations? Donations! Show your appreciation, whatever manner you feel is right."

Giggling, the aliens reach in and touch his card. Credit rushes into his account.

Even after they've paid him, they linger. They are fascinated by the way he grips the brim of his cap, the way I press my finger into the scrape on my knee and hiss as the sting flares and fades. George and I stand very still. Usually aliens don't leave unless you've really done nothing for a minute or two. They hate missing anything.

When they've gone, George flips them the bird. He checks the balance on his card and looks up at me, his mouth spreading into a grin. His eyes are hard and bright with opportunity. "We're *rich.*"

§

I tell my parents that waitressing interfered with my school work. The thought of this is so horrific that my mother drops the dust cloth and runs to smooth my hair. "Don't worry, honey, you do whatever you need to do. Eyes on that scholarship, right?"

"Sure, Mom. Whatever."

Really, Mr. Reade fired me for not being welcoming enough toward aliens. "I don't give a damn how you feel, Damia," he said. "We need them. They want to go behind the bar, you let them. They want to get right up next to people and watch them put fries in their mouths, you let them. Anything they want, you let them. Understand?"

I said I understood, but I couldn't help it. When one of them got near me, I froze up. I could hear my heart lurching, big as a cantaloupe, filling my whole torso. I was sure they could hear it too.

§

Sometime before the aliens found us, they discovered a way of divorcing their bodies from their minds. In cartoons and commercials here, the alien bodies are portrayed floating in pods of translucent goo, humanoid forms with wires running into them, rows of thousands upon thousands. The reality, I'm sure, is something totally different, something totally beyond any portrayal we might attempt.

Earth is visited, then, only by alien consciousnesses. They move through air, through concrete, through steel and polycarbonate with equal ease. They speak, or rather do not speak, in streams of thought directed toward our minds. Look at one straight, it's like the sunlight that plays on the hull of a boat in a lake. Only no boat, no lake, no sunlight.

Whatever splits them from themselves is not the only technology they have. They dole progress out to us in small doses. Cheap and infinite energy sources. Cures for genetic disorders. Earth governments turn into throngs of men clustered hungrily around the alien portals. Slowly now, the aliens say. You'll ruin yourselves.

Recently, reluctantly, they have agreed to take a small number of people each year back to their ship (or wherever they come from). The people will study alien technology so that it can be more unobtrusively incorporated on Earth. They will get to leave their bodies behind and move as pure consciousness. An alien came to our school to discuss the opportunity with us. If I hadn't been taking notes so frantically, I might have been unnerved at how silent the classroom was, the lecture delivered straight into our heads. But I was too busy panicking that I wouldn't get every thought down.

Halfway through the talk something hit my hand and made me start. George's copy of the brochure on alien exchange, folded into a paper football.

§

George doesn't mention his new source of income to his family. His mother and his sisters, they take what they can get. No questions. George's father split a long time ago, part of a NASA division to study alien tech. Or that's what he said. He also said he'd send them funds every month, enough alien credit to take a bath in. All they get is the government checks.

We've been friends since we were seven. At the beginning of third grade, this asshole Ross Tate followed us around for a week, singing "George and Damia, sitting in a tree—"

Punching Ross Tate was how I began my long and tumultuous relationship with in-school suspension.

Two days into my first suspension, I heard from another kid in the slammer that Ross Tate's desk had exploded. Firecrackers. He and three other kids ended up in the ER. The principal found a note in Ross's cubby, saying he had a plan to blow up my desk. He spelled my name wrong—D-a-m-Y-a. Tate spent a week in the hospital, and then two weeks in out-of-school suspension, crying about how he had no idea what happened. George's extralegal career was always more calculated than mine.

§

The aliens have no gender. When we asked them about it, they laughed and told us it was irrelevant. But it feels so strange to call a thinking being "it." "It" is more general than one being. We use the word all the time: *It* was irrelevant. *It* feels so strange.

Just in front of the Bean in Chicago, a patch of shimmering air hangs at eye level. If you walk straight at it, you can't miss the glint. If you come at it from the side it nearly disappears. Mostly people give it some space, though you could touch it, I guess. Every now and then, a bulge appears in the shimmer. It swells and grows and finally detaches, a scrap of light that floats away across Millennium Park. It's an alien, just arrived through the portal from shipside.

They could drift from shipside all the way to the surface of Earth, but it would take a long time. Or something. We're not totally clear where they come from, or how they perceive time. At some level, we assume, they value convenience.

They have no interest in the Grand Canyon or Everest or Victoria Falls. They put their portals in places where people gather. Parks, gas stations, fish markets. When we bump into each other or high five or blow our noses, their delight is palpable. They've been here ten years and it's still unsettling. Sometimes when aliens follow George and me as we walk down the street, he will spin around. Flail his arms. Shout, "What! What are we doing?"

Those times, he might as well be talking to air.

§

When I was in elementary school, a fun thing to do was play alien. Little mirrors or LED screens glued all over our clothes, reflecting back our surroundings and scenes from music videos. We stood stiffly in corners, flitted down the halls. Asked everyone, Did you see me? Was it like I wasn't there?

In high school it would be grotesque to be so overt. We still try to mimic them, though no one would admit it, and maybe no one could say exactly how it's done. Starving yourself is not the answer. The boniness of an emaciated kid is completely different from the gossamer presence of an alien. It's more a way of holding your body.

How to Live on Other Planets

A way of sliding your feet as you walk. A way of knowing how the light falls on your face.

I wonder if the aliens can tell when we try to mimic them. If they coo over us in private. How flattering. How cute.

George sticks to coyer, anachronistic forms of rebellion. George grows his hair long. George wears all black. George pierces the protrusions of his flesh ("You have no idea how many aliens were in that tattoo shop") and fills the holes with metal studs. George stands in the middle of the football field and kisses boys.

§

One day we're sitting outside the library after a fight, holding matching ice packs to our faces. George leans back. "I don't get it. Why would anyone want to leave their body? It's part of you. It is you." He flexes his fingers as he says this, clenches his fist. As though whatever anchoredness he feels from these gestures will pass to the rest of the world. He cannot mentally separate himself from his body. I'm jealous.

"It's these stupid aliens making people think like this," he says. "They're making people go crazy."

"No," I insist. "People thought this way before. We just never had an answer until the aliens came."

"It's a new thing to do. That doesn't mean it's an answer. That doesn't mean we've got the problem right."

A few days ago, George shaved himself a mohawk. He dyed it bright green and spiked it up with a glue stick. He has gold glitter on his face. His nails are painted bright red.

"How about this problem," I say. "I can't debate you when you look like a Christmas tree from Satan."

He pushes his ice pack into my face and I bite it and condensation trickles down my throat.

§

My father is an insurance agent. At the same firm, his father before him. They sat behind the same oak desk and took seriously the business of keeping people safe. On one side of his desk there's a framed picture of my mother and me at the beach. Also a drawing I made when I was four, of horses.

But the aliens have made health care cheap and technology safe. And hardly anyone gets sick anymore anyway. My father was never laid off—the aliens grow stern at the idea of people losing their livelihoods. But there are mornings when I leave for school and he is frozen at the sink, bathrobed, staring out the window. There are afternoons when I come home and wonder if he's moved.

He buys cookbooks. He says he will become a gourmet chef, which was always his dream. He spends hours watching the Food Network. I come home from school and make us tomato and cheese sandwiches. I say, Daddy, how about we watch something different for a while? He nudges the remote over to my side of the couch.

My mother substitute-teaches and cleans. She pretends she cannot hear him when my father asks, could she turn off the vacuum for a while? She sets her body between him and the TV, vacuums around each of his feet in their slippers as though he were an ottoman she'd rather not touch.

§

At night I peel off my gym shorts and T-shirt and stand in front of the bathroom mirror. My lips, too big for my face. My breasts, too small. It puzzles my mother, who says at least once a week, I don't understand it, Damia. All the other women in our family have gorgeous bods. I think she's trying to comfort me. I guess it could be worse if she said, I do understand it, Damia. You got exactly what you deserve.

My hips are too wide compared to my waist. The pores on my nose are visible from several feet away. My hands are huge, like a man's, like a giant's. The curve of my shoulders—no, the hulk of my shoulders—is abhorrent. It's weirdly satisfying, this rephrasing of my body into something grotesque. So when I finally peel off the whole thing, it will be deserved.

I slap water onto my face and tell myself to quit wallowing. I'm lucky. Other girls born at other times didn't get my choice. Write three essays, get two teacher recommendations, take a test, drop into the goo (if we choose to believe the cartoons). You're wrong, George. We've all always wanted this. To have the doubts fall away. Everything and nothing. Reborn. Glory-blinding.

§

I tell George I have to make up a comp-sci quiz, and I linger after school. There's an alien in the guidance counselor's office. Is it the one who told us about the exchange program?

I am, it says. You are interested?

"Uh, yeah. Yeah, I am."

Please, sit down. Or, actually— In the fluorescent light of the office, the alien is almost invisible. A dime of dull air rather than a plate-sized shimmer. —would you like to go outside?

Under a tree in the school courtyard, the alien says, First, let me try to dissuade you.

"Dissuade me?"

Yes. This program—I'm not sure it's entirely a good thing. We don't fully know what the effects will be. And your way of life has been in balance for so long. It's a terrible thing to disrupt.

"You don't think you've already disrupted a lot?"

Its response is not quite words this time, only shades of discomfort, regret, defensiveness. I have to backtrack. "I'm sorry. I get it, definitely. But I've been thinking about this for a long time. I've made up my mind."

The alien's projection morphs into acceptance. Well. If you're sure. I've always said what independent minds you have. You'd be doing a great service for your planet, certainly. What's your address? I'll send you the application file.

§

George is smoking outside the old gas station and when I get there he says, "Jesus, that took a long time."

"Don't tell me. I'm shit at writing code." I focus on his shoes, the scar on his elbow, the cobwebby gas pumps. Not his eyes.

§

He knocks on my door when I'm working on my application, and I let my mother answer. I can't see her but I can picture her with her arms crossed, filling up the doorway, lips bunched into a disapproving rose. "You two seem to get hurt a lot, don't you?"

"What the fuck, Damia?" George yells through her like she's a screen door.

His voice makes the bruise on my thigh, the scrape on my knee, the split on my cheek throb angrily. My fingers hang frozen over the keyboard until he's gone.

§

It's the afternoon after I submitted the application, and the aliens are asking for another fight. George sits on the curb, scuffing gravel into a pile and not looking up.

"Oh, come on, guys. You're good for business. Wouldn't believe how good." Mr. Reade, my former employer. He likes us to beat each other up in the parking lot beside the Stray Cat. "They come from shipside talking about you," he tells us. "One of them called it—wait, wait, I got it—something like, 'an authentic celebration of human physicality.' That great or what?"

George snorts. "As long as they keep putting money in the fucking hat."

"Hat? They're putting you in a *guidebook.*"

There's a sucking shrinking feeling in my chest. I edge toward George to sit down beside him, but without warning he kicks one leg out and swipes my shins. My palms smash into the grainy asphalt. The shrinking *feeling* is knocked out of me, replaced by something clean and pissed off. I take a deep breath and sweep gravel at George.

"Bitch!" He clutches his eye. "Rocks? Seriously?" Then he stands, brings his hands up, bounces on the balls of his feet. "Okay, cheater. Let's do this."

"What I'm *talking* about," says Mr. Reade.

§

The alien running the exchange program tells me its name is Lute. Or at least, it puts something in my head, and out of the jumble I get that word. Pretty, melodious name. Genderless as always. Lute says it came here to get away from responsibilities at home. Sometimes, when they talk about back home, the idea that fills me is "another dimension." Other times I only get "shipside." I put the two ideas to Lute. Were they different places? No, no. I feel Lute's patient smile. They are two slightly different ways of referring to the same place. Epithets. The distinction grows wider in translation.

I wonder what it's really saying. I suppose there's no way to know. "Understanding" is predicated on having the same apparatus translate things in the same way. One mouth must translate thoughts to sounds in the same way that other ears translate sounds to thoughts.

But Lute! Lute is sunlight falling on dust. Our apparatuses might not even lie in the same dimension. I am so lucky, that it can move through things as it does, bypass organs altogether. It lays down its intentions on my brain, and I give them meaning. The right meaning, I hope, though probably not. Inside the gnarled clod of my brain, something is always lost.

§

George shows up at my house one evening, looking like he's going to puke.

"My mother. Overdrew her card. Needed cash. Told the aliens, they could come and watch her pay bills. Watch her boil pasta." Something jumps in the soft skin under his left eye. "Those morons would tip to watch me shit."

"Maybe she deserves a break." I put my hands around his forearm. Whatever anchoredness I feel, let it pass to you. "Really. How's it different from what we do?"

"That's a *performance,*" he gasps out. "We can shuck that off. This is who she is."

"Right. She's a broke lady."

"She's a whore." He clutches my hand. Squeezes my knuckles white.

"And *you're* a terrible person." I go to flick him on the forehead, and somehow my hand doesn't fall away. Two of my fingers rest on the line of his jaw. His hands have moved up my arm now. His thumb brushes the inside of my elbow. He has been staring out at nothing but now his eyes move to me. And I fall in.

"You know, I don't think you're gay." I'm trying to make a joke. Trying to find a lifeline. "At best you're an asshole." Then I kiss him.

His lips are dry and his hands move across my shoulders, down my back, over all the places where he has opened cuts on me and seen them heal and opened them again. All the places I wish different, that I do not like, gouged or no. His hands don't shy away. He never breaks away.

Then somehow my sports bra is over my head and his jeans are coming off. Oh, I think, it's so simple. Simple as throwing that first punch. These barriers between people, these gulfs, how easily everything collapses.

There's a moment, later, when I revise: Really, that was not like fighting at all.

§

A cross section of how we are, George and I. My blood, my skin, some air, his skin, his blood. Sometimes: blood, skin, air, wall, air, skin, blood. During sex: blood, skin, skin, blood. As close as we can get. Seeking closer. But that final, perfect closeness? Blood, blood? That's not a place we can get, no matter how deep we pull. We strain against the boundaries of skin.

Except sometimes, when we fight. My knuckle into his lip, just the right way. The gouge in his elbow knocking off the scabs on my ear. Blood, blood.

We get there.

§

There is the night we lie against each other, naked, when George freezes, breath trembling in his throat. "Do you think—this—would they pay to see—"

I kiss him hard, but the thought is already out. It hangs like a marble on a string between us and grows foggy with our breath. Yes.

Is the answer. We both know and the marble grows bigger and presses a red welt into my chest. Yes.

Not only would they, but they will and they have and they probably are. Just because this thing is newly discovered to us doesn't mean it isn't old and tarnished to plenty. And plenty who wanted to eat or wanted to please could so easily say: You want human bodies? You want flesh? Come this way.

Not prostitution, exactly. No give and take of pleasure. Just watching. They would take the same kind of joy in it that they take in watching cashiers scan groceries, girls play clapping games, men fix a roof. Could sex still have beauty if it took place under such bland, curious eyes? Could it still have cruelty if that horror was supplanted by the blunt horror of being observed? Meanings warp, meanings dissolve. But still we let them in. Into the most Eleusinian mysteries, even when it breaks our hearts. The marble, giant now, weighs on my lungs and makes it difficult to breathe. Why is it never us, I wonder. Why are we never the ones who get to smile, to say—No, this is not for you. It's complicated. In a million years, you could not hope to understand.

§

One night, my father asleep in front of the television, I hear the newscaster say, "With us tonight, Johanna DeWitt, first human to return from shipside. If you think the studio looks emptier than it should, don't worry! Johanna has undergone the splitting process. On the street you'd be hard-pressed to tell her from your average alien. Tell us, Johanna, how are you feeling?"

Johanna's responses scroll as text along the bottom of the screen. They angle the studio lights so that we can see her shimmering a foot above the couch. Another woman sits next to Johanna. The caption on the screen informs us that this is Helene, Johanna's wife. She is small, with a round face. Her eyes look straight ahead but down, maybe at the cameraman's shoes.

The Johanna scroll informs us that she and Helene met in graduate school, that they devoted their lives to alien tech, that they were both so overjoyed when Johanna was selected as an ambassador. My body is safe, Johanna assures us. And I feel so indescribably free.

Helene hunches her elbows in, as though trying not to occupy the space that Johanna's body would need, if Johanna were there. She twists her wedding ring.

§

George comes up to me after school, squinting, hands jammed in his pockets.

"So, do you... should we go on a date, or something?"

I burst out laughing almost too hard to gasp out, "No."

"Thank god." Tension relinquishes his shoulders.

"But—want to swing by the library?"

That means, want to punch me until my skull rattles, but we never say that. The fights exist in a new vicious language, modulated by the color and spread of our bruises. Since we both speak it, there's no point in translating.

If you could lay your thoughts down on my brain, George. What would I understand?

When either of us lands a solid hit on the other, there is a ripple of excitement among the aliens. My elbow goes into George's stomach, and I can almost hear the chimes of their thoughts. Like starving men watching someone eat, I think. George hears it too. He clutches his stomach, his mouth frozen in the shape of pain. After a moment he catches my eye and grins, hard and grim.

I lean into his blows. Each punch he lands unmoors me a little more. If I can turn every inch of my body to bruise. Convert the entirety of my flesh to pain. Then by default, the mysterious points of anchor will sever. I will rise into the air.

When I sit down to dinner with blood crusted around my nose, my eye puddled purple and yellow, my mother stares. My father saws at his chicken without putting any pressure on the knife. My mother swallows. "We could buy you some new foundation," she says.

§

Protestors grow more active in the wake of Johanna's appearance. Will we let them disembody a generation of our children? No, we will not! Protect our human heritage! There are rallies around alien portals. A protestor grows wild, shoves his arm with his middle finger extended through the rippling air. His body convulses in a shudder—delight or anguish?—and he falls to the ground. They revive him with Gatorade and Cheetos.

I want to tell George how funny it is, the protestor slurping down *Blue Ice,* with *dangerously cheesy* dust around his mouth. Protect our human heritage! But George is not in school. He's not slouching behind the library or riding the kid swings at the park and drawing dark looks from the nannies. Four days go by.

I wake up feeling the imprint of his head against my chest. Every glimpse of dyed hair or glitter makes my heart lunge. I even try his mother's house and she says, "I'm sorry, who are you?"

§

The Chicago portal is destroyed. An organized act of terrorism, say the newscasters. No simple firecrackers, either; they used alien technology. Set fire to the air inside a tightly controlled ring, and devoured that unfathomable field. There's nothing there in the morning, when the cameras arrive. A crowd gathers in the shadow of the Bean, unwilling or unable to believe that it is gone. For the first time in a long time, they are actually staring at empty air.

The camera sweeps across the flock of faces, and my heart flips so hard I can hear the deafening clap in my ears. There in the crowd, a green mohawk. His arms are crossed over his chest as he stares at the spot where the portal used to hang. His smile is hard and grim.

§

I knew something would happen, says Lute. It and I are in the park. I sit with my back against a beech, a knot digging into my spine. We should not have given so much, so quickly. You could not deal with it.

"No," I say. "It's not that. Not exactly."

Lute is puzzled but I keep silent. They get our actions. Our angers, even. But not our reasons. Not this time.

Finally Lute says, In any case we should hurry things along. I know officials shipside. They could bump you to the front of the list.

Its presence is pale, diffuse. In my mind I catch fragments of distaste, anger that softens to grief. The sun is a low yolk in the sky. There is an ant crawling up my calf. Across the park two kids are trying to ride their Big Wheel bikes down the grassy hill. At the bottom they catch, go flying off, and for a moment their long shadows leap away from their feet.

Lute says, Could I—do you think—can I touch you?

I know Lute doesn't truly mean "touch," but I know it does mean "front of the list." And the front of the list means escape. Certain definitions can be made hazy. Some lines can be blurred. The change in density that marks the boundary between my skin and the air can be bridged. Touched.

My heart races. I pick at the gummy lines of my cuticles. My wide hands with their bulging knuckles. The loaves of fat lying under the skin of my thighs. I could never have to look at this body again. I could never have to breathe.

So I say, "Yeah, sure." Lute is a patch of air in front of me, and then is not. Lute is now the length of my forearm. My flesh glows if I watch from the corner of my eye but fades if I look straight on. Lute moves up my arm and through my torso. Lute is a gentle orb of heat, or else a chill that ripples through me. Lute is saying, Wow, wow, wow.

§

Deep inside my head, I picture my consciousness as a hot air balloon, harlequin red and blue and gold. It strains against a hundred ropes. One by one, they are struck through with an axe. The balloon trembles. Its basket tips back and forth.

§

Vessel. The word jumps into my mind so derisive it scorches my hair. Vessel. Now I am open to the mockery of late night talk show hosts, politicians, mothers who gossip at luncheons. They don't know it, but when they say it, vessel, they are talking about me. Imagine it, being probed by the unknown. Being… occupied. Their disgust tinged with the heat of fear.

Vessels hand over not just actions but the medium of flesh. It's what all the aliens want. It gives them bragging rights shipside. They tell horror stories of their close encounters with bodies. Their friends listen raptly, the ones who would never be brave enough to come down here. They think, shuddering, of their own bodies, wherever they have left them. When they sleep (or whatever) they have dreams (or something different) of being trapped.

I tell myself that this new kind of revulsion is just a temporary burden. I tell myself guilt is just another trapping of flesh. My body senses that its time is almost up, and so it casts out wild nets of feeling, trying to trap me and haul me back in. When I wake up retching at three a.m., sure that the gentle orb of heat has returned, that it has come through my neighborhood and my walls and my sheets to slide again up and down through my body, that's just muscle memory. Not a part of me.

And when I have no container? When I am no container? I will be nothing but myself.

§

I get out of bed and stand in front of the mirror. I cup a hand between my legs, cover everything up. I lay my other forearm over my breasts. More acts of self-censorship. Neuter. Neutral. It. *It* feels so strange. This is *it*.

§

George shows up at school the next Monday. He sits in the back of class with his head on the desk and the teachers don't bother calling on him. He ignores me at lunch. I stake out his locker after school but he doesn't pass by, and by the time I've figured that out and sprinted from the building he's halfway down the street. He freezes when I shout his name.

I catch up to him and spin him around by the shoulders. It's disconcerting how much he looks the same. What did I expect, some disfiguring scar? A brand on his forehead? Whatever words I had desert me.

He speaks instead. "You applied for exchange." It's not a question. And now his face is falling apart. "All those times—you said you hated them. You said how stupid they were."

Oh, George. Oh. You are not the only betrayer here. How can I explain that yes, I said that. But more than those things, I want to fly and I want speak in the music they speak and I want to touch and be touched the way they are. He would say they had tricked me. He would look at me with pity, and when pity didn't change my mind it would change in him to disgust. But it's my right to want those things. It's a want that is in myself, not my flesh.

He's not done. His voice cracks. "How can you hate yourself that much? How—you would go somewhere you're not even sure exists. You would leave your own body. And me."

You've already left me, I want to say. Not in the same way that I would leave, but it's your way, and it's as real to you as my way is to me. You know it is.

"Day. There are other ways to escape. We're fighting them. You should join us."

*Join,* ha! The word could mean so much more. The meaning he intends for it is sad, inadequate.

But the impossibility of that word brings me up short, and grief bells inside me. I want to stave off that truth as long as possible. I lean forward and kiss him, clutch him to me. Suddenly it doesn't matter whether the desire is in my flesh or in my mind, whether our words are adequate or not, whether everyone on the street is staring at us. Stay with me.

He pushes me off. "For fuck's sake, Damia. Sell yourself to the devil, sure. At least stand by your own position. This is pathetic."

Words calculated to smart. Words to reach where blows cannot. Where bodies refuse to go. It digs a honed edge into my chest and all the reasons why I can't lose him spill out like organs. I clutch my stomach—the points of anchor will be severed—and turn, and flee.

§

I plow through my house, upstairs into my room, punch the wall. Hot tears bully their endless way out from under my eyelids. Stupid girl. Typical girl. Crying because I would lose the boy I loved. Because my body was something people looked at as an artifact, and I was trapped inside it.

My mother comes into my room, holding the computer. She sees me slumped on the rug and kneels down next to me. "So you've heard."

I have no idea what she's talking about.

"You got a letter. From the regional exchange office." She hands me the screen.

*In light of recent terrorist attacks, the alien bureau regrets to announce that all scholarship exchange programs will be put indefinitely on hold. We regret the inconvenience and hope that amicable relations can be restored with all possible speed.*

*Postscript—Damia, I'm really very sorry about this. —Lute*

Behind their words, I can feel it, really feel it, for the first time. The bafflement. The seeds that will blossom into disgust. The aliens rustle and murmur, Look at what you did. After all we gave you. After all we sang your praises. How did we deserve that? How could you?

"Honey, I'm so sorry." Mom pats my hand. "I know how hard it is to feel you have nowhere to go."

But I drop the computer and ease out from under her palm. My eyes are dry. My nose isn't running anymore. I stand up and step into the doorway.

"Actually, I think I'm going outside."

How to Live on Other Planets

I jog into the center of town and stand outside the Stray Cat. Aliens spill out of it, following the end of the lunch rush. Aliens everywhere, following shoppers, watching toddlers drop ice cream.

"You want to fucking understand?" I scream at them. "Come here." The humans who are around look up too and cover their babies' ears. Fuck that. "Put this in your fucking guidebook."

The aliens follow me. They call to each other in their incomprehensible music and more come pouring out of shops and houses and Starbucks. They flock behind me, until I'm wearing a shimmering cloak of air that billows across the whole street.

I don't need to look more than one place. George. I know where you are.

I hope he gets my message, through my eyes and my set chin and my clenched knuckles. There are no more words between us. I will lay my thoughts down on his body, and he will give them meaning.

I round the corner of the library just as he's stubbing out his cigarette. He sees the aliens behind me, the flock, the exaltation, the avalanche. His eyes grow huge. I don't pause, just bring my fists up and heave myself into his chest. He catches me around the waist, eyes still wide. Yeah, this dance. Remember, George?

But he just pushes me back, barely any force, his lips parted in a silent question.

I slam my fist into the side of his face.

He staggers sideways, recovers. Bounces once on the balls of his feet and then lunges. Some restraint has been severed. Blows rain down from either side. He's stronger, he's always been stronger. He's a he, not an it. My head rings like a hundred aliens are screaming. A hundred aliens are screaming. There's something warm running through my hair. Lights in my skull explode. Light reflects off the sweat on his nose. I drop down, jut my shoulder into his stomach and feel his guts rearrange. He flips over my back, legs flailing, hits the asphalt with a noise of meat and wetness. I've always been faster. I'm a she, not an it.

The bar of his shin knocks my ankles out from under me and I drop. My head bounces on—softness. George's outstretched arm. My whole body peals with pain. Heartbeats flood my brain, drowning out the bray of alien projections. I can feel George's pulse through my scalp. His forearm is slickening with my blood. My body fills with the crashing of my breath, in and out and in. Dark arterial colors are leaching into my vision. I fight it, wrench my eyes into focus. Above us the sky is dazzling blue, and empty.

# CONTRIBUTOR BIOS

**Dean Francis Alfar** is a fictionist, playwright and the publisher of the Philippine Speculative Fiction annuals, beginning with the first volume in 2005. His fiction has appeared in *The Time Traveler's Almanac, The Year's Best Fantasy & Horror, Strange Horizons, Rabid Transit: Menagerie, The Apex Book of World SF,* and the *Exotic Gothic* anthologies, among others. His books include a novel, *Salamanca,* and two collections of short fiction, *The Kite of Stars and other stories* and *How to Traverse Terra Incognita.*

**Celia Lisset Alvarez** holds an MFA in creative writing from the University of Miami and teaches at Our Lady of Lourdes Academy. Her debut collection of poetry, *Shapeshifting* (Spire Press, 2006), was the recipient of the 2005 Spire Press Poetry Award. A second collection, *The Stones* (Finishing Line Press, 2006) followed that same year. Other work has appeared or is forthcoming in numerous journals and anthologies. Born in Madrid of Cuban parents en route to the United States, she grew up in Miami, where she lives with her husband, Cuban-American literary scholar and fellow poet Rafael Miguel Montes.

**RJ Astruc** lives in New Zealand and has written two novels: *Harmonica + Gig* and *A Festival of Skeletons.* RJ's short stories have appeared in many magazines including *Strange Horizons, Daily Science Fiction, ASIM, Aurealis* and *Midnight Echo,* as well as the short story collection *Signs Over the Pacific and Other Stories* (Upper Rubber Boot Books, 2013).

**Lisa Bao** is Chinese, Canadian, and American to various degrees. She studies linguistics and computer science at Swarthmore College. Her poetry has previously been published in *Strange Horizons* and *Eye to the Telescope.*

**Pinckney Benedict** grew up in rural West Virginia. He has published a novel and three collections of short fiction, the most recent of which is *Miracle Boy and Other Stories.* His work has been published in, among other magazines and anthologies, *Esquire, Zoetrope: All-Story,* the *O. Henry Award* series, the *Pushcart Prize* series, the *Best*

New Stories from the South series, *Apocalypse Now: Poems and Prose from the End of Days, The Ecco Anthology of Contemporary American Short Fiction,* and *The Oxford Book of the American Short Story.* Benedict serves as a professor in the MFA program at Southern Illinois University Carbondale.

Octavia E. Butler Scholar **Lisa Bolekaja** is a graduate of the Clarion Science Fiction and Fantasy Writers Workshop, an affiliate member of the Horror Writers Association, and a member of the Carl Brandon Society. She co-hosts a screenwriting podcast called "Hilliard Guess' Screenwriters Rant Room" and her work has appeared in "Long Hidden: Speculative Fiction from the Margins of History" (Crossed Genres Publishing), as well as "The WisCon Chronicles: Volume 8" (Aqueduct Press). Her story "Don't Dig Too Deep" will be in the upcoming *Red Volume,* an anthology of speculative fiction produced by her Clarion 2012 class with all proceeds going to support the Clarion Foundation.

**Mary Buchinger** is the author of *Aerialist* (Gold Wake Press, 2015; shortlisted for the May Swenson Poetry Award, the OSU Press/The Journal Wheeler Prize for Poetry and the Perugia Press Prize). Her poems have appeared in *AGNI, Cortland Review, DIAGRAM, Fifth Wednesday, Nimrod International Journal of Prose and Poetry, The Massachusetts Review,* and elsewhere. She is Associate Professor of English and Communication Studies at MCPHS University in Boston, Massachusetts. You can find her at yellowdogriver.blogspot.com.

**Zen Cho** was born and raised in Malaysia, and now lives in London. Her short story collection *Spirits Abroad* was published in summer 2014. Her short fiction has appeared most recently in anthologies *End of the Road* from Solaris Books, *Love in Penang* from Fixi Novo, and *The Alchemy Press Book of Urban Mythic.* She was a 2013 finalist for the John W. Campbell Award for Best New Writer.

**Tina Connolly**'s stories have appeared in *Lightspeed, Tor.com, Strange Horizons,* Rich Horton's *Unplugged: Year's Best Online SF* and URB's *Apocalypse Now: Poems and Prose from the End of Days.* Her books include the Nebula-nominated fantasy *Ironskin* (Tor, 2012) and its sequel *Copperhead.*

**Indrapramit Das** is a writer and artist from Kolkata, India. His fiction has appeared in *Clarkesworld, Asimov's* and *Apex Magazine*, as well as anthologies *The Year's Best Science Fiction: Thirtieth Annual Collection* (St. Martin's Press), *Aliens: Recent Encounters* (Prime Books) and *Mothership: Tales from Afrofuturism and Beyond* (Rosarium Publishing). His short story "The Widow and the Xir" is available as an ebook from URB. He is a grateful graduate of the 2012 Clarion West Writers Workshop and a recipient of the Octavia E. Butler Scholarship Award to attend the former. He completed his MFA at the University of British Columbia.

Tor Books published **Tom Doyle**'s first novel, *American Craftsmen*, in 2014. His novelette "While Ireland Holds These Graves" won third place in the Writers of the Future contest, and his novelette "The Wizard of Macatawa" (*Paradox* #11) won the WSFA Small Press Award. His stories have also appeared in *Daily Science Fiction, Futurismic,* and several other magazines. Paper Golem published his short fiction collection, *The Wizard of Macatawa and Other Stories.*

**Peg Duthie** is a Taiwanese Texan resident of Tennessee. She is the author of *Measured Extravagance* (Upper Rubber Boot, 2012), and there's more about her at www.NashPanache.com.

**Tom Greene** was born in Texas, grew up as a biracial Anglo/Latino science nerd, then moved to New England to study British Literature. He works as a full-time English professor and part-time lecturer on vampire literature. Recent publications include short stories in *Analog, Polluto* and *Strange Horizons.* He lives in Salem, Massachusetts with his wife and two cats.

**Benjamin S. Grossberg** is the author of *Space Traveler* (University of Tampa Press, 2014), *Sweet Core Orchard* (University of Tampa, 2009, winner of the 2008 *Tampa Review* Prize and a Lambda Literary Award), *Underwater Lengths in a Single Breath* (Ashland Poetry Press, 2007). His poems have appeared in many venues including the *Pushcart Prize* and *Best American Poetry* anthologies. He teaches creative writing at The University of Hartford.

**Minal Hajratwala** has inhabited San Francisco, New Zealand, Michigan, Bangalore, and several other earth sites. Her nonfiction epic, *Leaving India: My Family's Journey from Five Villages to Five Continents,* won four literary awards. She is the editor of *Out! Stories* *from the New Queer India* and creatrix of a one-woman performance extravaganza, *Avatars: Gods for a New Millennium*. Her poetry collection *Bountiful Instructions for Enlightenment* is forthcoming in 2014. Educated at Stanford and Columbia, she was a 2010-11 Fulbright-Nehru Senior Scholar. She is a writing coach and co-founder of The (Great) Indian Poetry Collective, publishing innovative poetry from India, and can be found at www.minalhajratwala.com.

**Julie Bloss Kelsey** started writing scifaiku in 2009, after the birth of her third child. Her short science fiction poems have since appeared in *Scifaikuest, Seven by Twenty, microcosms, Eye to the Telescope,* and other publications. She won the Dwarf Stars Award in 2011 for her poem "Comet." Julie lives in Maryland with her husband, kids, and an ever-changing assortment of pets. Connect with her on Twitter (@MamaJoules).

**Rose Lemberg** was born in Ukraine, and lived in subarctic Russia before immigrating to Israel with her family in 1990. She moved countries again in 2001, this time to the US, for graduate school. She officially became an immigrant in 2010, after living in the US for 9 years as a nonresident alien. Her fiction and poetry have appeared in *Strange Horizons, Beneath Ceaseless Skies, Apex,* and other venues. For more information, visit roselemberg.net.

An author and translator of speculative fiction, as well as a lawyer and programmer, **Ken Liu** is a winner of the Nebula, Hugo, and World Fantasy awards. His fiction has appeared in *The Magazine of Fantasy & Science Fiction, Asimov's, Analog, Clarkesworld, Lightspeed,* and *Strange Horizons,* among other places. He lives with his family near Boston, Massachusetts. His debut novel, *The Grace of Kings,* the first in a fantasy series, will be published by Simon & Schuster's new genre fiction imprint in 2015, along with a collection of short stories. He's online at http://kenliu.name.

**Alex Dally MacFarlane** is a writer, editor and historian. When not researching narrative maps in the legendary traditions of Alexander III of Macedon, she writes stories, found in *Clarkesworld Magazine, Strange Horizons, Heiresses of Russ 2013: The Year's Best Lesbian Speculative Fiction* and other anthologies. She is the editor of *Aliens: Recent Encounters* (Prime Books, 2013) and *The Mammoth Book of*

*SF Stories by Women* (Constable & Robinson, 2014).

**Anil Menon**'s short stories have appeared in *Albedo One, Chiaroscuro, Interzone, Interfictions, LCRW, Sybil's Garage, Strange Horizons*, among other publications. His debut novel *The Beast With Nine Billion Feet* (Zubaan Books, India) was nominated for the 2010 Parallax Prize and the Vodafone-Crossword award. Along with Vandana Singh, he co-edited *Breaking the Bow* (Zubaan Books, 2012), an anthology of speculative short fiction inspired by the Ramayana.

Editor **Joanne Merriam** is a Nova Scotian writer living in Nashville, Tennessee, and runs Upper Rubber Boot Books. Her writing has appeared in *Asimov's, Escape Pod, On Spec, Pank, Per Contra, Strange Horizons*, and *The Journal of Unlikely Entomology*. Her poetry collection, *The Glaze from Breaking*, was published by Stride Books in 2005 and was re-issued by URB in 2011. She is also the co-editor, with H. L. Nelson, of *Choose Wisely: 35 Women Up To No Good*.

**Mary Anne Mohanraj** wrote *Bodies in Motion* (a finalist for the Asian American Book Awards and translated into six languages) and nine other titles, most recently *The Stars Change* (Circlet Press, 2013). Mohanraj received a Breaking Barriers Award from the Chicago Foundation for Women for her work in Asian American arts organizing, and has also won an Illinois Arts Council Fellowship. Mohanraj is Clinical Assistant Professor of fiction and literature and Associate Director of Asian and Asian American Studies at the University of Illinois. She serves as Executive Director of *DesiLit*.

**Daniel José Older** is the author of the upcoming Young Adult novel *Shadowshaper* (Arthur A. Levine Books, 2015) and the Bone Street Rumba urban fantasy series, which begins in January 2015 with *Half-Resurrection Blues* from Penguin's Roc imprint. *Publishers Weekly* hailed him as a "rising star of the genre" after the publication of his debut ghost noir collection, *Salsa Nocturna*. He co-edited the anthology *Long Hidden: Speculative Fiction from the Margins of History* and guest-edited the music issue of *Crossed Genres*. His short stories and essays have appeared in *Tor.com, Salon, BuzzFeed, the New Haven Review, PANK, Apex* and *Strange Horizons* and the anthologies *Subversion* and *Mothership: Tales Of Afrofuturism And Beyond*. Daniel's band Ghost Star gigs regularly around New York and he facilitates workshops on storytelling from an anti-oppressive power analysis. You can find his thoughts on writing, read dispatches from his decade-long career as an NYC paramedic and hear his music at ghoststar.net and @djolder on twitter.

**Abbey Mei Otis** likes people and art forms on the margins. She studied creative writing at Oberlin College and is a graduate of the Clarion West Writers Workshop. She has taught poetry in the DC public schools with the DC Creative Writing Workshop, and is now a fellow at the Michener Center for Writers in Austin, Texas.

**Sarah Pinsker** is a writer and musician living in Baltimore, Maryland. Her fiction has been published in *Asimov's, Strange Horizons, Lightspeed, The Magazine of Fantasy & Science Fiction,* and the *Long Hidden* anthology, among others. Her novelette "In Joy, Knowing the Abyss Behind," was nominated for the Nebula and won the 2014 Theodore Sturgeon Memorial Award.

Manila-based **Elyss G. Punsalan** runs her own video production company. Some of her fiction can be found in the anthologies *Philippine Speculative Fiction* (Volumes 3, 6, and 9), *Philippine Genre Stories, A Time for Dragons, HORROR: Filipino Fiction for Young Adults,* and the webzine *Bewildering Stories.* At one point in her life, she produced and hosted the monthly Filipino audio fiction site *Pakinggan Pilipinas* (pakingganpilipinas.blogspot.com).

**Benjamin Rosenbaum** lives near Basel, Switzerland with his wife and children. His stories have been published in *Nature, Harper's, F&SF, Asimov's, McSweeney's,* and *Strange Horizons,* translated into 23 languages, and nominated for Hugo, Nebula, BSFA, Locus, World Fantasy, and Sturgeon Awards. He has collaborated with artist Ethan Ham on several art/literary hybrids. Find out more at www.benjaminrosenbaum.com.

**Erica L. Satifka**'s fiction has appeared in *Clarkesworld Magazine, Daily Science Fiction, Ideomancer, Lady Churchill's Rosebud Wristlet* and the Greek magazine supplement *εννέα*. She lives in Portland, Oregon. Visit her online at www.ericasatifka.com.

**Nisi Shawl**'s collection *Filter House* was a 2009 James Tiptree, Jr., Award winner; her stories have been published in *Asimov's, Strange Horizons, The Year's Best Fantasy and Horror* and both volumes of the

*Dark Matter* series. She was the 2011 Guest of Honor at the feminist SF convention WisCon and a 2014 co-Guest of Honor for the Science Fiction Research Association. She co-authored the renowned *Writing the Other: A Practical Approach* with Cynthia Ward, and co-edited the nonfiction anthology *Strange Matings: Science Fiction, Feminism, African American Voices, and Octavia E. Butler*. Shawl's Belgian Congo steampunk novel *Everfair* is forthcoming in 2015 from Tor Books. Her website is www.nisishawl.com.

**Lewis Shiner**'s latest novel is *Dark Tangos* (Subterranean Press, 2011). Previous novels include *Frontera* and *Deserted Cities of the Heart*, both Nebula Award finalists, and the World Fantasy Award-winning *Glimpses*. He's also published four short story collections, journalism, and comics. Virtually all of his work is available for free download at www.fictionliberationfront.net.

**Marge Simon**'s works appear in *Strange Horizons, Niteblade, DailySF Magazine, Pedestal Magazine, Dreams & Nightmares* and other places. She edits a column for the HWA Newsletter and serves as Chair of the Board of Trustees. She has won the *Strange Horizons* Readers Choice Award, the Bram Stoker Award (2008, 2012 & 2013), the Rhysling Award and the Dwarf Stars Award. Collections: *Like Birds in the Rain, Unearthly Delights, The Mad Hattery, Vampires, Zombies & Wanton Souls,* and *Dangerous Dreams*. Find her at www.margesimon.com.

**Sonya Taaffe**'s short fiction and poetry can be found in the collections *Postcards from the Province of Hyphens* (Prime Books), *Singing Innocence and Experience* (Prime Books), and *A Mayse-Bikhl* (Papaveria Press), and in anthologies including *Aliens: Recent Encounters, Beyond Binary: Genderqueer and Sexually Fluid Speculative Fiction, The Moment of Change: An Anthology of Feminist Speculative Poetry, People of the Book: A Decade of Jewish Science Fiction & Fantasy, The Year's Best Fantasy and Horror, The Alchemy of Stars: Rhysling Award Winners Showcase,* and *The Best of Not One of Us*. She is currently senior poetry editor at *Strange Horizons*; she holds master's degrees in Classics from Brandeis and Yale and once named a Kuiper belt object. She lives in Somerville with her husband and two cats.

**Bogi Takács** is a Hungarian Jewish author, a psycholinguist and a popular-science journalist. E writes both speculative fiction and poetry, and eir works have been published or are forthcoming in a variety of venues like *Strange Horizons, Apex* and *GigaNotoSaurus,* among others. E is online at www.prezzey.net.

**Deborah Walker** grew up in the most English town in England, but she soon high-tailed it down to London, where she now lives with her partner, Chris, and her two young children. Find Deborah in the British Museum trawling the past for future inspiration or on her blog: deborahwalkersbibliography.blogspot.com. Her stories have appeared in *Nature's Futures, Cosmos, Daily Science Fiction* and *The Year's Best SF 18.*

A South African clinical psychologist, **Nick Wood** has short stories in *AfroSF, Interzone, Infinity Plus, PostScripts, Redstone Science Fiction* and the Newcon Press anthology, *Subterfuge,* amongst other publications. His YA speculative novel, *The stone chameleon,* was published in South Africa. Nick has completed an MA in Creative Writing (SF & Fantasy) through Middlesex University, London and is currently training clinical psychologists in Hertfordshire, England. He can be found: @nick45wood or nickwood.frogwrite.co.nz.

**Bryan Thao Worra** is an award-winning Lao-American writer. An NEA Fellow in literature, he is a professional member of the Horror Writer Association and the Science Fiction Poetry Association. His work appears internationally, including in *Innsmouth Free Press, Tales of the Unanticipated, Illumen, Astropoetica, Outsiders Within, Dark Wisdom,* and *Mad Poets of Terra.* He is the author of the books of speculative poetry *On the Other Side of the Eye, Barrow,* and *Demonstra.* Visit him online at thaoworra.blogspot.com.

# ACKNOWLEDGEMENTS

Upper Rubber Boot Books would like to thank the following publications, in which these works first appeared:

Dean Francis Alfar, Ohkti—*Philippines Graphic,* December 2012

Celia Lisset Alvarez, Malibu Barbie Moves to Mars—*Eye to the Telescope,* January 2012

RJ Astruc, A Believer's Guide to Azagarth—*Third Order,* 2008

Lisa Bao, like father like daughter—*Eye to the Telescope,* April 2013

Pinckney Benedict, Zog-19—*Zoetrope: All-Story,* February 2000; *Prize Stories 2001: O. Henry Awards* (Anchor, 2001); *Zoetrope: All Story 2* (Harcourt, 2003)

Lisa Bolekaja, The Saltwater African—*Bloodchildren: Stories by the Octavia E. Butler Scholars* (Carl Brandon Society & Book View Café, 2013)

Mary Buchinger, Transplanted—*Journey, Anthology* (Eden Waters Press, 2009)

Zen Cho, The Four Generations of Chang E—*Mascara Literary Review,* October 2011; *Aliens: Recent Encounters* (Prime Books, 2013); *Spirits Abroad* (Fixi Novo, 2014)

Tina Connolly, Turning the Apples—*Strange Horizons,* 30 March 2009; *Pseudopod,* 15 January 2010; in Finnish translation, *Spin,* December 2013

Indrapramit Das, muo-ka's Child—*Clarkesworld Magazine,* September 2012; *Aliens: Recent Encounters*

(Prime Books, 2013)

Tom Doyle, The Floating Otherworld—*Strange Horizons*, December 20, 2004; *Kasma Science Fiction Magazine*, September 2011

Peg Duthie, With Light-Years Come Heaviness—*Eye to the Telescope*, April 2013

Tom Greene, Zero Bar—*Strange Horizons*, August 6, 2012

Benjamin S. Grossberg, The Space Traveler's Husband— *The Missouri Review*, Summer 2010; The Space Traveler and Boston—*Washington Square*, Winter/Spring 2011; The Space Traveler and the Promised Planet—*Literary Imagination*, Vol 13, No 1; All appear in *Space Traveler* (University of Tampa Press, 2014)

Minal Hajratwala, The Unicorn at the Racetrack—*Stone Telling*, Issue 9: Menagerie, 2013

Julie Bloss Kelsey, the itch of new skin—*Scifaikuest (online)*, November 2012

tongue lashing—*Eye to the Telescope*, April 2013

Rose Lemberg, Three Immigrations—*Strange Horizons*, November 2012

Ken Liu, Ghost Days—*Lightspeed*, October 2013

Alex Dally MacFarlane, Found—*Clarkesworld Magazine*, August 2013

Anil Menon, Into The Night—*Interzone*, January 2008; *Apex Book of World SF* (Vol 1, 2010); *Galaxies Revue Magazine*, 2010

Joanne Merriam, Little Ambushes—*Strange Horizons*, 20 August 2007

Mary Anne Mohanraj, Jump Space—*Thoughtcrime Experiments: nine stories* (co-operative publishing venture, May 2009)

Daniel José Older, Phantom Overload—*Salsa Nocturna* (Crossed Genres Publications, 2012)

Abbey Mei Otis, Blood Blood—*Strange Horizons*, 15 November 2010

Sarah Pinsker, The Low Hum of Her—*Asimov's Science Fiction*, August 2014

Elyss G Punsalan, Ashland—*Philippine Speculative Fiction Volume 6* (Kestrel Publishing, 2012)

Benjamin Rosenbaum, The Guy Who Worked For Money—"Shareable Futures" series, *shareable.net*, 12 July 2010; *Under the Needle's Eye* (Clarion West class of 2001, 2012); in German as "Der Mann, der für Geld arbeitet" in *Freier Fall und Der Mann, der für Geld arbeitet*, translated by Michael Drecker

Erica L. Satifka, Sea Changes—*Ideomancer*, September 2008; in Greek in *εννέα*

Nisi Shawl, In Colors Everywhere—*The Other Half of the Sky* (Candlemark & Gleam, 2013)

Lewis Shiner, Primes—*F&SF*, October/November 2000; *Collected Stories* (Blackstone Audio, 2013)

Marge Simon, South—*Aoife's Kiss*, 2006

Sonya Taaffe, Di Vayse Pave—*Moral Relativism Magazine*, January 2012

Bogi Takács, The Tiny English-Hungarian Phrasebook For Visiting Extraterrestrials— *Stone Telling*, Issue 9: Menagerie, 2013

Deborah Walker, Speed of Love—*Daily Science Fiction*, 12 November 2012

Nick Wood, Azania—*AfroSF*, December 2012

Bryan Thao Worra, Dead End In December—*Innsmouth Free Press*, December 2012; The Deep Ones—*On The Other Side Of The Eye* (Sam's Dot Publishing, 2007)

Additionally, the editor would like to thank Sharra Rosichan, Roz Spafford, Brent Altheim and Jay Cantrell for their valuable editorial comments, Alan Slone and Diana Flegal for their patience and support, and Joe Jones for the phrase "greeting tentacle."

# BOOKS BY UPPER RUBBER BOOT

Anthologies:
*140 And Counting: an anthology of writing from 7x20*, Joanne Merriam, ed.
*Apocalypse Now: Poems and Prose from the End of Days*, Andrew McFadyen-Ketchum and Alexander Lumans, eds.
*Choose Wisely: 35 Women Up To No Good*, H. L. Nelson and Joanne Merriam, eds.
*How to Live on Other Planets: A Handbook for Aspiring Aliens*, Joanne Merriam, ed.

Fiction:
*Bicycle Girl: a short story*, Tade Thompson
*Changing the World: a short story*, David M. Harris
*Heist: a short story*, Tracy Canfield
*Johnny B: a short story*, Phil Voyd
*The Mask Game*, Sergey Gerasimov
*The Selves We Leave Behind: a short story*, Shira Lipkin
*Signs Over the Pacific and Other Stories*, RJ Astruc
*The Suicide Inspector: a short story*, J. J. Steinfeld
*The Tortoise Parliament: a short story*, Kenneth Schneyer
*Twittering the Stars: a short story*, Mari Ness
*The Widow and the Xir: a short story*, Indrapramit Das

Poetry:
*Blueshifting*, Heather Kamins
*Floodgate Poetry Series*, edited by Andrew McFadyen-Ketchum
*The Glaze from Breaking*, Joanne Merriam
*Hiss of Leaves*, T. D. Ingram
*Marilyn Monroe: Poems*, Lyn Lifshin
*Measured Extravagance*, Peg Duthie
*The Sky Needs More Work*, Corey Mesler

# COPYRIGHT INFORMATION

*How To Live On Other Planets: A Handbook for Aspiring Aliens*
ISBN 978-1-937794-32-3
©2015 respective authors

Cover art and design by Joanne Merriam

Published in the United States of America

UPPER RUBBER BOOT

CPSIA information can be obtained at www.ICGtesting.com
Printed in the USA
LVOW11s0204200516

489132LV00001B/95/P